COGNITIVE CLASSROOM LEARNING

Understanding, Thinking, and Problem Solving

EDUCATIONAL PSYCHOLOGY

Allen J. Edwards, Series Editor
Department of Psychology
Southwest Missouri State University
Springfield, Missouri

A complete list of titles in this series is available from the publisher on request.

COGNITIVE CLASSROOM LEARNING

Understanding, Thinking, and Problem Solving

Edited by

Gary D. Phye
Thomas Andre

Department of Psychology
Iowa State University
Ames, Iowa

91-1551

ACADEMIC PRESS, INC.

Harcourt Brace Jovanovich, Publishers

San Diego   New York   Berkeley   Boston
London   Sydney   Tokyo   Toronto

ACADEMIC PRESS, INC.
San Diego, California 92101

United Kingdom Edition published by
ACADEMIC PRESS LIMITED
24-28 Oval Road, London NW1 7DX

Library of Congress Cataloging in Publication Data

Cognitive classroom learning.

(Educational psychology)
Includes index.
Contents: Cognition, learning, and education / Thomas
Andre and Gary Phye — Hemispheric laterality as a
basis of learning / Michael W. O'Boyle —Attentional
processes in education / Mark Grabe — Designing
instruction to produce understanding : an approach
based on cognitive theory / James M. Royer — [etc.]
1. Learning. 2. Cognition in children. 3. Memory
in children. I. Phye, Gary D. II. Andre, Thomas.
III. Series.
LB1060.C64 1986   370.15'23   86-7914
ISBN 0—12—554252—6 (alk. paper)

PRINTED IN THE UNITED STATES OF AMERICA
89 90 91 92 93   9 8 7 6 5 4 3

CONTENTS

8. METACOGNITIVE SKILLS   205
Orpha K. Duell

9. LEARNING TACTICS AND STRATEGIES   243
Jack Snowman

10. COGNITIVE DEVELOPMENT: LEARNING AND THE MECHANISMS OF CHANGE   277
Eric Lunzer

PREFACE

This book has its origin in many conversations with colleagues and graduate students concerning a need for a volume on classroom learning. During the last two decades, a major evolution has taken place in educational and psychological research. The cognitive information-processing perspective has changed the nature of psychological and education research and has, to our way of thinking, produced findings with tremendous potential for classroom application. Unfortunately little or no effort has been made to organize and integrate this new wealth of information at a level appropriate for a first-year graduate student. This volume is intended to provide the educational practitioner (classroom teacher, school psychologist, special educator, etc.) working on a graduate degree with a better understanding of the information processing involved when students learn. We view this effort as providing the basis for an awareness of the classroom learning processes of understanding, thinking, and problem solving.

A major change that current cognitive psychology offers to instructional psychology is a new perspective in which teaching activities are examined in light of the information processing carried out by students. Effective teaching processes are viewed as means of facilitating productive information processing by the student. As contrasted with a behavioral psychology, cognitive instructional psychology relegitimizes talk about what goes on inside a student's head when asked to learn!

While the volume was designed for use in a graduate-level course, it could also be used as a resource book by practicing school psychologists and educators in the field. The research cited is current and covers such areas as attention, memory functioning, practice, and problem solving. Of particular value to the educator in the field who may not have a background in neurology is the chapter by O'Boyle reviewing what we know and don't know about hemispheric laterality as a basis of learning. This chapter was included because of misconceptions about this topic that seem to be so prevalent in the popular literature.

This book is organized around the idea that learning occurs through the processing of information by structures in the student's learning/memory system. The learning/memory system is conceptualized as possessing many features that operate as the student learns. While different theorists propose models that differ in subtle ways, there are important commonalities among these models. The views expressed in the current volume of how students learn in the classroom assume that:

1. Attentional factors are important in learning and include such processes as orientation (focusing) and maintenance.

2. Short-term memory processes play a role in learning. Such processing involves what is commonly called working memory. Broadly speaking, working memory is a limited-capacity mechanism (e.g., 30 seconds) responsible for what is frequently called consciousness. Working memory is responsible for monitoring the ongoing activity of the learner as well as accessing long-term memory.

3. The representation of knowledge in long-term memory involves storage and retrieval. These processes influence what the student learns and remembers. Storage and retrieval processes are conceptualized as including the organizational strategies, e.g., "schemes," "scripts," etc., as well as a depth of processing factor.

4. Performance factors influence the learning process. Such factors include practice, the use of informative feedback, and the application of cognitive skills.

5. Metacognitive processes play a role in learning. Metacognitive processes refer to the goals the student has in the learning situation, the type of general learning skills the student brings to bear in the learning situation, and the learner's understanding and interpretation of the learning situation.

These features of the learning/memory system are discussed within the context of hemispheric laterality by O'Boyle in Chapter 2. In Chapter 3, Grabe reviews research related to attentional practices in education and provides suggestions for classroom practice. In Chapter 4, Royer provides the basis for designing instruction to produce understanding. In Chapter 5, Kulhavy, Schwartz, and Peterson review the literature on working memory and the encoding process. These authors provide a synthesis of the current research on "encoding" and develop a section on instructional applications that have direct application to the classroom. In Chapter 6, Phye introduces the topics of practice and skilled classroom performance. The development of classroom skills through practice is discussed, with special emphasis being given to error analysis and feedback. Andre introduces the topic of problem solving and education in Chapter 7. The nature of problem solving and the approaches to study that problem solving provides are initial considerations. The application of current theory and research findings is seen in a discussion of the learning of intellectual skills. In Chapter 8, Duell reviews the literature on metacognitive skills and summarizes the implications for class-room practice. Snowman introduces the topic of learning tactics and strat-egies in Chapter 9. Special attention is given to memory-directed learning tactics and comprehension-directed learning tactics. This chapter contains a review of learning strategy research that has direct implications for the classroom teacher or educational specialist working with learning disabled students.

Chapter 10 by Lunzer is devoted to the general topic of cognitive develop-ment. This chapter provides the reader with a resume of Piaget's theory with a critique of the errors of Piagetian theory and the positive legacy of Piaget. Lunzer also discusses the concept of continuity and the mechanisms of change. Of particular interest is the study of thinking as it applies to the classroom.

The contributors to this volume deserve a special expression of gratitude. We found all persons to be not only cooperative but also stimulating and dedicated scholars. The editorial staff at Academic Press deserves special mention for their efforts in the development of this book. A special thank you must go to Allen J. Edwards, series editor, who was willing to listen and then provide the opportunity for us to try a different approach.

Gary D. Phye
Thomas Andre

COGNITION, LEARNING, AND EDUCATION

Thomas Andre
Gary D. Phye

Department of Psychology
Iowa State University
Ames, Iowa 50011

While the social functions of schools are many and varied and have changed over the centuries, the facilitation of learning and development remains at the heart of the schools' purpose. Discovering and explaining how learning and development occur has also been a central issue in scientific psychology in its century of existence. This volume is intended to provide educators with a description of current psychological theory and research in the area of learning and cognition and the applications of that theory to educational problems. The volume is organized around a conception of the human cognitive system that has dominated research and theory in cognitive and learning psychology since the mid-1960s. We call this conception the cognitive information-processing view. Like most scientific perspectives, this view is based upon a central metaphor; that the brain–mind system is, in important ways, like a programmable computer. This metaphor implies that we can use concepts from the area of computer science to help us understand what human beings do when they learn, remember, and use knowledge.

I. THE COGNITIVE INFORMATION–PROCESSING (CIP) VERSUS EARLIER VIEWS

Earlier psychological conceptions of learning and cognition were dominated by two major traditions: behavioral learning theories and traditional cognitive theories. Behavioral learning theories are exemplified by the work of Thorndike, Skinner, Hull, and Spence. Traditional cognitive theories are illustrated by the Gestalt psychologists, by Piaget, and by Ausubel. Behavioral learning theory dominated American psychology for the first 6 decades of the century. Cognitive theories were primarily the work of European

COGNITIVE CLASSROOM LEARNING:
UNDERSTANDING, THINKING, AND PROBLEM SOLVING

TABLE 1   Comparison of Behavioral and Traditional Cognitive Theories of Learning and Cognition

Behavioral learning theory	Traditional cognitive theory
1. Learner is seen as passive and reactive to environment.	1. Learner is seen as active and mastering the environment.
2. Learning occurs because of associations among stimuli or between stimuli and responses.	2. Learning occurs because the learner actively tries to understand the environment.
3. Knowledge consists of whatever pattern of associations have been learned.	3. Knowledge consists of an organized set of mental structures and procedures.
4. Learning is the acquisition of new associations.	4. Learning consists of changes in mental structure brought about by mental reasoning.
5. Prior knowledge influences new learning primarily through indirect processes such as positive or negative transfer because of similarity of stimuli between situations.	5. New learning is based on using prior knowledge to understand new situations, and changing prior knowledge structures to deal with new situations.
6. Discussion of the activities of the mind is not permitted.	6. Discussion of activities of the mind is the central issue in psychology.
7. Strong experimental research tradition. Theories can only be verified through experiment.	7. Weak experimental research tradition. Observational research, thought experiments, and logical analysis can be used.
8. Education consists of arranging stimuli so that desired associations are made.	8. Education consists of allowing/encouraging, active mental exploration of complex environments.

psychologists. Table 1 illustrates some of the differences between behavioral and traditional cognitive theories.

As can be seen in Table 1, the behavioral tradition emphasized as its fundamental metaphor a mechanistic conception of learning that was based upon the concept of the mechanical (as opposed to the electronic) device. Stimuli acted as forces which forced the learner to engage in various behaviors much as dialed telephone numbers force the phone system to ring particular phones. The learner was not self-activated and only responded to environmental forces. The fundamental metaphor of the traditional cognitive view was that of the "logician-philosopher/rational-civilized man"[1] that pre–World War I, educated, middle-upper-class Europeans imagined them-

[1]The word *man* is used here not because we are sexist, but because we believe that it captures the view that was held by Europeans that we are trying to convey. In that view, logical–rational, nonemotional thought was male. We do not subscribe to that position.

selves to be. In this view, thinking and mental activity were the fundamental facts of human existence and had to be the basis upon which adequate psychological theories of cognition and learning were built.[2]

A. THE CIP VIEW

The CIP view in many ways represents an integration of the behavioral and traditional cognitive positions. Rather than seeing either the environment or the mind as the source of learning and behavior, the CIP view holds that learning and behavior emerge from an interaction of the environment and the previous experience and knowledge of the learner. The learner both responds to and acts upon the environment. Like the traditional cognitive view, the CIP model portrays the mind possessing a structure consisting of components for processing (storing, retrieving, transforming and using) information and procedures for using the components. Like the behavioral view, the CIP model holds that learning consists partially of the formation of associations. Rather than the simple undifferentiated associations of behavioral psychology, in the CIP model, associations vary in type and nature. In addition, the "things" associated are not simple stimulus–stimulus or stimulus–response connections but are connections among mental structures that are called schemata (schemes, scripts, frames, productions, etc). Besides acquiring associations among schemata (singular: schema), learning also consists of the acquisition of new schemata. In the CIP view, knowledge is represented in mental structure in a hierarchically organized network of associations among schemata.

Discussion of the processes occurring in the mind is central to the information processing view; but these processes are discussed in a more precise fashion than in the traditional cognitive view. The CIP view demands that each specific step and procedure of a postulated mental operation be described; the ideal is that the process be described in sufficient detail that it may be simulated upon a computer. In addition, the CIP model adopts the experimental attitude of the behaviorists. Mental processes are not simply postulated, but rather must be supported by experimental evidence. However, like the traditional cognitivists, researchers within the cognitive information-processing tradition make frequent use of informal observations and logical analyses of mental activities for the generation of hypotheses that are

---

[2]This contrast of the behavioral and traditional cognitive views is overdrawn for the pedagogical purpose of making the distinctions between the views clear. The contrasting views might be conceptualized as endpoints on a continuum upon which the specific theories of behavioral and cognitive theorists would fall. This description does not do justice to the rich traditions within either behavioral or traditional cognitive psychology and does not provide an adequate historical perspective.

later tested by experiment. This paragraph introduces many terms and ideas that appear very general. The purpose of this book is to flesh out and make more precise the general features described in this chapter and to show how these ideas can be used in education.

B. THE BASIC STRUCTURE OF THE MIND

While there is much debate within cognitive psychology about the exact nature of mental structure, models based upon the basic structure first proposed by Atkinson and Shiffrin (1968) have many adherents. Figure 1 presents an overview of a generic version of this model. According to Fig. 1, there are five basic components to the mental system: Input buffers or sensory registers; a short-term store or memory, a long-term memory, an executive routine, and output buffers. Thinking and learning consist of the movement and processing of information through and among the components of this system. In this chapter, we briefly describe each of these components and indicate how learning and thinking occur within this generic mode. Subsequent chapters provide an in-depth description of how information processing occurs.

1.   Input Buffers–Sensory Registers

The input buffers or sensory registers represent a portion of the memory system that is associated with the senses. Sensory registers are very short-term memories that function to hold incoming information for a brief period of time while it can be processed. Without sensory registers we would have more difficulty in perceiving the world because we would not have time to process many stimuli that are of very brief duration.

The existence of a sensory register for each of the senses is speculative.

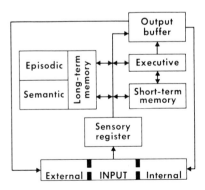

FIG. 1.   A model of the cognitive system.

Work by Sperling (1960), using stimulus arrays presented visually for very brief intervals through a device called a tachistoscope, led to the postulation of the visual sensory register. Work by Moray, Bates, and Barnett (1965) and Darwin, Turvey, and Crowder (1972) supports the existence of an auditory sensory register. The existence of sensory registers for the other senses is less well documented. While the sensory registers represent an interesting component of the memory system, their operation is pretty much an automatic part of perception, and they have little educational importance.

2. Short-Term Memory (STM)

Short-term memory is conceived to be that part of the memory system that contains information currently being thought about and processed. In many ways the concept of short-term memory is similar to the idea of consciousness. When we are currently conscious of ideas, they are in our short-term memory. Short-term memory is assumed to have a limited capacity to deal with information. As we devote attention to information, we bring that information into our short-term memory and process it. Because short-term memory is limited in its capacity, we have limits on the number of different ideas we can attend to. The capacity of short-term memory has been variously estimated at two to seven chunks of information. However, as Anderson (1980) points out, estimates are variously biased by the method used to make the estimate; he concludes that while we know that short-term memory capacity is limited, we do not know its exact capacity. In addition, information is lost very rapidly from short-term memory unless we continue to think about or rehearse it. *Rehearsal* is a term used to described the process of repeatedly saying something over and over to yourself. It is one way to maintain information in short-term memory. You have probably used rehearsal to keep a telephone number in your short-term memory.

Short-term memory acts as a kind of bottleneck in the memory system. Incoming information must be entered into short-term memory if it is to be learned. While it is being processed, our capacity to learn other information is reduced. Issues that we have to think about, such as constructing a sonnet, solving a math problem, or wondering what to do about our budget, use up short-term memory and attentional capacity. Again, our capacity to think of other things is reduced. One implication for instructional practice is that information should be presented no faster than it can be adequately processed. If information is presented too quickly, the memory system becomes overloaded and loss of information occurs.

3. Long-Term Memory

In order to learn and retain information for longer periods of time, we must transfer information from short-term to long-term memory. Long-term memory is conceived of as a very large-capacity, randomly-accessible, and content-addressable memory. *Large capacity* means that long-term memory can store a great deal of different information. As far as we know, there are no practical limits to the capacity of our long-term memory. By *random access*, psychologists mean that any item of information can be retrieved relatively independently of other items of information. The opposite of a randomly-accessible memory store is a serial memory store. In a serial memory store (like a tape recorder), you have to search through the entire memory in sequence until you find the item of information you want. A random-access memory store is somewhat like a library. If you know a book's call number and how the library is organized, you can find the book by going to that location in the memory without having to search through all the books in the library. By *content-addressable*, psychologists mean that the nature of the information to be learned determines where in long-term memory the information will be stored. If you learn about a certain topic, such as the sea life of Cape Cod, that information is stored in locations in your memory that can be accessed with cues based upon the content that you studied. So if you are asked questions about Cape Cod or sea life, you are likely to search that part of your memory that deals with those topics.[3]

Some theorists find it useful to divide long-term memory into two components: long-term episodic and long-term semantic memory (Calfee, 1981; Tulving, 1972). In Tulving's conception, long-term episodic memory is used to store the events of a person's life, whereas long-term semantic memory is used to store one's general knowledge of the language and the world. Knowledge in long-term memory is used to understand (give meaning to) the events one experiences and the language one hears. In Tulving's words episodic and semantic memory should be conceived as

> two information processing systems that (a) selectively receive information from . . . other cognitive systems, (b) retain various aspects of this information, and (c) . . . transmit specific retained information to other systems, including . . . conscious awareness. The two systems differ . . . in terms of (a) the nature of the stored information, (b) autobiographical versus cognitive reference, (c) conditions . . . of retrieval, and . . . (d) their vulnerability to interference. . . . Episodic memory receives and stores information about temporally dated episodes or events and temporal–spatial relations among these events. . . . Semantic memory . . . is a mental thesaurus, [containing] organized knowledge . . . about words . . . their

---

[3]This presentation of long-term memory uses a spatial metaphor and seems to imply that we hold that different memories are stored in different locations in the brain, and that brain organization is like a library or certain forms of database organization. We do not wish to imply any particular theoretical position on these issues. We are saying that long-term memory acts *as if* it had such an organization and features, and that a system with such features could simulate some features of long-term memory. We make no claim that such a system is any more than a metaphor useful for analysis.

meaning and referents . . . relations among them . . . and about rules, formulas, and algorithms. . . . (Tulving, 1972, pp. 385–386)

An important distinction between episodic and semantic memory is in the nature of the information stored in the memory system and the way in which that information is organized. *Episodic memory* contains our memory for the events of our lives. At a phenomenological level, the information is stored in the form of visual or other images.[4] The images seem to be organized on a temporal–spatial basis. In other words, we remember episodes in our lives on the basis of where they happened in space and when they happened in time (relative to other events). To demonstrate this to yourself, try to remember what you had for dinner a week ago today. Most people try to remember by figuring out when it was (e.g., what day of the week), what they were doing that day, and where they were that day. Even if you do not remember, the process of trying illustrates important aspects of episodic memory. The process is illustrated more strongly if you try to remember what you were doing at the time of day it is now 10 years ago this day.

Semantic memory contains the knowledge we have that has been abstracted away from the particular events that we have experienced. Semantic memory contains the generalizations we have drawn and acquired from experience. Semantic memory contains our knowledge of concepts, rules, principles, generalizations, skills, and metacognitive skills. In the current jargon of cognitive psychology, these elements of semantic memory can be collectively called *schemata*. We use schemata to give meaning to events, to understand language, and to solve problems. For example, if on a television show we see two vain middle-class women come to a party in the same outfit, we may be able to empathize with their chagrin and to expect some rude behavior on their part because we have generalized a rule from many situation comedies that have used this situation.

When we understand a particular sentence, such as Chomsky's famous FLYING PLANES CAN BE DANGEROUS, we do not simply decode the sentence and figure out its meaning. Rather, the words provide a set of signals that activate schemata in semantic memory, and from those schemata we try to construct a meaning for the sentence. That the meaning is in the act of construction and not in the sentence is shown by the fact that at least two meanings can be constructed from Chomsky's sentence. That the meaning of nonverbal events is similarly constructed by the observer is demonstrated by

---

[4]There has been debate in the literature about the exact nature of the storage of images in memory. The issues in the debate are not relevant for the discussion in this chapter, and we make no claims in this chapter about the "true" nature of storage in episodic or semantic memory. From the phenomenological perspective of what people report about their mental experience when they recall from episodic memory, images of some type seem to predominate.

the famous goblet/faces figure developed by Gestalt psychologists. Again, two meanings, either faces or goblets, can be constructed from the same figure. The meaning is not in the figure, but in what we do with the figure in our heads. As a further demonstration that meaning is an act of construction, consider the sentence displayed after this paragraph. This can be a meaningful sentence (the punctuation is removed), if you can construct the meaning. Trying to figure out what the sentence means certainly demonstrates that meaning is an act of mental construction.

Sentence: THAT THAT IS IS THAT THAT IS NOT IS NOT THAT THAT IS IS NOT THAT THAT IS NOT THAT THAT IS NOT IS NOT THAT THAT IS.

Schemata and Long-Term Semantic Memory.   The concept of schemata is an important and common one in current cognitive psychology. Long-term semantic memory is thought to consist of a network of schemata. A network consists of elements called *nodes* joined by connections or associations. A network can be represented graphically as in Fig. 2. The lines represent the connections or associations, and the places where they intersect are the nodes. In the current conception of cognitive psychology, the nodes in the semantic network are schemata and the lines are associations among schemata. This idea differs in two major ways from earlier associative theories: (1) Unlike the elements in previous associative theories, which were static internal responses to stimulation, schemata are conceived of as active dynamic entities which are able to transform incoming stimulation into more than is presented and to fill in missing details. (2) The connections among schemata are differentiated into varying types. This latter feature

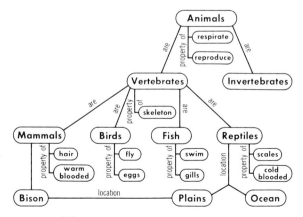

FIG. 2.   A portion of semantic memory.

allows information about superordinate, coordinate, subordinate, and case relationships among schemata to be easily represented in the network. The remaining chapters make extensive use of the concept of schemata and explicate its meaning and instructional utility.

4. The Executive

The executive is that component of our memory system that keeps track of what information is being processed and controls the flow of processing to determine which activities occur and which processing components receive system resources. The executive is conceptualized much as an operating system's program is conceptualized in a computer system. Both large-scale mainframe computer systems and small microcomputers typically have a component called the operating system. The operating system is a program that operates in the background while some other program or programs are running (being used). The operating system keeps track of what each program is doing, and when it needs to use some system resource such as a disk drive or printer, the operating system intervenes and controls the allocation and interface between the program and the resource. What an operating system does is determined by a pattern of priorities programmed by the system designers. In a large-scale mainframe computer system, for example, when two programs want to print something at the same time, the program with a higher priority code gets the printer first. In the human executive, the pattern of priorities is determined by our motivations and goals. A good example of how the executive changes our processing of information and actions is provided by the contrast between the behavior of a person who trips while carrying nothing and a parent who trips while carrying a child. The person carrying nothing flings out his/her limbs to break the fall. The parent moves to protect the child. The child-protection priority is greater than the self-protection priority in this case. It is important to realize that the executive is not conceived as a homunculus, a little human inside the head. Rather, it is a relatively simple control routine that makes decisions in a relatively mechanical way.

5. The Output Buffers

Output buffers are a somewhat speculative component of the processing system. We have included them to handle the fact that well-learned skills can operate without much conscious attention. This process is called automatization (Anderson, 1980; Schneider & Shiffrin, 1977; Shiffrin & Schneider, 1977). An experiment by Spelke, Hirst, and Neisser (1976) illustrates automatization. Undergraduates given the task of reading intently and also copying words dictated to them at first found that task very difficult. With 6 weeks of practice, they were doing the task well. Their comprehension scores on the reading were as good as when they were not copying. Surprisingly, they could not remember what they copied. The interesting point is that with practice, the copying task became automatic and could be carried out without attention. Driving and learning to ride a bicycle provide common examples of automatization. When we first learn to drive or ride, doing the act occupies all our attention. After months of practice however, we carry out many other tasks while driving or riding and sometimes can drive for long distances without much memory of the intervening road.

II.   THE FLOW OF INFORMATION DURING LEARNING

In order to understand how these components work together during learning and information processing, let us trace how the system might operate while engaged in an act of learning. This discussion is speculative and hypothetical, but it gives you an idea of how cognitive psychologists use these ideas about our cognitive system to explain learning and remembering.

Assume that the student is engaged in learning a list of sentences such as: THE DOCTOR MOPPED UP THE FLOOR. This sentence is part of a list of 20 such sentences. The student's task is to memorize the sentences so that he/she is able to recall the subject noun when given the predicate. All of the subject nouns refer to occupations of people, so it is a somewhat difficult task. The sentences are presented one at a time on a computer screen for 6 seconds. The aforementioned sentence is flashed on the screen. The sentence enters the visual sensory register. The student is still attending to and thinking about the previous sentence, so the item is not attended to for 10 milliseconds. Processing of the previous item concludes 10 milliseconds after the doctor sentence is flashed on the screen, and the student begins to attend to the doctor sentence in the visual sensory register. (Because the item stays on the screen for 6 seconds, the operation of the visual sensory register is not critical in this example.)

By attending to the sentence, the student forms a representation of it in the short-term store. This initial representation is probably based upon its perceptual features. The student uses perceptual schemata in long-term semantic memory to recognize the individual words of the sentence. This process changes the representation in short-term memory into a more linguistic than perceptual representation. The student begins to use meaning schemata in long-term semantic memory to construct meaning for the sentence. This process changes the representation to the direct and surface meaning of the sentence (a doctor moving a mop over a floor).

Because the student knows that sentence is to be remembered, he/she may try to elaborate upon and visualize the action of the sentence and a plausible context from it. The student may use world-knowledge schemata in long-term semantic memory to imagine a rural doctor discovering a man badly mauled by a bear. The doctor rushes to his cabin with the patient, operates successfully on his kitchen table, but must mop the floor because no orderly is present (of course many other plausible scenarios can be constructed).

As this elaboration is going on, the student begins to form an image in episodic memory of the elaborated sentence. For example, the image may be something like "I experienced this sentence in an experiment on this day. The sentence came after the sentence about the shepherd." When the test comes, the learner is presented with the test probe: THE _____ MOPPED UP THE FLOOR. This test probe is represented in short-term memory, is processed so as to reach a level of meaning, and activates the image in episodic memory. The response, "DOCTOR," is generated from that image. The response is entered into the output buffer, and the highly overlearned and automatic skill of writing is activated. The skill takes the response from the output buffer and uses it to generate a handwritten response. The student does not attend to the action of handwriting, but instead is thinking about the response to the previous question that he/she could not remember.

THE PURPOSE OF THE SCENARIO

What are the central features that are important about this scenario for understanding the learning process and what education needs to do to facilitate the process? It seems to us that there are several important features of the process.

1. Information to be learned must be attended to.
2. Information to be learned is processed through a series of stages into more complex forms.
3. The representation formed by the student of the information is determined both by the information itself (bottom-up processing) and by the previous general schemata of the student (top-down processing). This means that what a student acquires from instruction is determined as much by what the student already knows as by the nature of the instruction.
4. Using previous knowledge to elaborate upon the presented information facilitates its transfer into long-term memory. This latter point is very important. As you will see in this volume, most of the chapter authors believe that what the student already knows is an important determinant of subsequent learning. When the student relates new information to old information already in long-term memory, the student is more likely to learn and remember the new information. In addition, the way in which the student

processes the new information determines the nature of the representation formed in memory and the way in which the new information can be used.

III. THE NATURE OF MODELS IN THE COGNITIVE INFORMATION-PROCESSING APPROACH

The goal of the cognitive information-processing approach is to develop models of the specific processes that control the learning and the use of knowledge. One difference between the CIP approach and previous approaches is that the CIP approach attempts to develop very specific and precise models. Often such models are developed in the form of a computer program that attempts to simulate the behavior of humans doing the same task that the model is programmed to do. Even if the model is not programmed on a computer, it is described in such a way as to be theoretically programmable on a conceptual computer. By *conceptual computer* is meant a computer that would function computationally like current actual computers, but would have greater capabilities than can be technologically constructed at present (e.g., the conceptual computer would be assumed to have more memory or greater processing speed).

In this kind of model, it is assumed that even though the biological and electronic implementations of a conceptual process are physically different, they are computationally equivalent. For example, even though the biological processes that allow a human brain to see and recognize objects are physically different from the electronic processes that might allow a computer to see and recognize objects, the description of the two processes in terms of the computations performed would be the same.

The word *computation* requires description. In the sense we use it here, it refers to a description of the processes a computer would use to carry out an activity. These processes might include arithmetic computations, but they could also include comparison, moving of bits of information, and branching processes. A computer should be thought about as a symbol-manipulation system rather than a calculation device. A computational description is usually carried out to a systems-analysis or a programming level. It is usually not carried out to a level of description of the underlying electronics or even assembly language.

To make clear what is meant by a computational description, consider a systems-analytic description (flow chart) of how a computer proofreader might determine if a word in text is spelled correctly or not. In the flow chart in Fig. 3, the "word" is entered into a processing area, then compared with an internal dictionary, if the word is present, then it is assumed to be spelled correctly; if the word is not present, it is assumed to be spelled incorrectly.

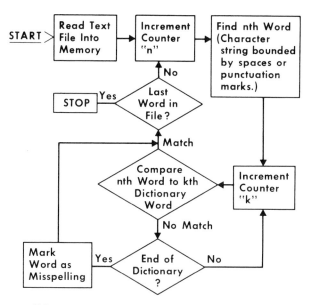

FIG. 3.   How a computer proofreader might operate.

What separates the psychology of cognition from the computer science programming of computers to carry out activities is the emphasis that each of the processes identified in a computational description must be subject to independent empirical measurement and experimental verification in humans. In other words, if as a psychologist I described a particular internal process as part of a description of problem solving, I have a responsibility to specify ways of measuring the process independently of the other processes I describe (Anderson, 1980, 1985; Calfee, 1976). (The preceding description of the spelling checker would *not* meet these criteria and is not a model of human spelling checking.)

IV.   AN ALTERNATIVE VIEW OF THE COGNITIVE SYSTEM

In 1972, Craik and Lockhart proposed an alternative model to the Atkinson–Shiffrin multicomponent model of the aforementioned cognitive system. What Craik and Lockhart suggested was that the various parts of the memory system described (sensory register, short-term store, etc.) did not exist. Rather, they proposed that the phenomena that seemed to support the existence of such mental components could be accounted for more parsimoniously if it was assumed that the result of different kinds of processing

was differentially memorable. They assumed that our cognitive system begins to process a piece of information from the time it is received at sensory
receptors. Each step in the processing yields a transformed piece of information. Each transformed piece of information can be remembered more easily
than the previous transformation.

To make this clear, let us work through an example. Suppose a word is
flashed on a screen and a student perceives it. The first stage of perceptual–
cognitive processing would be to break the letter down into its basic shapes:
lines, curves, overall pattern, etc. Thus, the original stimulus is transformed
into a stimulus that consists now of a patterns of lines, curves, etc. Let us call
this pattern *Output 1*; Output 1 serves as the input into the next stage of
processing. This second stage of processing constructs letters from the input
of the first stage of processing. It makes use of orthographic regularities such
as the spatial-frequency redundancy patterns of letters in English in order to
do so. The second stage yields, as *Output 2*, a pattern consisting of a visual
internal representation of the letters of the word. The third stage of processing combines these letters into a word and may activate an acoustical pattern
of information. Let us call this third transformed pattern *Output 3*. Output 3
is analyzed by semantic processes and yields a surface meaning for the word,
for example *dog*. This is *Output 4*. Output 4 can be analyzed and elaborated
upon further: the student may imagine a particular dog—a Lassie-like collie,
licking a small blond boy's face. This could be *Output 5*. Output 5 could be
further elaborated into a complete story; for example, how did the dog come
to be licking the boy's face?

The point made by Craik and Lockhart is that each stage of the output
would be easier to remember than previous stages. Output 2 would be easier
to remember than Output 1; Output 3 than Output 2; Output 4 than Output
3; and so on. They called this approach the *levels-of-processing* (sometimes
called *depth-of-processing*) *model*. The levels-of-processing model predicts
that material processed to deeper (more semantic and elaborated levels) will
be remembered more easily. The levels-of-processing model has developed
a wide following, and it has been applied to a variety of applied research
areas (Reynolds & Flagg, 1983). Reynolds and Flagg (1983) provide an eval-
uative comparison of these alternative models.

While the distinction between the models is important from a theoretical
psychological perspective, from an educational perspective both models
make similar predictions with regard to educationally useful activities. In
both the multicomponent and the levels-of-processing models, the activity
the student uses to encode and elaborate on presented information influences both the likelihood that the information will be remembered and the
situations in which the information will be remembered. Both models argue
that increases in the extent to which the student processes information for

meaning, relates information to previously stored information, and elaborates upon the information (such as fitting the word *dog* into a Lassie-type
story) will lead to increases in learning and retention. Educational activities
that promote increased semantic and elaborative processing should facilitate
learning.

V. LEARNING AND COGNITION

The general cognitive model described in this chapter emerged out of the
work in experimental psychology on simple verbal learning paradigms and
work in understanding language, problem solving, and other complex intellectual tasks. Since the early 1960s, work within this general perspective has
focused on describing the cognitive processes of adults who had already
acquired major concepts, skills, and abilities. In the area of language use, for
example, the major thrust has been to describe the cognitive systems that
support language use in the mature adult who already knows language. Less
emphasis has been placed on describing how the semantic knowledge that
supports language use was acquired in the first place. Cognitive psychology
focused on the *description* of ongoing cognitive processes, not on the *acquisition* of those processes. Happily, this situation has been changing over
the last several years. Considerably more attention has been devoted to how
cognitive processes are acquired and develop. This renewed attention to
learning is typified by the work of J. Anderson and others on the acquisition
of cognitive skills (e.g., Anderson, 1981), R. Anderson and others on the
acquisition of knowledge (e.g., Anderson, Spiro, & Montague, 1977), Siegler
on conceptual development (1980), Mayer and others on the development of
problem-solving skills (Mayer, 1980), as well as the work of many other
contemporary researchers. This change in emphasis is important because it
makes the relationship between cognitive psychology and educational practice more apparent.

VI. THE EDUCATIONAL UTILITY OF CURRENT
APPROACHES TO COGNITIVE PSYCHOLOGY

What is the value of the general information-processing approach to cognitive psychology for educational practice? Unlike models of behavior that
were developed earlier such as Skinnerian behaviorism, CIP psychology is
just beginning to lead to effective technologies for dealing with particular
educational problems. We believe that the general approach has many
important implications for education.

1. The general approach provides educators with a way of describing goals that goes beyond mere changes in behavior. Rather, the CIP approach suggests that the goals of education are to make changes in the cognitive structures (schemata) of students. Schools attempt to produce in students cognitive structures that provide them with socially common knowledge and ways of analyzing and dealing with problems. Calfee (1981) expressed it in this way:

> "*A theory of the educated mind.*" How does schooling affect the mind? In considering this question, let us assume a conventional notion of the school as a formal setting in which teachers present classical academics across a broad array of curriculum domains.
>
> Here is an answer that may at first seem overly simple, but which actually possesses great power: The effect of schooling is to create a set of well-organized mental structures that parallel the various curriculum programs, both those that are named (literacy, mathematics, science, physical education) and those that are implicit (self-discipline, responsibility, courtesy, competitiveness . . .). Thus, students who have been taught to *read* become the possessers of a complex "frame," if you will, which provides them *culturally designed and sanctioned tools* [italics added] for handling a set of tasks that are important for the society and for the individual. (p. 33)

Calfee goes on to argue that CIP psychology gives us a new and better set of tools for analyzing the mind of the student, the mind of the teacher, and the mind of the administrator. Such analysis can lead to a better understanding of the roles and tasks of students, teachers, and administrators and how to improve their functioning.

2. CIP psychology attempts to develop a more precise and detailed description of the mental processes of students as they carry out tasks. Such descriptions can lead to better specification of educational objectives; work by Greeno (1976) and Resnick (1976) on the cognitive objectives of education points in this direction.

3. Better and more precise description of student activities while they are doing meaningful tasks can lead to more effective procedures for testing and for description of students with typical and special abilities. Psychological testing in education has been primarily atheoretical, and scores even on diagnostic tests represent gross and undifferentiated descriptions of the ability of the student. We believe that the methodologies used for the analysis of cognitive events can also be used for the better analysis of individual patterns of ability. Recent work on the diagnosis of reading comprehension difficulties (e.g., Palincsar and Brown, 1984) illustrates this development.

4. Analysis of the relationship between existing knowledge and new learning may lead to the development of improved technologies for instructional design. A good example is the work of Mayer (1980), which shows how a metaphorical representation can facilitate the learning of problem-solving skills in computer programming.

These four examples of possible implications of the CIP model for educa-tion provide the flavor of the potentialities that exist, but do not exhaust the possibilities. We believe that the general CIP theoretical perspective offers education a model at least as productive and useful as the behavioral model has offered education. Just as in the mid-1950s, when the educational ramifi-cations of the behavioral model were just being to be explored, the implica-tions and possibilities of the CIP model are just beginning to be explored and developed. In our view, the future of the CIP model–educational practice relationship is now as bright as that of the behavioral model in 1955. We look forward to an exciting future.

VII.   THE CIP MODEL AND THE PLAN OF THIS BOOK

One major purpose of this volume is to provide graduate students in educational psychology and all its subfields (school psychology, instructional psychology, instructional design, etc.) and graduate students and practi-tioners in education with a comprehensive overview of the CIP model and its implications for education. This volume was organized around the CIP model, and its chapters provide a detailed presentation of current research and theoretical analysis of the ideas that are sketched in this introductory chapter.

Chapter 2 by O'Boyle discusses the biological components of the cognitive system and provides an overview of the research on laterality. The notion that the right and left hemispheres of the brain function differently has been uncritically accepted by some educators, and many programs have been developed that presumably take advantage of these differences. O'Boyle suggests that the differences are poorly understood and that some of the educational proposals emanating from hypothesized differences are prepos-terous.

Chapter 3 by Grabe discusses the role of attention in the educational process. Attention is the cognitive process that leads to the bringing of ideas into consciousness (STM). It involves the allocation of cognitive resources to tasks. Grabe provides an overview of the educationally important research on attentional processes and suggests how attention can be influenced in educational settings to facilitate learning.

Chapters 4, 5, and 6, by Royer, by Kulhavy, and by Phye, deal with the processing of information in working memory and its transfer into long-term memory. They discuss factors that inhibit and facilitate storage in and re-trieval from long-term memory. Royer focuses on the way in which knowl-edge is stored in long-term memory and presents an alternative that is similar to, but different from, models based upon computer metaphors. He applies his ideas to the measurement of reading comprehension. Kulhavy deals with the idea of schemata and the instructional factors which influence the encoding of information into cognitive structure. He discusses ways to improve the acquisition of knowledge from connected discourse. Phye discusses the roles of practice and informative feedback in the acquisition of skilled classroom performance. Following a review of models of skill development, the effects of timing, drill, and distribution of effort on practice are described. The role of feedback in the development of classroom skills is considered within the context of error analysis and error type.

Chapters 7–9, by Andre, Duell, and Snowman, respectively, deal with the nature of knowledge in long-term memory. Andre focuses on the development of schemata that are usually called concepts, principles, and problem-solving skills. He argues that these are essentially similar in the way they are stored in semantic memory, and he provides a model for designing instruction to facilitate their development. Duell and Snowman deal with a class of intellectual skills that are commonly called metacognitive learning skills or learning strategies. Such skills or strategies represent knowledge the student has about how to learn. They include knowledge about how to allocate resources and organize study as well as knowledge about particular mental activities to perform in particular learning situations. Duell discusses the development of such skills in children and pays particular attention to the development of skills necessary to comprehend and learn from language. Snowman focuses more on the skills used by adults (high school, college student, and older students) and discusses research on the effectiveness of particular learning techniques. These two chapters represent a particularly important thrust in current cognitive instructional psychology. There is a great emphasis on using cognitive psychology to produce better students as well as better instructional materials.

Chapter 10, by Lunzer, provides a bridge between traditional cognitive psychology and the CIP perspective. Lunzer reviews the general Piagetian model of cognitive change and points out its strengths and shortcomings. He provides a developmental context for a discussion of learning and the mechanisms of change. This concluding chapter provides a metatheoretical framework that previous chapters have, to differing extents, addressed. The final section of Chapter 10 provides a tentative model of CIP that accounts for learning and the mechanisms of change.

REFERENCES

Anderson, J. R. (1980). *Cognitive psychology*. San Francisco: Freeman.
Anderson, J. R. (1981). *Cognitive skills and their acquisition*. Hillsdale, NJ: Erlbaum.

Anderson, J. R. (1985). *Cognitive psychology and its implications* (3rd ed.). New York: Freeman.

Anderson, R. C., Spiro, R. J., & Montague, W., (1977). *Schooling and the acquisition of knowledge*. Hillsdale, NJ: Erlbaum.

Atkinson, R. C., & Shiffrin, R. M. (1968). Human Memory: a proposed system and its control processes. In K. Spence, & J. Spence (Eds.), *The psychology of learning and motivation* (Vol 2, pp. 301–355). New York: Academic Press.

Calfee, R. C. (1976). Sources of dependency in cognitive processes. In D. Klahr (Ed.), *Cognition and instruction*. Hillsdale, NJ: Erlbaum.

Calfee, R. (1981). Cognitive psychology and educational practice, in D. C. Berliner (Ed.), *Review of Research in Education*, 9, 3–79.

Darwin, C. J., Turvey, M. T., & Crowder, R. G. (1972). The auditory analogue of the Sperling partial report procedure: Evidence for brief auditory storage. *Cognitive Psychology, 3,* 255–267.

Greeno, J. G. (1976). Cognitive objectives of instruction: Theory of knowledge for solving problems and answering questions, in D. Klahr (Ed.), *Cognition and instruction* (pp. 123–160). Hillsdale, NJ: Erlbaum.

Mayer, R. (1980). Elaboration techniques that increase the meaningfulness of technical text: an experimental test of the learning strategy hypothesis. *Journal of Educational Psychology, 72,* 770–784.

Moray, N., Bates, A., & Barnett, T. (1965). Experiments on the four-eared man. *Journal of the Acoustical Society of America, 38,* 196–201.

Palincsar, A. S., & Brown, A. L. (1984). Reciprocal teaching of comprehension-fostering and comprehension-monitoring activities, *Cognition and Instruction, 1,* 117–175.

Resnick, L. B. (1976). Task analysis in instructional design: some cases from mathematics, in D. Klahr (Ed.), *Cognition and Instruction* (pp. 51–80). Hillsdale, NJ: Erlbaum.

Reynolds, A. G., & Flagg, P. W. (1983). *Cognitive psychology*. Boston: Little-Brown.

Schneider, W., & Shiffrin, R. M. (1977). Controlled and automatic human information processing: I. Detection, search, and attention. *Psychological Review, 84,* 1–66.

Shiffrin, R. M., & Schneider, W. (1977). Controlled and automatic human information processing: II. Perceptual learning, automatic attending, and a general theory. *Psychological Review, 84,* 127–190.

Siegler, R. S. (1980). When do children learn? The relationship between existing knowledge and learning. *Educational Psychologist, 15,* 135–150.

Spelke, E. Hirst, W., and Neisser, U. (1976). Skills of divided attention. *Cognition,4,* 215–230.

Sperling, G. A. (1960). The information available in brief visual presentation, *Psychology Monographs, 74,* Whole No. 498.

Tulving, E. (1972). Episodic and semantic memory. In E. Tulving & S. Donaldson (Eds.), *Organization of memory* (pp. 382–404). New York: Academic Press.

HEMISPHERIC LATERALITY AS A BASIS OF LEARNING: WHAT WE KNOW AND DON'T KNOW

Michael W. O'Boyle

Department of Psychology
Iowa State University
Ames, Iowa 50011

I. INTRODUCTION

One need only flick on the television set or skim a selection of current periodicals to get an idea of the popularity enjoyed by the topic of left brain–right brain differences. At present, it is quite chic in most advertising and educational circles to consider the left cerebral hemisphere (LH) as "verbal, analytic and dominant" while the right cerebral hemisphere (RH) is thought to be "artistic but mute and totally mysterious" (Pines, 1973). Over-simplification has always been a danger in the popular press; however, the extent of misinformation reported about brain laterality and the processing specializations of each hemisphere is staggering. Claims of dual consciousness or two separate persons competing inside the same head far exceed what we actually know about the two halves of the brain.

Unfortunately, the notoriety given to brain laterality has come to exert considerable social pressure on the educational community. Such pressure has influenced some schools to redesign teaching methods and testing procedures in an effort to capitalize on these presumed hemispheric specialties (Hardyck & Haapanen, 1979). Critics charge that our educational system, which places heavy emphasis on verbal and analytic skills, is solely attending to the left half of the brain while neglecting the right half. Appeals for whole-brain curricula are increasing, and fear is ever mounting that teachers may inadvertently be stifling creativity by failing to educate the RH (Bogen, 1975, 1977; Samples, 1975; Torrance, 1981). In order to avoid this danger, right brain–left brain proponents insist on scrapping a large portion of educational practice in favor of a more hemisphere-based curriculum—one which is more in tune with the unique processing capabilities of both cerebral hemispheres. According to these critics, the utilization of such a strat-

COGNITIVE CLASSROOM LEARNING:
UNDERSTANDING, THINKING, AND PROBLEM SOLVING

egy would effectively eliminate the potential for lopsided cognitive development.

Before making drastic changes in the school system, however, it seems wise to scrutinize the research literature to determine if claims about left brain–right brain differences have a solid scientific basis. Without an adequately established database, sweeping curriculum changes *do not* merit implementation.

The present chapter (1) briefly looks at the anatomical and historical precedence for left–right differences, (2) selectively reviews and critiques the hemispheric-specialization literature involving unilateral brain-damaged, split-brain, and normal populations, and (3) attempts to assess the implications and applications such findings may have for laterality as a basis of learning and educational practice.

II. ASYMMETRY IN THE MIDST OF SYMMETRY

At first glance, the human body seems quite balanced and symmetrical. We possess two arms, two legs, two eyes, two ears, and, interestingly, two cerebral hemispheres (two ostensibly symmetrical halves of the human brain). Each of the hemispheres is linked by several interconnecting fibers known as *commissures*, whose primary function is to relay information between the two halves of the brain. The most prominent of these pathways is the corpus callosum (see Fig. 1).

Despite this apparent bodily symmetry, there do exist several pronounced asymmetries, for instance, *hand dominance*. When greeting a friend by patting him on the back or threatening an enemy by waving our fist, most of us will use our right hand, though some are prone to using the left. Such hand preference is primarily genetic in origin (Carter-Saltzman, 1980; Levy & Nagylaki, 1972) and is demonstrated in various manipulospatial skills, from throwing a baseball to writing a letter or painting a picture. In addition, there are several other asymmetries which are equally pronounced, though less readily observed. For example, since the time of the ancient Greeks, it has been known that in females the two breasts are not quite identical in size, with the right one being slightly larger than the left (Bradshaw & Nettleton, 1983). Also, in males, the right testicle is situated slightly higher than the left, is larger in size, weighs more, and exceeds its counterpart in protein and DNA content (McManus, 1976). Moreover, researchers have recently pinpointed the existence of a small but reliable asymmetry in the incidence of tumors in bilateral organs (e.g., kidneys, adrenal glands, and ovaries) with the left being the predominantly affected (Robin & Shortridge, 1979).

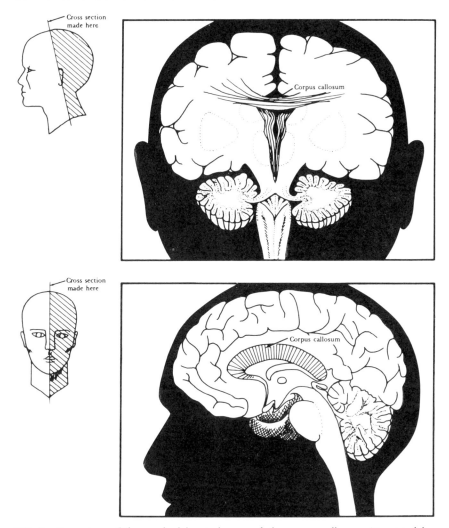

FIG. 1. Two views of the cerebral hemispheres and the corpus callosum. (Reprinted by permission from Lindsay and Norman, *Human Information Processing*, p. 442, Academic Press, 1977.)

In addition to these anatomical asymmetries, various cultures throughout history have emphasized a more mythological aspect to left–right differences. Since primitive times, the right has been regarded as the side of gods and life, while the left is considered the side of demons and death (Hertz, 1909, as cited in Bradshaw & Nettleton, 1983). Even in the Bible, there is evidence of a spiritual distinction between the two, with the "blessed" usually seated at the right hand of God (Matthew 22:44, 25:33–34). To this day, some believe that left-handedness is associated with a socially deviant personality (Hardyck & Petrinovich, 1977)—a carryover, perhaps, from this earlier biblical thinking.

III. MORPHOLOGICAL DIFFERENCES BETWEEN THE LEFT AND RIGHT HEMISPHERES

Given these anatomical and historical antecedents for differences between left and right, researchers in the neurosciences began to ask questions concerning the possibility of morphological asymmetries in the human brain. Specifically, were there verifiable structural differences between the left and right hemispheres, and if so, what impact do they have on mental operations?

Initially, the two cerebral hemispheres were thought to be mirror images of one another, identical in every way. In fact, any deviance from symmetry (be it chemical, electrical, or structural) was regarded as a neurological abnormality (Springer & Deutsch, 1985). Recent research, however, has done much to dispel the notion of symmetrical hemispheres, identifying several anatomical differences between the two. For example, it is now believed that the right hemisphere weighs more than the left (LeMay, 1976)—a finding which dovetails nicely with the fact that on the average, more tissue composes the right than the left hemisphere (Whitaker & Ojemann, 1977). Moreover, it was originally believed that the length and width of the two hemispheres were essentially equal. It is now known, however, that the frontal pole and the central portion of the right hemisphere tend to be wider, extending further forward than the left (Chui & Damasio, 1980). Contrastingly, the left occipital pole is wider and protrudes more to the rear than does the right (Rubens, 1977). These size and positional relationships between the two hemispheres are summarized succinctly by Bradshaw and Nettleton (1983) as giving the brain a "counterclockwise torque" (p. 24).

Other components which have been found to be asymmetrically represented in the human brain are the Sylvian fissure and the plenum temporale. The Sylvian fissure is a cortical fold which separates the temporal and parietal lobes of the brain. This crease is known to be longer on the left than the right (Cunningham, 1892). Similarly, the plenum temporale is an area of the brain located in the temporaparietal region of the association cortex, which is thought to be intimately involved in language-related functions. When examining a large number of postmortem brains, Geschwind and Levitsky (1968) found that in 65% of the cases this region was larger on the left and in 11% this area was larger on the right, whereas the remainder were not readily distinguishable.

IV. LEFT HEMISPHERE–RIGHT HEMISPHERE
SPECIALIZATION
IN COGNITIVE FUNCTIONING

As suggested by the aforementioned morphological differences, it appears that the two halves of the brain are not structurally identical. An important question remains, however: "Might not these anatomical asymmetries reflect specialization of the hemispheres for specific cognitive functions?" Extensive research has been conducted on three different subject populations in an effort to answer this question. Generally speaking, these studies attempt to determine what mental faculties are impaired or altered when subjects have (1) suffered a lesion or some form of tissue deterioration in one but not the other hemisphere (i.e., unilateral brain-damaged patients), (2) undergone surgical sectioning of the corpus callosum, leaving each of the hemispheres intact but unable to communicate with one another (i.e., "split-brain" patients), and (3) had no neurological impairment, but information is presented to them in such a way as to require either the LH or the RH to initiate processing (e.g., stimuli presented to the eye, ear, or hand on one side of the body are processed [at least initially] by the hemisphere on the opposite side).

The logic involved in these studies is to test each hemisphere's cognitive abilities in relative isolation and subsequently to identify some processes for which they may be uniquely specialized. A selective review of research involving each of the three groups follows.

A. EVIDENCE FROM UNILATERAL BRAIN-DAMAGED PATIENTS

Some evidence in support of a functional specialization of the hemispheres comes from studies involving unilateral brain-damaged patients. In these studies, individuals who have experienced some form of cerebral injury to one or the other hemisphere are examined for subsequent deficiencies in cognitive processing. As early as the nineteenth century, such examinations have revealed that language disorders (called *aphasias*) are more frequent and generally occur with greater severity when the injury is located in the left rather than the right hemisphere (Broca, 1865, as cited in Hellige, 1980a; Dax, 1836, as cited in Springer & Deutsch, 1985; and Wernicke, 1874, as cited in Benson, 1979). For example, both Broca's and Wernicke's aphasias (disorders involving speech production and comprehension deficits, respectively) occur almost exclusively as a result of damage to specific areas in the left hemiphere. Injury to identical locations in the right hemisphere alone only rarely produces either of these impairments (Benson, 1979; Caramazza & Martin, 1983). Conversely, performance deficits observed in tasks requiring visuospatial skills (e.g., face recognition, block design, finger mazes, and picture memory) are more likely to occur as a consequence of right rather than left hemisphere damage (DeRenzi, Faglioni, & Spinnler, 1968; Kimura, 1961; Milner, 1968, 1971). This verbal–visuospatial processing dichotomy, though somewhat oversimplified, has proven to be a popular framework for conceptualizing left–right differences in human brain functioning—typically linking most language-related functions to the left hemisphere and most spatial abilities to the right.

B.   CRITICISMS OF THE UNILATERAL BRAIN-DAMAGE STUDIES

That such a processing dichotomy is present in unilaterally brain-damaged patients is seemingly well established. However, are these findings on firm scientific ground, and if so, how accurately do they describe brain functions in neurologically normal individuals? Just how confident can we be that such hemispheric specialties are similarly lateralized in our students?

Despite the intuitive appeal and apparent support for a verbal–visuospatial processing dichotomy, several problems of interpretation arise when we attempt to attribute exclusive processing skills to one or the other hemisphere by juxtaposing the performance of left-brain-damaged patients against that of right-brain-damaged patients. First, even with recent advances in electronic brain scanning techniques (computerized axial tomography or CAT scans and positron emission tomography or PET scans), it remains a difficult task to determine the exact location and the extent of damage in either the right or the left hemisphere of these patients. This makes for serious difficulties in comparing the performance of each group on specific tasks, rendering conclusions about left hemisphere–right hemisphere advantages quite hazardous and perhaps misleading.

Second, in these patients, the source of the damage is oftentimes surgical intervention performed to correct some neurological disorder. In such instances, it is next to impossible to equate each of the patients' presurgery history. Pathology-related drug use and the etiology of the cerebral infirmity are likely to vary extensively from patient to patient, resulting in a set of individuals who on the surface appear quite similar (to the extent that they are all diagnosed as brain-damaged) but are only tangentially related with regard to other important psychological variables. Such presurgery characteristics may have a marked effect on hemispheric performance in a variety of postoperative tasks.

Finally and perhaps most importantly, one must be intimately aware of the fact that the substance of the conclusions drawn from research on unilaterally brain-damaged patients only addresses the issue of what the remaining tissue *can do*, not what it *does do* during normal functioning in the intact brain. Hence, the findings concerning left–right processing differences in brain-damaged patients are not necessarily representative of hemispheric processing in our students.

V. EVIDENCE FROM "SPLIT-BRAIN" RESEARCH

Additional evidence in support of a left brain–right brain specialization in cognitive functioning comes from what are commonly known as the "split-brain" studies. Initiated by Nobel Prize winner Dr. Roger Sperry at the California Institute of Technology, they are perhaps the most publicized research demonstrating the unique processing capacities of each cerebral hemisphere. In these studies, patients who have had their corpus callosum (see Figure 1) cut to reduce the severity of epileptic seizure are subjected to rigorous postoperative testing (for a detailed description of the actual surgical procedures utilized in splitting the brain see Gazzaniga, 1970, chapter 2, pp. 5–13). The effect of this operation is to disrupt the normal exchange of information between the right and left hemispheres, leaving only contralateral input for subsequent cognitive processing (i.e., as illustrated in Fig. 2, a signal presented to the left side is processed by the right hemisphere while one presented to the right side is analyzed by the left hemisphere). These lateralized processing responsibilities hold true for most perceptual modalities including vision, audition, and touch (Gazzaniga, Bogen, & Sperry, 1962).

Notably, the experiments performed on these commissurotomized patients are said to improve significantly upon the unilateral brain-damage experiments, in that they allow for the study of two intact, though relatively isolated and ostensibly undamaged hemispheres. Hence, several of the criticisms levied against the unilateral brain-damage studies are, for the most part, circumvented by the split-brain studies.

The results of this particular research program suggest the following with regard to left brain–right brain processing differences: (1) the left hemisphere in the split-brain patient is quite proficient in most language-related functions. These individuals are able to produce verbal and written responses to objects or words presented to the right visual field, and they can accurately retrieve with their right hand items which have been named, described, or defined by the experimenter, and (2) mathematical procedures like addition, multiplication, and division pose no particular problem (Levy, 1974; Nebes, 1974).

With regard to right-hemisphere capacities, the initial evidence indicated that it possessed little or no language-related abilities. The commissurotomized subjects were unable to name, verbally or in writing, any words seen in the left visual field or any objects felt with the left hand

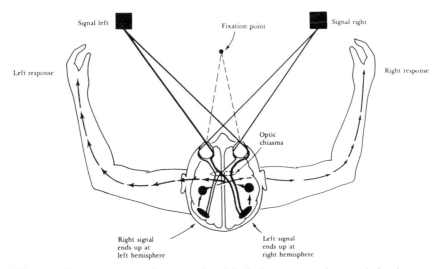

FIG. 2. Information presented to one side of the body is processed primarily by the contralateral hemisphere. (Reprinted by permission from Lindsay and Norman, *Human Information Processing*, p. 443, Academic Press, 1977.)

(Gazzaniga, Bogen, & Sperry, 1962, 1965, 1967). This deficit occurred despite the fact that the right hemisphere did indeed perceive and comprehend the requests as demonstrated by the ability to use nonverbal response modes to easily solve the task (i.e., patients could retrieve or point to the target object using the left hand but were unable to name the object aloud). In light of these results, researchers concluded that the "speech center" and perhaps all language-related functions were located in the left rather than the right hemisphere. There is, however, a considerable amount of research indicating that we have grossly underestimated the contribution of the RH to language processing (Searleman, 1977; Zaidel, 1978), particularly with regard to the verbal expression of anger and elation (Ross, 1982).

There also exist several other higher level mental processes which demonstrate lateralized locus of control in the split-brain patients. One such faculty is emotion. In the commissurotomized patients, appropriate emotional expressions are readily observed for both hemispheres. Sperry (1968) reports on a study in which a slide of a nude "pinup" was inserted by surprise into a set of neutral geometric figures. The subject's task was to verbally identify the stimulus presented. In this experiment, an interesting emotional response was observed, particularly when the pinup was flashed to the left visual field–right hemisphere (LVF–RH). In this instance, the subject would verbally report that she had seen nothing or just a flash of light. However, the patient was observed to be blushing and wearing a sneaky grin, and she proceeded to giggle over the course of the next several trials. Such behavior seemed to belie the verbal response. When the patient was asked, "What's all the grinning about?" the conversant LH provided a confabulated verbal response, which clearly demonstrated that it had no precise idea as to what the RH had observed (i.e., the LH would say something like, "Oh, you guys have a funny machine"). Such a response probably reflects the LH's perception of a change in facial musculature to a smile and/or the sound of the giggle rather than the content of the slide presentation per se. When the slide was presented to the right visual field–left hemisphere (RVF–LH), this patient would readily report verbally that she had indeed seen the pinup and subsequently would respond in a similar emotional fashion.

In addition, other investigators report that the RH often demonstrates various reactions of displeasure during experimental study. Such claims are based on observations of frowning, wincing, and head shaking by the RH for instances in which the RH knows the correct answer but cannot speak it, and in fact, the RH appears disgusted when it hears the LH provide an obvious verbal mistake (Gazzaniga, 1970; Gazzaniga & LeDoux, 1978; Sperry, 1966, 1968). As Sperry (1968) suggests, perhaps the RH is expressing a "genuine annoyance at the erroneous vocal responses of its better half" (p. 723).

One of the more intriguing questions associated with higher cognitive processes in commissurotomized patients is the possibility that the mechanisms responsible for human conscious experience may be doubly represented after brain bisection—that is, exhibiting a split-consciousness (Sperry, 1966). The aforementioned emotional expressions seem to be indicative of an RH which is indeed a "second conscious entity that is characteristically human and runs along in parallel with the dominant stream of consciousness in the major hemisphere (LH)" (Sperry, 1968, p. 732).

Gazzaniga and LeDoux (1978) have conducted several experiments in an attempt to substantiate this claim. Early on, they developed a methodology in which pictures of common objects were laterally presented to the mute RH of a rather unique split-brain patient (unique because preliminary testing indicated that he possessed some RH language ability). In these studies, the patient's task was to name the object presented by arranging letters into an identifying word. Gazzaniga and LeDoux believed that this experimental situation would provide the opportunity to assess whether or not the RH was capable of independently demonstrating properties of human consciousness. The procedure for testing this possibility is as follows.

First, a series of questions were formulated and subsequently presented to either the left or the right hemisphere. Exclusive presentation of these questions was assured by verbally stating the sentence except for the deletion of a "key word," which was replaced by the word *blank*. The specific key word for a given trial was then flashed very briefly to either the LVF–RH or the RVF–LH and the subject's task was to spell his answer using several sets of Scrabble® letters. This response was to be carried out by the patient's contralateral hand (left hand–RH or right hand–LH).

Using the preceding technique, the first question asked was "Who blank?" followed by the words *are you* laterally presented to the RH. The patient responded by spelling his name *Paul*. A second question asked was, "Would you spell your favorite *blank*?" Subsequently, the key word *girl* was flashed to the patient's LVF–RH. He responded by arranging the letters to form the word *Liz*, which was indeed the name of his current female friend. The most interesting exchange in this series of questions, however, transpired when the patient was asked, "What *blank* would you like to do? (key word *job*). When the key word was presented to the RVF–LH, the patient responded "draftsman." The result was markedly different, however, when the question was addressed to the LVF–RH, which spelled the term *automobile race*. These findings seem to suggest that the RH is indeed a separate conscious entity—one which exists independently of the LH.

CRITICISMS OF THE SPLIT-BRAIN RESEARCH

Despite the seemingly dramatic support for specialized differences between the left and right hemispheres for cognitive processing, serious problems of methodology and subsequent interpretation abound in the split-brain studies. One such problem involves the inevitable tissue destruction incurred as a result of the surgical procedure utilized to split the brain. When performing a commissurotomy, one of the hemispheres (typically the nonlinguistic one) is retracted to expose the corpus callosum for incision. This procedure can bruise the mesial surface of that hemisphere, as well as tear veins and arteries, which may provoke symmetrical degeneration of brain tissue in *both* hemispheres. This, of course, makes comparisons between LH and RH cognitive specialties quite tenuous, as each hemisphere (as a result of the operation) may be damaged to differing degrees, and each may be operating at less than full capacity. In addition, the incision process itself is a delicate one. If made too deeply, it essentially punctures the roof of the third ventricle, precipitating the release of cerebral spinal fluid, which can create some rather serious neurological complications. If the incision is too shallow, however, one cannot be totally sure that complete sectioning has occurred (Whitaker, 1978). Moreover, in these split-brain operations, it is sometimes the case that several interconnecting fibers (other than the corpus callosum) are left intact. Instances in which the anterior commissure, the hippocampal commissure, and/or the massa intermedia are spared may leave open alternate means of communication between the left and right hemispheres (this in addition to the fact that the intact brainstem can also serve to relay information, providing ample opportunity for "cross-talk" between the two). Although the extent and the nature of the information exchange via these alternative routes are not yet fully understood, it seems clear that any claim regarding total communicative isolation of the two hemispheres is less than completely accurate.

An additional problem of import concerning the split-brain, is that commissurotomy is performed only as a last resort, typically after a prolonged history of medication has failed to control epilepsy. Due to obvious differences in medical and psychological background, left–right processing specializations observed in these patients may not provide much direct information concerning the functions of each hemisphere in neurologically normal individuals like our students—individuals who have never suffered through a seizure or experienced the serious side-effects associated with the long-term use of potent medication. Moreover, only a very small number of individuals afflicted with epilepsy ever undergo this relatively drastic surgical measure. Given such a limited sample size (fewer than 40 patients in total, and usually no more than 2 or 3 involved in any given experiment), one must question the generalizability of the observed processing asymmetries, particularly when attempting to infer all normal brain processes from split-brain performance.

The fact that only a handful of commissurotomized patients are in existence has other ramifications beyond the mere generalizability of results. Given the interest and popularity of left brain–right brain processes, these unique individuals are in great demand for examination throughout the world. Once secured for study, they are subjected to an exhaustive, long-term research program involving thorough and rigorous testing. After participation in several such sessions, the tendency is for them to become extremely test-wise. In fact, commissurotomized patients demonstrate unparalled resourcefulness when forced to solve various laboratory tasks. Researchers have described several incidents in which split-brain subjects have successfully completed various tasks via cross-cuing techniques rather than relying on what appear to be specialized hemispheric capacities. For example, a patient is given an object to be held out of sight in his left hand. Typically, when asked to name the object aloud, the patient has extreme difficulty because of the RH's inability to contact the speech center, which is housed in the LH. On at least one occasion, however, a patient was indeed able to verbally identify the object held in his left hand as a comb. How did he successfully perform this task? P. J. Cox (personal communication, July 1978) reports that the patient would simply "thumb" the teeth of the comb producing a unique auditory cue for the LH. This bilateral information was then utilized by the LH to make a verbal guess, i.e., "comb." Similarly, in an effort to solve other tasks, split-brain patients have been reported to drop objects, tap them on the table and even flip them (coins in particular) above the curtain used to hide the objects from view (P. J. Cox, personal communication, July 1978; Gazzaniga, 1970; Gazzaniga & LeDoux, 1978). Because of this test-wise resourcefulness one must be exceedingly careful when attributing processing differences in these patients to hemispheric specialization when they might easily be the end result of some subtle interactive cross-cuing technique.

VI.   EVIDENCE FROM THE NEUROLOGICALLY NORMAL

Given the preceding research review, it appears that in neurologically impaired patients, the two halves of the human brain possess some unique processing skills. An important question, however, remains to be answered. Can we directly validate that such left-brain–right-brain differences are similarly exhibited in normal individuals?

Investigation of lateral processing asymmetries in the intact brain is actually quite a difficult task. Because all of the interconnecting fibers remain functional, it is impossible to examine the cognitive capabilities of each hemisphere in total isolation. Undoubtedly, the two hemispheres engage in extensive cross-talk (Kinsbourne, 1975) and are constantly exchanging information extracted from the environment (Moscovitch, 1979). Researchers have attempted, however, to minimize the problem of information exchange by studying performance on a variety of tasks as a function of which hemisphere receives the stimulus input directly and hence is forced to initiate cognitive processing. For neurologically normal subjects, stimuli presented to either the left or right side of the body are initially processed contralaterally (i.e., by the right and left hemispheres, respectively, as depicted in Fig. 2). This contralateral representation holds true for the auditory, visual (with some restrictions), and tactile modalities, though other senses (e.g., olfaction) are processed in a more ipsilateral fashion (Carlson, 1980).

The reasoning behind the side-of-presentation approach stems from the notion that performance should be best when the stimulus input travels directly to the hemisphere which is thought to be specialized for the analysis of the given information (e.g., verbal information presented directly to the LH and spatial–nonverbal information presented directly to the RH). In keeping with this notion, performance asymmetries may be attributed to the loss or the possible degradation of the stimulus information as a result of shuttling the representation from the hemisphere which receives the input to the hemisphere specialized for processing (Kimura, 1966, 1967, 1973). It should be noted that this side-of-presentation technique only ensures that the information will be *initially* processed by the contralateral hemisphere. Once the information has entered the brain, there is no guarantee that all subsequent processing is in fact completed solely by the left or the right hemisphere. In essence, we are really evaluating the interactive performance of the two hemispheres and their unique contributions towards successful completion of a given task. To illustrate by analogy, consider an automobile factory. Although all of the component parts arrive at the same loading dock, the assembly, the quality control, and the performance inspections may occur at various locations throughout the plant. Similarly, information presented directly to one hemisphere may be initially processed at that site, but subsequently may be sent to other locations in the brain for additional analyses.

One experimental method for investigating lateral processing asymmetries in the normal brain is referred to as *dichotic listening*. These experiments involve the simultaneous presentation of different auditory stimuli to the right and left ears. In this situation, input from each ear projects directly to the contralateral hemisphere (Milner, Taylor, & Sperry, 1968; Rosenzwieg, 1951). For example, by using stereo headphones, the digit *nine* is presented to the left ear/RH and the digit *five* is simultaneously presented to the right ear–LH. In a given experiment, several such stimulus pairs would be presented in rapid succession and the subject's task is to verbally recall as many of the digits as possible. In such studies, researchers have found that neurologically normal subjects tend to report more digits (Kimura, 1967) as well as more syllables (Hellige & Wong, 1983), words (McGlone & Davidson, 1973), and sentences (Zurif, 1974) when they are presented to the right ear and hence directly to the "linguistic" LH. The opposite-ear advantage is usually obtained if the stimuli presented are more nonverbal in nature, e.g., melodic patterns (King & Kimura, 1972), musical chords (Gordon, 1970), or various environmental sounds such as dishwashing, dogs barking, or clocks ticking (Knox & Kimura, 1970). The observed right-ear advantage is attributed to a LH specialization for the perception of speech as well as other stimuli requiring sequential processing—this finding dove-tails nicely with the unilateral brain-damage and split-brain results. Almost by default, the left-ear advantage is said to reflect a RH specialization for the processing of nonspeech sounds, which may involve a more holistic or simultaneous mode of analysis.

In the visual modality, similar left–right processing asymmetries are found using an experimental technique referred to as *tachistoscopic presentation*. In such studies, stimuli are presented to the left or the right of central vision for durations of 250 milliseconds (ms) or less. These short-on-time parameters all but eliminate eye movements, and due to the natural splitting of the visual system via the optic chiasm, the presentation of the stimulus input is restricted to the contralateral hemisphere (Bradshaw & Nettleton, 1981; Hellige, 1980a; Springer & Deutsch, 1985). Researchers using this particular method of investigation typically report a RVF/LH advantage for the recognition of words (Hines, 1976, 1977; O'Boyle, 1985, Exp. 1), nonsense syllables (Levy & Reid, 1978), single letters (Hellige, 1980b; O'Boyle & Hellige, 1982), and digits (Madden & Nebes, 1980). Conversely, a LVF/RH advantage is reported for the recognition of nonsense shapes (Hellige & Cox, 1976), faces (Hilliard, 1973; Moscovitch, Scullion & Christie, 1976; Rizzolatti & Buchtel, 1977), and depth perception (Durnford & Kimura, 1971).

Another source of evidence for lateral asymmetries in the normal brain comes from studies involving the sense of touch. These experiments typically involve the tactile perception of information (e.g., symbols or objects hidden from view) by either the left or right hand. This procedure is also thought to limit presentation of information (at least initially) to the right or left cerebral hemisphere. The bulk of the findings in these manipulospatial studies are reminiscent of those produced by dichotic listening and visual half-field experiments. For example, Witelson (1974) obtained a slight right hand–LH advantage for recognizing three-dimensional letters while reporting a pronounced left hand–RH advantage for recognizing three-dimensional shapes. Using a different paradigm, O'Boyle, Van Wyhe-Lawler, and Miller (1985) reported a strong recognition asymmetry associated with the identification of capital letters traced in the right and left palms. Specifically, those traced in the left palm–RH were more accurately identified than those traced in the right palm–LH—an effect they attribute to a RH advantage in the tactile perception of directionality and the codification of information along a spatial dimension (Benton, Levine, & Varney, 1973). Moreover, it has been reported that there exists a reliable left hand–RH advantage in Braille letter learning (Rudel, Denckla, & Splaten, 1974) as well as in subsequent reading speed and accuracy (Hermelin & O'Connor, 1971).

In addition to these relatively noninvasive procedures for studying left–right processing differences, there also exists a slightly more direct technique for measuring asymmetries in the normal brain. This methodology involves the monitoring of various anatomical responses when performing tasks designed to differentially engage either the right or left hemisphere. One such procedure is to measure regional cerebral blood flow (rCBF). In these studies, 133 Xenon (a low-grade radioisotope) is either injected or inhaled into the bloodstream. Subsequently, when performing either a verbal or a spatial task (e.g., reading a book or assembling a jigsaw puzzle, respectively), a sodium iodide crystal emission detector is affixed to the subject's head and monitors the flow of blood to different areas of the brain.

The assumption is that the metabolic activity will vary depending upon the extent to which right and left hemisphere functions are utilized (Lassen, Ingvar, & Skinhoj, 1978). Risberg, Halsey, Wills, and Wilson (1975) have indeed demonstrated differential rCBF in the LH and RH for verbal versus visuospatial task activation, respectively.

That the rCBF technique provides some support for left brain–right brain processing differences is apparent. There are, however, some distinct interpretive problems associated with the use of this experimental procedure. One such problem is that the process of metabolic exchange is a three-dimensional phenomenon which is being measured using a two-dimensional device (Bradshaw & Nettleton, 1983). By analogy, this is a process similar to estimating the volume of a cube by measuring only the dimensions of height and width while completely ignoring depth. Such a scaling mismatch in measuring rCBF may result in a misrepresentation of the extent to which each hemisphere contributes to performance in a given task. Hence conclusions about RH–LH processing specializations based on this procedure may be somewhat misleading.

Another issue which is problematic for the rCBF technique is that it remains a rather gross measure of metabolic activity, requiring sustained and continuous data collection for upwards of 20 minutes. Notably, the time frame associated with many cognitive events is considerably shorter than that required for rCBF measurement. This raises a question concerning just how accurately the procedure can index cognitive activity which has long since passed. Future technological advancements, however, should reduce the time necessary to collect measurements, making the technique considerably more useful in assessing left–right processing contributions (Wood, 1983).

An additional problem of interpretation involving this procedure stems from the recent discovery that various psychological factors like attention, motivation, and arousal exert considerable influence on the blood flow process. For example, when performing a complex cognitive task like mathematics, it has been demonstrated that rCBF to the LH can be altered as a result of monetary incentive (Warren, Butler, Katholi, McFarland, Crews, & Halsey, Jr., 1984). Hence, experiments involving subjects who have been paid for participation may produce results which differ relative to experiments with those who have not. This issue (which has heretofore been largely ignored) may make comparison of rCBF to each hemisphere a more complex matter than previously considered.

Another source of evidence from a similar physiological perspective is the electroencephalographic (EEG) studies. In these experiments, electrodes are placed at symmetrical locations above the right and left hemispheres to monitor the electrical activity at each of the brain sites. The logic underlying these studies is that differential electrical activity will index different degrees of specialized functioning by one or the other hemisphere.

Galin and Ornstein (1972) have demonstrated differential alpha wave suppression (8–12 hz activity—thought to reflect resting potential) as a function of verbal or spatial task involvement. Specifically, alpha activity was suppressed in the LH when the subjects were required to write a verbal passage from memory, whereas RH alpha suppression was obtained when they performed a modified version of the Koh Block Design task. Each of these observations was considered to be indicative of one hemisphere's being more actively involved in the processing operation, depending upon the specialized requirements of the task at hand (be they verbal or visuospatial, sequential or holistic).

As with the other methods, the EEG studies are not without problems of interpretation. One major concern is that lateral processing asymmetries are often claimed without reference to an adequately established baseline (for a review of this issue, see Donchin, Kutas, & McCarthy, 1977). The effect of this methodological flaw is to generate conclusions based on data which have no interpretive backdrop. Hence, phasic activities (i.e., increases or decreases in electrical activity levels) are reported but seldom specified in relation to tonic level activity (i.e., background or normal operating level) of each hemisphere. This is the equivalent of reporting a significant effect of an experimental manipulation without reference to a control group. In addition, the exact placement of electrodes at homologous locations above each hemisphere remains a troublesome task despite the utilization of the Jasper 10–20 mapping system (Jasper, 1958).

VII.   EDUCATIONAL IMPLICATIONS OF HEMISPHERIC LATERALITY

As can be seen from the research reviewed here, there is indeed a considerable amount of experimental evidence suggesting that the two cerebral hemispheres make distinct, interactive contributions to performance in a wide variety of cognitive tasks. These observed processing differences are normally quite small (a matter of milliseconds or percentage correct), are limited to relatively simple stimuli (e.g., letters, digits, words, shapes, or faces) observed under very specific laboratory conditions, and moreover, involve a rather unique and select group of subjects (e.g., split-brains, brain-damaged patients, or the college freshman). In addition, the generalizability (and in some instances the reliability) of the experimental findings are somewhat suspect in a fair number of these studies due to the methodological and interpretative problems discussed earlier. Despite these shortcomings, various educators have suggested that knowledge of hemispheric specialization should be incorporated into the educational system via the implementation of pedagogical techniques which would capitalize on these lateral asymmetries.

For example, Samples (1975) has accused the educational community of utilizing teaching methods which solely educate the left side of the brain while ignoring the right. Based on findings similar to those reviewed earlier, he contends that our students possess two separate minds (corresponding to the right and left hemispheres of the brain), which are responsible for two completely different styles of knowing. In the course of his paper, he extrapolates beyond the preponderance of findings in laterality research to conclude that the LH is specialized to perform "rational, linear, and digital functions" while the RH performs "intuitive, metaphoric and analogic functions." Though providing no data of his own in support of these uniquely lateralized abilities he suggests that

> In terms of mind functions, this means the left cerebral hemisphere tends to mediate inputs in a reductive or sorting out way, processing the variables systematically in order to find the best answer or solution. This is the blueprint for the rational, linear, cognitive domain. The other side of the mind, the right cerebral hemisphere, functions on relationships and multiple-image inputs. It tends to multiply affiliated ideas and mix pictures, images, experiences, emotions in a way that encourages invention. It thrives on invention. (p 25–26)

He goes on to suggest specific activities and classroom instructional hints to strengthen our students' neglected RH. For instance, writing sentences in a vertical rather than the normal left to right orientation is alleged to enhance creative thinking. Presumably, this is achieved by actively engaging the visuospatial capacity of the RH, a creative source which might otherwise have remained untapped.

Although I empathize with his concern for educational intervention, it is difficult to accept his conclusions because they require considerable leap frogging of the facts. As Geschwind (1979) has said, "Specialization of the isolated hemispheres should not be overstated" (p. 115). One must keep in mind that the classroom learning experience typically involves the teaching of complex, multidimensional skills like reading or mathematics. Each of these tasks comprises a small set of cognitive subprocesses which require the unique processing contributions of *both* cerebral hemispheres. For example, when solving an addition problem, the printed symbols must first be perceptually recognized (i.e., 1, 4, 5, +, =, etc.) using a process which undoubtedly involves visuospatial analysis. After this initial processing has taken place, we transform the information presented into several different formats (perhaps a *verbal code*, as in "four plus one equals five," or an *imagery code*, as in $////$ $+$ $/$ $=$ $/////$) and subsequently manipulate them via computational rules to arrive at a solution. Using Samples's own version of the processing specialties of the two hemispheres (which are only *grossly* correct at best), it should be readily apparent that both the LH and the RH are actively involved in successfully performing mathematics or any other complex cognitive skill.

Despite the fact that most classroom activity clearly requires interactive processes, misguided statements concerning exclusive hemispheric responsibilities persist. For example, Reisman (1979) has suggested that in the early grades the LH is specialized for the "verbal chaining of number names or counting in sequence" while the RH is responsible for "counting and bouncing [a] ball to 'One, my name is Alice, Two, my name is Becky, etc.'" (p. 354). Again, no actual data are offered in support of the position. In light of the laterality literature reviewed earlier, this clearly represents an oversimplification of the processing responsibilities of each hemisphere. In a similar speculative vein, Noyce (1979) has compiled a reading list of childrens' books for RH stimulation, based on Samples's (1975) notion of "guided fantasy." She selected these "RH texts" because she insists "they inspire inventiveness and cause ideas to multiply" as well as "stimulate the production of images and creative thinking" (p. 151). Can one truly believe that the LH has no part in such complex processing? In addition, Cashford (1979) claims to have established an interpretive link between the RH and the appreciation of poetry and mystic texts. Moreover, he contends that the LH is a "barrier to higher states of consciousness" (p. 59). Given the findings reviewed earlier, it seems inconceivable that these tasks, which so clearly involve verbal materials, could somehow exclude LH processing. Unfortunately, such speculation is oftentimes mistaken for fact by those not totally familiar with laterality research.

The preceding examples are far from isolated incidents in the literature. Other speculative descriptions and elaborations of left–right brain processes and their respective roles in learning abound. For example, some individuals have claimed that the difference in academic performance between certain socioeconomic groups can be ascribed to hemispheric laterality (Cohen, 1969; Lesser, 1971). Specifically, they contend that middle-class students are more likely to use a LH, verbal–analytic mode of processing while the urban poor are more likely to use a RH, spatial–holistic mode. From their perspective, our schools are considered to be "left-brained institutions" (Wolfe & Reising, 1978). Hence, the impoverished students are utilizing a cognitive learning style which is incompatible with that of a "LH curriculum," resulting in impaired classroom performance. Interestingly, these researchers never establish how dominant processing styles in these students are identified other than by the observed decrement in academic performance (a rather circular logic). In addition, it seems obvious that a large number of variables which are totally unrelated to hemispheric laterality are likely to contribute significantly to the academic plight of the urban poor. Moreover, if this theory were true and the difference between socioeconomic groups was as large as suggested, one would predict that urban poor students would outperform middle-class students on tests of spatial ability. There are, however, numerous studies involving various aspects of spatial processing which have failed to confirm this prediction (Sattler, 1982).

Torrance (1981) carries the notion of lateralized cognition one speculative level further by creating a taxonomy of functions which he believes are dichotomized to the right and left hemispheres. A select few of these "exclusive" processing responsibilities are listed below:

RH Functioning	LH Functioning
lying down and thinking	sitting erect and thinking
playing hunches	betting on a sure thing
writing fiction	writing nonfiction
learning geometry	learning algebra

(From Torrance, 1981, p. 102)

If one takes these suggestions to heart, some rather amusing educational hyperboles might be concocted. For example, when instructing our students on how to draft a technical essay or teaching them the principles of algebra, we should insist that they stand totally erect for the entire class period and write any assignments using only their right hand. Presumably, the implementation of such measures would serve to enhance the likelihood of LH involvement. Similarly, when assisting them in the creation of a poem or revealing the logic underlying the solution of a geometry problem, we should insist that all of our students lie down on the classroom floor and write using only their left hand. The use of such procedures should, theoretically, engage the specialized capacities of the RH in these tasks. (As an aside, perhaps when heading for the local race track we should consider wearing restrictive lenses and specialized headgear to limit information processing to solely the LH. In this way, using Torrance's dichotomy, we could rest assured of "betting on a sure thing").

In light of the research reviewed earlier, the left brain–right brain processing differences outlined by Torrance (1981) seem extremely simple minded and require a significant leap of faith extending far beyond any data concerning lateral processing asymmetries in the human brain. In general, it may be said that any attempt at characterizing hemispheric asymmetry in terms of such global processing capacities will inevitably result in oversimplification. Claims that the RH is emotional and the LH is rational or that one is urban poor while the other is middle class, or even suggesting a difference in the sex of the two hemispheres (indeed Kane & Kane, 1979, have speculated that the LH is masculine while the RH is feminine) are grossly inaccurate. It does an extreme disservice to our students to base educational practice on such ill-conceived notions.

A. SOME PROMISING EDUCATIONAL APPLICATIONS

Despite the aforementioned abuses, there do exist some rather promising applications of hemispheric assymmetry to the educational setting. One such application pertains to the teaching of reading skills. As suggested by Southgate and Roberts (1970), when teaching a student to read, instead of relying solely on the linguistically oriented phonetic method or the spatially oriented look-and-say method, teachers should combine the two into a whole-word technique. In this way, the student uses a balance of both phonetic and spatial cues in an effort to learn the word. Such multidimensional approaches to the instruction of other complex cognitive skills like mathematics or painting would also seem to benefit the student. The important point to remember is that in the classroom learning situation, the teacher should emphasize the *interactive* contributions of the right and left hemispheres to the mastery of any given skill. The utilization of various instructional designs, teaching techniques, and modes of presentation, each accentuating the processing propensities of both cerebral hemispheres, would seem to be the most effective classroom style (Ausburn & Ausburn, 1978). The logic here is simple. Multiple methods of instruction will typically result in better learning than will reliance on a single method. The crafting and construction of several techniques which highlight the contributions of *both* hemispheres to a given task (rather than designing methods to emphasize one at the exclusion of the other) may prove to be the most beneficial application of hemispheric laterality to the educational setting.

In a similar light, the relationship between hemispheric asymmetry and dyslexia may also prove useful to the educational system. *Dyslexia* is a clinical term which describes a specific performance deficit in a student's reading ability while he or she remains physically and psychologically normal. Although the learning-disabled individual is notoriously difficult to diagnose, and the disability is anything but an all-or-none phenomenon (Gaddes, 1980; Pirozzolo, 1979), our knowledge of lateral asymmetry may prove invaluable for the development of successful intervention and remediation techniques for such students.

Orton (1937) was one of the first researchers to suggest that dyslexia might be associated with incomplete or abnormal cerebral lateralization. Specifically, he noticed that dyslexic children tended to read and write in *mirror-*

form, reversing specific letters and letter sequences to form a pattern resembling the target word as it might be viewed in a mirror (e.g., *was* versus *saw* or *pool* versus *loop*). In addition, he observed that these children exhibited rather unstable hand preferences when asked to perform specific skills like writing or manipulating objects. By juxtaposing these findings, he proposed that the two were intimately related, perhaps the by-product of incomplete cerebral dominance. With regard to the origins of dyslexia, Orton believed that information about the visual world was represented differently in each of the cerebral hemispheres. Specifically, he hypothesized that the LH maintains information in the orientation perceived while the RH stores the information as a mirror image of the original form. Given that hemispheric dominance is not well established in these patients, a resultant confusion in reading and writing is experienced as both representations compete with each other during performance in the task. Orton referred to this phenomenon as "strephosymbolia." Though no longer accepted as an adequate explanatory model (Springer & Deutsch, 1985), Orton's work served to initiate a link between dyslexia and hemispheric laterality.

Recently, a more direct connection between the specialized processing capacities of the two hemispheres and dyslexia has been demonstrated by Witelson (1977). In this study, the performances of normal and dyslexic children were compared on tasks involving the recognition of three-dimensional letters and nonsense shapes via the tactile modality. Witelson found that normal children show the expected right hand–LH advantage for letters and a left hand–RH advantage for shapes. The dyslexic children, however, failed to demonstrate any hand advantage for the recognition of shapes and interestingly demonstrated a left hand–RH advantage for the recognition of letters. From these results, Witelson (1977) hypothesized that dyslexia may be the result of the spatial faculties' being equally represented in both cerebral hemispheres, a situation which is in contrast to the usual RH specialization for such processes. Specifically, she suggests that

> The bilateral neural involvement in spatial processing may interfere with the left hemisphere's processing of its own specialized functions and result in deficient linguistic, sequential cognitive processing and the overuse of the spatial, holistic mode. This pattern of cognitive deficits and biases may lead dyslexics to read predominantly with a spatial–holistic cognitive strategy and neglect the phonetic–sequential strategy. (p. 309)

The information garnered from various converging laterality experiments might assist educators in the development of teaching strategies for the learning disabled. Such methods might be designed to accentuate the spatial aspects of the reading process and thereby exploit (rather than contest) the unique hemispheric processing arrangement characterizing the dyslexic student.

B. CONCLUDING COMMENTS

Given the highly precise nature and limited scope of the experimental findings on hemispheric laterality, one must be extremely cautious when generalizing these results (derived within the confines of the laboratory) to learning applications in the classroom. One should bear in mind that the processing asymmetries observed between the two hemispheres are primarily quantitative rather than qualitative in nature. It is inaccurate to believe that in the normal brain one hemisphere can perform some specialized cognitive task while the other is totally devoid of such capacity. The difference is truly a matter of degree, not absolute ability. For example, it is *not* the case that only the RH can recognize faces while the LH cannot. Both possess the necessary capacity; however, when a face is presented initially to the RH, recognition processing seems to be handled with greater efficiency than when the face is presented first to the LH. In light of this fact, rather than declaring that one or the other hemisphere is specialized for a specific cognitive function, we should conceive of them as equally important partners of a processing team. Although a given hemisphere may indeed have a propensity to process information along a preferred dimension, we should bear in mind that when a person performs a complex task like learning to read or painting a picture, *both* cerebral hemispheres make substantial and unique contributions towards mastery of the skill. To develop educational curricula as if one hemisphere were totally responsible for a given cognitive ability (to the absolute exclusion of the other) is to ignore the complex interactive processes of the human brain.

An additional matter of significance concerning the educational implications of left brain–right brain differences is the realization that "neuroscience and education exist at different levels of study and abstraction" (Wittrock, 1981, p. 12). When viewed from this perspective, the translation of neuroscientific finding into classroom application often involves the proverbial mixing of apples and oranges. As Wittrock (1981) has said,

> In the everyday sense of the term, there are no educational implications in recent research on the human brain . . . attempts to develop educational implications by equating educational issues to neurological phenomena, by overlaying education upon neuroscience, or by reducing behavior and psychological function to neural structure and physiology are not likely to lead to useful educational implication, in the sense of answers to practical problems important to teachers and administrators. (p. 12)

Because the two disciplines engage in different levels of analyses, statements concerning the specialized cognitive capacities of the two hemispheres may imply one thing to the neuroscientist and quite another to the educator. Consider the following illustration.

A neuroscientist conducts an experiment in which two symbols are flashed very briefly to one or the other hemisphere and the subjects' task is to determine if the two forms are identical in shape. The experimenter finds that such comparisons are made more accurately and several milliseconds faster when the symbols are initially presented to the RH. Subsequently, the neuroscientist summarizes his or her findings by theorizing that the RH is specialized for "visuospatial processing." In a limited neuropsychological sense, the data do indeed suggest that such is the case.

To the educator, however, the statement concerning RH specialization for visuospatial processing (taken outside the context of the neuroscientific experiment) suggests several classroom applications. For example, educators may mistakenly conclude that to better instruct their students in art class, they must alter their teaching methods to capitalize on the specialized spatial abilities of the RH (a link established *only* at the neuropsychological level). They may have students draw with their left hand or paint with their right eye closed, all in an effort to engage the spatial capacities of the RH and disengage the stifling verbal contributions of the LH. Oversimplifications of this sort typically mushroom into the development of popularized texts and teaching curricula based on the mistaken notion that the RH alone is the neurological seat of artistic endeavor. Such developments occur despite the fact that no hard evidence is provided from research conducted by educators in the art class setting itself. Educational overgeneralizations such as these far exceed the safety of the neuroscientific data upon which they were originally formed. Clearly, it is one thing to conclude that the RH is specialized for visuospatial processing on the basis of a superior ability to match various shapes. It is quite another matter to conclude from the same data that we "draw from the right side of the brain" (Edwards, 1979). Translation errors like this are undoubtedly responsible for many of the misguided educational applications of left brain–right brain differences as reviewed earlier.

Perhaps the largest risk we take when applying hemispheric laterality to the educational setting stems from the possibility that such applications will replace rather than supplement existing pedagogical methods. This concern is succinctly expressed by Chall and Mirsky (1978):

> The greatest danger of all is that what has been learned about teaching and learning from educational research and practice may be abandoned in the rush to study the effects of various neurological factors, particularly the condition of being left- or right-brained. Some pupils may not learn to read or write well, not because they are right-brained or left-brained, but because they may have not been taught well, or were not sufficiently motivated at home and/or school. (p. 376)

To rely on hemispheric laterality as a panacea for all of our educational woes would be a serious mistake. We as teachers should acknowledge the vast potential that neuropsychological research has for educational application; however, at this point in time, we should remain cautious with regard to specific classroom uses. What we do know about the hemispheres and how they operate in the normal brain is minute relative to what we do not know. At this stage of the game, it is difficult to determine if left brain–right brain differences applied to the learning situation are an educational salvation or merely "snake-oil" (Hutson, 1982). Until further research is conducted, particularly in the actual classroom setting, changes in curricula or teaching methods predicated on hemispheric laterality seem premature. Only after extensive investigation can we begin to fully understand and wisely apply hemispheric laterality as a basis of learning.

REFERENCES

Ausburn, L. J., & Ausburn, F. (1978). Cognitive styles: Some information and implications for instructional design. *Educational Communication and Technology, 26,* 337–354.

Benson, D. F. (1969). Aphasia. In K. M. Heilman & E. Valenstein (Eds.), *Clinical neuropsychology* (pp. 22–58). Oxford: Oxford University Press.

Benton, A. L., Levine, H., & Varney, N. (1973). Tactile perception of direction in normal subjects: Implications for hemispheric cerebral dominance. *Neurology, 23,* 1248–1250.

Bogen, J. E. (1975). Some educational aspects of hemispheric specialization. *UCLA Educator, 17,* 24–32.

Bogen, J. E. (1977). Some educational implications of hemispheric specialization. In M. C. Wittrock, J. Beatty, M. S. Gazzaniga, H. J. Jerison, S. D. Krashen, R. D. Nebes, and T. J. Teyler (Eds.), *The human brain* (pp. 133–152). Englewood Cliffs, NJ: Prentice-Hall.

Bradshaw, J. L., & Nettleton, N. C. (1981). The nature of hemispheric specialization in man. *Behavioral and Brain Sciences, 4,* 51–63.

Bradshaw, J. L., & Nettleton, N.C. (1983). *Human cerebral asymmetry.* Englewood Cliffs, NJ: Prentice-Hall.

Caramazza, A., & Martin, R. C. (1983). Theoretical and methodological issues in the study of aphasia. In J. B. Hellige (Ed.), *Cerebral hemisphere asymmetry* (pp. 18–45). New York: Praeger.

Carlson, N. R. (1980). *The physiology of behavior.* Boston: Allyn & Bacon.

Carter-Saltzman, L. (1980). Biological and sociocultural effects on handedness: Comparisons between biological and adoptive families. *Science, 209,* 1263–1265.

Cashford, J. (1979). The integration of the cerebral hemispheres in poetry and mystic texts. *The Gifted Child Quarterly, 23,* 56–70.

Chall, J. S., & Mirsky, A. F. (1978). The implications for education. In J. S. Chall and A. F. Mirsky (Eds.), *Education and the brain* (pp. 371–378). Chicago: University of Chicago Press.

Chui, H. C., & Damasio, A. R. (1980). Human cerebral asymmetries evaluated by computed tomography. *Journal of Neurology, Neurosurgery and Psychiatry, 43,* 873–878.

Cohen, R. (1969). Conceptual styles: Cultural conflict and non-verbal tests of intelligence. *American Anthropologist, 71,* 828–856.

Cunningham, D. F. (1892). *Contribution of the surface anatomy of the cerebral hemispheres.* Dublin: Royal Irish Academy.

De Renzi, F., Faglioni, P., & Spinnler, H. (1968). The performance of patients with brain damage on face recognition tasks. *Cortex 4*, 17–33.

Donchin, E., Kutas, M., & McCarthy, G. (1977). Electrocortical indices of hemispheric utilization. In S. Harnad, R. W. Doty, L. Goldstein, J. Jaynes, & Krauthamer (Eds.), *Lateralization in the nervous system* (pp. 339–384). New York: Academic Press.

Durnford, M., & Kimura, D. (1971). Right hemisphere specialization for depth perception. *Nature, 231*, 394–395.

Edwards, B. (1979). *Drawing on the right side of the brain*. Los Angeles: J. P. Tarcher.

Gaddes, W. H. (1980). *Learning disabilities and brain function: A neuropsychological approach*. New York: Springer-Verlag.

Galin, D., & Ornstein, R. (1972). Lateral specialization of cognitive mode: An EEG study. *Psychophysiology, 9*, 412–418.

Gazzaniga, M. S. (1970). *The bisected brain*. New York: Appleton.

Gazzaniga, M. S., Bogen, J. E., & Sperry, R. W. (1962). Some functional effects of sectioning the cerebral commissures in man. *Proceedings of the National Academy of Sciences, 48*, 1765–1769.

Gazzaniga, M. S., Bogen, J. E. & Sperry, R. W. (1965). Observations on visual perception after disconnexion of the cerebral hemispheres in man. *Brain, 88*, 221–236.

Gazzaniga, M. S., Bogen, J. E., & Sperry, R. W. (1967). Dyspraxia following division of the cerebral commissures. *Archives of Neurology, 16*, 606–612.

Gazzaniga, M. S., & LeDoux, J. E. (1978). *The integrated mind*. New York: Plenum.

Geschwind, N. (1979). Specializations of the human brain. *The brain*. San Francisco: Freeman.

Geschwind, N., & Levitsky, W. (1968). Human brain: Left–right asymmetries in the temporal speech region. *Science, 461*, 186–187.

Gordon, H. W. (1970). Hemispheric asymmetry in the perception of musical chords. *Cortex, 6*, 387–398.

Hardyck, C., & Haapanen, R. (1979). Educating both halves of the brain: Educational breakthrough or neuromythology? *Journal of School Psychology, 17*, 219–230.

Hardyck, C., & Petrinovich, L. F. (1977). Left-handedness. *Psychological Bulletin, 84*, 385–404.

Hellige, J. B. (1980a). Cerebral hemisphere asymmetry: Methods, issues and implications. *Educational Communication and Technology, 28*, 83–98.

Hellige, J. B. (1980b). Effects of perceptual quality and visual field of probe stimulus presentation on memory search for letters. *Journal of Experimental Psychology: Human Perception and Performance, 6*, 639–651.

Hellige, J. B., & Cox, P. J. (1976). Effects of concurrent verbal memory on recognition of stimuli from the left and right visual fields. *Journal of Experimental Psychology: Human Perception and Performance, 2*, 210–221.

Hellige, J. B., & Wong, T. A. (1983). Hemisphere specific interference in dichotic listening: Task variables and individual differences. *Journal of Experimental Psychology: General, 112*(2), 218–239.

Hermelin, B., & O'Connor, N. (1971). Functional asymmetry in the reading of Braille. *Neuropsychologia, 9*, 431–435.

Hilliard, R. D. (1973). Hemispheric laterality effects on a facial recognition task in normal subjects. *Cortex, 9*, 246–258.

Hines, D. (1976). Recognition of verbs, abstract nouns and concrete nouns from the left and right visual half-fields. *Neuropsychologia, 14*, 211–216.

Hines, D. (1977). Differences in tachistoscopic recognition between abstract and concrete words as a function of visual half-field and frequency. *Cortex, 13*, 66–73.

Hutson, B. A. (1982). Brain based curricula: Salvation or snake oil? *Midwestern Educational Researcher, 2,* 1–33.

Jasper, H. H. (1958). The ten-twenty electrode system of the International Federation. *EEG Clinical Neurophysiology, 10,* 371–375.

Kane, N., & Kane, M. (1979). Comparison of right and left hemisphere functions. *The Gifted Child Quarterly, 23,* 157–167.

Kimura, D. (1961). Some effects of temporal-lobe damage on auditory perception. *Canadian Journal of Psychology, 15,* 166–171.

Kimura, D. (1966). Dual functional asymmetry of the brain in visual perception. *Neuropsychologia, 4,* 275–285.

Kimura, D. (1967). Functional asymmetry of the brain in dichotic listening. *Cortex, 3,* 163–178.

Kimura, D. (1973). The asymmetry of the human brain. *Scientific American, 228,* 70–78.

King, F. L., & Kimura, D. (1972). Left-ear superiority in dichotic perception of vocal nonverbal sounds. *Canadian Journal of Psychology, 26,* 111–116.

Kinsbourne, M. (1975). The control of attention by interaction between the cerebral hemispheres. In P. M. A. Rabbit and S. Dornic (Eds.), *Attention and Performance* (Vol. 5, pp. 81–97). New York: Academic Press.

Knox, C., & Kimura, D. (1970). Cerebral processing of nonverbal sounds in boys and girls. *Neuropsychologia, 8,* 227–237.

Lassen, N. A., Ingvar, D. H., & Skinhoj, E. (1978). Brain function and blood flow. *Scientific American, 239,* 50–59.

LeMay, M. (1976). Morphological cerebral asymmetries of modern man, fossil man and nonhuman primate. *Annals of the New York Academy of Sciences, 280,* 349–366.

Lesser, G. (1971). *Psychology and educational practice.* New York: Scott, Foresman.

Levy, J. (1974). Cerebral asymmetries as manifested in split-brain man. In M. Kinsbourne and W. L. Smith (Eds.), *Hemispheric disconnection and cerebral function* (pp. 165–183). Springfield, IL: Thomas.

Levy, J., & Nagylaki, T. (1972). A model for the genetics of handedness. *Genetics, 72,* 117–128.

Levy, J., & Reid, M. (1978). Variations in cerebral organization as a function of handedness, hand posture in writing, and sex. *Journal of Experimental Psychology: General, 107,* 119–144.

McGlone, J., & Davidson, W. (1973). The relation between cerebral laterality and spatial ability with special reference to sex and hand preference. *Neuropsychologia, 11,* 105–113.

McManus, I. C. (1976). Scrotal asymmetry in man and ancient sculpture. *Nature, 259,* 426.

Madden, D. A., & Nebes, R. D. (1980). Hemispheric differences in memory search. *Neuropsychologia, 18,* 665–674.

Milner, B. (1968). Visual recognition and recall after right temporal-lobe excision in man. *Neuropsychologia, 6,* 191–209.

Milner, B. (1971). Interhemispheric differences and psychological processes. *British Medical Bulletin, 27,* 272–277.

Milner, B., Taylor, L., & Sperry, R. W. (1968). Lateralized suppression of dichotically presented digits after commissural section in man. *Science, 161,* 184–186.

Moscovitch, M. (1979). Information processing and the cerebral hemispheres. In M. S. Gazzaniga (Ed.), *Handbook of behavioral neurobiology: Vol. 2. Neuropsychology* (pp. 379–446). New York: Plenum.

Moscovitch, M., Scullion, D., & Christie, D. (1976). Early versus late stages of processing and their relation to functional hemispheric asymmetries in face recognition. *Journal of Experimental Psychology: Human Perception and Performance, 2,* 401–416.

Nebes, R. D. (1974). Hemispheric specialization in commissurotomized man. *Psychological Bulletin, 81,* 1–14.

Noyce, R. M. (1979). Children's books for right hemisphere stimulation. The *Gifted Child Quarterly*, *23*, 151–156.

O'Boyle, M. W. (1985). Hemispheric asymmetry in memory search for four-letter names and human faces. *Brain and Cognition*, *4*, 104–132.

O'Boyle, M. W., & Hellige, J. B. (1982). Hemispheric asymmetry, early visual processes and serial memory comparison. *Brain and Cognition*, *1*, 224–243.

O'Boyle, M. W., Van Wyhe-Lawler, F., & Miller, D. (1985). Lateral asymmetry in the identification of letters traced in the right and left palms. *Journal of Clinical and Experimental Neuropsychology*, *7*(2), 153.

Orton, S. T. (1937). *Reading, writing and speech problems in children*. New York: Norton.

Pines, M. (1973, September 9th). We are right-brained or left-brained. *New York Times Magazine*, pp. 32–33, 121–122, 124–127, 132, 136, 137.

Pirozzolo, F. J. (1979). *The neuropsychology of developmental reading disorders*. New York: Praeger.

Reisman, F. K. (1979). Mathematics for both cerebral hemispheres in the early grades. *The Gifted Child Quarterly*, *23*, 352–355.

Risberg, J., Halsey, J. H., Wills, E. L., & Wilson, E. M. (1975). Hemispheric specialization in normal man studied by bilateral measurements of regional cerebral blood flow. *Brain*, *98*, 511–524.

Rizzolatti, T., & Buchtel, H. A. (1977). Hemispheric superiority in reaction time to faces: A sex difference. *Cortex*, *13*, 300–305.

Robin, D. E., & Shortridge, R. T. J. (1979). Lateralization of tumors of the nasal cavity and paranasal sinuses and its relation to aetiology. *Lancet*, *8118*(1), 695–696.

Rosenzweig, M. R. (1951). Representations of the two ears at the auditory cortex. *American Journal of Physiology*, *167*, 147–158.

Ross, E. D. (1982). The divided self. *The Sciences*, *22*, 8–12.

Rubens, A. B. (1977). Anatomical asymmetries of the human cerebral cortex. In S. Harnad, R. W. Doty, L. Goldstein, J. Jaynes, & G. Krauthamer (Eds.), *Lateralization in the nervous system* (pp. 503–516). New York: Academic Press.

Rudel, R. G., Denckla, M. B., & Splaten, E. (1974). The functional asymmetry of Braille letter learning in normal, sighted children. *Neurology*, *24*, 733–738.

Samples, R. E. (1975). Are you teaching only one side of the brain? *Learning*, *3*, 24–30.

Sattler, J. (1982). *Assessment of children's intelligence and special abilities* (2nd ed.). Boston: Allyn & Bacon.

Searleman, A. (1977). A review of right hemisphere linguistic capabilities. *Psychological Bulletin*, *84*, 503–528.

Southgate, V., & Roberts, G. R. (1970). *Reading—Which approach?* London: University of London Press.

Sperry, R. W. (1966). Brain bisection and mechanisms of consciousness. In J. C. Eccles (Ed.), *Brain and conscious experience* (pp. 298–313). New York: Springer-Verlag.

Sperry, R. W. (1968). Hemisphere disconnection and unity in conscious awareness. *American Psychologist*, *23*(10), 723–733.

Springer, S. P., & Deutsch, G. (1985). *Left brain, right brain* (2nd ed.). San Francisco: Freeman.

Torrance, E. P. (1981). Implications of whole-brained theories of learning and thinking for computer-based instruction. *Journal of Computer-Based Instruction*, *4*, 99–105.

Warren, L. R., Butler, R. W., Katholi, C. R., McFarland, C. E., Crews, E. L., & Halsey, J. H., Jr. (1984). Focal changes in cerebral blood flow produced by monetary incentive during a mental mathematics task in normal and depressed subjects. *Brain and Cognition*, *3*(1), 71–85.

Whitaker, H. A. (1978). The fallacy of split-brain research. *Brain Theory Newsletter, 11*(1), 8–10.

Whitaker, H. A., & Ojemann, G. A. (1977). Lateralization of higher cortical functions: A critique. *Annals of the New York Academy of Sciences, 299,* 459–473.

Witelson, S. F. (1974). Hemispheric specialization of linguistic and non-linguistic tactual perception using a dichotomous stimulation technique. *Cortex, 10,* 3–17.

Witelson, S. F. (1977). Developmental dyslexia: Two right hemispheres and none left. *Science, 1977, 195,* 309–311.

Wittrock, M. C. (1981). Educational implications of recent brain research. *Educational Leadership, 39*(1), 12–15.

Wolfe, D. T., & Reising, R. W. (1978). Politics and English teaching or (can, should, will) we teach the whole brain? *English Journal, 67,* 28–32.

Wood, F. (1983). Laterality of cerebral function: Its investigation by measurement of localized brain activity. In J. B. Hellige (Ed.), *Cerebral hemisphere asymmetry* (pp. 383–410). New York: Praeger.

Zaidel, E. (1978). Auditory language comprehension in the right hemisphere following cerebral commissurotomy and hemispherectomy: A comparison with child language and aphasia. In A. Caramazza and E. Zurif (Eds.), *Language acquisition and language breakdown: Parallels and divergencies* (pp. 229–275). Baltimore: Johns Hopkins University Press.

Zurif, E. B. (1974). Auditory lateralization: Prosodic and syntactic factors. *Brain and Language, 1,* 391–404.

ATTENTIONAL PROCESSES IN EDUCATION

Mark Grabe

Department of Psychology
University of North Dakota
Grand Forks, North Dakota
58202

I. INTRODUCTION

As is sometimes the case with education and psychology, the term *attention* appears frequently within the vocabulary of each discipline and applies to approximately the same phenomena, but it is often used with different levels of precision. Teachers use the concept of attention in a variety of ways. They may admonish students to "pay attention" and describe the inadequacy of a particular student as having a "short attention span." They may also describe one merit of a certain instructional technique or an interesting book or film as "holding the students' attention." These uses of the term *attention* do carry meaning. Individuals familiar with the classroom environment can easily visualize the difficulties or advantages being described.

While appreciating the validity of the ways in which teachers commonly view attention, psychologists would like to see the term used more precisely to refer to the actual mechanics of student behavior and thought (Pointkowski & Calfee, 1979). For instance, in its educational use, it is often unclear whether the term *attention* is used in reference to motivation or cognition. Is the student unable or unwilling to attend to the teacher's presentation? Although intending to explain student behavior, the teacher is more likely using the term *attention* in describing student behavior. Psychologists would prefer definitions that discriminate between motivation and action and between description and explanation. In all fairness, psychologists display their own lack of precision in referring to attention. In a summary of research, Moray (1969) has noted at least seven different processes described as attention; included were mental concentration, vigilance, selective attention, search, activation, set, and analysis by synthesis.

This chapter is organized in the following way. First, an attempt is made to describe a single, general model of attention. As part of this task, the

COGNITIVE CLASSROOM LEARNING:
UNDERSTANDING, THINKING, AND PROBLEM SOLVING

various facets of attention as described by other authors are integrated into a single conceptual system. Special emphasis is given to the ways in which attention has been operationalized in research. This general model is then applied to the explanation of classroom function and malfunction. Because the number of possible topics could be nearly limitless, two examples were selected for detailed consideration. One example concerns an academic skill (directed reading) and the other an individual difference that is of educational importance (hyperactivity). Finally, some specific suggestions for ways in which teachers might improve the classroom attention of their students are given. I hope that this approach will provide an interpretive bridge between basic laboratory research and classroom concerns.

II. A MODEL OF ATTENTION

An attempt will be made to discuss attention in a very general way. While such an approach obviously lacks the precision emphasized in theories built by researchers to explain a specific type of cognitive behavior, a general approach should be of greater use to individuals wanting to conceptualize a variety of educational applications. Of the uses of the term *attention* listed earlier, an expanded use of selective attention would seem best suited to the focus of this discussion. Such a model of attention can be broadly applied to a variety of situations in which there would be an advantage in concentrating limited mental resources on specific external or internal information or a particular processing activity. The external versus internal distinction implies that competing sources of information can exist either in the student's environment or memory stores. The reference to processing activities implies that at any given instant the student may have to choose among several possible cognitive activities. The proposed general model thus emphasizes the ability and (as is shown here later) the necessity of making choices and controlling the allocation of resources among competing alternatives.

Attention within this model is represented as a limited resource by which particular cognitive processes are mobilized and maintained. Researchers (e.g., Britton, Glynn, Meyer, & Penland, 1982; Kahneman, 1973) taking a perspective similar to that utilized here have alternatively described attention as energy, capacity, effort, resources, and fuel. Each of these descriptors will be considered as roughly equivalent. The important point is that each label describes a resource that exists within the information-processing mechanism, in limited supply, and that this resource is expended to accomplish desired goals.

Some examples may be useful in illustrating the range of behaviors that could be considered using this general model. One should note in each example that the student is concentrating on one source of information or activity rather than another.

1. In learning to distinguish one letter from another (e.g., *d* and *b*), a reader learns that certain features of letters are important in making decisions and should be considered more carefully than other features of letters. In distinguishing the *b* from the *d*, the young reader carefully notes whether the vertical line is on the left or the right side of the circle.

2. To do well in class, the second-grade student must be able to listen carefully to the teacher's voice and ignore the noise coming from the music room just down the hall.

3. In preparation for tomorrow's quiz, a high school student has been told to carefully note certain issues in his or her reading assignment. Efficient reading behavior allows the student to somehow emphasize material related to these goals in studying the day's assignment.

4. In listening to a biology lecture, the college student concentrates carefully on the instructor's description of dominant and recessive genes and daydreams during a story about the instructor's childhood.

To understand how attention operates within the total cognitive system it is first necessary to provide a model of the total system. Again, a very simple model will suffice. The components of this model have been utilized by Britton, Piha, Davis, and Wehausen (1978) to explain attention allocation during reading, but the components are general enough to describe stages in any form of information acquisition. The model contains three stages: a perceptual stage, a comprehension stage, and an elaboration stage. The *perceptual stage* involves the recognition of information collected from the environment by the sensory receptors. The labeling of a visual form as an *A* would be an example. The *comprehension stage* results in the attachment of meaning to the recognized input. Stored information, rules, and experiences are matched to the perceptual input to provide meaning. For instance, words or phrases are given meaning by accessing the internal lexicon, and when grammatical rules are applied to the words, sentence comprehension results. The *elaborative stage* was included to indicate that the system has the capacity to go beyond the information provided by the environment. Problem solving, inferencing, and activities such as memorization or study would exist at this stage. For instance, a student reading a text may realize her teacher often asks test questions about the meaning of technical terms and may make a special effort to retain the meaning of a new term just encountered.

The deceptive simplicity of this model may mask the fact that feats of great complexity are actually being accomplished. Much more is going on in each stage than is readily apparent from the present discussion. During the execution of a complex cognitive activity such as reading in preparation for an examination, the cognitive system must coordinate and execute many component processes within a limited period of time. If these component processes all require attention, the total effort or capacity available will simply be exceeded, and the attempted task will meet with failure. Returning to our example, the student cannot afford to carefully note that the word being fixated begins with a letter formed by a vertical line attached at its base to the left side of a small circle and that the individual letters b-i-s-o-n collectively spell the word *bison* if she hopes to glean from her book facts about the history of the bison in the United States. While it is true that a student could not simultaneously attend to all the reading tasks just described, it is also true that students at some level of competence can study a text to meet prescribed goals. This is true in part because in becoming a competent reader the student has developed certain cognitive skills to the point that they no longer require attention.

The processing of information without attention is referred to here as *automatic processing*. Kahneman (1973) suggests that the difference between automatic and effortful processing can be understood by considering what must be fed into the system to trigger a particular information-processing activity. In effortful processing, the inputs include some type of information and effort. Automatic processing activities are triggered solely by an input of information.

Because automatic processing plays such an important role in the limited-resource information-processing system, a more detailed example is provided to acquaint the reader with work in this area. LaBerge and Samuels (1974) have developed a theory to explain the involvement of automatic processing in reading. If a person is to read for meaning, these authors believe, information has to be passed among several memory systems (visual, phonological, episodic, and semantic). Their model has been most clearly worked out and tested only in regard to the most basic of reading activities. Consider for example the LaBerge and Samuels model for grapheme learning. This is the process by which letters, spelling patterns, and words come to be perceptually coded. These activities are accomplished within visual memory. Visual memory consists of several types of codes. These visual codes exist in a person's long-term memory. Incoming information from the eyes is first analyzed by feature detectors which feed into letter codes. The letter codes potentially activate spelling-pattern codes, which in turn may feed into word codes. Within this model, it is assumed that feature detectors are activated by incoming information in the form of lines, curvature, angles, intersections, etc. (Gibson, 1969).

In the first stage of perceptual learning, the subject may not know which lower level codes are required to signify the presence of a higher level code.

For instance, the young reader at this point has to discover that a horizontal line, a vertical line, and an intersection identify the letter *T*. Mistakes are quite possible at this stage. The young reader might frequently mistake a *b* for a *d* because there is but a single unique feature differentiating these letters. With experience, the child begins to reliably check the lower level codes, but this process requires attention. The reader may have to purposefully check for the presence of a *d*, an *o*, and a *g* before recognizing the word *dog*. This represents the second stage in the learning process. Errors are infrequent, but attention is still involved. As a given set of codes is repeatedly checked, the set of codes takes on a unitary nature and is associated automatically with the higher level code. This represents the final stage at which the next–higher level code is available to be recognized without attention.

A brief description of two experiments conducted by LaBerge and Samuels (1974) illustrates both the concept of automaticity and the two stages involved in learning. In the first experiment, subjects were asked to indicate whether two simple forms represented a match. For the second experiment, they were asked to provide the name of the form. For the majority of trials in each experiment, the graphic forms were taken from a restricted set of letters (*bdpq*). On some trials, a pair of stimuli (first experiment) or a single stimulus (second experiment) was displayed from an unexpected set of letters (*agns*) or other symbols (↑↓). In the second experiment, the non-alphabetic symbols were given names. When one of the unexpected stimuli was presented, the subject first had to shift attention to the new internal codes. If the subject expected to see a given stimulus, attention could be directed to the related codes ahead of stimulus presentation. If the processing was automatic, the use of unexpected stimuli made little difference. The lower codes were already activated by the time the subjects could shift attention to the new codes, and no additional time was required. Because adults (who would have had a great deal of experience with letters) were employed as subjects, this was initially the case for the letters but not for the symbols.

Subjects returned periodically to the laboratory for a number of days to perform either the matching or naming task. This extended period of training was intended to develop automatic coding of the symbols. Error rates and reaction times were recorded during each session. With experience, it was shown that the nonalphabetic symbols came to produce reaction times similar to those for the letters. In the matching task, the reaction rates became statistically identical. In the naming task, the reaction speeds also became more alike. Error rates for the letters and nonalphabetic symbols became statistically equal, but after fewer days of practice. The combination of error and latency data allowed the three stages in the achievement of automaticity to be differentiated (see Fig. 1). The stage marked by significant error and latency differences identifies the unlearned condition. The stage marked by equal error rates but significant latency differences indicates the stage of effortful or attention-demanding processing. The stage of equal error rates and latencies indicates that automaticity has been achieved.

LaBerge and Samuels (1974) believe that teachers should be aware of the stages of automaticity—especially the difference in student performance between the second and third stages of learning. The researchers are concerned that teachers may misinterpret low student error rates as mastery of a particular skill and proceed to a subsequent skill. If the lower level skill is still requiring attention, rapid advancement to more demanding tasks may overload processing resources and cause the student difficulty. For instance, a child may recognize all of the words in a paragraph and still have difficulty understanding what the paragraph is about. The effort required to decode the words may require so much attention that requirements for comprehension cannot be met.

What does it take for a student to learn to process in an automatic manner? Certainly, the major determinant is practice. This was noted by Huey in 1908. In discussing the process of learning to read, he stated that "repetition progressively frees the mind from attention to detail, makes facile the total act, shortens the time, and reduces the extent to which consciousness must concern itself with the process" (Huey, 1968, p. 104). LaBerge and Samuels (1974) believe other factors are also involved. They claim that organization of lower level codes into a higher level code will not be attempted unless necessary. Thus, learning tasks must be difficult enough to provide an advantage for automatizing some aspect of the task. Finally, they suggest that students need to feel confident that they can function at the higher level of coding. An overly critical teacher may prevent a student from risking transi-

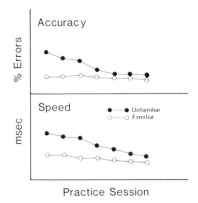

FIG. 1.   Stages in the acquisition of automaticity, as indicated by latency and error rate.

tions to more advanced codes. For example, the student may read by employing a conservative word-by-word approach rather than risk errors produced by efforts to read for meaning.

At this point, it might be useful to refer to the list of representative selective-attention tasks mentioned earlier. These tasks differ along a number of important dimensions. One important dimension concerns whether the basis for the selectivity exists concurrently or sequentially. In concentrating on the most meaningful features of an alphabet letter or in trying to follow the teacher's presentation in the midst of background noise, the student is attempting to concentrate resources on a subset of the information available at a given instant in time. In attending more carefully to one paragraph of text or one segment of a lecture than to other paragraphs or lecture segments, the student is controlling the expenditure of effort across time. The expenditure of resources across time can be further differentiated into those cases in which the student can and cannot control the input of new information. In reading, the student has the freedom to stop or to reread information before proceeding. In listening, this same freedom is not available. While the student may ignore new input and concentrate instead on an important point just presented, the student listening to a presentation cannot prevent the presentation from continuing. It is thus in skills like reading that attention can be utilized with the greatest degree of flexibility.

Successful utilization of attention may depend on different skills in concurrent and sequential situations. In a concurrent task, success may be influenced more by the extent to which subtasks can be accomplished automatically and the extent to which the limited resources available can be concentrated on the most essential tasks. This implies that the student knows what the appropriate tasks are and can direct resources to the accomplishment of these tasks. These same skills come into play in sequential activities, but the greater freedom to continue processing activities when necessary makes the ability to determine when desired goals have been accomplished (see Chapter 8 by Duell on metacognition) an important additional skill. Using more processing resources than necessary would be inefficient, but not checking to determine that desired goals have been accomplished and responding with additional activities when necessary would fail to take advantage of the full power of the processing system. Sequential attentional tasks may thus allow certain unique diagnostic and remedial activities to be employed.

III. MEASUREMENT OF ATTENTION IN RESEARCH

Researchers conducting experiments in this area or teachers attempting to understand the behavior of their students look to various behaviors or physiological variables to draw inferences about attention. The purpose of this section will be to describe some of the variables used as indicators of attentional allocation.

Variables employed in selective-attention research can first be differentiated as process or product measures. A process variable attempts to provide an immediate or on-line indicator of what the processing system is doing. A good example of a process variable might be eye fixations. The object being fixated at a given point in time provides an immediate way to define the focus of the subject's attention. In contrast, a product measure represents an assessment of the output or results available when the processing operations have been completed. Differential recall of one category of information in comparison to another probably represents the most common use of a product variable to argue for selective attention. The assumption is that the information most available to recall was the information receiving the most attention during processing.

The following section provides a brief discussion of the most frequently employed product and process variables. The intent is to acquaint the reader with application of these variables and not to provide an exhaustive review.

A. PRODUCT VARIABLES

1. Retention

Many studies have employed the recall of subjects as evidence for the ability to attend selectively or to provide an indication of what has been attended to. Dichotic listening (e.g., Bryden, 1971) represents one of the classical experimental methods for studying selective attention. The technique uses recall as an indication of the impact of focusing attention. In this technique, simultaneous but different messages (digits, words, or connected discourse) are delivered to a subject. The most common approach is to use stereo earphones to present one input to the right ear and a second input to the left. The subject is told to pay particular attention to one source of input, but is asked to recall both. As might be expected, the attended input is recalled at a higher level than the input that is not the focus of attention.

Recall has also been a frequent measure of attention in research appearing in the educational or developmental journals. The majority of these studies have probably involved written prose (e.g., Faw & Waller, 1976; also see Section IV.A), but other presentation methods have also been involved (e.g., Collins, 1970). Recall in this research is used to indicate what content subjects attend to naturally or to determine if subjects have focused their attention in a particular way as the result of some orienting device (objectives, questions, etc.).

2. Other Product Variables

Many studies have employed product variables other than recall. Often, these studies have compared the quality of some type of performance with and without a source of distraction (see Douglas & Peters, 1979, or Piontkowski & Calfee, 1979, for reviews of some of these studies). As an example, Baker and Madell (1965) asked college students defined as achievers or underachievers to take two equivalent forms of a standard reading-comprehension test. One of the forms was administered under standard conditions and the other was administered while humorous recordings were played as a source of distraction. No differences in comprehension were observed when the test was administered under standard conditions. However, the underachievers did perform at a lower level when distracted. The product variable (i.e., comprehension test performance) is used in this case to argue that underachievers may have greater difficulty maintaining a particular attentional focus in the face of distraction. In a similar type of study, Samuels (1967) had good and poor students read a passage with and without pictures. The pictures in this case served as potential distracting stimuli. The study demonstrated that the less able students were adversely influenced by the presence of the pictures.

B. PROCESS MEASURES

1. Secondary Task Technique

As the name implies, subjects involved in an experiment utilizing this technique are presented with a primary and secondary task. *Primary* and *secondary* in this case refer to the priority that subjects are asked to place on the two activities. The validity of the technique relies on the assumption that attentional capacity has a limit and both the primary and secondary tasks must operate within this limited capacity. Even when one is not engaged in purposeful activity (i.e., a primary task), some capacity is being occupied in continuous monitoring of the environment. This capacity, which Kahneman (1973) refers to as *spare capacity*, represents the attentional resources which will be devoted to the secondary task. A measure of this spare capacity can be obtained by requiring the subject to respond at unpredictable intervals to a probe task (Kahneman, Beatty, & Pollack, 1967; Posner & Boies, 1971). The *probe task* often requires the subject to press a key as quickly as possible whenever a tone is sounded. The more the primary task takes up available capacity, the less attention can be allocated to the monitoring activity. As attention is withdrawn from the monitoring function, the task is likely to be performed with less proficiency. In a practical sense, this means it takes the subject longer to respond to the signals being monitored. Reaction times increase as the primary activity takes up more and more of the capacity available.

The secondary-task technique is used to determine the relative attentional requirements of different activities (e.g., Britton, Glynn, Meyer, & Penland, 1982; Britton, Holdredge, Curry, & Westbrook, 1979; Britton, Piha, Davis, & Wehausen, 1978; Britton, Westbrook, & Holdredge, 1978) or to detect fluctuations in the allocation of attention to a particular task (e.g., Anderson, 1982).

2. Pupil Dilation

The claim that the dilation of the pupils can serve as a measurement of mental effort was originally made by Hess and Polt (1964). These researchers noted that there was a correspondence between the degree of dilation and the difficulty of arithmetic problems (e.g., 7×8 vs. 16×23) subjects were attempting to solve. Kahneman (1973) noted that pupil diameter serves as an indicator of arousal and as such may reflect the effort invested in an activity, the interest an environmental situation generates, or a state of the organism such as might be induced by drug or drive states. With the imposition of appropriate experimental controls, alternate explanations of pupil diameter can usually be dismissed, and differences in diameter can serve as a rather immediate indication of effort. A wide variety of tasks have demonstrated the relationship between difficulty and pupil dilation (see Kahneman, 1973, for a summary). Of particular interest within the present context are studies showing a relationship between the degree of pupil dilation and the difficulty or arithmetic problems (Bradshaw, 1968) or sentence comprehension (Wright & Kahneman, 1971). In light of the relatively nonobtrusive nature of the pupil dilation technique, it is interesting to note that this technique has not been frequently applied to many of the educational tasks discussed in other sections of this chapter.

3. Eye Fixations

Two aspects of eye fixations provide measures of attentional allocation: frequency and duration. The frequency of fixations devoted to one component of a visual display in comparison to another represents one indication of attentional allocation. For example, studies have demonstrated that subjects attend to different components of pictures (Yarbus, 1967) or text (Rothkopf & Billington, 1979), depending upon the focus of questions they have been asked. In a somewhat similar manner, Brenner and Stern (1976) have determined hyperactive boys' ability to resist distraction by determining the frequency of non-task-related fixations. The second measurable aspect of the fixation is its duration. Longer fixation durations are used as an indication of the expenditure of greater mental effort. For instance, Inhoff (1983) showed that words which were difficult to predict within the context in which they were read were fixated for longer periods of time than were more predictable words. Rothkopf and Billington (1979) found that in attending to written material that had been defined as important and thus the expected focus of greater attention, subjects produced reading behaviors that provided some evidence of longer fixation durations.

4. Viewing Times

In certain situations, the amount of time devoted to particular stimuli can be determined. This is done either by having the subject control stimulus presentation (e.g., Cirilo & Foss, 1980; Geiselman, 1977; Goetz, Schallert, Reynolds, & Radin, 1983; Grabe, 1980; McConkie, Rayner, & Wilson, 1973; Reynolds & Anderson, 1982; Reynolds, Standiford, & Anderson, 1979; Rothkopf & Billington, 1979) or by having the subject indicate what he/she is attending to at regular intervals (Rankin, 1970–1971). Greater time commitments are equated with a greater commitment of attentional resources.

It is important to note that the studies cited emphasize two kinds of flexibility. The first demonstrates that the same task can be completed with varying degrees of effort (e.g., McConkie, Rayner, & Wilson, 1973), the second that effort can be differentially expended on different segments of material within the total task (e.g., Reynolds, Standiford, & Anderson, 1979).

5. Classroom Observational Systems

Observational measures of attention require that a classroom rater make some judgment regarding the focus of student attention (Cobb, 1972; Lahaderne, 1968; Meyers, Attwell, & Orpet, 1968; Samuels & Turnure, 1974; Shannon, 1942). Observational procedures often require that the rater judge which of several categories of behavior best describes a student's actions during a brief interval of time. A behavioral definition of attentiveness–inattentiveness within such a system may include a list of specific activities (orients eyes to text or teacher, observes chalkboard, closes eyes, works or plays with nonassigned materials, etc., Samuels & Turnure, 1974) or a general description of focus (e.g., pupil is doing what is appropriate in the situation, Cobb, 1972). A variable indicating the proportion of time on task can be calculated and related to potential causes and consequences.

C. OTHER MEASUREMENT CONCERNS

The variety of attentional variables just described is necessary because of the variety of research situations in which attention is studied. Certain attentional variables are best suited to certain research questions. In addition, it appears that multiple measures of attention may sometimes be necessary within the same study. Reynolds and Anderson (1982) contend that in some situations attention is multidimensional and the various aspects of attention must each be measured to provide an accurate description of processing activity. When processing can be extended in time (e.g., reading activities), Reynolds and Anderson claim that attention is a joint function of duration and intensity. In their research, duration was represented by inspection time and intensity by the secondary-task technique. These researchers were able to demonstrate that the two measures of attention were independent and potentially compensatory. Had only one variable been considered, the impact of attention would have appeared less impressive than was actually the case. Other research has demonstrated that when multiple measures of differential attention are available, some attentional variables may be influenced by a treatment condition while others remain unaffected (Britton, Glynn, Meyer, & Penland, 1982). Again, these researchers might have reached a very different conclusion had not several different attentional variables been studied. Finally, Rothkopf and Billington (1979) were able to demonstrate in a careful analysis of the behavior of individual subjects that a process variable (inspection time) showed variations in attention only among some of the subjects showing attentional differences in a product variable (differential recall). The single process variable employed was not sufficient to explain the manner in which all subjects responded to produce evidence of differential attention. While it is certainly possible that nonattentional processes were responsible, the work of Reynolds and Anderson (1982) suggests an alternative the Rothkopf and Billington (1979) methodology would have missed. Some readers may have responded to the task by varying inspection time and others by varying intensity. Taken collectively, this research demonstrates the importance of utilizing multiple measures of attention in future research. Of special interest may be studies investigating the unique ways in which individual subjects use alternative attentional resources in response to a particular task.

A second issue of great importance to researchers in this area concerns the necessary methodological procedures for demonstrating the causal impact of differential attention (Reynolds & Anderson, 1982). The researcher wants in some way to show that differential allocation of attentional resources produces some detectable differences in task performance. In making a case, the researcher can gather product data, process data, or both. The weakest case for causality exists when only product data (e.g., differential recall or task performance) are available. In this case, an assumption is being made that the allocation of attention and not some other component or function of the information-processing system is responsible for the observed differences in performance. The assumption may be incorrect, and alternate explanations always remain as possibilities. In a somewhat more advanced procedure, the researcher gathers both product and process data and assumes that if both data sets show the hypothesized differences, the process differences are responsible for the product differences. Taking goal-directed reading as an example, the greater inspection time accorded goal-relevant information is assumed to be the cause of the superior recall of this same information. The difficulty here is the possibility that the process and product results are only associated and not related to each other in a causal manner. This possibility has been noted in several sources (Reynolds & Anderson, 1982; Reynolds, Standiford, & Anderson, 1979; Rothkopf & Billington, 1979).

Reynolds and Anderson (1982) propose that a still more rigorous procedure be employed. This procedure is utilized in situations in which the subject has been asked to attend to one of several categories of information and later required to recall all the information possible. The procedure is based on the logic that if differential attention is the causal link between stimulus relevance and differential recall, then discounting or removing the link between stimulus importance and the process measure should also eliminate the significant relationship between stimulus importance and differential recall. This test can be accomplished statistically using a stepwise multiple regression technique. After analyzing several different studies of attention in this manner, Reynolds and Anderson (1982) found that some studies did and some did not meet this standard. At this point, this technique has been used so infrequently that the theoretical value of the procedure is difficult to evaluate.

IV. EXAMPLES OF EDUCATIONAL APPLICATIONS

Attention research has focused on many specific topics of educational significance. Rather than attempting a general survey, we will consider two specific but different topics in some depth. The first topic is concerned with understanding the role of selective attention in purposeful or goal-directed reading. Research topics such as this primarily focus on understanding how the information-processing system functions when confronted with a particular task. The second topic is concerned with the identification of the attentional deficiencies of hyperactive children. Research topics such as this investigate group differences in the functioning of the information-processing system. Group differences in functioning should be apparent across a variety of tasks tapping the critical processing skill or skills.

A. ATTENTION CONTROL IN READING

Anderson (1982) claims that one of the most consistent findings in reading is that text elements that are important are likely to be recalled more successfully than less important elements. To structure reasons that text elements become important, a model, suggested in its basic form by Kozminsky (1977), will be employed. In this model (see Table 1), the determinants of importance are represented as being present within the text, within the experience of the reader, or within any task given to the reader. While these determinants of importance probably interact in most reading situations, and assignment of a task to a category is thus somewhat arbitrary, the three-part system appears to represent a straightforward and intuitive method for organizing existing research and theory. This brief consideration of importance is intended to set the stage for the following discussion of selective attention in reading. Explaining the details of Table 1 is beyond the scope of this

TABLE 1   Factors Determining the Importance of Elements in Text

Text
    Idea unit structure
        Kintsch and van Dijk, 1978
        Meyer and McKonkie, 1973
    Text signals
        Syntactic signals
            Haviland and Clark, 1974
        Imposed text signals
            Titles
                Kozminsky, 1977
            Typographical cues
                Glynn and DiVesta, 1979
Reader
    General story grammar
        Mandler and Johnson, 1977
        Thorndyke, 1977
    Interest
        Asher, 1980
    Existing perspective
        Anderson, Reynolds, Schallert, and Goetz, 1977
        Steffensen, Joag-dev, and Anderson, 1979
Assigned purpose
    Assigned perspective
        Pichert and Anderson, 1977
    Assigned questions–goals
        Reynolds, Standiford, and Anderson, 1979
        Rothkopf and Billington, 1979
        Rothkopf and Bisbicos, 1967

chapter. I hope that the subtitles are self-explanatory and many of the references are already familiar to the reader. The point being established is that there are many dimensions on which a reader may differentiate important from unimportant text information. If the learner can discriminate the more important content, selective attention should then allow the purposeful reader to process the important information in a manner that optimizes the retention of that material.

A simple explanation (Anderson, 1982) can be provided for the advantage that "important" text elements enjoy in reading. First, this explanation assumes that text elements must be processed to some minimal level so that their degree of importance can be evaluated. On the basis of this evaluation, the text element then either receives additional attention or is dismissed in favor of considering the next text element. Because of this differential treatment, the preferred text elements may be better retained. While other explanations are possible (Ausubel, 1963; Kintsch & van Dijk, 1978) and are considered in other chapters of this text, this section will consider data related to the hypothesis that importance influences recall because of differential attention.

This review would quickly grow beyond the limits of this chapter if every study investigating directed reading were included. There are literally scores of studies in the area of interspersed questions alone (for reviews see Anderson & Biddle, 1975; Andre, 1979). A more reasonable domain can be established by considering studies in which both a process and a product variable were obtained during the completion of a reading task. A summary of 13 studies providing both types of dependent measures is provided in Table 2. The columns in this table indicate how importance was established in a particular study, the process variable that was employed, whether the product or process variables indicated differential sensitivity to the important text elements, and whether the study attempted to determine that an individual difference variable influenced attentional control. The product variable in all studies was some measure of prose retention.

The study by Reynolds et al. (1979) serves as a good example of the type of research done in this area. This study focused on the indirect effect of *inserted postquestions.* For those unfamiliar with this type of research, inserted postquestions require that the reader stop during the reading task and answer a question about the material that has just been read. The indirect effect of questions means that if the reader is continually asked one type of question (e.g., the meaning of technical terms), this type of information begins to receive more careful consideration in anticipation of future questions. In the Reynolds et al. (1979) study, subjects read pages of text from the screen of a computer-controlled terminal. Depending upon whether or not the contents of a given page contained information of the type the subject

TABLE 2 Reading Studies Employing Product and Process Variables to Investigate Attentional Control

Study	Importance established	Process variable	Significant outcomes	Individual difference interactions
Anderson, 1982	Interest	Probe task reading times	Recall, probe task, reading time	
	Assigned perspective	Probe task reading times	Recall, probe task, reading time	
Cirilo & Foss, 1980	Story grammar	Reading time	Recall, reading time	
Geiselman, 1975	Assigned theme	Reading time	Recall, reading time	
Geiselman, 1977	Emphasized topic	Reading time	Recall, reading time	
Goetz, Schallert, Reynolds & Radin, 1983	Assigned perspective	Reading time	Recall, reading time	(Background), recall—no; reading time—yes
Grabe, 1979 Study 1	Assigned perspective	Reading time	Recall	
Grabe, 1981 Study 1 Study 2	Assigned perspective Questions	Reading time	Recall	
Just & Carpenter, 1980	Story grammar	Eye movements	Recall, eye movement variables	
Ramsel & Grabe, 1983	Questions	Reading time	Recall, reading time	(Age) recall—yes; reading time—no
Reynolds & Anderson, 1982	Questions	Probe task reading time	Recall, probe task, reading time	(Ability) recall—yes
Reynolds, Standiford & Anderson, 1979	Questions	Reading time	Recall, reading time	
Rothkopf & Billington, 1975	Questions	Reading time	Recall, reading time	
Rothkopf & Billington, 1979 Study 1, 2 Study 3	Questions Questions	Reading time Eye movement	Recall, reading time Recall, eye movement variables	

was being asked to answer questions about, the contents of each text page could be defined as high or low in importance. The use of the computer allowed for precise measurement of the amount of time spent on each text segment. After reading the passage in the manner just described, subjects were asked to answer some of the questions that had previously been used as inserted questions, some new questions about the same type of content, and questions about other types of content. As might be expected, subjects did better on questions that repeated questions asked while they were reading. This finding represents a direct effect of the inserted questions. Subjects who received a particular type of inserted question also did better than other groups on new posttest questions of that type. This finding demonstrates the indirect effect of inserted questions. The reading-speed data also demonstrated that subjects spent more time on the pages containing the type of information they were being questioned about. Reynolds et al. (1979) described their results as reflecting the time-intensive process of selective attention.

Reynolds et al. (1979) and the other studies summarized in Table 2 strongly suggest that readers respond to the importance of text elements with a differential allocation of attention. All studies cited demonstrated that the important components of the text were more likely to be available for recall. In addition, the vast majority of studies also indicated that on-line measures of attention showed that important material was processed differently. Of course, the tempting conclusion is that the differential allocation caused the differences in retention. As was discussed earlier (see Section II.C), a causal relationship has been established in only a few cases (Anderson, 1982; Reynolds & Anderson, 1982).

An important application of this research area may eventually involve the study of individual differences in reading skill. A number of studies (Eamon, 1978–1979; Grabe, 1980; Grabe & Prentice, 1979; Ramsel & Grabe, 1983; Reynolds & Anderson, 1982; Sanders, 1973) have demonstrated that more capable readers are able to adapt their reading behavior more successfully to an assigned task. Perhaps these differences imply that less capable readers are preoccupied with basic reading tasks (e.g., decoding, lexical access) and are either incapable of controlling or lack the reading skills to control processing activities. Unfortunately, the group differences to date have been evident only in product variables. Studies of individual differences in attention (Ramsel & Grabe, 1983; Reynolds & Anderson, 1982) have not been able to demonstrate a special attentional deficiency in the reading behavior of the less able reader. Both good and poor readers appear to locate the important material and attend to this material for a longer period of time. However, this additional processing seems to benefit the better readers more than the poorer readers. What is not evident from the existing research is what good and poor readers are doing during this period of extended processing. It is very possible that during this extra time better readers are engaging in activities that are in some way more purposeful, intensive, or appropriate to the assigned task. Future work may profitably center on this issue.

B.   ATTENTIONAL FUNCTIONING IN HYPERACTIVE CHILDREN

This section examines the role that the ability to control attentional resources may play in differentiating a partcular category of students from their peers. No battles of cause and effect are fought here. Rather, it is only noted that differences in the ability to control attention have clearly been associated with age (Hagen & Hale, 1973; Miller & Weiss, 1981), hyperactivity (Douglas & Peters, 1979; Rosenthal & Allen, 1980), intelligence (Stankov, 1983), and learning disabilities (Douglas & Peters, 1979; Samuels & Edwall, 1981; Santostefano, Rutledge, & Randall, 1965). The references provided contain exemplary reviews of many studies in the areas mentioned. Hyperactivity is the only topic given additional consideration here. Hyperactivity is a syndrome present in children of at least normal intelligence who demonstrate excessive motor activity and seem highly distractible (Rosenthal & Allen, 1980). Hyperactive children have difficulty functioning in the school environment. Unlike learning disabled children, who suffer from a specific difficulty, hyperactive children are likely to fall consistently behind their classmates in many academic areas (Minde, Lewin, Weiss, Lavigueur, Douglas, & Sykes, 1971).

This brief comment on hyperactivity and attention draws heavily on the thorough literature review and theoretical arguments provided by Douglas and Peters (1979). The interested reader is directed to this source for a complete discussion of this area. Douglas and Peters (1979) argued that theoretical explanations for the academic difficulty of hyperactive children could be organized into two general categories: failures of selective attention and failures to sustain attention. The model of attention utilized in this chapter has acknowledged these two facets of attention, but has chosen to deal with both within the same general model. As has been stated previously, others have found it more useful to maintain clear distinctions among various attentional processes and have developed theoretical explanations for each process.

Researchers attempting to demonstrate that hyperactive children are deficient in selective attention have viewed attention as a filter mechanism (originally Broadbent, 1958). In this conceptualization, information impinges on the person through several parallel sensory pathways. However, the person's ability to process information is limited to a single pathway. Attention serves the purpose of filtering out the surplus input. The hyperactive child is claimed to have a defective filter that fails to block out irrelevant stimuli from further processing and thus may overload the processing system. In other words, the hyperactive child is controlled by the stimulus environment rather than being able to exercise control over that environment. The intended task may be lost among other competing stimuli.

Researchers focusing on the ability to sustain attention have adopted a conceptualization of attention similar to that advocated by Kahneman (1973). The difficulty in this case is a failure not to direct attention, but to sustain a focus when tasks require self-sustained and self-directed effort (Douglas & Peters, 1979). Because the selective-attention and the sustained-attention positions can be clearly delineated, it should be possible to use field and laboratory investigations to determine if either position accurately explains the difficulties of the hyperactive child.

1. Hyperactive Children and Selective Attention

Studies assessing the hypothesis that the hyperactive child suffers from a deficiency of selective attention fall into two categories. The first category of studies seeks to demonstrate that the hyperactive child is particularly susceptible to distraction. Researchers attempt to demonstrate that the presence of irrelevant stimuli impair the performance of an assigned task. The second category attempts to show that hyperactive and control children perform differently on incidental learning tasks. In essence, these two categories of research reflect the opposite sides of the same premise. By attending less successfully to the targeted stimuli (distraction) the hyperactive child may acquire more knowledge of nontargeted stimuli (incidental learning).

a. Distractibility Research. To demonstrate that hyperactive children are unable to screen out task-irrelevant stimulation, researchers hope to show differential deterioration of the performance of hyperactive and normal children as their responses to tasks with distractors are compared with their performance on tasks without distractors. It is important to note that group differences in performance are not enough to demonstrate the greater distractibility of the hyperactive group. The researcher must show that the difference in group performance is significantly greater in the presence of the distractor than without it. A study by Cohen, Weiss, and Minde (1972) provides a good example. Hyperactive and control adolescents were asked to (1) read color names (printed with black ink), (2) name the color of colored patches, and (3) read color names printed in a conflicting colored ink. The dependent variable was naming latency. The hypothesized attentional deficit was to be evidenced in a group by task interaction; the largest group difference was expected when the colored names were printed in a conflicting colored ink.

Major summaries of the research regarding the hypothesis that hyperactives are more distractible do not appear to agree. Douglas and Peters (1979) concluded from their own research and from the research of others that hyperactive children are not more distractible. In spite of the fact that essentially the same research is summarized, Rosenthal and Allen (1980) reached the opposite conclusion. Rosenthal and Allen (1980) concluded that many of the studies failing to demonstrate group differences employed distractors that were tangential to the assigned processing task. A 90-dB horn (employed in Dykman, Walls, Suzuki, Ackerman, & Peters, 1970) sounded during a reaction time task would represent a good example, In this case, different input modalities would clearly differentiate the central and tangential stimuli. To determine how hyperactive children were influenced by an intratask distractor, Rosenthal and Allen (1980) asked subjects to match one of two visual displays to a target. The displays could vary in the shape of the form present in the display, the color of the display, and the position of a star placed within the display. Only one of these dimensions was relevant to a particular matching task. The other dimensions were either included or not included on a particular trial to vary the level of distraction. The hyperactive group was more adversely influenced by the addition of the irrelevant dimensions. However, other studies in which irrelevant dimensions were either present or not have failed to demonstrate that hyperactive children are most distractible. The study by Cohen, Weiss, and Minde (1972) discussed at an earlier point is a good example. There appears no clear resolution of these conflicting results. However, some researchers (Douglas & Peters, 1979) argue that differences in the way hyperactive subjects are defined (perhaps learning-disabled students have been included) and whether a particular distraction task may actually require sustained attention or search behavior can often explain the seemingly discrepant findings.

Field studies investigating the impact of providing stimulus-reduced learning environments actually predated the laboratory studies of selective attention. Zentall and Zentall (1976) reported that reducing sensory input (e.g., Cruickshank, Betnzen, Ratzenburg, & Tannhauser, 1961) was once the preferred method for handling hyperactive children in the classroom. A common approach was to isolate hyperactive children in cubicles in an attempt to reduce the distractions found in a normal classroom environment. Hyperactive children might join their peers for group activities, but had to complete their seatwork in an isolated booth or cubicle at the rear of the classroom. These isolation studies represent a good example of the fact that commonsense educational solutions are not always successful. Studies of this type (Rost & Charles, 1967; Somervill, Warnberg, & Bost, 1973) have failed to reveal any advantage in academic performance. In fact, studies have indicated that the behavioral problems of the hyperactive child increase in isolation (Zentall & Zentall, 1976). Like the laboratory studies, field studies have failed to consistently indicate that hyperactive children are primarily impaired by their distractibility.

b. *Incidental Learning Studies.* While studies of distraction assume that the hyperactive child is attending to irrelevant stimuli because performance on the assigned task deteriorates, incidental learning studies attempt to directly assess the processing of irrelevant information. In most cases this technique requests recall of the irrelevant information and either makes a direct group comparison on this variable (e.g., hyperactive subjects would probably be expected to recall more irrelevant information than a matched control group) or attempts to demonstrate a relevance by group interaction (e.g., the more able group might be significantly better on the relevant task and the less able group might be better on the irrelevant task). Some of the tasks discussed in the section on purposeful reading (Section IV.A) could also be interpreted as providing information about incidental learning.

Only Peters (1977) has used an incidental learning task with hyperactive and normal children. In this study, children were shown cards containing a picture of an animal and a household object. The subjects were told only to remember the animals, but were later tested on the household objects. No group differences were present. It should be noted that a task of this type has been used successfully to demonstrate age differences in incidental learning (Miller & Weiss, 1981), and thus the technique cannot be dismissed as insensitive.

2. Hyperactive Children and Sustained Attention

Earlier in this chapter, a distinction was made between the selective and intensive aspects of attention. This same distinction has been made repeatedly by other authors (Anderson, 1982; Kahneman, 1973). It appears that this distinction is critical in pinpointing the attentional difficulty of hyperactive children. Douglas and Peters (1979) argued that distractibility and selective attention do not represent major difficulties for the hyperactive child, but that the hyperactive child has difficulty when he or she must sustain "the concentration of consciousness." This type of difficulty is likely to show up on tasks that reward both strategic and thorough processing. While the research to be described here does not include typical school tasks, certainly academic activities such as reading an assignment or listening to a class discussion require strategic and thorough processing.

A variety of tasks have been used to study the hyperactive child's ability to sustain attention. Douglas and Peters (1979) differentiate these tasks as vigilance tasks and a more general category of complex tasks.

a. *Vigilance Studies.* Vigilance essentially represents a state in which the subject is waiting for a particular event to happen. Responding before the event occurs represents an *error of commission*, and failing to respond to the event represents an *error of omission*. A common vigilance task used with hyperactive subjects is the Continuous Performance Test (e.g., Sykes, Douglas, Weiss, & Minde, 1971; Weingartner, Rapoport, Buchsbaum, Bunney, Ebert, Mikkelsen, & Caine, 1980). In this task, a series of single letters is presented to the subject. The subject must respond to a particular letter (e.g., A), but only after it is preceded by another letter (e.g., X). Hyperactive children are more likely to fail to respond when appropriate and are also more likely to fail to inhibit responses when the target letter is presented without the required preceding letter. The fact that both types of errors can be made less frequent when hyperactives are given methylphenidate (Ritalin) (Sykes, Douglas, & Morganstern, 1973) has been used to argue that hyperactives have an underaroused nervous system. However, recent data (Weingartner et al., 1980) showing that the performance of normals can also be improved with Ritalin brings this theory into serious question.

b. *Complex Tasks.* An interesting example of a complex task showing a consistent difference between hyperactive and control subjects is Kagan's Matching Familiar Figures Test (Kagan, Rosman, Day, Albert, & Phillips, 1964). In this task, a subject is shown a picture of a common object and is then asked to pick a perfect match from among a group of alternatives. With the exception of the target figure, the alternatives differ from the original in a number of subtle ways. In one case, the picture shows a teddy bear sitting on a chair. The incorrect alternatives differ from the standard on such dimensions as the shape of the chair back, the shape of the bear's feet, and the position of the bow around the bear's neck. Error frequency and decision-making latencies were originally used to differentiate the problem-solving strategies of children. Reflective children took longer than average but made few errors. Impulsive children responded quickly but made frequent errors. Even on an intuitive level it should be clear why researchers interested in the strategic behavior of hyperactive children began to use this task. Several studies (e.g., Cohen, Weiss, & Minde, 1972; Juliano, 1974) have successfully demonstrated that hyperactive children and adolescents perform in a more impulsive manner than their classmates. Hyperactive children often lack the systematic search strategies necessary to perform this task successfully. This inability to sustain strategic behavior may contribute to deficient performance in a variety of tasks.

It appears that tasks that require sustained attention or processing represent a clear difficulty for the hyperactive child. Certainly these skills are a prerequisite to many school activities. Future research might show more directly how this inability to sustain attention is involved in school difficulties. It would seem that some of the reading tasks described previously (e.g., the imposed-perspective or imposed-question technique) would represent a technique with greater face validity for school situations. Because stimulant drug therapy produces effects in the lab that appear more questionable in the classroom (Barkley, 1977), research with more school-like tasks and existing drug treatments might be particularly interesting.

V.   SUGGESTIONS FOR CLASSROOM PRACTICE

The growing body of information concerning the factors which focus and maintain human attention will most likely influence classroom practice in an indirect manner. Even research presented in previous sections of this chapter, which dealt with typical classroom materials and situations (e.g., reading text in preparation for an examination) and demonstrated a significant way to improve student functioning (e.g., inserted questions), can only suggest approaches that teachers might take. Research on the direct classroom application of these techniques is often lacking. For the most part, teachers should expect to use general principles gained from research, in combination with insights drawn from experience and knowledge of situational factors, to guide their decisions. This final chapter segment attempts to outline some of these general principles and to summarize some of the studies most directly attempting to influence the attention of students in classroom situations. Before suggestions for classroom practice are given, an important prerequisite should be considered. Teachers must make conscious decisions to utilize techniques for maintaining or focusing student attention or to terminate an activity when students are no longer involved. Such decisions require that the teacher be aware of the level of student attentiveness. Unfortunately, there is evidence that not all teachers are able to distinguish attentive from inattentive students (Brophy & Good, 1974). In discussing the level of teacher awareness, Kounin (1970) has coined the term "withitness." Among behaviors evidenced by more "withit" teachers was a constant scanning of the entire class while presenting a lesson, working with a single student, or preparing materials. Not only does this scanning behavior result in a more informed teacher, but students aware that the teacher is monitoring their behavior may attend more diligently to their work.

What should teachers watching for inattentive students look for? Good and Brophy (1984) recommended that teachers note (1) eye focus, (2) whether students begin working after directions are completed, and (3) physical signs (e.g., writing) that students are engaged in seat work. These authors and others (Brophy & Good, 1974; Jecker, Maccoby, Breitrose, & Rose, 1964) cautioned that visible signs are not always enough. Strict teachers may be able to produce classroom settings in which students sit quietly doing nothing. Teachers should ask students questions to obtain the most reliable information concerning student task involvement.

While this chapter has attempted a common view of attention, it will be most useful in this section to differentiate two forms attention might take. The first form might contain student behaviors that exemplify alertness or task involvement. While these terms do not refer to exactly the same phenomena, both terms imply that the student is pursuing an appropriate task with some degree of intensity. Teachers sometimes use the buzzword *on-task* to refer to this situation. The second form involves selective attention, or discrimination. According to Piontkowski and Calfee (1979), *selective attention* includes the ability to (1) locate the components of a situation that may be important to a particular decision or task, (2) expend attentional resources on these critical features, and (3) ignore other noncritical features.

In attempting to organize ways in which attention might be improved, one further distinction might be useful. Changes in alertness or selective attention could occur because of changes in some characteristic of the student or some characteristic of the instructional environment. While the teacher can most easily change the instructional environment (e.g., seating assignments, design of materials, use of questions), these changes cannot help the student in other situations. The modification of student strategies or capabilities would improve student functioning in many learning situations.

A.   MAINTAINING STUDENT ALERTNESS AND INVOLVEMENT

1.   Environment-Based Techniques

Educational critics (e.g., Silberman, 1970) have frequently commented on the dullness, repetitiveness, and passivity that exist in many classrooms. Maintaining an optimal level of alertness under such circumstances is asking a lot of the student. Good and Brophy (1984) offered many suggestions for ways in which teachers can motivate students and keep them involved. One key to student alertness is to prevent the classroom from becoming too predictable and repetitive. Teachers themselves may become monotonous and should attempt to vary voice quality and facial expressions, the type of presentation (e.g., lecture, discussion), and the type of questions asked. Lessons should also not extend beyond the point where students are actively involved. In many cases, this would require that instruction proceed by a series of brief lessons (elementary worksheets or the format of "Sesame

Street" may illustrate this approach). Good and Brophy (1984) also recommended that teachers interact with students in such a way that students are continually involved in the learning process. First, they recommend that teachers carefully focus the attention of students before beginning an activity. They recommend that teachers employ a standard signal (e.g., "All right, let's begin") to draw student attention, pause briefly, and then begin. Second, teachers are encouraged to keep lessons moving. Attention can wander when the teacher spends too much time rehashing a point already understood, engaging in needless review, becoming preoccupied with an individual student, or struggling with a piece of instructional equipment. Finally, teachers should make students accountable for their involvement. Part of teacher–student interaction should include questions. From time to time, students can also be asked to provide comments on the answers of other students so they will actively follow the entire discussion.

Other aspects of the classroom environment which teachers may be able to control also seem to influence student attentiveness. One intriguing example concerns the physical arrangement of the classroom. Dunkin and Biddle (1974) describe an area within the classroom that they label the "action zone." The action zone consists of the seats across the front and down the center aisle and represents the part of the classroom in which the teacher spends most of his or her time and carries on the major proportion of teacher–student interactions. Students sitting in this area are more attentive and achieve at a higher level. Schwebel and Cherlin (1972) moved students either into or out of the action zone and found related changes in attentiveness. Based on these results, Piontkowski and Calfee (1979) suggested that teachers may improve the work of inattentive students by moving them to the action zone. Why does sitting in or out of the action zone influence attention? Piontkowski and Calfee (1979) suggested that being in the action zone leads to greater student participation and more attention from the teacher. Alternatively, Schwebel and Cherlin (1972) suggested that students may think of themselves differently because of the seats they occupy and may act according to their perceptions. In either case, teachers should be aware that the spatial relationships that exist within a classroom in one way or another can influence student attentiveness.

2. Student-Based Techniques

Some practitioners have assumed that the observed relationship between task involvement and academic achievement was due to some characteristic of the student. This perspective has led to attempts to change the student rather than the environment. Cobb and Hops (1973) included the ability to attend to the teacher as one of several essential academic survival skills. Students lacking competence in survival skills were found to do poorly academically (Cobb, 1972). Cobb and Hops attempted to modify student behavior through behavior modification techniques. A clock and light signalled to the teacher and students when the entire class was engaged in appropriate behavior. The entire group received reinforcement when time on task met the necessary criterion for the day. Additional behavioral techniques were used with students who still had difficulty attending. The behavioral program improved both student survival skills and academic performance in comparison to a control group, who received no special treatment. Based on this and other research, Piontkowski and Calfee (1979) suggested that student attention can be improved if the school environment rewards students for attending. Several specific examples of applications can be obtained from this source.

One reason behavioral approaches may be more productive than other approaches in improving school performance (e.g., amphetamine therapy—Barkley, 1977) is that the student is taught and rewarded for appropriate behavior. Some students may not know how to attend to a lesson and may have to be taught what attentive behavior is. Two studies with impulsive students provide some insight into how direct instruction might be accomplished. Egeland (1974) and Learner and Richman (1984) attempted to improve performance on the type of tasks employed in the Matching Familiar Figures Test (MFFT, Kagan et al., 1966) and then to determine if this skill newly acquired would transfer to measures of reading comprehension. The MFFT task requires that students match a target picture with an identical picture presented among several alternatives. Impulsive children both respond more quickly and make more errors than the typical child. Egeland (1974) believed impulsive children make more errors because they fail to note component parts and respond instead on a global basis. Direct instruction in both studies consisted of two components: (1) children were taught to take more time in responding—in training, answers would not be accepted until a certain amount of time had passed, and (2) children were given a scanning strategy to use—find components, compare target to alternatives on each component, and eliminate alternatives not producing a match. The children were found to be more reflective (slower and fewer errors) on the MFFT task after training. Surprisingly, both studies also showed that the children improved their scores on tests of reading comprehension!

While a great deal more work has yet to be completed, it appears that the ability to maintain attention can be directly taught. As a possible place to start, Biehler and Snowman (1982) suggested that younger students be allowed to play games that require attention. Simon Says or Concentration may represent good examples for younger students. It also appears that teachers or researchers wishing to improve attention may have to give some thought to what the students will be doing as they attend and then find a way to develop those particular skills. Finally, Egeland (1974) said that practical applications require that the student learn to utilize the strategy in an automatic manner. He suggested this can be accomplished by gradually increasing the difficulty of the task in a way that minimizes errors. For instance, in the game of Concentration just mentioned, the number of pairs in a given game could be gradually increased as the children become more adept at the game.

B. FACILITATING SKILL IN SELECTIVE ATTENTION

1. Environment-Based Techniques

In a novel area, learning to selectively attend is a two-stage process. First, the students must gain some appreciation for the dimensions of the stimuli they have been asked to work with. Then, the students must attend to the dimensions that are relevant to a particular task and ignore the dimensions that are irrelevant. An example may help illustrate this distinction. Students in an adult-education program are taking a course in wine tasting. Before the students will be able to compare several wines on a particular characteristic (e.g., fruitiness), the instructor will have to help the students understand what feature of taste, smell, or color a particular characteristic describes.

Piontkowski and Calfee (1979) argued that people are usually pretty good at picking out salient dimensions. Usually, the teacher's major task will be to help the student identify important sources of information and avoid distractions. Many practical examples of how to help the student focus attention on important information appear to involve some variant of the Von Restorff (1933) effect. Von Restorff claimed that the isolation of an item against a homogeneous background facilitated the retention of that item. Stimulus features such as bright colors, loud sounds, and novelty can be used to control the focus of attention. A teacher can print key words on the blackboard in large letters or in color; important lecture points can be emphasized with a loud voice, and particularly important lectures can be initiated in a novel way (e.g., dressing in a costume from a particular historical period) (Biehler & Snowman, 1982). Selective attention can also be encouraged in a more purposeful manner. Students can be asked to "really concentrate on this, it's important" (Biehler & Snowman, 1982), can be given textual material in which important terms or phrases have been underlined (Cashen & Leicht, 1970; Mayer, 1984), or can be given questions to answer. Such techniques are probably most useful when the student is unfamiliar with the material being presented or has poor selection skills (Mayer, 1984).

Finally, selective attention can be improved by reducing distractions. Piontkowski and Calfee (1979) discussed an example in which young children were being taught to listen to the sound generated by a single instrument within the context of an orchestra performance. For instructional purposes, the music had been specially recorded so that the sounds generated by all but the key instrument were muted. While this example is probably a bit extreme and most teachers could not be expected to go to such lengths, teachers should be aware that the classroom setting can be quite hectic and some students may suffer because of distractions. Piontkowski and Calfee (1979) suggested that the movement of many educational institutions toward more open-classroom and multigrouped approaches has produced learning situations in which some students may have difficulty. To combat these difficulties, they recommended that teachers make sure that there are quiet retreats within the classroom so that as needed students could find a location free of distraction. These suggestions should not be interpreted to mean that classrooms should be absolutely barren and quiet. Research (Wilkinson, 1963) seems to indicate that there is an optimal level of arousal and noise (and perhaps other sources of distraction or tension) that can, in some circumstances, facilitate learning. Teachers should observe their students individually and determine when distractions are impeding learning and when the learning environment could benefit from increased stimulation (e.g., background music).

2. Learner-Based Techniques

Students can acquire skills that will allow them both to more effectively differentiate the dimensions of a particular situation and to selectively focus on relevant dimensions. The key to learning to recognize the features present in a particular situation is learning a way to operationalize the features. A frequently cited example of concept learning (Mechner, 1971) can be used to illustrate how the function of operationalization can be accomplished. The learning problem in this example is to acquire the skills necessary to diagnose certain heart conditions from electrocardiographic patterns. The stimuli are pen tracings that are the output of an electrocardiograph. To the uninitiated, the tracings look like a series of squiggly lines. Some of the variability in the lines is significant and some is not. The first step in the learning process is to give students a system with which to label the components of the tracings (see Fig. 2). Each heartbeat produces five distinctive deviations from a straight line, and these are labelled in the order of their appearance P, Q, R, S, and T. Once the features can be identified, a relatively simple rule is applied to produce a particular diagnosis. For example, an infarction—severe heart damage—is present when the width of the Q

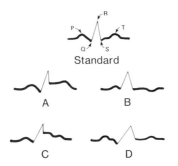

FIG. 2. Dimensions involved in the categorizing of electrocardiographic patterns.

wave is greater than a certain value (example D in Fig. 2). When students can label or describe stimulus dimensions, they have acquired the knowledge on which selective attention can be based.

Students can also learn strategies that help them selectively attend. One example might be underlining or copying (Mayer, 1984; Rickards & August, 1975). In selecting certain segments of text, the reader may be able to enhance the prominence of that material. One caution must be noted. Several studies (Idstein & Jenkins, 1972; Stordahl & Christensen, 1956) have failed to produce a special advantage for underlining. Rickards and August suggest this may have occurred because students were allowed to engage in unlimited underlining. In the Rickards and August (1975) technique, students were limited in the number of sentences that could be marked, and this approach may have resulted in greater focusing on those sentences actually underlined. Students can learn activities that may help them differentiate material they think is important from material of lesser significance.

VI. SUMMARY

The goal of this chapter has been to link theory and research on attentional processes to the activities of the classroom. To accomplish this goal, a general model of attention was first developed. Within this model, attention was essentially represented as a limited quantity of conscious effort that could be expended on alternative information sources or cognitive tasks. To make this definition a little more concrete, various ways in which attention has been operationalized were presented.

Attention is such an integral component of day-to-day school functioning that a review of all possible applications would have been beyond the possible scope of a single chapter. Two exemplary topics, the role of attention in purposeful reading and the attentional difficulties of hyperactive children, were selected to illustrate how the role of attention is studied as a component of an academic skill and as a source of individual variability. It is hoped that these extended examples and the brief comments on classroom applications will provide the reader with an understanding of the cognitive role attention plays in educational tasks.

REFERENCES

Anderson, R. (1982). Allocation of attention during reading. In A. Flammer & W. Kintsch (Eds.), *Discourse processing* (pp. 292–305). Amsterdam: North Holland Publishing Co.

Anderson, R., & Biddle, B. (1975). On asking people questions about what they are reading. In G. Bower (Ed.), *Psychology of learning and motivation* (Vol. 9, pp. 89–132). New York: Academic Press.

Anderson, R., Reynolds, R., Schallert, D., & Goetz, E. (1977). Frameworks for comprehending discourse. *American Educational Research Journal, 14,* 367–381.

Andre, T. (1979). Does answering higher-level questions while reading facilitate productive learning. *Review of Educational Research, 49,* 280–318.

Asher, S. (1980). Topic interest and children's reading comprehension. In R. Spiro, B. Bruce, & W. Brewer (Eds.), *Theoretical issues in reading comprehension* (pp. 525–534). Hillsdale, NJ: Erlbaum.

Ausubel, D. (1963). *The psychology of meaningful verbal learning.* New York: Grune & Stratton.

Baker, R., & Madell, T. (1965). A continued investigation of susceptibility to distraction in academically underachieving and achieving male college students. *Journal of Educational Psychology, 56,* 254–258.

Barkley, R. (1977). A review of stimulant drug research with hyperactive children. *Journal of Child Psychology and Psychiatry, 18,* 327–345.

Biehler, R., & Snowman, J. (1982). *Psychology applied to teaching* (4th ed.). Boston: Houghton-Mifflin.

Bradshaw, J. (1968). Pupil size and problem solving. *Quarterly Journal of Experimental Psychology, 20,* 115–122.

Brenner, D., & Stern, J. (1976). Attention and distractibility during reading in hyperactive boys. *Journal of Abnormal Child Psychology, 4,* 381–387.

Britton, B., Glynn, S., Meyer, B., & Penland, M. (1982). Effects of text structure on use of cognitive capacity during reading. *Journal of Educational Psychology, 74,* 51–61.

Britton, B., Holdredge, T., Curry, C., & Westbrook, R. (1979). Use of cognitive capacity in reading identical texts with different levels of discourse level meaning. *Journal of Experimental Psychology: Human Learning and Memory, 5,* 262–270.

Britton, B., Piha, A., Davis, J., & Wehausen, E. (1978). Reading and cognitive capacity usage: Adjunct question effects. *Memory and Cognition, 6,* 266–273.

Britton, B., Westbrook, R., & Holdredge, T. (1978). Reading and cognitive capacity usage: Effects of text difficulty. *Journal of Experimental Psychology: Human Learning and Memory, 4,* 582–591.

Broadbent, D. (1958). *Perception and communication.* London: Pergamon.

Brophy, J., & Good, T. (1974). *Teacher–student relationships: Causes and consequences.* New York: Holt.

Bryden, M. (1971). Attentional strategies and short-term memory in dichotic listening. *Cognitive Psychology, 2,* 99–116.

Cashen, V., & Leicht, K. (1970). Role of the isolation effect in a formal educational setting. *Journal of Educational Psychology, 61,* 484–486.

Cirilo, R., & Foss, D. (1980). Text structure and reading time for sentences. *Journal of Verbal Learning and Verbal Behavior, 19,* 96–109.

Cobb, J. (1972). Relationship of discrete classroom behaviors to fourth-grade academic achievement. *Journal of Educational Psychology, 63,* 74–80.

Cobb, J., & Hops, H. (1973). Effects of academic survival skill training on low achieving first graders. *Journal of Educational Research, 67,* 108–113.

Cohen, N., Weiss, G., & Minde, K. (1972). Cognitive styles in adolescents previously diagnosed as hyperactive. *Journal of Child Psychology and Psychiatry, 13,* 203–209.

Collins, W. (1970). Learning and media content: A developmental study. *Child Development, 41,* 1133–1142.

Cruickshank, W., Betnzen, F., Ratzenburg, F., & Tannhauser, M. (1961). *A teaching method for brain injured and hyperactive children.* Syracuse, NY: Syracuse University Press.

Douglas, V., & Peters, K. (1979). Toward a clearer definition of the attentional deficit of hyperactive children. In G. Hale & M. Lewis (Eds.), *Attention and cognitive development* (pp. 173–247). New York: Plenum.

Dunkin, M., & Biddle, B. (1974). *The study of teaching.* New York: Holt.

Dykman, R., Walls, R., Suzuki, T., Ackerman, P., & Peters, J. (1970). Children with learning disabilities: Conditioning, differentiation, and the effect of distraction. *American Journal of Orthopsychiatry, 40,* 766–782.

Eamon, D. (1978–1979). Selection and recall of topical information in prose by better and poorer readers. *Reading Research Quarterly, 14,* 244–257.

Egeland, B. (1974). Training impulsive children in the use of more efficient scanning techniques. *Child Development, 45,* 165–171.

Faw, H., & Waller, T. (1976). Mathemagenic behaviors and efficiency in learning from prose materials: Review, critique and recommendations. *Review of Educational Research, 46,* 691–720.

Geiselman, R. (1975). Semantic positive forgetting: Another cocktail party problem. *Journal of Verbal Learning and Verbal Behavior, 14,* 73–81.

Geiselman, R. (1977). Memory for prose as a function of learning strategy and inspection time. *Journal of Educational Psychology, 69,* 547–555.

Gibson, E. (1969). *Principles of perceptual learning and development.* New York: Appleton.

Glynn, S., & DiVesta, F. (1979). Control of prose processing via instructional and typographical cues. *Journal of Educational Psychology, 71,* 595–603.

Goetz, E., Schallert, D., Reynolds, R., & Radin, D. (1983). Reading in perspective: What real cops and pretend burglars look for in a story. *Journal of Educational Psychology, 75,* 500–510.

Good, T., & Brophy, J. (1984). *Looking in classrooms.* New York: Harper.

Grabe, M. (1979). Reader imposed structure and prose retention. *Contemporary Educational Psychology, 4,* 162–171.

Grabe, M. (1980). Utilization of imposed structure: The impact of reading competence and grade level. *Journal of Reading Behavior, 12,* 31–39.

Grabe, M. (1981). Variable inspection time as an indicator of cognitive reading behaviors. *Contemporary Educational Psychology, 6,* 334–343.

Grabe, M., & Prentice, W. (1979). The impact of reading competence on the ability to take a perspective. *Journal of Reading Behavior, 11,* 21–25.

Hagen, J., & Hale, G. (1973). The development of attention in children. In A. Pick (Ed.)

Minnesota symposium on child psychology (Vol. 7, pp. 117–140). Minneapolis: University of Minnesota Press.

Haviland, S., & Clark, H. (1974). What's new? Acquiring new information as a process in comprehension. *Journal of Verbal Learning and Verbal Behavior, 13,* 512–521.

Hess, E., & Polt, J. (1964). Pupil size in relation to mental activity during simple problem-solving. *Science, 140,* 1190–1192.

Huey, E. (1968). *The psychology and pedagogy of reading.* Cambridge, MA: MIT Press. (first published in 1908 by Macmillan Co.)

Idstein, P., & Jenkins, J. (1972). Underlining versus repetitive reading. *Journal of Educational Psychology, 65,* 321–323.

Inhoff, A. (1983). Attentional strategies during reading short stories. In K. Rayner (Ed.), *Eye movements in reading: Perceptual and language processes* (pp. 181– 192). New York: Academic Press.

Jecker, J., Maccoby, N., Breitrose, H., & Rose, E. (1964). Teacher accuracy in assessing cognitive visual feedback from students. *Journal of Applied Psychology, 48,* 393–397.

Juliano, D. (1974). Conceptual tempo, activity and concept learning in hyperactive and normal children. *Journal of Abnormal Psychology, 83,* 629–534.

Just, M., & Carpenter, P. (1980). A theory of reading: From eye fixations to comprehension. *Psychological Review, 87,* 329–354.

Kagan, J., Rosman, B., Day, B., Albert, J., & Phillips, W. (1964). Information processing in the child: Significance of analytic and reflective attitudes. *Psychological Monograph, 7B* (1, no. 578).

Kahneman, D. (1973). *Attention and effort.* Englewood Cliffs, NJ: Prentice-Hall.

Kahneman, D., Beatty, J., & Pollack, I. (1967). Perceptual deficit during a mental task. *Science, 157,* 218–219.

Kintsch, W., & van Dijk, T. (1978). Toward a model of text comprehension and production. *Psychological Review, 85,* 363–394.

Kounin, J. (1970). *Discipline and group management in classrooms.* New York: Holt.

Kozminsky, E. (1977). Altering comprehension: The effect of biasing titles on text comprehension. *Memory and Cognition, 5,* 482–490.

LaBerge, D., & Samuels, S. (1974). Toward a theory of automatic information processing in reading. *Cognitive Psychology, 6,* 293–323.

Lahaderne, H. (1968). Attitudinal and intellectual correlates of attention: A study of four sixth-grade classrooms. *Journal of Educational Psychology, 59,* 320–324.

Learner, K., and Richman, C. (1984). The effect of modifying the cognitive tempo of reading disabled children on reading comprehension. *Contemporary Educational Psychology, 9,* 122–134.

Mandler, J., & Johnson, N. (1977). Remembrance of things parsed: Story structure and recall. *Cognitive Psychology, 9,* 111–151.

Mayer, R. (1984). Aids to text comprehension. *Educational Psychologist, 19,* 30–42.

McConkie, G., Rayner, K., & Wilson, S. (1973). Experimental manipulation of reading strategies. *Journal of Educational Psychology, 65,* 1–8.

Mechner, F. (1971). Complex cognitive behavior: the teaching of concepts and chains. In M. Merrill (Ed.), *Instructional design: Readings* (pp. 264–284). Englewood Cliffs, NJ: Prentice Hall.

Meyer, B., & McConkie, G. (1973). What is recalled after hearing a passage? *Journal of Educational Psychology, 65,* 109–117.

Meyers, C., Attwell, A., & Orpet, R. (1968). Prediction of fifth grade achievement from kindergarten test and rating data. *Educational and Psychological Measurement, 28,* 457–463.

Miller, P., & Weiss, M. (1981). Children's attention allocation, understanding of attention, and performance on the incidental learning task. *Child Development*, 52, 1183–1190.

Minde, K., Lewin, D., Weiss, G., Lavigueur, H., Douglas, V., & Sykes, E. (1971). The hyperactive child in elementary school: A 5 year, controlled, followup. *Exceptional Children*, 38, 215–221.

Moray, N. (1969). *Attention: Selective processes in vision and hearing.* London: Hutchinson Educational.

Peters, K. (1977). *Selective attention and distractibility in hyperactive and normal children.* Unpublished doctoral dissertation, McGill University, Montreal.

Pichert, J., & Anderson, R. (1977). Taking different perspectives on a story. *Journal of Educational Psychology*, 69, 309–315.

Piontowski, D., & Calfee, R. (1979). Attention in the classroom. In G. Hale & M. Lewis (Eds.), *Attention and cognitive development* (pp. 297–329). New York: Plenum.

Posner, M., & Boies, S. (1971). Components of attention. *Psychological Review*, 78, 391–408.

Ramsel, D., & Grabe, M. (1983). Attention allocation and performance in goal-directed reading: Age differences in reading flexibility. *Journal of Reading Behavior*, 15, 55–65.

Rankin, E. (1970–1971). How flexibly do we read? *Journal of Reading Behavior*, 3, 34–38.

Reynolds, R., & Anderson, R. (1982). Influence of questions on the allocation of attention during reading. *Journal of Educational Psychology*, 74, 623–632.

Reynolds, R., Standiford, S., & Anderson, R. (1979). Distribution of reading time when questions are asked about a restricted category of text information. *Journal of Educational Psychology*, 71, 183–190.

Rickards, J., & August, G. (1975). Generative underlining strategies in prose recall. *Journal of Educational Psychology*, 67, 860–865.

Rosenthal, R., & Allen, T. (1980). Intratask distractibility in hyperkinetic and nonhyperkinetic children. *Journal of Abnormal Child Psychology*, 8, 175–187.

Rost, K., & Charles, D. (1967). Academic achievement of brain-injured children in isolation. *Exceptional Children*, 34, 125–126.

Rothkopf, E., & Billington, M. (1975). Relevance and similarity of text elements to descriptions of learning goals. *Journal of Educational Psychology*, 67, 745–750.

Rothkopf, E., & Billington, M. (1979). Goal-guided learning from text: Inferring a descriptive processing model from inspection times and eye movements. *Journal of Educational Psychology*, 71, 310–327.

Rothkopf, E., & Bisbicos, E. (1967). Selective facilitative effects of interspersed questions on learning from written materials. *Journal of Educational Psychology*, 58, 56–61.

Samuels, S. (1967). Attentional process in reading: The effect of pictures on the acquisition of reading responses. *Journal of Educational Psychology*, 58, 337–342.

Samuels, S., & Edwall, G. (1981). The role of attention in reading with implications for the learning disabled student. *Journal of Learning Disabilities*, 14, 353–361, 368.

Samuels, S., & Turnure, J. (1974). Attention and reading achievement in first-grade boys and girls. *Journal of Educational Psychology*, 66, 29–32.

Sanders, J. (1973). Retention effects on adjunct questions in written and aural discourse. *Journal of Educational Psychology*, 65, 181–186.

Santostefano, S., Rutledge, L., & Randall, D. (1965). Cognitive styles and reading disability. *Psychology in the Schools*, 2, 57–62.

Schwebel, A., & Cherlin, D. (1972). Physical and social distancing in teacher–student relationships. *Journal of Educational Psychology*, 63, 543–550.

Shannon, J. (1942). Measures of validity of attention scores. *Journal of Educational Research*, 35, 623–631.

Silberman, C. (1970). *Crisis in the classroom: The remaking of American education*. New York: Random House.

Somervill, J., Warnberg, L., & Bost, D. (1973). Effects of cubicles versus increased stimulation on task performance by first grade males perceived as distractible or non-distractible. *Journal of Special Education, 7,* 169–185.

Stankov, L. (1983). Attention and intelligence. *Journal of Educational Psychology, 75,* 471–490.

Steffensen, M., Joag-dev, C., & Anderson, R. (1979). A cross-cultural perspective on reading comprehension. *Reading Research Quarterly, 15,* 10–29.

Stordahl, K., & Christensen, C. (1956). The effects of study techniques on comprehension and retention. *Journal of Educational Research, 49,* 61–70.

Sykes, D., Douglas, V., & Morganstern, G. (1973). Sustained attention in hyperactive children. *Journal of Child Psychology and Psychiatry, 14,* 213–220.

Sykes, D., Douglas, V., Weiss, G., & Minde, K. (1971). Attention in hyperactive children and the effect of methylphenidate (Ritalin). *Journal of Child Psychology and Psychiatry, 12,* 129–139.

Thorndyke, P. (1977). Cognitive structures in comprehension and memory of narrative discourse. *Cognitive Psychology, 9,* 77–110.

Von Restorff, H. (1933). Über die Wirkung von Bereichsbildungen im Spurenfeld. *Psychologie Forschung, 18,* 299–342.

Weingartner, H., Rapoport, J., Buchsbaum, M., Bunney, W., Ebert, M., Mikkelsen, E., & Caine, E. (1980). Cognitive processes in normal and hyperactive children and their response to amphetamine treatment. *Journal of Abnormal Psychology, 89,* 25–37.

Wilkenson, R. (1963). Interaction of noise with knowledge of results and sleep deprivation. *Journal of Experimental Psychology, 66,* 332–337.

Wright, P., & Kahneman, D. (1971). Evidence for alternative strategies of sentence retention. *Quarterly Journal of Experimental Psychology, 23,* 197–213.

Yarbus, A. (1967). *Eye movements and vision* (B. Haigh, Transl., pp. 192–193). New York: Plenum.

Zentall, S., & Zentall, T. (1976). Activity and task performance of hyperactive children as a function of environmental stimulation. *Journal of Consulting and Clinical Psychology, 44,* 693–697.

DESIGNING INSTRUCTION
TO PRODUCE UNDERSTANDING:
AN APPROACH BASED ON
COGNITIVE THEORY

James M. Royer

Psychology Department
University of Massachusetts
Amherst, Massachusetts 01002

I. INTRODUCTION

Somewhere around the transition from the 1960s to the 1970s, a change of some importance occurred in American psychology. During this period, the psychology of human learning, which was far and away the most influential area of psychology, was transformed into the psychology of memory. This transformation was considerably more than a change of topic labels; it consisted of a very different way of thinking about human behavior, and it involved a radical change in the thrust of psychological theory and research. This transformation has had a tremendous impact not only on basic psychological topics, but also on the attempt to apply psychological knowledge to educational practice.

For at least 30 years prior to the late 1960s, the study of learning in the United States was dominated by a perspective that focused on attempts to develop "transition rules" that would describe how and why behavior changed from one state to the next (Kessen, 1962). This perspective was associative learning theory (or *connectionism*), and it was such a dominant force that the general term *learning theory* came to be synonymous with the more specific, *associative learning theory*. Learning theory was a general theory that was said to be able to explain learning in areas as diverse as animal learning (e.g., Kimble, 1961), adult learning (e.g., Dixon & Horton, 1968), child development (e.g., Munn, 1954), and mental retardation (e.g., Estes, 1970). Moreover, at first glance, the theory would seem to be ideally suited as a theoretical basis for approaches to education. It contained guidelines for establishing appropriate motivational states, for designing instructional sequences, for arranging appropriately spaced review sessions, and for building in procedures and elements that would encourage positive transfer between instructional units.

In the late 1960s, the general consensus about the utility of learning theory began to unravel. Psychologists who were previously interested in verbal learning and verbal behavior began to place increasing emphasis on verbal memory (Tulving & Madigan, 1970). Developmental psychologists began to express second thoughts about the theoretical adequacy of learning theory (White, 1970), and educational psychologists began to question the utility of the theory that provided the underpinnings for at least 10 years of infatuation with educational technology (e.g., Rothkopf, 1968).

The main force of the theoretical shift away from learning theory began with the explicit or implicit consideration of whether humans process information in a manner similar to that of computers (e.g., Hunt 1971; Shiffrin & Atkinson, 1969) and then quickly moved to a concern with describing the structure and content of the human mind (e.g., Kintsch, 1974; Tulving & Donaldson, 1972). This latter move resulted in an unfortunate state of affairs for educational psychologists interested in developing theory-based approaches to instruction. The goal of education is the production of desirable changes in behavior, and theories that are best suited for educational purposes are those that focus on why and how behavior changes. The problem with trying to apply the newly formulated cognitive theories to educational practice was that the theories placed very little emphasis on how the structure and content of the mind came to be, or how it might be changed. The cognitive revolution had resulted in the curious situation in which learning theory had been replaced by newer theories that could not learn!

Whereas early cognitive theories placed little emphasis on the development and change of cognitive structure, more recent theories have been concerned with these topics. In the present chapter, recent cognitive theory and research are reviewed, and the implications of this theory and research for educational practice are discussed.

The thesis developed is that cognitive theory can provide the basis for approaches to the development of understanding and problem solving. More specifically, in this chapter, a definition of what it means to understand is proposed, a way of measuring understanding is described, and empirical literature is reviewed that describes techniques that can be used to assist students in acquiring understanding.

The aforementioned thesis is developed in several of the following sections. The section following this introduction presents a taxonomy of educational problems that delineates them into two types: those that can be approached using cognitive theory and those that are best approached using other theories. The next section (Section III) reviews the relationship between working memory and long-term memory and describes how two different theories view the process whereby incoming information interacts with prior knowledge. The fourth and fifth sections are concerned with how cognitive theory can be transformed into educational practice: Section IV suggests an approach to the critically important problem of how understanding can be defined and measured, and Section V reviews several empirically documented procedures for inducing understanding. The sixth and final section of the chapter presents a modified Instructional Systems Design model that could be used as a general approach to the development of instructional materials designed to induce understanding and problem-solving skills.

II.   A TAXONOMY OF EDUCATIONAL PROBLEMS

There are some things that cognitive theory can reasonably be expected to do, and some things that it cannot do. In order to decide which is which, we need to begin with a taxonomy of educational problems.

One way of thinking about educational problems is to divide them up into four types: (1) problems involving observable student behaviors; (2) problems involving the mastery of basic low-level information; (3) problems involving the understanding of complex materials; and (4) problems involving the acquisition and utilization of problem-solving techniques.

A.   PROBLEMS INVOLVING OBSERVABLE BEHAVIORS

Problems involving observable behaviors most often entail getting students to engage in task-appropriate behavior and getting them to not engage in task-inappropriate behavior. Cognitive learning theory is ill-suited for developing approaches to problems involving observable behaviors. A theory of the structure and processes of the mind is little help in designing a program to change the behavior of an unruly student. Problems of this sort can be dealt with effectively, however, through the use of behavior modification principles (e.g., Sulzer-Azaroff & Mayer, 1977). Operant learning theory, which provides the theoretical basis for behavior modification techniques, is ideally suited for problems involving observable behavior, given its emphasis on environmental events and their consequences.

B.   PROBLEMS INVOLVING MASTERY OF BASIC INFORMATION

The second type of problem entails the mastery of basic, low-level knowledge. This kind of knowledge includes the mastery of low-level terms, vocabulary, quantitative entities, and concepts that provide the foundation of any area of study. Cognitive learning theory is again not particularly well suited for developing approaches to this type of problem. However, associative learning theory does provide valuable approaches to problems involving the acquisition of basic information. An enormous amount of instructional research was conducted in the 1960s and early 1970s that was based in large part on associative learning theory (e.g., Anderson, Faust, Roderick, Cunningham, & Andre, 1969; Snelbecker, 1974). This research provides guidelines on developing practice schedules, review intervals, and conditions of transfer, all of which are valuable components of an instructional sequence designed to assure mastery of basic information.

C. PROBLEMS INVOLVING UNDERSTANDING

The understanding of complex information is a third kind of educational problem. *Understanding* is one of those terms that early proponents of behavioral objectives urged us to purge from our vocabularies because it was so hopelessly vague that it could never serve as a meaningful educational goal (e.g., Mager, 1962). But, our understanding of what it means to understand has increased considerably in recent years, principally because the question of what it means to understand is at the very heart of cognitive theory. Moreover, this new insight into what understanding is has implications for the design of educational approaches having as their goal the development of understanding.

Michael Reddy (1979) has written an interesting paper illustrating the differences between old and new perspectives on understanding. Reddy invoked contrasting metaphors to illustrate the erroneous implicit belief we have about meaning in language. Reddy (1979) pointed out that the way we describe meaning documents the existence of an unconscious acceptance of what he has called the *conduit* metaphor of meaning in language. Consider the following examples, which are merely a smattering of the hundreds of examples Reddy has collected: "Did you catch what I meant?" "Your ideas just don't come across in your writing." "Your speech effectively conveyed your beliefs," "Did you get the author's message?"

Reddy argued that the preceding statements reflect the acceptance of a model of meaning that says that the sender of a message packages the meaning of the message in the form of speech or writing and sends that message through some communication conduit, whereupon the receiver of the message unpackages it and extracts the meaning. Reddy argues that acceptance of the conduit metaphor means that one accepts the position that the meaning of a message resides within the message itself. This is essentially the implicit view of understanding contained in associative learning theory. Within the framework of associative learning theory, memory is merely the blackboard that experience writes upon, and meaning must be contained in the message on the blackboard.

Reddy (1979) argued that the conduit metaphor was wrong, and he offered a substitute that he called the *tool maker* metaphor, which he believed to more accurately represent the process of deriving meaning. Reddy began his metaphor with the suggestion that communication between individuals was analogous to interactions between people in slightly different environments. Imagine, he wrote, that a resident of a heavily wooded area has invented a rake to collect fall leaves. Proud of his invention, he transmits the plans for the rake to a person living in an environment with few trees. The person in the treeless environment cannot make sense of the original design, but with some modifications transforms it into a pick or a hoe—implements that make sense in terms of the environment.

Reddy's point was that people must interpret the plans for the rake in terms of their own environment. Moreover, he argued, the process of deriving meaning from language involves an individual interpreting a message in light of his or her own experiences and knowledge.

The perspective that the derivation of meaning from language involves an interaction between a message and a person's knowledge and experience has come to be known as the *constructivist* view of learning and memory (e.g., Bransford & McCarrell, 1974; Brown, Bransford, Ferrara, & Campione, 1983; Jenkins, 1979; Royer & Cunningham, 1981). We do not receive the meaning of a message. Instead, we must *construct* a meaning by interpreting a message in light of our own knowledge.

The constructivist interpretation of learning and memory is at the core of the cognitive explanation of understanding. Something is understood when it has been integrated in a meaningful way into the learner's existing knowledge structure. When the learner does not have any relevant knowledge that can be used to construct an interpretation of a message, memorization may occur, but understanding will not.

The argument that understanding involves the integration of new material into existing knowledge structure is an interesting theoretical statement, and, as I argue here later, it provides guidelines for developing educational approaches designed to enhance understanding. But before such approaches can be developed, we must devise ways of differentiating between the student who has understood and the one who has not. In a later section, an operational definition of understanding is proposed, but first let us describe a fourth kind of educational problem.

D. PROBLEM SOLVING AND THINKING

The fourth kind of educational problem involves teaching students the higher order skills of problem solving and thinking. When Glaser (1984) reviewed the history of attempts to teach problem solving and thinking, he noted that there were two general approaches. The first approach was to view problem solving and thinking as a domain-free cognitive activity that could be generalized to many content areas and activities. The instructional strategy derived from this perspective was to attempt to isolate the sequence of steps a skilled problem solver engages in, and to then teach a student to perform the skills in a systematic and sequential manner.

Glaser (1984) noted that the idea of problem solving and thinking as a set of sequentially activated skills not tied to any particular domain of knowledge was a perspective that followed naturally from the associative learning theory tradition mentioned in the introduction of this chapter. However, he also noted that there was a new perspective emerging—one which emphasized an integral connection between the cognitive activity of problem solving and thinking and knowledge within a *specific* content area. From this perspective, problem solving is not thought of as a domain-free set of cognitive activities, but instead is linked, and perhaps even restricted to, a particular domain of knowledge.

The domain-specific view of problem solving and thinking is naturally linked to recent cognitive theory, just as the domain-free perspective was naturally linked to learning theory. In a later section, the link between this perspective and cognitive theory is discussed in more detail, along with techniques for translating the perspective into instructional design.

E. SUMMARY

To sum up this section, educational problems can be divided into four types: problems involving observable behaviors, problems involving the acquisition of basic information, problems involving the understanding of complex material, and problems involving problem solving and thinking.

Cognitive theory is not well suited to guide approaches to the first two types of problems. Instead, operant learning theory is ideally suited as the basis for the development of approaches to problems involving observable behaviors, and associative learning theory is ideally suited for developing approaches to problems involving the acquisition of basic information. Cognitive learning theory can, however, be valuable in developing approaches to problems involving understanding and those involving problem solving and thinking. Both of these types of problems can be thought of as involving the development of appropriate relationships between incoming information and the learner's existing knowledge, and the explication of such relationships is at the heart of cognitive theory.

III. WORKING MEMORY AND LONG-TERM MEMORY

Theories that have been proposed since the late 1960s have compartmentalized memory in a variety of ways. These include divisions into short- and long-term memory (e.g., Shiffrin & Atkinson, 1969), episodic and semantic memory (e.g., Tulving, 1972), and declarative and procedural knowledge (e.g., Winograd, 1975). One distinction that has remained fairly constant, however, is the differentiation between one aspect of memory that is the repository of previously acquired information, and a second aspect of memory that deals with that material that is currently and actively involved in ongoing processing. The *repository memory* is referred to here as *long-term memory*, and the *active memory* is referred to as *working memory*.

Working memory is generally thought of as the place where the constructive process occurs—that is, the place where incoming information makes contact with prior knowledge and the interaction between the two produces an interpretation of the incoming information. Theories that provide a comprehensive perspective on this constructive process must do at least four things. First, they must specify the nature and the organization of the material that is represented in memory. Second, they must specify how some subset of long-term memory (working memory) becomes active when processing verbal information. Third, they must specify how incoming information interacts with knowledge already in working memory during the process of constructing an interpretation of the incoming message. And fourth, the theory must specify how the newly interpreted information becomes part of long-term memory. In order to provide examples of how theories satisfy these requirements, two quite different theories of cognition are now reviewed.

A. KINTSCH'S THEORY

Walter Kintsch and his colleagues (e.g., Kintsch, 1974; Kintsch & van Dijk, 1978) have developed one of the most comprehensive of the new cognitive theories. Kintsch's theory indicates that written text (and presumably language in general) can be divided into elemental units called *propositions*. Propositions can then be arranged into a hierarchical structure called a *coherence graph* that describes the position and thematic importance of the propositions in the text. This description of a text (called a *text base*) has been shown to have psychological utility, in that variables like propositional density, thematic importance of ideas, and thematic redundancy of the text have all been shown to be related to a subject's ability to recall a text after reading or listening to it (e.g., Kintsch & Vipond, 1977).

Kintsch and his colleagues have proposed that readers process a text base in a number of steps. First, at the start of reading, a limited number of propositions are drawn into working memory. Long-term memory is then searched for relevant material, and one or more propositions are transferred to working memory to serve as an anchor point for the construction of a memory representation. When a representation is constructed, highly important propositions are selected to remain in working memory to serve as anchor points for the next cycle of incoming propositions, and then recently constructed memory representation is transferred to long-term memory. New propositions are then drawn into working memory, and the process is repeated without a search of long-term memory. A search of long-term memory (called a *reinstatement search*) is initiated on subsequent cycles only if the propositions retained in working memory are irrelevant to the propositions coming in on any given cycle.

In Kintsch's theory, text processing results in two kinds of memory representations. The first, called the *microstructure representation*, preserves the explicit details of the text base. The second type, called the *text macrostructure*, encodes the gist of the text. Both the microstructure and macrostructure text representations are represented and organized in memory in accordance with the semantic aspects of the material. That is, materials having similar meanings will be stored in the same location.

The constructive principle of meaning is clearly operative in Kintsch's theory. Representations of the meaning of incoming text is constructed in working memory in a process that involves the interaction between incoming material and prior knowledge. Moreover, if it were the case that the reader did not have any prior knowledge that could be used as the starting point for the construction of a text representation, the process could not occur, and the reader could not comprehend the text.

Kintsch conceptualizes working memory as a location in memory that serves as an interface point between long-term memory and incoming information. Incoming information and prior knowledge are drawn into working memory, processed, and then transferred back to long-term memory for storage. A very different conceptualization of working memory is present in the next theory.

B.   ROYER'S NUROGEN THEORY

Royer (1985) has presented a model of reading that is based on a biological metaphor as contrasted to the computer metaphor that underlies most of the current cognitive theories. The most elemental units in the model are *nurons* that have many of the basic properties of neurons. That is, they can be excitatory or inhibitory; they have thresholds for firing; and they can connect with other nurons. Connections between nurons form when two nurons that are physically next to one another become simultaneously active. Networks of interconnecting nurons build up and become units, called *nurogens*, that have some of the properties of nurons. For example, they have thresholds for firing, and they can spread activation to other nurogens. Nurogens are organized into a hierarchical system having six levels (called

echelons) (see Fig. 1). At the lowermost echelon are nurogens that correspond to letters. These nurogens are formed by the simultaneous activation
of a set of feature detectors that correspond to a particular letter. Letter
nurogens feed upward to the second echelon, which contains nurogens representing particular spelling patterns that are formed as a function of frequency of encounter. For example, there is a spelling pattern nurogen corresponding to "AD" but not one corresponding to "YQ". At the next echelon
are nurogens corresponding to words. Word nurogens are defined by their
connections to lower level spelling pattern nurogens. As an instance, the
nurogen corresponding to "BIRD" is connected to the spelling pattern
nurogens "BI" and "RD"

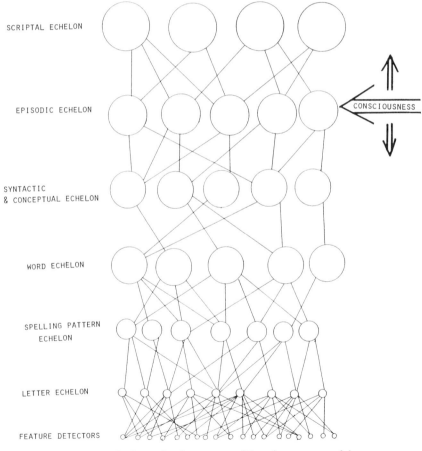

FIG. 1.   The hierarchical structures of Royer's nurogen model.

Word nurogens are connected to nurogens in the higher level conceptual–syntactic echelon. These nurogens consist of conceptual and syntactical categories. For example, there is a nurogen that represents "BIRD" in the conceptual sense and noun in the syntactical sense. The fifth echelon contains episodic nurogens that represent frequently experienced events. At the uppermost echelon are nurogens that represent scriptal events that correspond to the repeated contiguous activation of a number of episodic nurogens. The final component of the model depicted in Fig. 1 is consciousness. Consciousness can move from one echelon to another, but in general, it is directed to the uppermost active echelons. Thus, if the reader is reading familiar material that poses no comprehension problems, he or she will not be consciously aware of letters, words, or even the conceptual nature of the incoming material. Instead, the reader will be aware of how the incoming information relates to larger scriptal and episodic units.

Nurogens fire when the level of activation rises above a firing threshold. When they fire, they spread activation to those nurogens to which they are connected. Therefore, when the spelling pattern nurogens "BI" and "RD" are simultaneously firing, activation feeds upward activating the word nurogen "BIRD" and the firing word nurogen, in turn, feeds activation upward resulting in the activation of the concept nurogen corresponding to "BIRD."

In addition to spreading activation upward, a firing nurogen also spreads activation to the adjacent lower echelon. This can result in a sensitization of the lower echelon nurogens. *Sensitization* is a term used to refer to a raising of the firing potential of any nonactive nurogen. As an example, when the concept nurogen "BIRD" is active it feeds activation downward to word nurogens such as "ROBIN," "WREN," etc. This sensitization of word nurogens connected to the active concept nurogens means that less excitation feeding upward from spelling pattern nurogens is required to fire the sensitized word nurogens.

The nurogen model assumes that both listening and reading comprehension are heavily interrelated processes. At the time that a child begins to learn to read, the speech comprehension system is well developed. This includes development up through the episodic and perhaps even the scriptal echelons. The development of reading skill is assumed to be the process of developing the reading analysis system to a point where decoded words are fed into the conceptual echelon of the speech analyses system at a rate sufficient to initiate firing activity in the episodic echelon.

The nurogen model proposes that reading entails the successive activation of nurogens up through each echelon of the nurogen system. The model assumes that when a nurogen fires, it continues to fire for a matter of seconds in a steadily decreasing reverberatory firing pattern. When in the reverberatory firing pattern, the nurogen continues to pass excitation to upper-level nurogens, and it continues to sensitize lower echelon nurogens. When the reverberatory firing of a nurogen dampens below firing threshold, it does not immediately return to a resting state level of activation. Complete return to resting state takes time, and a for matter of time following the decline to below-threshold activation, the nurogen is sensitized relative to resting state nurogens.

The reverberatory firing assumption allows one to define working memory as that part of the system that is either actively firing or in a highly sensitized state. Conceptualized this way, working memory is a time-constrained cognitive capacity. Some individuals may have relatively long reverberatory firing patterns, others relatively short patterns. Long patterns would be particularly advantageous when processing long clausal strings, as in the sentence, "There are writers who believe not only that the concepts underlying language antedate the acquisition of language but that they antedate experience." Long clausal strings require that many conceptual–syntactic nurogens be kept in a firing state in order to feed enough excitation upward to activate an episodic nurogen and thereby provide an interpretation of the sentence. For instance, a reader with a short reverberatory pattern might begin reading the example sentence and have that part of the nurogen system corresponding to "there are writers" dampen below firing level before reaching the end of the clause. If so, the reader would have to reread the sentence in order to understand it. In comparison, a reader with a long firing pattern would have much less difficulty in maintaining firing until the end of the clause was reached. The same principle would influence the comprehension of readers differing in decoding skill. A proficient reader having highly automatized decoding skills could rapidly activate nurogens up to the conceptual–syntactic level, which in turn would activate an episodic nurogen. In contrast, a reader having poor decoding skills might find that nurogens activated by words at the beginning of a clause would dampen before the end of the clause was reached.

C. Summary

This section began with the observation that most theories of verbal cognition divided memory into a dormant repository of acquired information and an active section of memory where interpretations of incoming messages were constructed. The first of these types of memory was called long-term memory and the second was called working memory.

Two different conceptualizations of working memory and long-term memory were then reviewed. Walter Kintsch views working memory as a limited-capacity memory structure that receives incoming information and information retrieved from long-term memory, combines the two, and then sends the newly constructed representation back to long-term memory for storage. In comparison, Royer's nurogen model defines working memory as *that part* of long-term memory that is currently in an active firing state. Another difference is that working memory in the nurogen model is imagined to be time-constrained rather than capacity-constrained as it was in the Kintsch model.

Despite the differences between the two models with respect to how working memory functions, they do agree on the central role of working memory in the cognitive process. Moreover, they both assume that understanding is a constructive process involving both prior knowledge and incoming information, and that the constructive process itself operates within working memory.

IV. TRANSFER OBJECTIVES AS AN OPERATIONAL DEFINITION OF UNDERSTANDING AND PROBLEM SOLVING

To this point, it has been suggested that cognitive theory provides a viable approach to educational problems concerned with understanding and problem solving, and two theories of how memory representations of incoming information are constructed have been reviewed.

We are now ready to take the first step toward translating cognitive theory into educational practice. That step is to develop an operational definition of understanding and problem solving.

One powerful element of the technology-of-instruction approach popular during the 1960s was the use of behavioral objectives as a standard of instructional success. However, understanding was one of those terms that educators were urged to purge from their vocabularies because it was hopelessly vague. In this section, a procedure for defining understanding is described that would allow an educator to include understanding as a well defined and measurable behavioral objective.

There are several educationally relevant ways to define understanding. One way refers to the reception of a verbal message. If a teacher tells a student something and then asks, "Do you understand?" a positive response would indicate that the message had been received and the student had a subjective sense of comprehension. Although asking students whether they have understood something is an acceptable way of ascertaining whether a message has been passed from one person to another, it is frequently not a good way to determine whether students have understood the instruction they have received. In these situations, a much better index of whether a student has understood the instruction is the demonstration that the student can *use* the instruction in a meaningful way.

The idea that understanding can be assessed by the ability to use knowledge is simply an extension of the idea that the comprehension of instructions can be ascertained by having the recipient perform the actions described in the instructions. Thus, an index of whether a student "understands" long division can be obtained by having the student complete long-division problems. If one thinks about use as an operational definition of understanding, it quickly becomes apparent that there are various degrees of use associated with most forms of knowledge. Taking the long-division illustration as an example, successful completion of problems identical to or very similar to those experienced during instruction is a lesser accomplishment than solving completely new problems. Extending this idea further, it would be even more impressive if the student used his or her long division skills in situations encountered outside the classroom.

UNDERSTANDING AND THE TRANSFER OF LEARNING

Use as an index of understanding is equivalent to the idea that the ability to *transfer* learned information is evidence that understanding is present. Moreover, the literature on the transfer of learning can be used to provide some focus to the idea that the ability to use knowledge provides an objective index of understanding.

In his review of theories of the transfer of learning, Royer (1979) made several distinctions about transfer that are relevant to the present discussion. One distinction, for example, was between near and far transfer. *Near transfer* involves a situation in which there is a great deal of overlap between the stimulus elements present during instruction and those present when the transfer task is completed. An example of near transfer would be a situation in which a test for acquisition of long-division skills is given in the same room where instruction occurred, and the test involves problems very similar to those encountered during instruction. In comparison, *far transfer* would be evident if the student performed the skill in a context very different from that of the classroom. An example of far transfer of long division would be if a student appropriately reduced the ingredients in a recipe for 10 people to a recipe for 4 people, without being told that long division could be used to accomplish this task.

A second distinction that Royer made about transfer is also relevant to developing an operational definition of understanding. Royer (1979) suggested a distinction between what he called literal and figural transfer. *Literal transfer* was said to involve the transfer of an intact skill or bit of knowledge to a new learning task. The utilization of long division skills both in and out of school settings would be an instance of literal transfer. *Figural trans-fer*, on the other hand, was said to involve the use of some segment of our world knowledge as a tool for problem solving, thinking, or learning about a particular problem or issue. Royer suggested that the clearest instances of figural transfer could be found in the use of figural language such as metaphor, analogy, and simile. When one says that "encyclopedias are gold-mines" or "man is like a computer," the listener is being asked to use the knowledge they have about the referent of the statement as a tool for understanding or thinking about the subject of the statement. The link between figural transfer and understanding has been explicitly made by other writers. For example, the physicist, Robert Oppenheimer (1956), wrote, "Whether or not we talk of discovery or of invention, analogy is inevitable to human thought, because we come to view things in science with what equipment we have, which is how we have learned to think about this relatedness of things. We cannot, coming into something new, deal with it except on the basis of the familiar and the old fashioned" (p. 129). Donald Schon (1963) has made an even more detailed argument that true invention (including the development of scientific understanding) always involves the displacement of metaphor. That is, the utilization of a well-understood body of knowledge in an entirely new context.

The distinctions between near and far transfer and literal and figural transfer can be used as a basis for providing an approach to the degrees-of-understanding problem mentioned before. The near–far transfer distinction reflects the degree to which the conditions of transfer task performance resemble those of instruction. The idea is that far transfer, in which there are few cues available that would indicate that a particular skill should be used, represents a higher level of understanding than near transfer task performance. The reason is that a student who performs successfully in far transfer situations is almost certain to be able to perform successfully in near transfer situations when both situations involve the same skill. However, the converse is not true. Students who can perform successfully in near transfer situations may not be able to successfully perform a far transfer task.

The literal–figural distinction adds a complementary dimension to the near–far distinction. Whereas the near–far distinction is a distinction about the *conditions* under which instruction and transfer tasks are performed, the literal–figural distinction is a distinction about the *nature* of the skills themselves. Literal transfer involves the transfer of an intact skill or bit of knowledge. Declarative knowledge (e.g., Winograd, 1975) is an example of the kind of information that is involved in literal transfer. In contrast, figural transfer involves the transfer of a much more abstract and general form of knowledge. Procedural knowledge (e.g., Winograd, 1975) and high-level

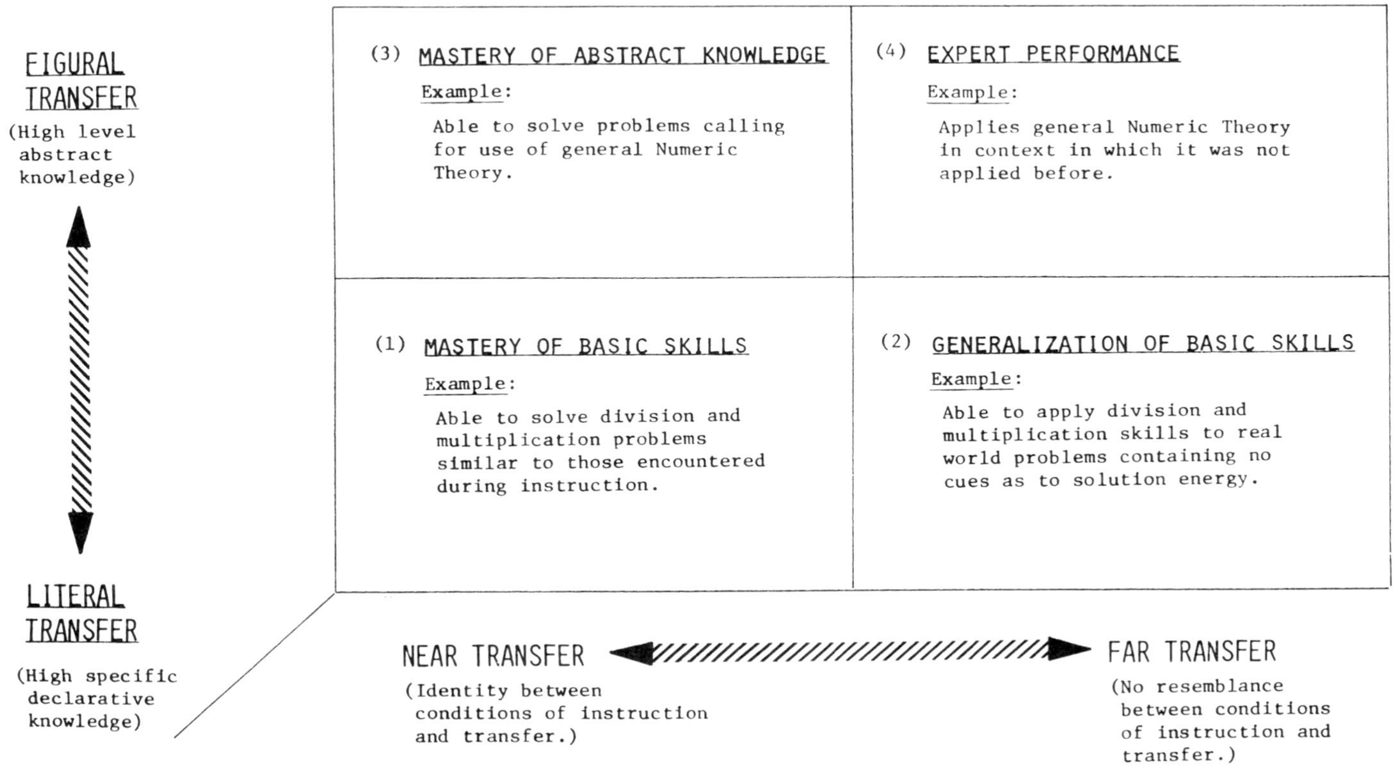

FIGURAL
TRANSFER

(High level
abstract
knowledge)

LITERAL
TRANSFER

(High specific
declarative
knowledge)

(3) MASTERY OF ABSTRACT KNOWLEDGE

Example:

Able to solve problems calling
for use of general Numeric
Theory.

(4) EXPERT PERFORMANCE

Example:

Applies general Numeric Theory
in context in which it was not
applied before.

(1) MASTERY OF BASIC SKILLS

Example:

Able to solve division and
multiplication problems
similar to those encountered
during instruction.

(2) GENERALIZATION OF BASIC SKILLS

Example:

Able to apply division and
multiplication skills to real
world problems containing no
cues as to solution energy.

NEAR TRANSFER

(Identity between
conditions of instruction
and transfer.)

FAR TRANSFER

(No resemblance
between conditions
of instruction and
transfer.)

FIG. 2. A scheme for describing varying degrees of understanding.

schematic knowledge (e.g., Chi, Feltovich, & Glaser, 1981) is characteristically the kind of knowledge involved in figural transfer.

Examples of the literal and figural distinction can be found in Chi et al.'s
(1981) research on the differences between experts and novices when solving
physics problems. Novices tended to group problems together on the basis
of their surface-structure features (e.g., the objects mentioned in the problems or the physics terms mentioned). In contrast, the experts tended to
group problems in terms of the major physics principle governing the solution of each problem (e.g., the law of conservation of energy, Newton's
Second Law). After suggesting that the concept of schemata best captured
the nature of the knowledge being utilized in their problems, Chi et al.
(1981) went on to describe the differences between the schemata of experts
and novices: "Experts' schemata contain a great deal of procedural knowledge, with explicit conditions for applicability. Novices' schemata may be
characterized as containing sufficiently elaborate declarative knowledge
about the physical configuration of a potential problem, but lacking abstract
solution methods" (p. 151).

The near–far distinction and the literal–figural distinction can be combined to provide a means of characterizing transfer tasks. Figure 2 provides a
graphic representation of such a system. If the goal of instruction is the
understanding of basic skills or concepts, such understanding can be demonstrated by selecting transfer tasks that would be contained in Quadrant 2 of
Fig. 2. If the instructional goal is concerned with the understanding of high-
level abstract knowledge, transfer tasks could be selected from Quadrant 4 of
Fig. 2.

V.   APPROACHES TO ENHANCING UNDERSTANDING

Given that the goal of instructional efforts based on cognitive theory is to
develop understanding, and given that understanding can be assessed by
determining if instruction transfers, the next question is, what does cognitive research and theory provide in the way of guidelines for developing
instruction that will encourage understanding? First, there is a very general
answer to this question: Understanding will be enhanced when the instructional material can be integrated into the learner's existing knowledge structure. This general answer breaks down into two more specific answers. The
first of these is that understanding can be enhanced by increasing the likelihood that students will bring appropriate knowledge to bear when receiving instruction. Second, understanding can be enhanced by providing the
student with new information that will assist in integrating the instructional
material into existing knowledge structure.

A. ACTIVATING EXISTING PRIOR KNOWLEDGE

The first approach to encouraging understanding is to activate knowledge that the students already have so that incoming information can then be integrated into the activated structure. One of the simplest techniques for doing this is the use of mnemonics. The most thoroughly documented educational use of mnemonic procedures is a technique called the keyword method.

1. The Keyword Method as an Example of a Mnemonic Technique

The term *keyword method* was coined by Richard Atkinson (Atkinson, 1975) to describe the technique of foreign language vocabulary learning that involves associating the foreign word with a well-known concrete English word that is called the *keyword.* The keyword need not have a meaning relationship to the foreign word. It must, however, be similar in sound. For instance, the keyword used by Raugh and Atkinson (1975) to teach the Spanish word for duck (*pato*—pronounced pot-o) was *pot.* As another example, the keyword for learning the Spanish word for horse (*caballo*—pronounced cob-eye-yo) was *eye.*

The keyword method divides vocabulary learning into two stages. The first step requires the student to associate spoken foreign words with the keyword. This association is generally learned quickly because of the sound similarity between the foreign word and the keyword. The second stage requires the subject to form a mental image of the keyword "interacting" with the English translation of the foreign word. For example, the student might form an image of a duck with a pot on its head as an aid in learning the meaning of *pato.* As another example, the student might imagine a horse with a large eye in the middle of its forehead as an aid in learning the meaning of *caballo.*

The keyword technique has proven to be a remarkably effective technique for acquiring foreign language vocabulary words in a variety of settings and with a number of different kinds of students. Atkinson and Raugh (1975) had one group of Stanford University undergraduates study a 120-word Russian vocabulary list using the keyword method while a control group instructed to learn the words in any way they chose studied the same list. At the end of a set period of time, the group using the keyword technique had learned an average of 86 words whereas the control group learned an average of 55 of the words. In addition, this learning advantage persisted over time. When tested 6 weeks later, the keyword group remembered the meaning of 43% of the 120 words, whereas the control group remembered only 28% of the words. In another study involving college students, Raugh and Atkinson

(1975) reported that a group using the keyword method mastered 88% of a 60-word Spanish vocabulary list whereas a control group studying the list for the same period of time mastered only 28% of the list.

The keyword method has also proven to be a very effective means of learning foreign language vocabulary with much younger students. Pressley and Levin (1978) and Levin, Pressley, McCormick, Miller, and Shriberg (1979) have reported a number of experiments that involve teaching elementary age children the meaning of Spanish words. In every study involving children in this age group, those students who used the keyword method learned the meaning of more words than did students who used their own methods to learn the words. Moreover, the margin of advantage for the keyword students was frequently greater than 2:1.

Thus far, the reviewed research has focused on the *acquisition* of foreign words. We now consider evidence that not only does the keyword method produce superior acquisition, it also meets the criterion for understanding in that it produces superior *transfer*. Pressley, Levin, and Miller (1980) reported several studies in which college students learned the definitions of infrequently used English words using either the keyword technique or using a technique of the student's own devising. The students then performed a variety of tasks that included identifying when a targeted word was used correctly or incorrectly in a sentence, selecting the correct sentence into which a targeted word could be inserted, and constructing a sentence that involved the correct usage of a targeted word. In all of these transfer tasks, the groups that learned the words using the keyword technique performed at a level superior to that of the control group.

Using mnemonics represents one of the simplest means of activating prior knowledge as an aid in achieving meaningful learning of new material. The research reviewed focuses on the acquisition of vocabulary words, but it should be noted that the technique could be used for acquiring a variety of kinds of information such as technical names and the names of people or places (Lorayne & Lucas, 1974).

2.   Using Analogies to Facilitate Subsequent Learning

Another way of activating prior knowledge that can then be used to facilitate subsequent learning is through the use of analogies.

Royer and his associates (Royer & Cable, 1975, 1976) have reported several studies using this technique. They wrote two passages, one of which was concerned with the transfer of electricity through metals and the other of which was concerned with the transfer of heat through metals. Each of these passages was then rewritten in two forms. One form—called the concrete form—was written in an easily understandable way that made extensive use of analogies to assist in the understanding of difficult concepts. The other version—called the abstract version—was purposely written in a highly abstract style that was supposed to be difficult to understand. Royer and Cable (1975) chose heat and electrical conduction through metals as topics for their passages because of the considerable similarities between the two phenomena. Metals are excellent conductors of both heat and electricity because they are crystalline in structure and they have a great many free-floating electrons. These properties were explained by analogy in the following way:

> Heat transfer actually involves the transfer of molecular motion. In the case of heat conduction through metals this transfer of motion occurs through a solid substance such as a bar of iron. If we were able to examine a bar of iron through an extremely powerful microscope, we would see that the interior consists of a series of regularly shaped and spaced structural units known as crystal lattices. In order to picture these lattices, imagine a box made of many tinker-toys with smaller boxes inside consisting of other joined tinker-toys. The solid round parts of the tinker-toys would correspond to the molecules within the crystal lattice. In our bar of iron, which is a good conductor of heat, each of the bonded molecules within the lattice has associated with it several "free floating" electrons. Each crystal lattice then is an orderly array of molecules surrounded by a cloud of electrons that are not attached to any particular molecule, but are free to move at random through the lattice. You can picture this by imagining many tiny particles floating through the series of tinker-toy boxes. (From an experiment reported in Royer & Cable, 1975)

By using analogies such as the tinker-toy analogy in the preceding passage, Royer and Cable (1975) hoped to activate prior knowledge that could be used to facilitate the understanding of the material being presented in the passages. This understanding could then be assessed by presenting the students with related material and seeing if what they had learned previously *eased* the learning of the related material—in short, determining whether the learned material would positively transfer to the learning of additional material.

The results of the Royer and Cable (1975) experiment supported the prediction that activating knowledge by using an analogy would ease the learning of subsequent related material. Students who read the analogy material prior to reading a second passage learned at least 40% more from the second passage than did a group that did not read the analogy material.

The results of the initial Royer and Cable (1975) study have been replicated many times (Perkins, 1978; Royer & Cable, 1976; Royer & Perkins, 1977). In addition, Royer and Perkins (1977) were able to demonstrate that the meaningful learning produced by using analogies persisted over time. They presented college students with an initial passage with analogies, or with a control passage, and they then had the students read a second transfer passage immediately, after 2 days, or after 1 week. Their results indicated that the positive transfer attributable to using analogies was as strong after 1 week as it was immediately.

Coming up with exactly the right analogy to achieve meaningful learning of conceptually difficult material is a truly creative act. This is especially true because many analogies do not work very well. Describing a living organism, for example, as being like a factory that takes in raw materials and puts out waste products may capture one attribute of the living organism; but the fit of the analogy is so poor and may generate so much confusion that it negates any benefits that might occur with its use. For example, a discerning student might point out that one of the defining features of factories is that they produce a product. If living organisms are like factories, what products do they produce?

Another caution against using analogies to assist in achieving meaningful learning is that the supposedly known part of the analogy must, in fact, be part of the learner's knowledge. If you were told that Aplysia (a large sea snail) is a favorite organism of study by neurobiologists because it has a nervous system characteristic that is similar to that of the also favored squid, chances are you would not have been enlightened in the least. Only if you know that squid have very large nerve cells and thus are easy to examine and study would you benefit from being told that Aplysia was a favorite organism of study for the same reason. Teachers should be very careful to make sure that the supposedly known part of the analogy is, in fact, part of the learner's knowledge. Otherwise, using the analogy certainly will not help the learner and, in fact, may be worse than nothing, in that the learner now has two things he or she does not understand rather than one.

Questions such as the aforementioned are very fruitful issues for future researchers. Moreover, analogy research is receiving increasing attention in both the basic and the applied literatures. An example of the former is the insightful analysis presented by Gick and Holyoak (1983); as an example of the latter, Simons (1984) has reported six experiments that evaluate the instructional utility of analogies.

B. ENHANCING MEANINGFUL LEARNING BY TEACHING STUDENTS
    INFORMATION THAT WILL EASE SUBSEQUENT LEARNING

In the previous section, techniques were discussed for achieving meaningful learning by *activating* information the student had already learned. In this section, techniques for achieving meaningful learning are examined that involve *teaching* the student new information that can then be used to ease subsequent learning.

Advance Organizers

In the early 1960s, David Ausubel (1960, 1963) suggested *advance organizers* as a device for easing the learning of subsequently presented material. Advance organizers are statements that are "presented at a higher level of abstraction, generality, and inclusiveness than the new material to be learned" (Ausubel, Novak, & Hanesion, 1978, p. 171).

Ausubel envisioned advance organizers as a bridge between "what the learner already knows and what he needs to know before he can meaningfully learn the task at hand" (Ausubel, Novak, & Hanesion, 1978, p. 172). Ausubel and his fellow researchers conducted many studies during the 1960s (Ausubel, 1960; Ausbel & Fitzgerald, 1961, 1962; Ausubel & Youssef, 1963; Fitzgerald & Ausubel, 1963) that demonstrated the efficacy of presenting students with advance organizers before they engaged in a learning task. A typical study by Ausubel and Youssef (1963) involved having college students read a passage on Buddhism after reading a "comparative advance organizer" (examining the relationship between Buddhism and Christianity) or a control passage. They found that the students who had initially read the organizer passage retained more from the Buddhism passage than did the students who initially read the control passage. In addition to Ausubel's studies, which have shown greater acquisition of subsequently presented material, other studies have shown beneficial effects of advance organizers using more remote transfer tasks. Grotelueschen and Sjogren (1968), Merrill and Stolurow (1966), and Scandura and Wells (1967) have all shown that material preceded by advance organizers is more likely to transfer to remote tasks than material not preceded by advance organizers.

At this point, there seems to be little doubt that advance organizers can improve the learning of subsequent material under certain conditions. Ausubel (Ausubel, Novak, & Hanesion, 1978) has indicated two of these conditions. First, the material to be presented must involve unitary topics or related sets of ideas. If the ideas to be presented are highly varied, as might be the case, for example, in a college-level survey class (e.g., introductory psychology), then it would not be possible to generate a single advance organizer to encompass all of the ideas. This does not preclude, however, breaking the subject matter into unitary topics and then preparing advance organizers for each topic.

Ausubel's second circumstance is that a true advance organizer must be developed with an awareness of the learner's existing knowledge structure. This means that if advance organizers are to serve as a bridge between material to be presented and material the learner already knows, it is essential to know what the learner already knows. Otherwise, a teacher might end up presenting a learner with two things (the advance organizer and the target material) that the student has difficulty in learning rather than just one (the target material).

Models as a Form of Concrete Advance Organizer. Ausubel defined an advance organizer as a statement that was at a higher level of abstraction than the target material to follow. Another kind of advance organizer that has received considerable investigation is the model or "concrete advance organizer."

A model or concrete advance organizer is either a statement or an illustration that provides a concrete general overview of a system the student is going to study in detail. An example of the use of a model as an advance organizer can be found in Mayer's research on teaching college students a computer programming language (Mayers, 1975, 1976; Mayer & Bromage, 1980). Mayer (1975) presented his model students with a text which began with a diagram of the inside working components of a computer. The diagram included an input window (described as a ticket window), and output pad (described as a pad of message paper), a memory scoreboard (described as an eight-space, erasable scoreboard), and a program list with pointer arrow (described as a shopping list). The use of descriptions such as a ticket window for the input window was designed to make the unfamiliar components more familiar by relating them to information the students already possessed. After the students had become familiar with the model, they received instruction on computer programming that made continued reference to the model. In effect, the student was asked to role play what the computer did with each of the programming statements.

Another group of students in Mayer's (1975) study were instructed on computer programming in a more traditional manner. They were given definitions of programming statements and examples of the appropriate usage of each of the statements. Following instruction, students in each of the groups were asked to write a number of short computer programs that varied in type of problem and in complexity. A comparison of the performance of the groups revealed that students who had received the model as an advance organizer performed significantly better on the programming transfer task than did students who received the traditional instruction. The results were replicated in later studies (Mayer, 1976; Mayer & Bromage, 1980).

Mayer's research on computer programming represents one instance where a system or process model can be beneficial in any area of study involving a concrete system. Imagine, for example, that you were teaching an automotive repair course. A good strategy would be to begin the course with a model overview of the functioning of an automobile. Moreover, it would probably be beneficial to review the model as the students moved from one system to another. So, for example, if the students had been working on the carburetor, and were ready to move to the ignition system, it would probably be worthwhile to present the model of the entire car again so that they could relate the functioning of the ignition system to the operation of the entire car.

C.   Summary

This section has indicated that there are two general techniques that can be used to enhance the understanding of instructional material. The first technique entails *activating* some segment of prior knowledge that the student already has and then relating incoming instruction to the newly activated prior knowledge. This strategy encourages the constructive memory process described in the early parts of this chapter, and it facilitates the meaningful representation in memory of the newly presented instruction. The second technique involves *teaching* the student new information that can subsequently be related to incoming instruction, thereby facilitating the constructive learning process.

Two well-researched methods of activating prior knowledge were described. The first was the keyword technique, in which a foreign word, a new concept, a proper noun, or a new vocabulary word are learned by first associating the new term to a well-known concrete English word called a *keyword*, and then constructing a mental image of the interaction between the keyword and the meaning of the new word. The second technique for activating prior knowledge was the use of analogies. Analogy entails drawing a specific relationship between something that is well known and familiar, and something that is new and unfamiliar.

Two techniques were described for teaching the student new information that could be used to ease the learning of subsequently presented instruction. The first of these techniques was the use of advance organizers, and the second technique entailed presenting a concrete model as a means of assiting the understanding of instructional material. The idea involved in both techniques is that the advance material will encourage the process of constructing a meaningful representation of the instructional material.

At this point in the chapter, a definition of what it means to understand has been proposed, a way of measuring understanding has been described, and several techniques for enhancing understanding have been reviewed. In the next section, a means of pulling these pieces together into a systematic instructional development framework is described.

VI. AN INSTRUCTIONAL SYSTEMS DESIGN (ISD) MODEL DESIGNED TO PRODUCE UNDERSTANDING

Another aspect of the instructional technology movement of the 1960s that lent power and order to the instructional development process was the Instructional Systems Design (ISD) model. One version of an ISD model is depicted in Fig. 3. ISD models were a powerful force in the development of instruction during the 1960s. However, they were utilized only in situations where the goal of instruction was low-level knowledge that could be readily defined in behavioral terms and when the objective could be attained using principles borrowed from associative learning theory. In this section, a revised version of an ISD model is proposed—one that begins with a procedure for identifying and defining tasks the successful performance of which would indicate that the student had understood the instruction that had preceded. The revised version of the model is presented in Fig. 4.

A. TRANSFER GOALS

The model begins with the formulation of a general transfer goal.

In essence, this means deciding which quadrant of the transfer task surface depicted in Fig. 2 contains the desired instructional goal. If the intent of instruction is to have students master content and skills that are to be utilized in situations very similar to those encountered in instruction and that will involve problems similar to those experienced before, the goal of instruction would reside within the first quadrant. Notice that either or both of the transfer surface dimensions can come into play when selecting an instruction goal. If the interest is in determining if a particular intact basic skill can be used in other situations, the goal would be chosen by holding the level of the goal constant along the literal–figural dimension and moving out along the near–far dimension. In other words, the goal of instruction would involve performing a learned skill in circumstances that differed to some degree from instructional circumstances and with tasks that differed in specifics (but not form) from those received during instruction.

In comparison, if the intent of instruction was to teach a basic skill so that this skill could be used to ease the learning of a more complicated skill, the goal of instruction would involve holding the conditions of task performance constant along the near–far dimension and allowing the position along the literal–figural dimension to vary.

Finally, it may be that the goal of instruction involves the teaching of a skill so that the skill can be used to ease the learning of a more complicated skill under conditions that differ from those encountered during instruction.

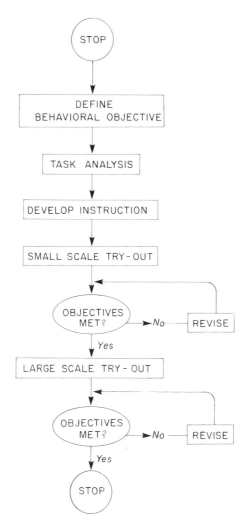

FIG. 3.   The traditional Instructional Systems Design (ISD) model.

In other words, the instructional goal involves simultaneously moving out on both the near–far dimension and the literal–figural dimension.

Instructional goals could also be located in Quadrants 2, 3, or 4. A goal in Quadrant 2 might be exemplified by a situation in which a school-learned basic skill is expected to transfer to out-of-school situations. A goal in quadrant 3 would involve a situation in which complex skills are expected to transfer to situations similar to those encountered during instruction. Final-

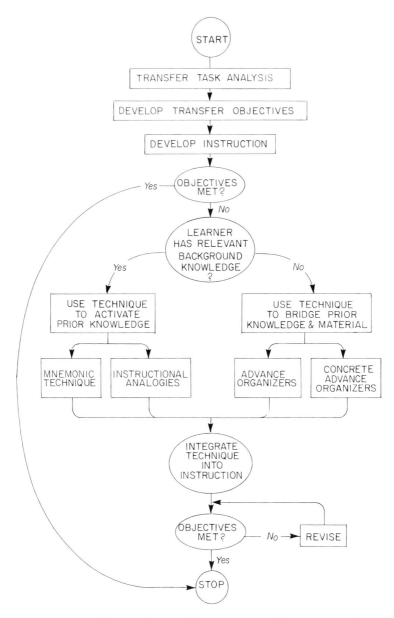

FIG. 4.   An Instructional Systems Design (ISD) model that could be used to produce instruction that will be understood.

ly, if the goal of instruction were the training of complicated skills to be performed under variable and different situations, as would be required of experts for example, the goal would be located in Quadrant 4. Licensure exams for physicians or lawyers might be examples of goals located in the fourth quadrant.

B. Transfer Task Analysis

After a general transfer goal has been selected, the next step in the revised ISD model is performing a transfer task analysis. The idea behind a transfer task analysis is to examine the nature of the tasks to which the instruction is expected to transfer so that their general properties can be ascertained. These general properties can then guide both the selection of specific transfer objectives and the instructional development process.

C. Selecting Transfer Objectives

The selection of specific transfer objectives should be guided by the area of the transfer surface identified in the selection of the transfer goal and by the properties of the transfer tasks identified in the task analysis. With respect to detail, transfer objectives should be described in the kind of careful detail characteristic of the instructional objectives that provide the basis for criterion-referenced tests (see Popham, 1978, pp. 216–230).

D. Developing and Trying Out Instruction

The next phase of the revised ISD model would entail developing instruction and then trying it out in a small-scale test. Instructional development at this point would not involve any special attempts to enhance understanding. After the instruction was developed, it could be tried out on a small scale to see if the transfer objectives were satisfied. If they were, no further instructional development would be necessary.

E. Building In Techniques to Enhance Understanding

If performance on the transfer objectives is not satisfactory, the next step in the model is to build in techniques designed to enhance understanding. The first stage of this process entails determining whether students have background knowledge upon which an approach to developing understanding could be based. In general, this would probably be done intuitively. For example, if the instructional designer has an analogy in mind that might enhance understanding, he or she would also be likely to have a good sense of whether the students have the knowledge upon which the analogy is based. Alternatively, if there did not appear to be a knowledge base from which an approach to understanding could be developed, a technique that bridged the gap between prior knowledge and the material to be learned would be called for.

The knowledge-enhancing technique that was chosen would depend on the nature of the material to be learned. For instance, if the instruction involved the acquisiton of a set of terms or concepts, it would be appropriate to use a mnemonic strategy. Alternatively, if a more complex principle or rule were involved, analogies, advance organizers, or concrete models might be appropriate.

F.   INTEGRATING UNDERSTANDING TREATMENTS INTO INSTRUCTION

After an approach to enhancing understanding had been selected and instruction developed, the final stage of the model would entail integrating the new material into the previously developed instruction. This would be followed by another tryout and revision cycle until the transfer objectives had been satisfied.

VII.   FINAL COMMENTS

Instructional psychology naturally lags behind the theory and research that provides the foundation for particular educational approaches. As this chapter and other chapters in the book have indicated, cognitive theory is very new, and instructional techniques based on cognitive theory are newer yet. Moreover, cognitive theory is in a period of rapid evolution, with important findings and insights appearing in each issue of major research journals. This means that very few of the instructional implications have been explored, and additional implications are constantly being generated.

This chapter has barely scratched the surface of utilizing cognitive theory as a guiding framework for the enhancement of educational understanding. This is most obvious in the area of designing techniques that can be embedded within instructional materials as a means of facilitating student understanding. There are undoubtedly a great many techniques that can be used to facilitate the constructive memory process that must take place before understanding can occur. The discovery of such techniques will contribute greatly to the design of instruction that will be understood.

REFERENCES

Anderson, R. C., Faust, G. W., Roderick, M. C., Cunningham, D. J., & Andre, T. (1969). *Current research on instruction.* Englewood Cliffs, NJ: Prentice-Hall.

Atkinson, R. C. (1975). Mnemotechnics in second-language learning. *American Psychologist, 30,* 821–828.

Atkinson, R. C., & Raugh, M. R. (1975). An application of the mnemonic keyword method to the acquisition of a Russian vocabulary. *Journal of Experimental Psychology: Human Learning and Memory, 104,* 126–133.

Ausubel, D. P. (1960). The use of advance organizers in the learning and retention of meaningful verbal material. *Journal of Educational Psychology, 51,* 267–272.

Ausubel, D. P. (1963). *The psychology of meaningful verbal learning.* New York: Grune & Stratton.

Ausubel, D. P., & Fitzgerald, D. (1961). The role of discriminability in meaningful verbal learning and retention. *Journal of Educational Psychology, 52,* 266–274.

Ausubel, D. P., & Fitzgerald, D. (1962). Organizer, general background, and antecedent learning variables in sequential verbal learning. *Journal of Educational Psychology, 53,* 243–249.

Ausubel, D. P., Novak, J. D., & Hanesion, H. (1978). *Educational psychology: A cognitive view* (2nd ed.). New York: Holt.

Ausubel, D. P., & Youssef, M. (1963). Role of discriminability in meaningful parallel learning. *Journal of Educational Psychology, 54,* 331–336.

Bransford, J. D., & McCarrell, N. S. (1974). A sketch of a cognitive approach to comprehension: Some thoughts about understanding what it means to comprehend. In W. B. Weimer & D. S. Palermo (Eds.), *Cognition and the symbolic processes.* Hillsdale, NJ: Erlbaum.

Brown, A. L., Bransford, J. D., Ferrara, R. A., & Campione, J. C. (1983). Learning, remembering, and understanding. In J. H. Flavell & E. M. Markman (Eds.), *Carmichael's manual of child psychology* (Vol. 1). New York: Wiley.

Chi, M. T. H., Feltovich, P. J., & Glaser, R. (1981). Categorization and representation of physics problems by experts and novices. *Cognitive Science, 5,* 121–152.

Dixon, T. R., & Horton, D. (Eds.). (1968). *Verbal behavior and general behavior theory.* Englewood Cliffs, NJ: Prentice-Hall.

Estes, W. K. (1970). *Learning theory and mental development.* New York: Academic Press.

Fitzgerald, D., & Ausubel, D. P. (1963). Cognitive versus affective factors in the learning and retention of controversial material. *Journal of Educational Psychology, 54,* 73–84.

Gick, M. L., & Holyoak, K. J. (1983). Schema induction and analogical transfer. *Cognitive Psychology, 15,* 1–38.

Glaser, R. (1984). Education and thinking: The role of knowledge. *American Psychologist, 39,* 93–104.

Grotelueschen, A., & Sjogren, D. D. (1968). Effects of differentially structured introductory materials and learning tasks on learning and transfer. *American Educational Research Journal, 5,* 191–202.

Hunt, E. (1971). What kind of computer is man? *Cognitive Psychology, 2,* 57–97.

Jenkins, J. J. (1979). Four points to remember. A tetrahedral model and memory experiments. In L. S. Cernak & F. I. M. Craik (Eds.), *Levels of processing in human memory.* Hillsdale, NJ: Erlbaum.

Kessen, W. (1962). "Stage" and "structure" in the study of children. In W. Kessen & W. Kuhlman (Eds.), *Thoughts in the young child. Monograph of the Society for Research in Child Development, 27,* 65–86.

Kimble, G. A. (1961). *Hilgard and Marquis' conditioning and learning.* New York: Appleton.

Kintsch, W. (1974). *The representation of meaning in memory.* Hillsdale, NJ: Erlbaum.

Kintsch, W., & van Dijk, T. (1978). Toward a model of text comprehension and production. *Psychological Review, 85,* 363–394.

Kintsch, W., & Vipond, D. (1977). Reading comprehension and readability in educational practice and psychological theory. In L. G. Nilsson (Eds.), *Proceedings of the University of Uppsala conference on memory.* Hillsdale, NJ: Erlbaum.

Levin, J. R., Pressley, M., McCormick, C. B., Miller, G. E., & Shriberg, L. K. (1979). Assessing the classroom potential of the keyword method. *Journal of Educational Psychology, 71,* 583–594.

Lorayne, H., & Lucas, J. (1974). *The memory book.* New York: Ballantine.

Mager, R. F. (1962). *Preparing instructional objectives.* Palo Alto, CA: Feron.

Mayer, R. E. (1975). Information processing variables in learning to solve problems, *Review of Educational Research, 45,* 525–541.

Mayer, R. E. (1976). Some conditions of meaningful learning of computer programming: Advance organizers and subject control of frame sequencing. *Journal of Educational Psychology, 68,* 143–150.

Mayer, R. E., & Bromage, B. K. (1980). Different recall protocols for technical texts due to advance organizers. *Journal of Educational Psychology, 72,* 209–225.

Merrill, M. D., & Stolurow, L. M. (1966). Hierarchical preview vs. problem oriented review in learning an imaginary science. *American Educational Research Journal, 3,* 251–261.

Munn, N. L. (1954). Learning in children. In L. Carmichael (Ed.), *Manual of child psychology* (2nd ed.). New York: Wiley.

Oppenheimer, R. (1956). Analogy in science. *American Psychologist, 11,* 127–135.

Perkins, M. R. (1978). *Measures of cognitive structure: Do they really assess learning at the level of comprehension?* Unpublished doctoral dissertation, University of Massachusetts, Amherst.

Popham, W. J. (1978). *Criterion-referenced measurement.* Englewood Cliffs, NJ: Prentice-Hall.

Pressley, M., & Levin, J. R. (1978). Developmental constraints associated with children's use of the keyword method of foreign language vocabulary learning. *Journal of Experimental Child Psychology, 26,* 359–372.

Pressley, M., Levin, J. R., & Miller, G. E. (1980, March). *How does the keyword method affect vocabulary comprehension and usage?* (Working paper No. 278). Madison, WI: Wisconsin Research and Development Center for Individualized Schooling.

Raugh, M. R., & Atkinson, R. C. (1975). A mnemonic method for learning a second-language vocabulary. *Journal of Educational Psychology, 67,* 1–16.

Reddy, M. (1979). The conduit metaphor—A case of frame conflict in our language about language. In A. Ortony (Ed.), *Metaphor and thought.* New York: Cambridge University Press.

Rothkopf, E. Z. (1968). Two scientific approaches to the management of instruction. In R. M. Gagne & W. J. Gephart (Eds.), *Learning research and school subjects.* Itasca, IL: Peacock.

Royer, J. M. (1979). Theories of the transfer of learning. *Educational Psychologist, 14,* 53–69.

Royer, J. M. (1985). Reading from the perspective of a biological metaphor. *Contemporary and Educational Psychology, 10,* 150–200.

Royer, J. M., & Cable, G. W. (1975). Facilitated learning in connected discourse. *Journal of Educational Psychology, 67,* 116–123.

Royer, J. M., & Cable, G. W. (1976). Illustrations, analogies, and facilitative transfer in prose learning. *Journal of Educational Psychology, 68,* 205–209.

Royer, J. M., & Cunningham, D. J. (1981). On the theory and measurement of reading comprehension. *Contemporary Educational Psychology, 6,* 187–216.

Royer, J. M., & Perkins, M. R. (1977). Facilitative transfer in prose learning over an extended time period. *Journal of Reading Behavior, 9,* 185–188.

Scandura, J. M., & Wells, J. N. (1967). Advance organizers in learning abstract mathematics. *American Educational Research Journal, 4,* 295–301.

Schon, D. A. (1963). *Displacement of concepts.* London: Tavistock.

Shiffrin, R. M., & Atkinson, R. C. (1969). Storage and retrieval processes in long-term memory. *Psychological Review, 76,* 179–193.

Simons, P. R. J. (1984). Instructing with analogies. *Journal of Educational Psychology, 76,* 513–527.

Snelbecker, G. E. (1974). *Learning theory, instructional theory, and psychoeducational design.* New York: McGraw-Hill.

Sulzer-Azaroff, B., & Mayer, G. R. (1977). *Applying behavior-analysis procedures with children and youth.* New York: Holt.

Tulving, E. (1972). Episodic and semantic memory. In E. Tulving & W. Donaldson (Eds.), *Organization of memory.* New York: Academic Press.

Tulving, E., & Donaldson, W. (Eds.). (1972). *Organization of memory.* New York: Academic Press.

Tulving, E., & Madigan, S. A. (1970). Memory and verbal learning. *American Review of Psychology, 21,* 437–484.

White, S. H. (1970). The learning theory tradition for child psychology. In P. H. Mussen (Ed.), *Carmichael's manual of child psychology* (Vol. 1). New York: Wiley.

Winograd, T. (1975). Frame representations and the declarative/procedural controversy. In D. G. Bower and A. Collins (Eds.), *Representation and understanding: Studies in cognitive science.* New York: Academic Press.

5

WORKING MEMORY: THE ENCODING PROCESS

Raymond W. Kulhavy
Sarah Peterson*

*Department of Educational
Psychology
Arizona State University
Tempe, Arizona 85281*

Neil H. Schwartz

*Department of Educational
Psychology
Northern Arizona University
Flagstaff, Arizona 86011*

I. INTRODUCTION

In this chapter, we look at some of the ways in which people work at the task of learning and remembering instructional materials. Our discussion centers on those activities which influence *working memory*, which is a concept that can be broadly defined to include all parts of the human processing system responsible for the effort associated with study (Baddeley & Hinch, 1974; Daneman & Carpenter, 1980). Within the realm of working memory, we are specifically interested in the process of *encoding*, especially in the sense that this term refers to acts which influence how information is stored and remembered. Encoding denotes a wide variety of activities performed by students while they are attempting to acquire target information from a lesson, and we are willing to extend our definition to include any overt or covert act that has as its goal the transformation of an instructional stimulus such as a text or lecture, into an accessible part of what we know.

In the second section of this chapter, we explore the attributes of three separate systems which appear to have a strong effect on encoding in working memory and together are thought to influence both the type of encoding that occurs and the manner in which that encoding determines later memory performance. In this section, our first task is to talk briefly about how learners allocate their attention to particular parts of a lesson, and about how such an allocation appears to influence the encoding process. Second, we review various aspects of the schema models of cognitive perception and look at ways in which a specific schema works, to determine what it is that we are

*Present address: Department of Education, Indiana–Purdue University at Fort Wayne, Fort Wayne, Indiana 46805

COGNITIVE CLASSROOM LEARNING:
UNDERSTANDING, THINKING, AND PROBLEM SOLVING

likely to encode from an instructional communication. The end of the second section describes the general form of depth-of-processing theories and discusses how such theories account for what is learned and remembered from different encoding processes.

The third section of the chapter focuses initially on the types of changes in instruction that seem to affect how encoding is accomplished. Because the majority of the research on instructional encoding has emphasized written text, our discussion touches on the effects of changes in text structure and then moves to instructional accessories such as themes, organizers, questions, mnemonics, and spatial adjuncts like reference maps. Here, we attempt in each case to summarize the research done and boil it down to specific statements about what works and what does not. In all cases throughout this section, we try to integrate facts about stimulus changes and instructional variables with the theoretical frameworks described in the second section.

In the fourth and final section of the chapter, we evaluate how one might apply the things we know about encoding to the practice of instruction. In this last instance, we are less interested in what the research shows, and more interested in how the results can be applied to facilitate the learning and retention of instructional content.

II. PRIMARY INFLUENCES ON ENCODING

A. ATTENTIONAL VARIABLES

Few persons would question the notion that for encoding of instruction to take place, the learner must pay attention to the lesson material. Unfortunately, such an assumption is not quite as simple as it sounds because there is good evidence that the raw amount of time one spends attending to instruction correlates less than perfectly with what is learned and remembered (Reynolds & Anderson, 1982). However, both common sense and research data suggest that even if the relationship between attention and learning is not absolute, attending behavior itself still represents one of the more powerful determinants of what people will gain from study.

For the purposes of our current discussion, we can distinguish between two types of attending phenomena which operate in the instructional environment. First, we have what we call *primary attention*, which is merely the act of selectively focusing one's receptors on a stimulus set and then filtering the information through the sensory system (cf. Norman, 1968). Primary attention is probably important to volitional learning in the sense that it represents the point at which the learner determines which segments of the stimuli are to be treated as critical and which are not. However, acts of primary attention are relatively basic in nature, and other than to point out the fact that they are necessary for encoding, we pass over them in this chapter.

Of far more interest to our discussion is the second type of attending behavior, which we have labeled *processing attention*. We view processing attention as the effective agent for directing encoding activities, and for fixing the limits on what will and will not be learned and remembered. When students expend effort trying to acquire the content of a lecture or book, they make a number of choices regarding what information they will concentrate on and how closely they will study it. It is at the point when such attending choices are made that the student constrains the domain of what specific information will be processed in the system. For example, if a person studying text sees content that is underlined, capitalized, or emphasized in some other fashion, the probability that they will learn the emphasized material increases dramatically—but at the expense of other material which is not accentuated (Anderson & Faust, 1967). A number of the variables used to increase the acquisition of critical instruction are designed to take full advantage of a student's ability to allocate processing attention, and they do so by giving overt cues concerning what is critical material (Glynn & DiVesta, 1979), or by telling students which domains of content they should attend to while studying (Anderson & Biddle, 1975; Rothkopf & Billington, 1979). Hence, one of the ways in which processing attention is manipulated is by adding stimulus elements to the material, which act to direct and control the attending process.

On the other hand, in the absence of specific stimulus prompts, people still tend to focus their processing attention toward those aspects of a lesson which they judge to be important to understanding the message (Meyer, 1975). In this later case, the locus of processing attention is probably controlled by two types of variables: (1) those which are intrinsic to the structure of the message, and (2) those which form a part of the learner's prior knowledge and current expectations. In fact, a current conception of processing attention, based on Kahneman's (1973) work, suggests that people bring a relatively fixed volume of processing attention to an instructional task, and then are able to make selective allocations of their available attending capacity to those instructional segments which they perceive as having the greatest potential payoff (Anderson, 1982; Reynolds & Anderson, 1982). It is this selection and allocation process that is brought under the control of various text prompts, adjunct materials such as questions, and the cognitive characteristics of the learner.

Our conclusion regarding attention is that it acts as a front-line manager for controlling what specific information will be encoded into the working memory system. As we show in the third section of this chapter, a good part of the research on effective instructional variables is really research on ways in which one can add to or change lesson material so that learners will allocate processing attention toward content which is critical to the lesson.

B. SCHEMA STRUCTURES

Another major way in which the instructional process is influenced involves the selection and use of cognitive structures called *schemata* (Anderson, 1977; Rumelhart, 1980). Essentially, schemata are generally described as information-based structures which determine how a learner will view, approach, and interpret instructional content. In other words, the particular schema (the singular form of schemata) a person activates when studying an instructional communication will have a great deal to do with what new information that person will mark for entry into the working-memory encoding system (Anderson, Pichert, & Shirey, 1983). Schemata appear to have their main effect on encoding by helping the learner to determine what things are semantically important in the instructional message (Goetz, Schallert, Reynolds, & Radin, 1983) and for providing an interpretative vehicle for placing the important information into memory.

At this point, readers of this chapter are probably saying to themselves, "Schemata sound impressive, but what exactly are they?" Unfortunately, the answer to this question is not an easy one because no one has ever seen a schema, and there are even those who argue that the entire concept is too loose to be of much use except as a verbal description (Thorndyke & Yekovich, 1980). However, our judgment is that there is enough research supporting the schema process to make it a valuable addition to our discussion, even if the concept itself is still less than perfectly defined (see Schallert, 1982). Probably the best way to describe schemata is first to say that they are structures which represent bodies of information available to the learner, and second, that they depend on the person's prior experience and knowledge of the world for their effects. Finally, people tend to activate particular schemata for use in given situations, depending on the context in which they perceive that particular situation and on the specific expectations they have regarding how the lesson material should be used.

There is no doubt that there are many potentially available schemata for a given instructional task. Hence, what the learner generally does is to use contextual cues to help determine which specific schema is most likely to apply to the instructional problem at hand. Not surprisingly, there is a large body of research showing that variables such as theme-related titles (Dooling & Mullet, 1973; Schmid & Kulhavy, 1981) and context-oriented pictures

(Bransford & Johnson, 1972) work to direct people in making their choice of schemata. For example, Kulhavy, Sherman, and Schmid (1978) presented subjects with short stories written in a convoluted manner which was difficult to understand. One group of subjects received titles before the passages, which were related to the theme of the stories, and a control group received no titles. One result from the study was that people who saw theme-related titles were able to remember more of the content than their no-theme counterparts. What this study shows is that statements which provide a context for interpretation tend to increase what is remembered from prose material, presumably because they assist the subject in activating an appropriate schema vehicle for use in effectively encoding the text. In an instructional environment, the schema activation process is probably also influenced by what students expect to have to do with the material once they have learned it. In fact, there is a fair sized, but confusing, literature dealing with variables such as what type of test students expect to receive following instruction. However, as yet there has been no consistent empirical verification that test expectancy determines schema selection—although the idea makes intuitive sense (Rohwer, 1984).

The prior knowledge component of a schema is central to our understanding of what schemata are and how they work. The general sense in the field is that schemata are formed from our prior experiences and knowledge of the world and that they represent dynamic systems which are constantly being created, added to, and expanded by new information which becomes available to the learner (cf. Schallert, 1982). In the absence of specific contextual direction, people seem to activate particular schemata and apply their inherent interpretations to new information based on the simple fact of what they already know the most about.

A good example of this phenomenon is contained in an insightful study by Anderson, Reynolds, Schallert, and Goetz (1977). In this experiment, a group of music education majors and a second group of physical education majors read two short passages, each of which could be interpreted in two different ways. The first passage could be interpreted as describing either a wrestling match or a prison break, and the great majority of the physical education subjects selected the wrestling interpretation as being consistent with the meaning of the passage, whereas the music education subjects chose the prison break option a large percentage of the time. The second passage in the study could also be interpreted in two ways: either as a group of friends getting together for a card game, or as a rehearsal session of a woodwind ensemble. As expected, music education subjects overwhelmingly interpreted the second passage in terms of the woodwind alternative, while the physical education group emphasized the card-playing possibility. The results of the Anderson et al. study clearly show that the meaning a person assigns to a unit of information depends on the prior knowledge milieu within which that person is used to operating.

One way in which specific schemata are activated is controlled by the particular perspective the learner takes on some new unit of information (Goetz, Schallert, Reynolds, & Radin, 1983; Pichert & Anderson, 1977). Although schemata are flexible in their application (Hertel, Cosden, & Johnson, 1980), and specific perspectives can be changed under certain conditions (Anderson & Pichert, 1978), it still appears true that how the learner conceptually views stimulus content determines, to a great degree, exactly which knowledge set will be applied during study. One of the important aspects of the work on perspective is that it soundly supports the notion that what an instructional communication means to a learner is more determined by the learner than by the instruction.

In fact, we tend to agree with Spiro (1980), who rejects the meaning-in-text position in favor of a constructivist approach which assumes that words, sentences, and paragraphs do not themselves possess a fixed meaning, but depend on the learner to construct a meaning from them. The constructivist model presupposes that when people process information, they not only interpret what is in the text, but also add new information to it, change it in accord with their own views, and create inferences about it to make it better match the prior knowledge base already available to them (Goetz, 1979). We believe then that in a direct sense, what instruction means to a learner depends more on what the learner thinks it means than on any fixed interpretation of the instruction itself.

In conclusion then, it appears that the concept of schemata is an important one for understanding how people go about encoding and storing target information. There is little doubt that if we are able to get students to approach and interpret a lesson in the fashion intended by the instructor, we are likely to increase the amount and type of relevant material that the students take with them as a result of study (Brooks & Dansereau, 1983).

C. DEPTH OF PROCESSING

The phrase *depth of processing* is often used to describe a variety of interrelated theories dealing with how information is encoded into the memory system. The basic assumption underlying depth of processing is that what people remember depends, to a great extent, on the *way* in which they encode information during learning (Anderson, 1970). The general form of these theories postulates that encoding itself can take place at any one of several levels in the processing system, and that the deeper the level of processing, the better the chance that the target information will be remembered (Craik & Lockhart, 1972). According to various statements of the depth relationship, incoming stimuli are analyzed in a hierarchical fashion which begins with an evaluation of surface features (e.g., letter forms), moves downward in the hierarchy toward processing of individual words, and eventually ends up at the deepest levels where the focus is on what the stimulus information means, and the analysis becomes semantic and elaborative in nature (Anderson, 1972; Craik & Tulving, 1975). From an instructional point of view, what all of this boils down to is the simple principle that the more the encoding process relies on meaning, the greater the chance that the material will be remembered at some later time.

While many of the defining experiments in depth-of-processing research have been performed with individual words and sentences, the same effects still seem to hold with more complex materials such as text, where the processing of meaning at deeper levels has led to more effective encoding and better memory with such materials as ambiguous paragraphs (Schallert, 1976), college science text (Kunen, Cohen, & Solman, 1981), and lengthy descriptive passages containing much detail (Bretzing & Kulhavy, 1979).

In fact, the research by Bretzing and Kulhavy provides a good example of how depth of processing has been experimentally manipulated. In this study, subjects read a 2000-word description of a fictitious African tribe and were required to take notes on each page read by either writing a summary, paraphrasing main ideas by putting them into their own words, or copying essential information in its verbatim form. Two control groups either copied capitalized words from every page or simply read the passage without writing at all. On a posttest on the passage content, both summary and paraphrase writers remembered more than either the verbatim group or the no-writing controls, and all four groups were able to recall significantly more information than the subjects who simply copied capitalized words. The depth-of-processing approach predicts exactly these relationships because conditions like summary writing and paraphrasing should result in higher recall performance because these acts require subjects to closely process the meaning of the text in order to be able to produce their specific types of notes. Obviously, learners must process deeply in order to understand the meaning of the passage and to be able to put it into their own words or summarize what it says. Alternately, just reading the text or copying essential content can be viewed as processing of a shallower nature, and the act of writing down capitalized words should have the least depth because it emphasizes letter and word forms at the expense of processing what the words mean when taken together.

In spite of the amount of research it has generated, the depth-of-processing concept has been criticized a number of times, mostly because no independent measure of depth has been available and the basic assumption of the model then becomes circular, i.e., that which is processed deeply is remembered, and that which is remembered is processed deeply (Baddeley, 1978; Postman, Thompkins, & Gray, 1978). The strongest response to this criticism has attempted to overcome the circular problem by emphasizing components of the encoding process like distinctiveness and elaboration (Craik & Tulving, 1975; Jacoby & Craik, 1979). According to such arguments, the distinctiveness of a stimulus item is increased when the encoding of that stimulus requires more effort and elaboration to achieve. Under these conditions, the depth at which a processing event occurs can be described in terms of both the amount of effort needed to produce the encoding, and the number of elaborations of the stimulus element that are associated with it in memory. Hence, various scales of effort–elaboration become metrics against which depth of processing can be measured, and the issue of circularity becomes moot.

From an instructional perspective, a number of studies by Glover and his associates have repeatedly shown that effort–elaboration formulations are good predictors of how students encode and remember text material (Benton, Glover, & Bruning, 1983; Glover, Bruning, & Plake, 1982). The amount remembered by subjects in these experiments was a direct function of the amount of encoding effort needed to acquire the target information and the degree to which subjects were able to associate elaborations with the stimulus text material. Further, as the encoding-specificity hypothesis predicts (Tulving, 1979), operations performed on the text to produce distinct and elaborative encoding also increased memorability for adjacent text information, making it apparent that such depth-related operations may have a lapover benefit for material outside of the instructional target area (Glover, Bruning, & Plake, 1982). What this body of work indicates is that the depth-of-processing concept and its distinctiveness–elaboration extensions are useful models for both understanding and predicting what students are likely to successfully encode and remember from an instructional episode.

So, what then are we able to deduce from our discussion of depth of processing? The inescapable conclusion is that people will probably learn more if we can find ways of making them work harder at the business of encoding and if they are encouraged in some fashion to attempt to deal with new information in terms of its meaning and semantic content. Research on depth of processing also tells us that getting students to simply repeat material or spend more time looking at it is probably not the most efficient way to ensure that they will learn and remember the content. Rather, our instructional goals would probably be better met if we were able to provide strategies that helped to ensure that what they do process, they process deeply.

III. FACTORS WHICH AFFECT ENCODING

A. OVERVIEW

This section of the chapter addresses some of the multitude of variables which appear to affect the instructional encoding activity. In order to build a framework for our discussion, we have decomposed the process of study into a series of general components, each of which has attracted the attention of those who produce research in the area of instruction. An outline of our framework is shown graphically in Fig. 1, and although there is no good reason to suppose that these components operationally relate to one another in a simple linear fashion, the framework still provides us with a way (schema?) of organizing the types of variables in which we are interested.

The leftmost side of the figure expresses our view that it is the interaction between learner and stimulus characteristics which is primarily responsible for the initial selection of the knowledge and task schemata which will be applied to a particular block of information. It is our argument that what learners do is to approach the stimulus materials with some set of instructional expectations concerning what they should learn and remember following study, and that it is at least partly these expectations which determine what encoding strategies or task schemata are chosen for use during a specific instructional episode. In addition, the content and structure of the material itself serves to activate a particular knowledge schema, which will then be used as a base for interpreting the new information.

Here, it is our notion that the interaction between learner and stimulus characteristics works to produce not one, but two instructionally useful schemata. The first such structure we have labeled the *task schema*, which is a goal-oriented set of procedures that control the ways in which the learner will activate both overt and covert encoding activities in order to achieve the desired instructional outcome. The second type of structure is a *knowledge schema*, which we have already discussed in section II, and which acts to represent the type of interpretation that the learner will apply in attempting to acquire the new information. It is our belief that a task schema is selected as a result of the expectancies associated with a particular instructional episode, but that a corresponding knowledge schema is activated because the material in the lesson matches well with a particular block of semantic experience available to the learner. Following the reasoning of people like Endel Tulving (1979), we conclude that it is the interaction between episodic and semantic expectancies which are the initial determinants of how new information will be processed, and of where it will be deposited in the learner's cognitive storehouse.

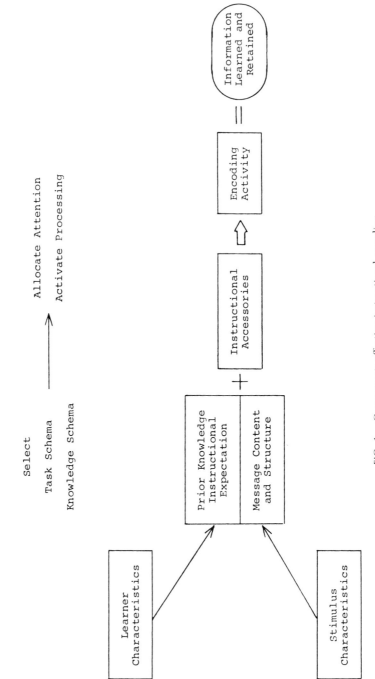

FIG. 1. Components affecting instructional encoding.

The final set of factors which seem to influence what information is emphasized and how it is encoded we have called *instructional accessories* in Fig. 1. As we use this label here, instructional accessories include all of the cues, directions and adjunct devices which are not a part of the primary lesson content but which relate to the instruction in such a fashion that they influence what and how learning takes place. Our definition includes vague manipulations such as simple instructions to study in a certain way, obvious prompts like the underlining and capitalization of important information, graphic organizers like pictures and maps which are not a critical part of the instruction, and adjunct variables such as theme statements, questions, and mnemonic memory devices which direct the learner toward what he or she should work to remember. Defining instructional accessories as a separate category of variables has the advantage of making it easier to evaluate the effects of our various components on the end product of learning.

B. TEXT STRUCTURE

In this section, we intend to briefly review the effects of message structure on what students encode and remember from a lesson. Because much of this research has been done with written texts, our discussion emphasizes the text presentation mode, although there seems to be no good reason to believe that the learning outcomes would markedly change with lecture material—except for obvious differences in the task demands. Here, we are interested in how the characteristics of instructional stimuli act to influence learning prior to the point at which any of the more common instructional accessories are appended to the text information.

Studies on text structure have most often emphasized differences in the importance of various text segments as being a major determinant of what will be learned and remembered from reading. In this case, the term *importance* generally refers to how necessary a particular text element is for the learner to comprehend and process the coherent substance of the discourse. Both Meyer and Kintsch have heavily influenced the way in which structural characteristics have been viewed experimentally. For example, Meyer (e.g., Meyer, 1975) has developed a quasi-linguistic procedure which allows her to decompose a passage into a hierarchical form, where more prominent information is placed at the top levels and less prominent information at the bottom levels of the hierarchy. Material at the top level is seen as more important in the sense that it serves a superordinate or organizing function for less important information located deeper in the structure. At the bottom level, one finds elements, details, and facts which are of little integrative value to the overall meaning of the passage. A somewhat different approach to structure has been developed by Kintsch and his associates (Kintsch & van

Dijk, 1978), in which texts are seen as having a similar top-to-bottom arrangement, only the basic unit for the analysis is the proposition rather than the linguistic units adopted by Meyer. For Kintsch, the individual propositions in a text, each of which forms a complete informational unit, are also arranged in an importance hierarchy, where the upper levels exist as a macrostructure for information lower in the passage.

In spite of the procedural differences in these two models, both of them appear to do a relatively good job of predicting what information a reader will remember after contact with the passage. In both cases, there is substantial research to show that higher level information is learned better than lower level units under a wide variety of experimental conditions. Such data do serve to tell us that in the general case, it is possible to use the structural characteristics of text as one way of determining what people will probably encode while reading them.

An alternate way in which the structural characteristics of text can be conceptualized is by examining the structural elements, or grammars, of short, narrative stories (Mandler & Johnson, 1977). In most story-grammar studies, the prose is dissected in terms of its narrative value in much the same fashion as one might expect in a college literature class—e.g., plot structure, episode organization, and so on. The resulting story grammar units are then experimentally manipulated and analyzed in various ways to determine how they influence memory for the text content (Thorndyke, 1977). By and large, such research has been successful in showing that the elements of story grammars can act as guides to what people encode and remember from a tale (Haberlandt, Berian, & Sandson, 1980), especially if the story components present a well-defined sequence of problem-solution links in the narrative chain (Black & Bower, 1980).

Based on this brief overview, what can we now deduce about the relationship between text structure and the process of encoding in instruction? First, it seems clear that there *are* structural characteristics in discourse, such as perceived importance and narrative architecture, which can serve to direct the encoding process and lead to relatively uniform predictions about what will be remembered. However, such phenomena appear to be of less importance in many instructional settings, where design patterns and the addition of instructional accessories may have a marked impact on what material students pay attention to and actually process. Also, if one accepts the constructivist view offered earlier, then the importance value or emphasis that a segment of text receives is at least partially a function of what the learners expect to do with the information and how they choose to interpret it in the first place. Hence, in spite of the impressive amount of data generated by those interested in structural variables, we are unsure about how wide the applicability of such research is to the types of planned learning sequences which form the typical instructional unit.

C. INSTRUCTIONAL ACCESSORIES

In this section, we intend to cover research done with several of the more common instructional accessories. We first review work done with a class of accessories that we call schema activators, which include such instructional additions as theme statements, passage headings, and advance organizers— all of which appear to affect encoding by providing the learner with an appropriate knowledge schema for interpreting and integrating new information.

Next, we discuss the effects of presenting passage-relevant questions before, after, or during the reading of a text. Research on such adjunct questions has blossomed since the mid-1960s, and the area is an important one for understanding how people allocate attention and develop a task schema during study of a lesson.

Our third group of accessories involve the structure and function of mnemonic procedures as a way of enhancing the encoding process. As we choose to define it, the term *mnemonics* subsumes all of the artificial devices or procedures which are developed to make lesson information easier to learn and remember. Although a number of mnemonics are created by students themselves to fit their own needs, there is a substantial literature on how one goes about building in mnemonics as a part of the instruction; hence, we are willing to treat both classes of devices under our definition of instructional accessories. Finally, we overview data which have focused on how spatial processing influences the encoding and retention of text-based information. Here, we deal primarily with research done using reference maps as a way of increasing the amount one remembers from reading prose.

1. Schema Activators

As we mentioned earlier in our overview of schema theory, the influence of theme statements, titles, and headings on text interpretation has been a popular topic in the literature on instruction and cognition. In our view, *schema activators* include any semantic stimuli which work to provide people with a way of organizing or interpreting the information contained in a passage they are about to encode. Such activators seem to have their main effect at the point of encoding where the students are searching for a way to place the new information in memory so they can get it out again, and the activation of an appropriate knowledge schema greases the wheels of their processing mechanism.

In the previous section on schema theory, we described how the act of providing a theme or title for a difficult passage works to make the material understandable and, therefore, easier for the learner to process effectively. The same facilitative effect can also be achieved by placing a contextually relevant picture before a text, which has the effect of helping the learner to organize and interpret the material.

For example, in the first experiment of a now-classic article by Bransford and Johnson (1972), subjects read a short, difficult-to-interpret passage and saw a picture which supplied a context for the text either before or after reading. Control groups simply read the passage once or twice without a picture or saw a picture of the same objects rearranged so that they made little sense relative to the prose content. Those learners who saw the contextually relevant picture before reading produced comprehension and recall scores which were dramatically higher than any of the remaining groups. Such data clearly show that an appropriate schema activator cues the reader to select an applicable schema structure within which to process and interpret the new material. Further, this same positive effect is produced not only by theme statements and pictures, but also by such basic manipulations as placing headings in text (Dee-Lucas & DiVesta, 1980) and putting quotation marks around passage segments which are critical to the desired interpretation (Pratt, Krane, & Kendall, 1981). The conclusion, then, is that any device which guides the activation of an appropriate schema, especially for convoluted or unfamiliar material, will increase the probability that the learners will be able to acquire the new information in such a fashion that they can reproduce it at some point in the future.

There is yet a second body of research which deals with schema activation under the label *advance organizers* (e.g., Ausubel, 1960, 1968). Unlike simple titles, headings, and so forth, advance organizers generally consist of a fair-sized block of information which is presented before the student tackles the main instructional content. The purpose of such organizers is to provide the learner with a knowledge vehicle for subsuming or assimilating the target material into memory. Hence, advance organizers may be more abstractive and inclusive than the material to follow (Ausubel, 1968), include rules and analogies that will apply to the target content (Mayer & Bromage, 1980), or perhaps supply concrete instances which can later be used to organize the primary text during encoding (Royer & Cable, 1975, 1976). Whatever their format, advance organizers should help the student bridge the knowledge gap between what the person already knows and what he or she is going to try to learn from the instructional episode. In other words, organizers activate critical schematic information which will provide a sound base for incorporating the new content (Derry, 1984).

In general, it appears that advance organizers do have a positive effect on at least the conceptual information contained in a later lesson (Luiten, Ames, & Ackerson, 1980). In fact, studies which have shown no organizer effects have probably not done so because they emphasized the direct learning of easy-to-measure detail, rather than the learning of concepts and superordinate information which is central to theories of advance organization (Barnes & Clawson, 1975; Mayer, 1979). It does seem that some form of advance organizer may be of greater instructional use than are themes or headings, because the latter have been shown to work best with ambiguous or convoluted materials of relatively short length (Dooling & Mullet, 1973). Such an effect probably occurs because themes and headings simply cue an applicable knowledge schema for interpretation, while organizers attempt to provide a portion of the schema framework in order to speed integration of the new information.

2. Adjunct Questions

There is now a good deal of evidence to suggest that the act of identifying important elements of a lesson either before, during, or after reading has a strong influence on what people will encode and remember from their study. This positive influence holds for basic teaching components such as instructional objectives (Duell, 1974; Klauer, 1984), but the bulk of such research has involved adjunct questions which are related to the text content as the primary way of identifying important elements within the lesson (cf. Anderson & Biddle, 1975; Rothkopf & Bisbicos, 1967). Although there are many variations, the typical adjunct questions study takes a set of text-related questions and allows the learner to study them either before or after reading some portion of the target passage. The most general finding in research of this sort is that when a group receiving text-related questions is compared to a no-questions control group, questions placed *before* the text lead to a significant increase in what people remember about the specific information related to the questions themselves. Alternately, when the same questions are placed *after* the text, they tend to increase what is remembered both from question-related material and from adjacent content which is not specifically referenced in the questions. When the presence of adjunct questions increases performance on material related specifically to the item content, the questions are said to have a direct effect, in the sense that seeing the question causes the learner to encode information directly related to its content. On the other hand, while postquestions have the same direct effect, they also have an indirect effect, where people remember more information which was not directly addressed in the question proper.

The important issue for us is, of course, identifying the mechanism responsible for both the direct and the indirect effects of adjunct questions.

The best available answer seems to be that adjunct questions act to provide a task schema which controls the allocation of processing attention during study. The assumption is that questions placed before the passage work simply to focus learner attention on text segments which are directly related to the questions themselves (e.g., Reynolds & Anderson, 1982). In the case of postquestions, the answer is more complex and seems to involve both a mental rehearsal component where learners spend time reviewing question-relevant information in memory, and an additional attention-priming effect where later segments in the passage are read more closely merely because the reader learns to expect that questions will follow segments of the text (Anderson & Biddle, 1975; McGaw & Grotelueschen, 1972; Wixson, 1984).

Now that we have defined how adjunct questions act to facilitate learning, it seems logical to ask whether or not the content or form of the questions is influential in determining the type of information that people are likely to remember from reading. Unfortunately, the literature on this point is unclear. On one side, it has been convincingly argued that both the form and the focus of adjunct questions should have at least a qualitative influence on what the learner encodes from the text.

For example, Watts and Anderson (1971) found that application questions which required the learner to apply information from his or her reading worked to increase the student's ability to apply principles and concepts. In a similar vein, subjects in a study by Rickards and DiVesta (1974) produced higher recall scores when they saw meaningful learning questions, as opposed to rote-learning-of-ideas questions. On the other hand, there are numerous studies in which question content and/or format has failed to show a reliable effect, and what conclusion one draws about such variables appears to depend on which study they read. For instance, inconsistent results materialize in comparisons involving lexically paraphrased questions (Anderson & Biddle, 1975; Andre & Sola, 1976; Swenson & Kulhavy, 1974), questions oriented toward the application of target material (Andre, Mueller, Womack, Smid, & Tuttle, 1980; Watts & Anderson, 1971), and questions that have emphasized higher-order informational concepts as their locus of effect (Andre, 1979). This lack of uniform results for different question types leaves us with no distinct set of recommendations concerning how questions other than those lifted straight from the text are likely to influence what is learned from the instruction. The idea that different types of questions should yield different types of learning has great intuitive appeal; however, we feel compelled to table our judgment about how such effects might work until future research adds the weight of fact to our intuition.

Our summary comment then, is that adjunct questions which are close to the content form of the target material will have a reliable facilitative effect on what people are likely to encode and remember from reading a text.

Further, when the questions are seen before reading, they focus attention directly on similar information in the passage; and when they are placed after a discourse, they have the same direct effect, but also tend to increase memory for other information not directly related to the question content.

3. Mnemonic Devices

In the general sense, the phrase *mnemonic devices* spreads out to cover any and all of the procedures which students are either taught or develop themselves for use in making the task of learning easier. When a person makes up a rhyme to help remember a list of names, tries to imagine a target object in their mind so they will not forget it, or links a series of terms together by using their first letters to form a word, they are implementing various mnemonic procedures to make their study more effective. Further, there is evidence both abundant and clear that mnemonic devices generally have a positive effect on how much is learned, and typically work to increase what people are able to produce on a later test (e.g., Bellezza, 1981).

Mnemonic devices have a long and well-documented history in terms of their ability to facilitate learning (Yates, 1966). For example, centuries ago Greek orators spent a great deal of time and resourcefulness in developing a mnemonic technique called the "method of loci," which they used to help them remember the series of facts needed for public speeches. In fact, the method of loci is still used by professional mnemonists today, and represents a good illustration of a spatial–sequential procedure for ensuring that information is remembered both properly and in the proper order. In the method of loci, the user expends great effort constructing a durable mental picture of a place they are closely familiar with; for instance, the layout of a well-known building. Next, the mnemonist takes the sequential parts of the target material (say an outline for a speech) and distributes in the required order throughout the landmarks (loci) in the mental image of the building. Now, all that is necessary for the person to correctly retrieve the information, is for them to mentally pass through the building and collect the separate parts of the material in their appropriate sequence. Using this method, people are able to encode and remember tremendous amounts of information accurately and within a relatively short time span. These same dramatic increases in learning have also been found with mnemonics which emphasize linking units of information together in a meaningful sequence by using an easy-to-remember rhyme like "On Old Olympus Towering Top . . ." for the cranial nerves, or by embedding the units within the context of a short story which is made up by the learner (Bower & Clark, 1969). Alternately, there exists an entire family of mnemonics grouped under the rubric pegword, keyword, or cueword, which allow the student to remember words, definitions, and the like simply by associating them with familiar words, numbers, or images already known to them (Bellezza, 1981). Finally, there is some evidence that mnemonic-like procedures involving organizational encoding or forming images while reading may have a similar facilitative effect on prose materials of the type found in textbooks (Kintsch, 1982; Kulhavy & Swenson, 1975).

Perhaps the most popular mnemonic for those interested in educational research is the *keyword* procedure. This technique has been widely tested, and there is now substantial experimental evidence that it facilitates learning of foreign language vocabulary and other materials which involve direct associate pairings (Atkinson, 1975; Pressley, Levin, & Delaney, 1982). A common version of the keyword method involves three associative steps in order to produce its beneficial effect (Hall, Wilson, & Patterson, 1981). For example, in foreign language learning, the student takes the word to be learned and derives a common English word from it, which is related in some way to its form or spelling—this derived word is the keyword. In the next step, the student repeatedly associates the foreign word with the keyword until a strong associative bond is formed. Finally, the learner forms a visual image in their mind, which closely relates the keyword with the English translation of the foreign word. Although the procedure sounds lengthy, it can be learned by students in a relatively short time.

Now, let us borrow an actual example of the keyword process from Hall and his associates (1981). Suppose that our target word were *candada* which means padlock in Spanish. In order to follow the three-step procedure, we might: (1) derive the keyword (say) *candy*, which is easy to remember and relates well to the target, (2) rehearse the pairing *candada–candy* over and over so that the two are strongly associated together, and (3) produce a visual image which combines the keyword and the translation together—for instance, a padlocked box of candy. This general type of associative encoding strategy has yielded learning gains with subjects in the primary grades, high school, and college, and with a number of associable content units other than foreign language words.

It should be clear from this discussion that there are various mnemonic techniques which can have a fruitful existence within the instructional milieu. However, one does well to remember that the actual learning of a useful mnemonic may require much practice and effort to achieve, and that not all subject domains or content elements are amenable to the more popular mnemonic devices. More importantly, it has been argued that the effects of many mnemonics are neither durable over time nor particularly capable of generalizing to tasks other than the specific one being measured (Pressley, Borkowski, & O'Sullivan, 1984).

One response to such criticisms has been the argument that we should shift our focus away from specific applications of particular mnemonic devices, and begin to concentrate on teaching students about mnemonics as a class of instructionally useful procedures which can be applied to a variety of materials and content elements (Pressley et al., 1984). Such a process would emphasize supplying the student with information about how a mnemonic works and how to use it effectively, rather than restrict the mnemonic to a specific task demand with little explanation of how or why it works. It is possible that a move in the direction of providing more process as opposed to product information will allow mnemonics to have a wider appeal within the instructional enterprise.

4. Spatial Processing

Our discussion of spatial processing centers on how coherent structures such as reference maps act to increase learning from related prose content (e.g., Dean & Kulhavy, 1981). Here, we are interested primarily in instances where instructional goals are served by the spatial relations portrayed in a stimulus, rather than in the context referents provided by illustrations, or in different arrangements of words or study patterns (Bellezza, 1983; Schallert, 1980).

Research exploring the relationship between maps and prose has clearly shown that students remember significantly more discourse information when that information is related to elements which are depicted spatially on an adjunct map (Kulhavy, Lee, & Caterino, 1985). For example, in a definitional study by Schwartz and Kulhavy (1981), undergraduates listened to a narrative involving the activities of a fictitious group of pirates living on a Pacific island. While they listened to the story, subjects either studied a map of the island with features mentioned in the story distributed over the island area, saw an outline of the island with the same features listed in a column to the right of the page, or saw only an outline of the island without any features depicted. In all cases, the features consisted of both a line drawing and a verbal label. Following the study–listen phase of the experiment, one of the tests the learners received over the passage content consisted of fill-in-the-blank items requiring responses which were either related to or not related to specific features on the map—none of these questions could be answered by studying the map alone. People who saw the spatially distributed map produced substantially more correct test responses on feature-related items than either of the control groups who saw the list of features or only the outline. Performance on items not related to map features was about the same for all groups. What the results of this study show is that the relation between maps and discourse is a facilitative one, and that the spatiality of the map is an important variable for producing such facilitation.

Given such results, the real question becomes, what mechanism is responsible for the positive interaction in map–prose combinations? In responding to this question, we are inclined to agree with Kulhavy et al. (1985) that the answer lies in an evaluation of the differences between how verbal and spatial information are encoded into the processing system. Kulhavy and his associates offer a model, which they call the "conjoint retention hypothesis" in order to account for map–prose facilitation. Basically, their argument is

> Conjoint retention hypothesis is essentially a rendition of the dual coding approach in the sense that linguistic/verbal and perceptual/spatial representations in the cognitive milieu are treated as separate coding processes, at least portions of which are nonoverlapping in memory. In the general case, we think that much of discourse content is stored in a linguistic/verbal mode with few perceptual referents whereas, the geography of a map is stored primarily as a perceptual/spatial representation which probably possesses at least quasi-pictorial characteristics. (Kulhavy et al., 1985, p. 29)

Under this set of assumptions, facilitation occurs simply because the learner is able to draw on both encoded representations at retrieval—an act which increases the probability of remembering conjointly stored information, as opposed to information which has only one code available. In other words, the encoded map seems to act as a spatial schema which provides additional distinct retrieval cues for prose information related to the features. This reasoning is supported by research showing that the cognitive representation of a map is more spatial than not (Kulhavy, Schwartz, & Shaha, 1983), and by analyses which demonstrate that memory for verbal information is significantly related to whether or not the learner can conjointly recall a spatially related feature from the map (e.g., Schwartz & Kulhavy, 1981).

Our conclusion then is that coherent spatial structures such as reference maps are a powerful means for increasing the amount of information people are able to remember from a related prose passage. Further, performance increases probably result as a function of the way in which the two stimulus types are differentially encoded, and the degree to which learners can use both spatial and verbal cues as a base for recalling target information.

IV. EDUCATIONAL APPLICATIONS

In our discussion to this point, we have seen that what people learn from study is a complex function not only of the characteristics of what they study, but also of their previous experience, what they expect to learn in the first place, and the ways in which the instruction is modified or added to in order to increase its effectiveness. Given this state of affairs, it comes as no surprise that people have encountered difficulty in attempting to transform instructional research into instructional practice. However, in spite of such difficulties we now do our best to outline possible applications of the material we have reviewed.

Remember that the second section of this chapter summarizes research done on three major classes of activity which influence instructional encoding. We reviewed work (1) on allocation of processing attention, (2) on schema conceptions of how old knowledge is activated in order to acquire new information, and (3) on the various approaches to depth of processing activities. Based on this initial analysis, we are able to begin our discussion of applications by describing three important principles.

A. PRINCIPLE 1

The allocation of processing attention is critical in order for encoding to take place. Hence, any procedure that directs processing attention to target portions of the instruction increases the probability that students will learn what is expected of them.

B. PRINCIPLE 2

The activation of an appropriate knowledge schema provides a useful semantic framework for interpreting incoming information. Thus, any manipulation which acts to produce an interpretation schema that is similar to that of the author and/or tester of the instruction, will heighten the chance of the content being successfully encoded.

C. PRINCIPLE 3

Depth of processing in terms of both effort and complexity is important for producing durable encoding. Consequently, any instructional method that compels the student to work harder at learning, or helps to semantically increase the elaboration–integration process will lead to more effective instructional outcomes.

D. UNIFYING THE THREE PRINCIPLES

Taken together, these three principles provide us with a set of guidelines, both for evaluating the various instructional accessories we have discussed, and for thinking generally in terms of teaching practice. For instance, in the examples we have previously used, the allocation of attention is probably influenced to the greatest extent by variables such as text structure and adjunct questions. Other things being equal, the structural hierarchy and author-generated cues within a text become a determinant of what the learner will pay attention to while reading. If the inherent text structure fits tested instructional goals, then this form of attention control will facilitate acquisition of target material. The same effect holds true for adjunct questions, in the sense that they provide the student with a task schema for what is to be learned, and help to define those parts of the lesson which will receive processing attention during study. In addition, adjunct questions are relatively easy to generate and are more likely to increase attention allocation to critical content than is text structure because such questions are acquired as separate units outside of the context of the lesson itself.

In terms of the second principle, knowledge schemata are triggered by the class of accessories we have labeled "schema activators." We have previously shown that a wide variety of contextual and semantic cues serve to assist the learner in selecting an appropriate interpretation vehicle for incoming information. Also, feature-based structures such as maps may provide a type of spatial schema which itself is later useful for the accurate recall of target information. From an application point of view, there is little doubt that any mechanism which catalyzes an appropriate schema also establishes the appropriate information base on which to focus processing attention and depth-of-processing strategies.

The mnemonic devices we have discussed provide a good example of how one might tap depth of processing within an applied framework. The successful use of mnemonics does, indeed, depend on the *way* in which new information is handled and encoded. Research on procedures, such as the method of loci and the keyword method, represents a somewhat concrete instance of how specific processing strategies can be brought to bear on a particular stimulus combination. However, virtually any procedure which aims at making the target instruction more distinct and elaborates its meaning fits within the depth-of-processing category.

The formula for instructional application then involves first determining which of the attending, schema, and processing components is to be influenced, and then selecting one or more accessories that will act to maximize learning yields per unit of time. It has come as no surprise to us that the preceding process is highly similar to that which is practiced by many master teachers, who follow essentially the same sequence of instructional events, but base their selections on years of teaching experience, rather than on the research immediately available in the literature domain we have just reviewed.

REFERENCES

Anderson, R. C. (1970). Control of student mediating processes during verbal learning and instruction. *Review of Educational Research, 40*, 349–369.

Anderson, R. C. (1972). How to construct achievement tests to assess comprehension. *Review of Educational Research, 42*, 145–170.

Anderson, R. C. (1977). The notion of schemata and the educational enterprise. In R. C. Anderson, R. J. Spiro, & W. E. Montague (Eds.), *Schooling and the acquisition of knowledge* (pp. 415–431). Hillsdale, NJ: Erlbaum.

Anderson, R. C. (1982). Allocation of attention during reading. In A. Flammer & W. Kintsch (Eds.), *Discourse processing* (pp. 292–305). New York: North Holland.

Anderson, R. C., & Biddle, W. B. (1975). On asking people questions about what they are reading. In G. Bower (Ed.), *Psychology of learning and motivation* (Vol. 9, pp. 89–132). New York: Academic Press.

Anderson, R. C., & Faust, G. W. (1967). The effects of strong formal prompts in programmed instruction. *American Educational Research Journal, 4*, 345–352.

Anderson, R. C., & Pichert, J. W. (1978). Recall of previously unrecallable information following a shift in perspective. *Journal of Verbal Learning and Verbal Behavior, 17*, 1–12.

Anderson, R. C., Pichert, J. W., & Shirey, L. L. (1983). Effects of the reader's schema at different points in time. *Journal of Educational Psychology, 75*, 271–279.

Anderson, R. C., Reynolds, R. E., Schallert, D. L., & Goetz, E. T. (1977). Frameworks for comprehending discourse. *American Educational Research Journal, 14*, 367–381.

Andre, T. (1979). On productive knowledge of levels of questions. *Review of Educational Research, 49*, 280–318.

Andre, T., Mueller, C., Womack, S., Smid, K., & Tuttle, M. (1980). Adjunct application questions facilitate later application, or do they? *Journal of Educational Psychology, 72*, 533–543.

Andre, T., & Sola, J. (1976). Imagery, verbatim and paraphrased questions and retention of meaningful sentences. *Journal of Educational Psychology, 68*, 661–669.

Atkinson, R. C. (1975). Mnemotechnic in second-language learning. *American Psychologist, 30*, 821–828.

Ausubel, D. P. (1960). The use of advance organizers in the learning and retention of meaningful verbal material. *Journal of Educational Psychology, 51*, 267–272.

Ausubel, D. P. (1968). *Educational psychology: A cognitive view.* New York: Holt.

Baddeley, A. D. (1978). The trouble with levels: A reexamination of Craik and Lockhart's framework for memory research. *Psychological Review, 85*, 139–152.

Baddeley, A. D., & Hinch, G. (1974). Working memory. In G. A. Bower (Ed.), *The psychology of learning and motivation* (Vol. 8, pp. 36–78). New York: Academic Press.

Barnes, B. R., & Clawson, E. V. (1975). Do advance organizers facilitate learning? Recommendations for further research based on an analysis of 32 studies. *Review of Educational Research, 34*, 637–659.

Bellezza, F. S. (1981). Mnemonic devices: Classification, characteristics, and criteria. *Review of Educational Research, 51*, 247–275.

Bellezza, F. S. (1983). The spatial-arrangement mnemonic. *Journal of Educational Psychology, 75*, 830–837.

Benton, S. L., Glover, J. A., & Bruning, R. H. (1983). Levels of processing: Effects of number of decisions on prose recall. *Journal of Educational Psychology, 75*, 382–390.

Black, J. B., & Bower, G. H. (1980). Story understanding as problem-solving. *Poetics, 9*, 223–250.

Bower, G. H., & Clark, M. C. (1969). Narrative stories as mediators for serial learning. *Psychonomic Science, 14*, 181–182.

Bransford, J. D., & Johnson, M. K. (1972). Contextual prerequisites for understanding: Some investigations of comprehension and recall. *Journal of Verbal Learning and Verbal Behavior, 11*, 717–726.

Bretzing, B. H., & Kulhavy, R. W. (1979). Notetaking and depth of processing. *Contemporary Educational Psychology, 4*, 145–153.

Brooks, L. W., & Dansereau, D. F. (1983). Effects of structural schema training and text organization on expository prose processing. *Journal of Educational Psychology, 75*, 811–820.

Craik, F. I. M., & Lockhart, R. S. (1972). Levels of processing: A framework for memory research. *Journal of Verbal Learning and Verbal Behavior, 11*, 671–684.

Craik, F. I. M., & Tulving, E. V. (1975). Depth of processing and the retention of words in episodic memory. *Journal of Experimental Psychology: General, 104*, 268–294.

Daneman, M., & Carpenter, P. A. (1980). Individual differences in working memory and reading. *Journal of Verbal Learning and Verbal Behavior, 19*, 450–466.

Dean, R. S., & Kulhavy, R. W. (1981). Influence of spatial organization in prose learning. *Journal of Educational Psychology, 73*, 57–64.

Dee-Lucas, D., & DiVesta, F. J. (1980). Learner-generated organizational aids: Effects on learning from text. *Journal of Educational Psychology, 72*, 304–311.

Derry, S. J. (1984). Effects of an organizer on memory for prose. *Journal of Educational Psychology, 76*, 98–107.

Dooling, D. J., & Mullet, R. L. (1973). Locus of thematic effects in retention of prose. *Journal of Experimental Psychology, 97*, 404–406.

Duell, O. K. (1974). Effect of type of objective, level of test question, and the judged importance of tested materials upon posttest performance. *Journal of Educational Psychology, 66*, 225–232.

Glover, J. A., Bruning, R. H., & Plake, B. S. (1982). Distinctiveness of encoding and recall of text materials. *Journal of Educational Psychology, 74*, 522–534.

Glynn, S. M., & DiVesta, F. J. (1979). Control of prose processing via instructional and typographical cues. *Journal of Educational Psychology, 71*, 595–603.

Goetz, E. T. (1979). Inferring from text: Some factors affecting which inferences will be made. *Discourse Processes, 2*, 179–195.

Goetz, E. T., Schallert, D. L., Reynolds, R. E., & Radin, D. I. (1983). Reading in perspective: What real cops and burglars look for in a story. *Journal of Educational Psychology, 75*, 500–510.

Haberlandt, K., Berian, C., & Sandson, F. (1980). The episode schema in story processing. *Journal of Verbal Learning and Verbal Behavior, 19*, 635–650.

Hall, J. W., Wilson, K. P., & Patterson, R. J. (1981). Mnemotechnics: Some limitations of the mnemonic keyword method for the study of foreign language vocabulary. *Journal of Educational Psychology, 73*, 345–357.

Hertel, P. T., Cosden, M., & Johnson, P. J. (1980). Passage recall: Schema change and cognitive flexibility. *Journal of Educational Psychology, 72*, 133–140.

Jacoby, L. L., & Craik, F. I. M. (1979). Effects of elaboration of processing at encoding and retrieval: Trace distinctiveness and recovery of initial context. In L. S. Cermak & F. I. M. Craik (Eds.), *Levels of processing and human memory* (pp. 1–22). Hillsdale, NJ: Erlbaum.

Kahneman, D. (1973). *Attention and effort.* Englewood Cliffs, NJ: Prentice-Hall.

Kintsch, W. (1982). Memory for text. In A. Flammer & W. Kintsch (Eds.), *Discourse processing* (pp. 186–204). New York: North Holland.

Kintsch, W., & van Dijk, T. A. (1978). Toward a model of text comprehension and production. *Psychological Review, 85*, 363–394.

Klauer, K. J. (1984). Intentional and incidental learning with instructional texts: A meta-analysis for 1970–1980. *American Educational Research Journal, 21*, 323–339.

Kulhavy, R. W., Lee, J. B., & Caterino, L. C. (1985). Conjoint retention of maps and related discourse. *Contemporary Educational Psychology, 10*, 28–37.

Kulhavy, R. W., Schwartz, N. H., & Shaha, S. H. (1983). Spatial representation of maps. *American Journal of Psychology, 96*, 337–351.

Kulhavy, R. W., Sherman, J. L., & Schmid, R. F. (1978). Contextual cues and depth of processing in short prose passages. *Contemporary Educational Psychology, 3*, 62–68.

Kulhavy, R. W., & Swenson, I. (1975). Imagery instructions and the comprehension of text. *British Journal of Educational Psychology, 45*, 47–51.

Kunen, S., Cohen, R., & Solman, R. (1981). A levels-of-processing analysis of Bloom's taxonomy. *Journal of Educational Psychology, 73*, 202–211.

Luiten, J., Ames, W., & Ackerson, G. (1980). A meta-analysis of the effects of advance organizers on learning and retention. *American Educational Research Journal, 17*, 211–218.

Mandler, J. M., & Johnson, N. S. (1977). Remembrance of things parsed: Story structure and recall. *Cognitive Psychology, 9*, 111–151.

Mayer, R. E. (1979). Can advance organizers influence meaningful learning? *Review of Educational Research, 49*, 371–383.

Mayer, R. E., & Bromage, B. K. (1980). Different recall protocols for technical texts due to advance organizers. *Journal of Educational Psychology, 72*, 209–225.

McGaw, B., & Grotelueschen, A. (1972). Direction of the effect of questions in prose material. *Journal of Educational Psychology, 63*, 580–588.

Meyer, B. J. F. (1975). *The organization of prose and its effects on memory.* Amsterdam: North Holland.

Norman, D. A. (1968). Toward a theory of memory and attention. *Psychological Review, 75*, 522–536.

Pichert, J. W., & Anderson, R. C. (1977). Taking different perspectives on a story. *Journal of Educational Psychology, 69*, 309–315.

Postman, L., Thompkins, B. A., & Gray, W. D. (1978). The interpretation of encoding effects in retention. *Journal of Verbal Learning and Verbal Behavior, 17*, 681–706.

Pratt, M. W., Krane, A. R., & Kendall, J. R. (1981). Triggering a schema: The role of italics and intonation in the interpretation of ambiguous discourse. *American Educational Research Journal, 18*, 303–316.

Pressley, M., Borkowski, J. G., & O'Sullivan, J. T. (1984). Memory strategy instruction is made of this: Metamemory and durable strategy use. *Educational Psychologist, 19*, 94–107.

Pressley, M., Levin, J. R., & Delaney, H. D. (1982). The mnemonic keyword method. *Review of Educational Research, 52*, 61–91.

Reynolds, R. E., & Anderson, R. C. (1982). Influence of questions on the allocation of attention during reading. *Journal of Educational Psychology, 74*, 623–632.

Rickards, J. P., & DiVesta, F. J. (1974). Type and frequency of questions in processing textual material. *Journal of Educational Psychology, 66*, 354–362.

Rohwer, W. D. (1984). An invitation to an educational psychology of studying. *Educational Psychologist, 19*, 1–14.

Rothkopf, E. Z., & Billington, M. J. (1979). Goal guided learning from text: Inferring a descriptive processing model from inspection times and eye movements. *Journal of Educational Psychology, 71*, 310–327.

Rothkopf, E. Z., & Bisbicos, E. E. (1967). Selective facilitative effects of interspersed questions on learning from written materials. *Journal of Educational Psychology, 58*, 56–61.

Royer, J. M., & Cable, G. W. (1975). Facilitated learning in connected discourse. *Journal of Educational Psychology, 67*, 116–123.

Royer, J. M., & Cable, G. W. (1976). Illustrations, analogies and facilitative transfer in prose learning. *Journal of Educational Psychology, 68*, 205–209.

Rumelhart, D. E. (1980). Schemata: The building blocks of cognition. In R. J. Spiro, B. C. Bruce, & W. F. Brewer (Eds.), *Theoretical issues in reading comprehension* (pp. 33–58). Hillsdale, NJ: Erlbaum.

Schallert, D. L. (1976). Improving memory for prose: The relationship between depth of processing and context. *Journal of Verbal Learning and Verbal Behavior, 15,* 621–632.

Schallert, D. L. (1980). The role of illustrations in reading comprehension. In R. J. Spiro, B. C. Bruce, & W. F. Brewer (Eds.), *Theoretical issues in reading comprehension* (pp. 503–524). Hillsdale, NJ: Erlbaum.

Schallert, D. L. (1982). The significance of knowledge: A synthesis of research related to schema theory. In W. Otto & J. White (Eds.), *Reading expository material* (pp. 13–48). New York: Academic Press.

Schmid, R. F., & Kulhavy, R. W. (1981). Theme and prose comprehension: Understanding or depth-of-processing. *Contemporary Educational Psychology, 6,* 66–75.

Schwartz, N. H., & Kulhavy, R. W. (1981). Map features and the recall of discourse. *Contemporary Educational Psychology, 6,* 151–158.

Spiro, R. J. (1980). Constructive processes in prose comprehension and recall. In R. J. Spiro, B. C. Bruce, & W. F. Brewer (Eds.), *Theoretical issues in reading comprehension* (pp. 245–278). Hillsdale, NJ: Erlbaum.

Swenson, I., & Kulhavy, R. W. (1974). Adjunct questions and the comprehension of prose by children. *Journal of Educational Psychology, 66,* 212–215.

Thorndyke, P. (1977). Cognitive structures in comprehension and memory of connected discourse. *Cognitive Psychology, 9,* 77–110.

Thorndyke, P. W., & Yekovich, F. R. (1980). A critique of schemata as a theory of human story memory. *Poetics, 9,* 23–49.

Tulving, E. (1979). Relation between encoding specificity and level of processing. In L. S. Cermak & F. I. M. Craik (Eds.), *Levels of processing and human memory* (pp. 405–428). Hillsdale, NJ: Erlbaum.

Watts, G., & Anderson, R. C. (1971). Effects of three types of inserted questions on learning from prose. *Journal of Educational Psychology, 62,* 387–394.

Wixson, K. K. (1984). Level of importance of postquestions and children's learning from text. *American Educational Research Journal, 21,* 419–433.

Yates, F. A. (1966). *The art of memory.* London: Routledge.

PRACTICE AND SKILLED CLASSROOM PERFORMANCE

Gary D. Phye

Department of Psychology
Iowa State University
Ames, Iowa 50011

I. INTRODUCTION

In this chapter, the topic is practice and skilled performance. The effects of practice on the development of cognitive skills are reviewed, and suggestions are made for the incorporation of cognitive skill development into a model of study behavior.

In section II, the nature of a cognitive skill is discussed and consideration is given to how skills are acquired. Based on a two-process model of skill development by Shiffrin and Schneider (1977), cognitive skills are defined in terms of controlled and automatic processing. Following the discussion of the Shiffrin and Schneider model that is generic in nature, Anderson's model (1982) of skill acquisition is reviewed. This model is similar to the Shiffrin model in that it is also a two-process model based on controlled and automatic processing. A third view of skill acquisition, an iterative model, has been proposed by Hayes-Roth, Klahr, and Mostow (1981). The iterative model is viewed as complementary to the previously discussed models. The iterative model is based on the idea that following the try-out of new knowledge, a number of potential problems and learning opportunities exist.

In a classroom situation, advice by a teacher is usually provided when a student is asked to acquire new knowledge. This advice usually takes the form of rules, concepts, or heuristics. New learning is not required when the advice is successful in meeting new demands. On the other hand, learning occurs following an episode where expectations of success are not met and errors are made that must be corrected. Thus, learning is seen as the correction of errors and the modification of existing schemata. It is the error analysis component of the iterative model that makes it unique.

The final topic in section II is a discussion of expert performance. The role of practice over a period of years is seen as crucial in the development of skill demonstrated by eminent mathematicians, musicians, and sports figures.

COGNITIVE CLASSROOM LEARNING:
UNDERSTANDING, THINKING, AND PROBLEM SOLVING

This discussion serves as a lead-in to section III, which is devoted to the topic of practice.

Section III is divided into three major subsections: (1) einstellung, (2) practice schedules, and (3) processing variables necessary for improvement to occur as a result of practice. *Einstellung* is discussed within the context of a narrowing of focus as a result of practice that may produce a deleterious effect when more than one strategy can be used for problem solution. Practice schedules are discussed in terms of the influences of whole or part practice, massed or distributed practice, and the timing of the initial practice session. These factors are considered in terms of their impact on skill acquisition. The section on processing variables includes a discussion of the concept of feedback and the role of informative feedback in skill acquisition. The nature of feedback and its corrective or confirmatory functions are introduced within the context of error analysis. The role of error analysis and diagnosis within the context of practice and skill acquisition is presented as an iterative approach to instruction and classroom learning.

Section IV provides a summary statement about the role of practice in skill acquisition. Also, the presentation topics are related to a call for the development of an educational psychology of studying (Rohwer, 1984).

II. COGNITIVE SKILL

In previous chapters, consideration has been given to the role of various memory components (e.g., attention and working memory) involved in the process of learning. Each chapter author has provided examples of how these components function and the role they play in classroom learning. The present chapter is an attempt to integrate some of the current research findings that relate to skilled performance in the classroom.

How does a consideration of cognitive skills relate to the processing components discussed in the preceding chapters? Such a relationship has been developed elsewhere (Hudgins, Phye, Shau, Theissen, Ames, & Ames, 1983) and can be conceptualized as a hierarchical arrangement involving a combination of superordinate–subordinate relationships among academic tasks, cognitive skills, and cognitive processes (see Table 1).

The list of cognitive skills in Table 1 is certainly not exhaustive. This becomes obvious when one reflects on the content of other chapters. In this section, the focus is on defining what is meant by *skill* and exploring how *skill* is acquired.

A commonly heard maxim is that "practice makes perfect." This should be corrected to read "almost always, practice brings improvement and more practice brings more improvement" (Newell & Rosenbloom, 1981). In a real

TABLE 1 Hierarchy of Cognitive Tasks, Skills, and Processes

Cognitive academic tasks
  Language development
  Reading
  Mathematics
  Writing
Cognitive skills
  Thinking skills (inductive and deductive reasoning)
  Comprehension skills
  Attention skills
  Remembering skills
  Study skills
  Transfer skills
  Inferential skills
  Problem-solving skills
  Critical thinking skills
  Creative thinking skills
Cognitive processes
  Attention
  Short-term memory
  Working memory
  Long-term memory
  Metacognition

Note. From Hudgins et al. (1983).

sense, a skill is a highly overlearned rule, schema, etc., that is initially processed in a slow, halting, error-prone fashion to a point that through practice it becomes fast, automatic, and relatively error free. Practice used to be a basic topic in many educational psychology texts, in some cases even being a separate chapter (e.g., Ausubel, 1968; Ausubel & Robinson, 1969). At the present time, many texts devote only a page or two, if that, to the topic. But as Newell and Rosenbloom point out, in the first edition of Woodworth's *Experimental Psychology*, the statement was made that "there is no essential difference between practice and learning except that the practice experiment takes longer" (Newell & Rosenbloom, 1981, p. 1). Consequently, practice has not remained a separate topic but has become a term for talking about learning skills through the repetition of their performance.

The concept of practice as a means of promoting skill acquisition in motor learning has continued to appear in both the research literature and physical education classrooms. However, a comparable interest in multiple trial learning (practice) has not been as persistent in the verbal learning literature.

A. The Nature of a Skill

In the generic sense, what is a skill? If desired, one could list a number of individual skills said to be necessary for competence in any academic task. While such a list would be descriptive, it would not address the issue of "what is the nature or role of a skill in human information processing?"

For present purposes, a *skill* can be viewed as a highly developed sequence of procedures that acquire the characteristics of automatic processing. An *automatic process* is a set of highly practiced sequences (schema, plans, frames, etc.) that provides the basis for an integration of processing components. For example, good readers are those students who understand what they are reading without consciously paying attention to such things as the number of eye fixations per line of text, organizing what is being read so that it can be related to existing knowledge, or going into long-term memory to decode the meaning of a word, etc. This emphasis on automatic as well as controlled processing is a current focus in cognitive psychology (Gagne, 1985). The development of automatic processes seem to be predicated on practice. Practice gives rise to a high level of error-free performance that we designate as skill. Here, concern is only with those automatic procedural sequences we call cognitive skills.

B. A Model of Skill Development

Where do skills fit into the picture when considering learning in the classroom? Going back to Table 1, it becomes apparent that many of the teaching activities in a classroom are devoted to the learning and refinement of cognitive skills. In some cases, the current Zeitgeist (spirit of the times) of "back to the basics" is defined in terms of basic skills like critical thinking, problem solving, studying, etc. When these cognitive skills are developed to such a high level that their appropriate use is highly automatic, one makes reference to the skilled learner. So what is implied is a highly specific mode of information processing that requires little or no conscious monitoring. These highly developed schemata, rules, procedures, plans, etc., involve sequences of processing stored in long-term memory storage that, along with controlled processing in short-term working memory, provides the basis for skilled performance.

Automatic and Controlled Processing

A formal model of automatic and controlled processing is the two-process theory of human information processing proposed by Shiffrin and colleagues (Schneider & Shiffrin, 1977; Shiffrin & Dumais, 1981; Shiffrin & Schneider, 1977). This two-process theory identifies controlled and automatic processing as the basis for human information processing. Controlled processing involves the conscious processing of information, frequently referred to as working memory. Automatic processing involves overlearned schema or sequences stored in long-term memory. Once activated, automatic processing operates independently of a learner's conscious control. These automatic sequences located in long-term memory were originally learned via conscious effort (controlled processing). In other words, skilled performance is based on the automatic processing of sequences originally learned as a result of conscious effort. Through practice, the overlearned sequences stored in long-term memory can be automatically processed once they have been activated via controlled processing (working memory) or stimuli from the environment.

> *Automatic processing* [emphasis mine] is activation of a learned sequence of elements in long term memory that is initiated by appropriate inputs and then proceeds automatically—without subject control, without stressing the capacity limitations of the system, and without necessarily demanding attention. *Controlled processing* [emphasis mine] is a temporary activation of a sequence of elements that can be set up quickly and easily but requires attention, is capacity limited [usually serial in nature], and is controlled by the subject. (Schneider & Shiffrin, 1977, p. 1)

A student involved in classroom learning uses both types of processing. For example, a skilled reader, reading material aloud for the first time, can think about what is being read (comprehension) while not paying attention to such automatic skills as number of fixations per line of text, having a good return sweep to the left margin, good word attack skills, phonic skills, etc. Examples of skilled writers or mathematicians could also be developed. From the context provided in the present volume, we could probably substitute the concept of schema, rule, or plan, for Shiffrin and Schneider's concept of a collection of nodes. Conceptually, one could also substitute Royer's neurogen theory based on a biological metaphor without violating the basic heuristic value of the two-process theory. As will be noted shortly, Anderson (1982,1985) has incorporated some basic elements of the two-process theory in his model of skill acquisition that is associationistic in nature (Anderson, 1976).

A controlled process is under the conscious control of the learner. Because a controlled process requires the attention of a learner, only a single sequence may be controlled at a time. Also, because a controlled process utilizes short-term store in working memory, it is also capacity limited. Further, controlled processing may involve input of information from receptors or the retrieval of information from long-term memory store. Conversely, an automatic process is located in long-term memory store and may be activated in response to inputs from outside the learner or from short-term memory store. The schema, plan, skill, etc., that has become an automatic process is activated automatically without the necessity of active control or attention. Hence the possibility of the parallel processing of a controlled and automatic sequence of cognitive activities (e.g., our oral reading example).

C. SKILL ACQUISITION

A more detailed account of how skills are learned is provided by Anderson (1982,1985). Anderson has proposed a stage theory of skill acquisition that incorporates elements of the aforementioned two-process theory, the work of Fitts (1964), and the ACT model of language, memory, and thought (Anderson, 1976; Anderson & Bower, 1973). For a detailed explanation of the acquisition process, the reader is referred to the *Psychological Review* article "Acquisition of cognitive skill" (Anderson, 1982).

Briefly, Anderson proposes a two-stage learning model of skill acquisition that includes a declarative stage and a procedural stage. The *declarative stage* involves declarative knowledge that consists of information and/or facts. This declarative stage marks the initial point in the learning process where the learner knows facts or has information about what is to be learned. This stage is where facts or information about the learning task is interpreted and encoded in terms of a general problem-solving strategy or schema appropriate to the task at hand. In order to get to a point where the learner can use the facts and information to produce a solution or product, a transition must be made to the *procedural stage*, where a person "knows how" to use the facts and/or information. Once the procedural stage has been reached, continued practice will produce a level of proficiency characterized by relatively rapid, error-free performance that has domain specific (geometry, reading, algebra, writing, etc.) application.

An overview of the ACT acquisition model is provided in Table 2. This skeleton is not intended to be complete and any errors of misrepresentation are strictly the responsibility of the present author.

What we generally call *practice* would involve the transition of knowledge from the declarative stage to the procedural stage and beyond. In fact, much learning goes on after a skill has been compiled into a task specific procedure. As can be noted in Table 2, the processes of generalization, discrimination, and strengthening are operative. Generalization is the ability to apply procedures adequately in a new or novel situation. The discrimination process restricts the range of application of procedures to those most appropriate. In order for the discrimination process to work, both negative feedback indicating an error and information as to what the correct action should be must be available to the learner. The strengthening process in the ACT model is analogous to the concepts of positive reinforcement and punishment. The strengthening process provides the basis for increasing the

TABLE 2   ACT Model—Stages of Skill Acquisition

Skill encoding	Stage 1:	*Declarative stage*	
		Component:	Short-term working memory
		Processes:	Initial encoding and general interpretation of facts about skill domain to be learned. This is the development of general problem-solving strategy relative to the task at hand (e.g., geometry problems, chemistry problems)
Skill transition		*Knowledge compilation:*	The process by which a skill transits from the declarative stage (Stage 1) to the procedural stage (Stage 2)
		Components:	Short-term and long-term working memory
		Processes:	Composition and proceduralization
			Composition takes sequences of productions that follow each other in a problem strategy and collapses them into a single prodution
			Proceduralization eliminates clauses in the condition of a production that requires information to be retrieved from long-term memory and held in working memory
Skill refinement	Stage 2:	*Procedural stage*	
		Components:	Long-term working memory, metamemory
		Processes:	Declarative knowledge has become proceduralized and procedures undergo continual refinement as a result of processes of (1) generalization, (2) discrimination, and (3) the strengthening of procedures

strength of an appropriate application of a procedure and lessening the strength of an incorrect application.

In summary, I refer the reader back to Table 1 and the hierarchy of academic tasks, cognitive skills, and processes. A bit of reflection on what we have required of teachers would suggest that most of their training and most of what they teach are related to the first level—cognitive tasks. I have tried to make the case that cognitive skills of one type or another are integral parts of any academic task. Unfortunately, when we train prospective teachers, we tend to ignore cognitive skills. Assuming that skills are basic to the successful mastery of an academic task, how can teachers offer corrective remediation, prompts, guidance, etc., unless they are aware of the role of cognitive skills?

Further, what about those instances when a learner cannot engage in appropriate information processing because of a component weakness or disability. Again, most teachers are better prepared to modify the physical classroom environment than identify or diagnose processing errors involving component or skill deficits. Many such learners get diagnosed learning disabled and removed from the regular classroom. This may be appropriate in such cases as dyslexia that would be an instance of a component disability. However, I suspect that the majority of students labeled "learning disabled" suffer from a skill deficiency that could be dealt with by a regular classroom teacher with an understanding of the learning process.

D.   ADVICE TAKING AND KNOWLEDGE REFINEMENT

An iterative view of skill acquisition has been proposed by Hayes-Roth, Klahr, and Mostow (1981). The iterative view should not be viewed as a model of skill acquisition that is in opposition to the Shiffrin–Schneider (1977) or the Anderson (1982) models. Rather, it could be viewed as an extension and complement.

The theoretical focus underlying the Hayes-Roth et al. model differs from that of earlier models. The *iterative view of development* is one that emphasizes the dynamic nature of change and assumes that as change occurs, the nature of the acquisition process changes both quantitatively and qualitatively. The iterative view has a long history in the cognitive developmental literature. An iterative model is one that builds upon itself in a repetitive manner. Following the try-out of new knowledge, a number of potential problems and learning opportunities exists. A diagnosis of potential problems and errors stimulates a refinement of previous knowledge. At this point, the cycle is reinitiated and the refined knowledge is tried out.

Hayes-Roth et al. assume that when we acquire intellectual skill, three types of knowledge are learned. These include (1) concepts and algorithms within an area or domain, (2) increasingly effective means for achieving goals in that area or domain, and (3) an improved awareness of the consequences of our plans. More frequently, these three types of knowledge have been referred to as "knowing," "knowing how," and "knowing how to know," respectively. "Knowing" is frequently used as a synonym for declarative knowledge. For example, "knowing" consists of information such as concepts and algorithms that are domain specific. Reference by Hayes-Roth et al. to an increasingly effective means for achieving goals in a domain appears to be comparable to "knowing how." In this instance, "knowing how" means being able to appropriately use the knowledge one has. An improved awareness of the consequences of one's plans appears comparable to the metacognitive skill of "knowing how to know." This skill involves an awareness that the present problem is similar to problems successfully solved in the past using the concepts and/or algorithms used successfully in the past.

Because most intellectual skills are acquired in a formal educational setting, some form of instruction is typically available. The learner must also learn via experience when new knowledge is tried out. Consequently, Hayes-Roth et al. have proposed a two-phase learning cycle. The *first phase* requires the learner to follow the advice of an instructor. In the first phase of learning, advice is provided in the form of concepts, rules, heuristics, etc., that define a domain. However, before learners can use the advice, they must interpret it and relate it to previous knowledge. This process of understanding has transformed the advice into knowledge that can be used. Actual putting the knowledge to use in the form of plans or strategies and carrying out the plans produces the behavior that the advice initiated. The *first phase* of the learning cycle involves the acquisition of declarative knowledge and the transformation of declarative knowledge to procedural knowledge, as demonstrated by the learner trying to use concepts and/or algorithms for problem solution.

Typically, this processing is not learned in a single trial, and errors occur. These errors may arise from several sources as information is transformed from declarative to procedural knowledge and must be diagnosed and rectified. These activities initiate the *second phase* of the learning cycle. In this phase, errors are diagnosed and the knowledge base constructed in Phase 1 is refined.

Errors can arise from several sources. The learner might have misinterpreted the advice that was initially offered. Second, the plan or heuristic that was developed to guide behavior might be wrong. Also, the plan or heuristic might be appropriate, but its implementation might be faulty. In each case, the learner must reevaluate and refine knowledge and/or strategies in accordance with the diagnosed deficiencies. It is this error-analysis feature of the advice-taking model that makes it unique as an acquisition model. This model largely ignores positive learning cycles that are assumed to be strengthened as a result of successful completion and focuses on negative learning experiences that require diagnosis and refinement.

The implications of such a focus is that new learning is not required when advice (a plan, concept, or heuristic) is successful in meeting expectations. In other words, learning is triggered when errors occur and our expectations of success are violated. "We can think of behavior as theory driven, because behaviors derived from assumptions, plans and theoretically appropriate transformations of expressions; learning is triggered by events that disconfirm the expectable consequences of such theories" (Hayes-Roth, Klahr, & Mostow, 1981, p. 243). From this perspective, a skilled learner is one who is adept at Phase 2 activities within an area or domain. Also, the learner who has attained a high degree of ability to "know how to know" within an area is frequently referred to as an expert.

E. EXPERT PERFORMANCE

As has been mentioned in various chapters, the examination of performance differences between experts and novices has become a topic of considerable interest. The various skill areas that have been explored include, among others, chess (Chase & Simon, 1973), physics (Larkin, McDermott, Simon, & Simon, 1980), algebra (Lewis, 1981), and the social sciences (Voss, Tyler, & Yengo, 1983). The focus in these studies has been attempts to identify how experts and novices process information differently when engaged in particular tasks. Keep in mind that the processing differences are observed relative to the skill under observation (e.g., chess or algebra). Processing differences of a general nature that cut across skill domains have not been observed. In other words, the expert chess master may have no processing advantages on tasks other than playing chess. Processing differences between experts and novices is not the focus of the present chapter. Rather, I want to introduce the topic of practice by considering its role in the *development* of expert performance.

Bloom (1982,1986) has begun to publish results of a 3-year study of talent. The subjects in this study were world-class Olympic swimmers, pianists, and research mathematicians. All of these individuals had attained "world class" status in their fields prior to the age of 35. Three characteristics possessed by all participants in the study appeared to transcend the particular fields of sport, music, or mathematics. The three characteristics that made these persons good students in their chosen fields were (1) an unusual willingness to practice, (2) great competitiveness, and (3) the ability to rapidly learn new techniques, ideas, or processes in the talent field.

Interestingly, the first characteristic (willingness to work to achieve a high standard) was not present at early ages (5 to 8 years), but it became apparent following several years of instruction. This willingness to work or practice appears to be related to early socialization in the home and the early training provided by teachers. "In general, it was discovered that during a minimum of at least 10 years all of the individuals had devoted more time, energy, and thought to their talent areas than to any other activity or area of their life" (Bloom, 1982; p. 511).

III. PRACTICE

From our discussion of skill acquisition, it is obvious that practice is essential for automatic processing to develop. When analyzing the suggestion "of no essential difference between practice and learning except that the practice experiment takes longer" (Newell & Rosenbloom, 1981; p. 1), one comes to the conclusion that components involved in learning are also involved in practice. The distinguishing feature that characterizes the practice experiment is repetition. As a result of practice, commonly observed effects of repetition are an increase in the speed of task completion, a decrease in error rate, and a decrease in flexibility (Einstellung effect).

Langley and Simon (1981) have specifically addressed the central role of learning in cognition. By implication, practice plays a major role in any attempt to explain an increase in the efficiency (increased speed and decreased error rate) with which the learner performs. This information-processing perspective gives rise to certain basic principles that define the conditions under which learning through practice can take place. Although the list is not exhaustive, Langley and Simon (1981) have identified six of the most prominent and central conditions for learning from an information-processing perspective. These conditions include (1) knowledge of results, (2) generation of alternatives, (3) causal attribution, (4) hindsight, (5) learning from instruction and (6) automation.

Generally speaking, in order for practice to be effective, the learner must be able to detect improvement or degradation in performance. Thus, knowledge of results is essential in any practice situation. In the recent psychological literature, *knowledge of results* is a cognitive mechanism that provides information used to monitor practice. This cognitive mechanism is one side of the coin called *reinforcement*, that also embraces a motivational mechanism called *reward*. Here, because of our cognitive frame of reference, we are concerned only with the knowledge-of-results issue of reinforcement.

This ability of the learner to monitor performance through the use of knowledge of results must be coupled with the ability to *generate alternatives*. This is particularly the case when knowledge of results indicates an impasse in the increase in speed of task completion and a decrease in error rate, or a degeneration in performance. The analysis of errors can contribute greatly to the learning process only if new behaviors can be attempted. The ability to use knowledge of results to identify types of errors and then generate alternative modes of performance can occur only if the learner can successfully identify the source and nature of the error(s). Students can learn from mistakes only if they can discover the source of their errors (causal attribution). In a real sense, we are talking about aspects of metacognitive functioning discussed in Chapter 8. Because knowledge of results follows performance, hindsight must be used to analyze and improve performance. *Hindsight* (a metacognitive skill?) involves the reexamination and reevaluation of past performance in light of knowledge of results and causal attribution received following performance. This principle of learning is known to most good students and to a relatively few poor students.

According to this view, the repetition (practice) of a learning event must contain provisions for knowledge of results, an opportunity to generate alternative responses, the ability to identify the source of good or poor performance and then the use of such information in a manner called *hindsight* in order for automation to occur which is characterized by an improvement in speed and accuracy of performance.

The effects of practice can be facilitated by instruction. As we have seen in previous chapters, a teacher can provide knowledge of results, information to be encoded, the organization to be used in encoding, knowledge about the source of good performance or errors, and the use of hindsight. Also, the upcoming chapter on learning strategies is predicated on the assumption that instruction during practice facilitates the learning of complex skills.

A.   EINSTELLUNG EFFECT

In this discussion of practice, we have emphasized the characteristics of (1) increase in speed and (2) accuracy in performance as a result of repetition. It must also be acknowledged that performance may at some point reach a plateau, in which case new alternatives in responding must be considered. It appears that the observed plateau (no increase in speed or accuracy) may be the result of the Einstellung effect (the set which predisposes a learner to one type of motor or conscious act).

While practice provides the basis for an increase in speed and accuracy, there is a potential trade-off effect. The price one pays as speed and accuracy increase is a growing inflexibility and a resistance to adopting or generating alternatives. This resistance to change was first reported in the problem-solving literature by Luchins (1942). Although the Einstellung effect was observed in several different kinds of tasks, the most well-known experiment was the water-jar problem. The basic task and the problems used to demonstrate the effect are given in Table 3.

Subjects were told that they had three empty jars they could use to obtain a specified amount of water. They could use the jars in any combination they wished as long as they obtained the exact specified amount. They could not use any other measuring devices.

The first problem in Table 1 can be solved in two steps using two jars. The successful strategy can be proceduralized using the formula A − 3B. However, Problems 2 through 6 are more complex because three jars must be used and more steps are required for successful solution. Problem 2 can be proceduralized using the formula B − A − 2C. Both problems were given as examples with solutions provided.

Then, subjects were told to practice using problems 3 (E_2) through 11 (C_4). Problems were presented on the blackboard one at a time at intervals of

TABLE 3   Example of Luchin's Water Jar Type Problems

Problems	Given the following empty jars as measures			Obtain the required amount of water
	Jar A	Jar B	Jar C	
1	21	2	—	15
2 E_1	20	115	3	89
3 E_2	24	153	5	119
4 E_3	20	43	2	19
5 E_4	8	32	3	18
6 E_5	30	69	4	31
7 C_1	26	58	6	20
8 C_2	15	39	3	18
9	30	84	2	28
10 C_3	20	58	6	26
11 C_4	18	42	6	12

$2\frac{1}{2}$ minutes, or more often if students required less time. If a person works problems 3 (E_2) through 6 (E_5), it becomes obvious the B − A − 2C strategy is successful. At this point, verify for yourself that while the B − A − 2C strategy works for problems 7 (C_1) and 8 (C_2), a more simple and direct solution for problem 7 is A − C and for problem 8 A + C. In the original study, not one of the subjects (Ph.D. or M.D. degree holders) used the more direct method in problems 7 and 8. Problem 9 cannot be solved using the B − A − 2C formula. But, it can be easily solved using an A − C strategy. The effect of problem 9 was to improve performance on problems 10 (C_3) and 11 (C_4), in that there was a 15% increase in the number of subjects using the simpler more direct A + C and A − C strategies.

Einstellung is "the set which immediately predisposes an organism to one type of motor or conscious act" (Luchins, 1942, p. 3). In the water-jar experiment, problems 2 through 6 were problems that generated the Einstellung effect for problems 7 and 8. The Einstellung effect was demonstrated when subjects used the B − A − 2C formula and not the more simple and direct A − C (Problem 7) and A + C (Problem 8) strategies.

B. TASK VARIABLES

Ausubel (1968) and Ausubel and Robinson (1969) devoted a chapter to the topic of practice. However, current authors tend not to give much attention to the topic. It is hoped that the current interest in "study behavior" will regenerate interest in practice. This lack of interest in the topic can be observed in many classroom activities. The Zeitgeist during the decade of the 1970s seemed to be one where the practices of homework, skill development, drill and practice, and structured seatwork was deemphasized. The process of schooling was supposed to be fun, and practice looked too much like work. The current Zeitgeist suggests that while the socialization and social skill aspect of the schooling process may be fun, the development of academic skills entails work in the form of practice. While the recent decline in SAT scores is, no doubt, due to a multitude of factors, I am convinced that a decline in emphasis on practice and skill development has been a contributing factor.

Major variables to be considered when designing an optimal practice schedule are the task variables of (1) the nature of practice and (2) distribution of practice. Both of these variables are influenced by such factors as the subject matter being practiced, and the age of the learner. Of course, consideration must be given to the outcome of practice. Is the objective one of short-term retention (studying for next exam and then forgetting it), long-term retention (acquiring skills that can be used again and again throughout academic career), or transfer (the ability to use acquired skills when appropriate, independent of subject matter)?

1. Whole versus Part Practice

One of the first considerations when developing a practice schedule is the nature of the practice session. Should one try to cover the whole assignment at one time, or should the task be broken into smaller parts? In the latter case, the student practices parts of the assignment independently and then puts the parts together. As one would guess, it is difficult to state unequivocally which approach is best for all students. In reality, this decision must be made by the learner on the basis of trial and error with various subject matters. A student with good reading skills may be able to read an entire chapter and organize it for further study. A student with less ability or skill may cover only the first half of the chapter during the first study period and the rest of the chapter on the next day. In addition to the ability dimension and its influence on how much can be covered in one sitting, the age of the learner is an influencing factor. For instance, a fifth grader can memorize the Declaration of Independence as well as a tenth grader. However, the fifth-grader will probably have to learn and practice the speech one paragraph at a time while the tenth-grader might tackle the speech in its entirety. One last example of the relative nature of what is meant by whole or part learning comes to mind in terms of subject matter.

As a college undergraduate, I found that a chapter of 30 to 50 pages in the social sciences was about right for a single study period. In other words, the whole chapter was studied at one sitting. However, when reading a chapter in a chemistry text, the progress was much slower. Typically, a chapter would be divided in half and covered in two sittings on successsive days. Thus, when reviewing (practicing) a chapter in psychology, the chapter would be studied in its entirety. However, when reviewing chemistry, the first part of a chapter would be studied and then the last half of the chapter reviewed at another time. To complicate things a bit further, when breaking a study assignment into parts for practice, three possibilities exist. These possibilities include (1) the pure part method, (2) the progressive part method, and (3) the repetitive part method (McGeogh & Irion, 1952). Again, using the Declaration of Independence as an example, the three part methods can be demonstrated. For purposes of demonstration, assume that the Declaration of Independence has been divided into three parts (A, B, & C).

In the *pure part method*, each subpart would be practiced separately, starting with subpart A. If the criterion is one perfect recitation, subpart A is practiced until the learner can recite the material with no errors. Then, subpart B is practiced in the same way. When B can be recited with no errors, subpart C is practiced in the same manner. When the last subpart has been recited perfectly, all subparts are put together (A, B, & C) and practiced as a whole until the entire speech can be recited perfectly.

The *progressive part method* is like the pure part method up to a point. For instance, subpart A is practiced until mastery occurs, and then subpart B is practiced in the same way. At this point, rather than attack subpart C as would be the case in the pure part method, subparts A and B are combined and practiced until the criterion of a perfect recitation is reached. Only then does the learner attack subpart C and practice until the criterion is reached. When subpart C is mastered, subpart A and B is combined with subpart C until the entire task (A & B, + C) is mastered. With this practice strategy, the learner is dealing with two parts of a task with the initial subpart becoming progressively larger as practive proceeds.

The *repetitive part method* is the last part-practice strategy considered. Here, the learner first masters subpart A. Then, subpart A is combined with subpart B to produce subpart A&B, which is then practiced. When subpart A&B is mastered, subpart C is combined with part A&B to produce A&B + C (the whole task), which is then practiced until mastery is reached.

These part-practice strategies are simply various combinations of new learning and review, which we call *practice*. The most effective strategy for any learner is undoubtedly influenced by such factors as age and ability, meaningfulness of the task, the type of subject matter, and subject matter sophistication. A learner's ability to adopt the study strategy best suited to her or his needs is certainly demonstrating the type of metacognition referred to by Brown (1981) as "regulation of cognition activities" (see Chapter

8 of this volume). Quite obviously, these practice approaches could be incorporated into the development of learning tactics and strategies to be used within the context of training and/or instruction. It would appear that such practice strategies would facilitate the encoding processes employed by working memory when attempting to store information in long-term memory.

2. Massed versus Distributed Practice

While the part–whole schedule addresses practice strategies in terms of quantity or the size of a learning assignment, the massed vs. distributed practice schedule addresses the issue of timing of practice. Obviously, the part versus whole and massed versus distributed practice schedule issues are not independent. A student studying for a weekly quiz or a midterm exam considers both the size of the assignment and the test date when developing a study strategy. However, for didactic purposes, the two topics have been separated.

The massed versus distributed practice issue has a history comparable to that of the part versus whole practice issue (Ausubel, 1968; Stroud, 1942). Nonetheless, recent research has focused more on the issue of massed versus distributed practice (Zechmeister & Nyberg, 1982). This possibly is due to the less nebulous nature of the massed versus distributed practice strategy because this strategy is more easily and clearly operationalized. It should also be recognized that in certain instances, a part or whole practice strategy may be identical to a distributed or massed practice strategy. But, this need *not* be the case. For example, a student studying a chapter for a weekly quiz may read the chapter in its entirety (whole method) on Wednesday and Thursday for Friday's quiz (distributed practice). An alternative strategy might be to use the pure part method on Thursday night in order to cover the chapter twice that night (massed practice).

In the classroom, we frequently tell students that cramming (massed practice) the night before an exam is not a good practice strategy. Is this truism accurate? As one would guess, the answer is not straightforward. First of all, if the cramming session is an all-night session or one that lasts until the early hours, fatigue becomes a confounding factor. For example, if one stays up all night to study for an exam at 10:00 a.m. and must attend 8:00 a.m. and 9:00 a.m. classes prior to the exam, fatigue will influence the efficiency with which you can retrieve information or solve problems on a timed test regardless of how well the material was learned the night before. However, if we assume the assignment is a short one and can be learned by regular bedtime, fatigue is not a factor. Now, what does the literature say about the massed versus distributed practice issue?

A review of the current research literature pertaining to the distributed versus massed practice controversy has been provided by Zechmeister and Nyberg (1982). An overall conclusion reached by these authors is that when fatigue is not a confounding factor, no difference exists in the total amount of time to learn material regardless of strategy. However, when the issue is one of long-term retention, the situation changes. In this instance, distributed practice promotes better long-term retention for verbal materials than does massed practice. If you are enrolled in a course having 3-hour exams and a comprehensive final, cramming (massed practice) may produce as good a grade on an hourly exam as distributed practice—provided fatigue is not a factor. However, it is on the comprehensive final where distributed study appears to pay off in terms of better memory storage. Consequently, if one can do as well on hourly exams using distributed practice and at the same time ensure yourself of better performance on the comprehensive final, distributed practice would appear to be one's first choice as a study schedule. It would follow that an undergraduate who uses a distributed practice study schedule should experience positive transfer from one exam to another within a course. Also, this student should, theoretically, require less time to review for a comprehensive final exam than a student who used a massed practice study strategy.

3. Timing of Initial Practice Session

When a lesson (text, list of spelling words, names of presidents, etc.) has been covered for the first time, should a review be introduced immediately or at a later point in time? Should you review classnotes immediately following class? This issue has not been unequivocally answered, although the issue has significant implications for a student's study habits.

This line of research has dealt with the question of whether or not immediate feedback is better than delayed feedback in improving performance when learning meaningful material. One of the primary postulates of operant conditioning theory is that immediate feedback is superior to delayed feedback (Skinner, 1968). However, the "delayed retention effect" has been found with some types of classroom tasks like prose learning (Peeck & Tillema, 1978; Sturges, 1969), multiple-choice test performance (Kulhavy & Anderson, 1972), written instruction (Kulhavy, 1977), and computer-assisted testing (Sturges, 1978). The delayed-retention effect states that delayed feedback is superior to immediate feedback when dealing with meaningful verbal material. The explanations for this phenomenon have ranged from the "interference perseveration hypothesis" (Kulhavy & Anderson, 1972), to a "depth of processing and spread of encoding" explanation (Peeck & Tillema, 1978; Sturges, 1978). Not all of the research investigating the "delayed retention effect" has been supportive. Published studies that have failed to support a "delayed retention effect" have investigated such tasks as prose learning (Phye & Baller, 1970), multiple-choice test performance (Phye, 1979; Phye, Gugliemella, & Sola, 1976), and other forms of classroom learning (Newman, Williams, & Hiller, 1974; White, 1968).

This lack of agreement as to the occurrence of the delayed retention effect is hardly surprising when considering such factors as (1) what is meant by feedback, (2) nature of learning tasks, (3) differing definitions of "immediate" and "delayed," and (4) two differing paradigms to test for the "delayed retention" effect. Kulhavy (1977) has pointed out that definitions of feedback have varied considerably in the research literature. Such terms as knowledge of results, knowledge of correct response, knowledge of response, correctional review, et cetera, have appeared in the literature, and all deal with feedback issues. Further, a review of individual studies supports the position that "If we are willing to treat feedback as a unitary variable, we can speak of its form or composition as ranging along a continuum from the simplest 'yes–no' format to the presentation of substantial corrective or remedial information that may extend the response content, or even add new material to it," (Kulhavy, 1977, p. 212).

Adding further confusion, the complexity of tasks have ranged from a simple discrimination task (Brackbill, Bravos, & Starr, 1962), through prose material especially prepared for the experiment (Sassenrath & Yonge, 1969), to a regularly scheduled exam in an educational psychology class (Phye & Baller, 1970). Also, immediate and delayed intervals have varied widely in the way they were operationally defined. In some studies, immediate feedback is provided following each test item, while in others, immediate feedback is defined as feedback given immediately following the completion of the entire set of items (i.e., multiple-choice test). With such variation in the nature of tasks, the nature of feedback, and the timing of feedback, it is not surprising that there is a lack of consensus as to the occurrence of the "delayed retention effect."

4. Drill

Drill in the classroom has undergone periods of favor and disfavor. In an early review of practice in the classroom, Stroud (1942) traced the history of practice and drill. Enthusiasm for drill has waxed and waned over the years and we are presently coming out of a period when drill in the form of spelling words, math problems, and oral reading was frowned upon. However, the current Zeitgeist, which calls for a return to the "basics" suggests a renewed interest and an awareness that skilled performance is in part predicated on the automatic processing of subskills acquired through drill.

As was noted in the foregoing discussion of practice, the basic principles of drill and practice have been available for the past 30 to 50 years. What we are currently seeing in the research literature is a renewed interest in using these principles in combination with new research paradigms in an attempt to improve skill development. For instance, Snowman reviews the literature on learning strategies in Chapter 9. A careful reading of this literature reveals that principles of drill and practice are incorporated into many of the learning strategies that have been devised to promote the acquisition of academic skills. Also, Duell's discussion of self-monitoring as a metacognitive skill reveals elements of practice and drill. In other words, when a student is asked to master complex academic subject matter and demonstrate such cognitive skills as critical thinking or problem solving, practice in the form of multiple trials and/or drill on essential subtasks is critical to the learning process.

Technical innovations have also set the stage for a renewed interest in drill. Specifically, the microcomputer in the classroom makes possible the use of software designed to promote the practice and drill of subject matter content. The teacher no longer has to be physically present (e.g., flash card drill in math) in order to carry out drill and practice in the classroom. The microcomputer and available software make possible individualized practice and drill sessions. In this respect, the microcomputer is viewed as a teaching aid that allows the teacher to focus on other aspects of teaching. In this regard, the computer ensures that drill and practice can be part of the curriculum, while freeing the teacher to focus on the many other teaching activities required in the classroom.

A current example of computer-based drill and practice programs has been provided by Merrill and Salisbury (1984; Salisbury, 1984). Many of the available educational computer programs are admittedly boring, dry, and unpleasant. This need not be the case. An awareness of the principals of drill and practice can eliminate such features of current programs. For instance, many of the current programs do little more than expose the learner to material in a manner similar to the simple drill and practice strategy often employed by parents, teachers, or students learning on their own. Typically, this simple strategy involves nothing more than repeated exposure to a list of words or a set of flashcards. While this strategy works to a degree, it is not very efficient or effective. First of all, the learner typically has to deal with every item in the series regardless of whether or not he or she knew an item prior to the practice session. Also, the learner is usually required to learn all the items at a single sitting, and an equal amount of time is frequently spent on learned and unlearned items. When all items are encountered on every series, a *serial position effect* may occur, where an item serves as a cue for the next item. In such a case, the possibility exists that the learner may not know an item when the sequence is altered or the item is encountered in a new context.

Merrill and Salisbury (1984) have developed sophisticated drill-and-practice software for a microcomputer that corrects the aforementioned problems observed in many available software programs. For instance, the Merrill–Salisbury drill-and-practice program incorporates the principle of whole or part learning and breaks the learning task down into a subset of 5 to 9 items. Rather than practicing all items at once, a student works with a limited subset. The size of the subset depends on the difficulty of items and the age or level of development of the learner. In order to avoid unnecessary practice on learned items, this program has the capacity to move items from the working pool to a review pool (see Fig. 1). At the time a learned item is moved to the review pool, a new item is moved from the item pool to the working subset as a replacement for the learned item. As a means of eliminating a serial learning effect, items in the working subset are randomly reordered each time the learner goes through the working subset of items. Once items have been learned to a specific criterion and have been moved to the review pool, they can be retrieved for periodic review. This review procedure is one means of taking advantage of the positive aspects of distributed practice.

Of particular interest to us is the way Merrill and Salisbury (1984) have incorporated principles of learning and practice into the software design. As can be seen from this example, the incorporation of practice principles into computer-assisted drill programs can change the learning experience. Where traditional drill-and-practice software is not very efficient, more sophisticated software can be developed that will increase considerably the efficiency of computer-assisted drill.

C. PROCESSING VARIABLES

In the discussion of task variables, the focus was on those environmental factors (e.g., massed practice, part–whole practice, and timing of feedback) that influence learning and retention. In the present consideration of process

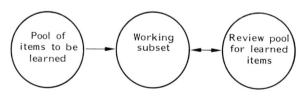

FIG. 1.   Practice elements incorporated into a computer-assisted instructional program.

variables, we take an information-processing perspective and analyze the cognitive nature of reinforcement, informative feedback, and the analysis of errors.

When the topic of reinforcement and human behavior is introduced, one immediately thinks of Thorndike's "Law of Effect" (1935) and Skinner's (1968) operant conditioning principles. More recently, Estes (1972) has provided a cognitive explanation of reinforcement in human behavior and concludes that reward and punishment influence human action via an informational and cybernetic process. Any event that meets the definition of a positive reinforcement (reward) contingency serves both an informational and a motivational function. The reward is assumed to satisfy a motive. However, this event also provides the learner with information about what to do that will lead to reward in the future in a like or similar situation. As Estes points out, these two aspects of reinforcement have not been clearly delineated in the literature. In a series of experiments, Estes (1972) rather convincingly points up the necessity of an informational interpretation of reinforcement in the case of the normal learner. "The new insights arising from our novel manipulations of normal reward contingencies call for a change in our usual way of looking at the law of effect. We are led to infer that the occurrence of a rewarding or punishing event does not act backward in some sense to strengthen the response which proceeded it, but rather provides an opportunity for the organism to learn a relationship between the stimulus which evoked its response and rewarding or punishing consequence" (Estes, 1972, p. 726). According to this perspective, one needs to take into account not only the relationship between the stimulus and the reinforcing event but also the information available to the learner concerning the probability that the same relationship will hold in the future. This would suggest that at any decision point, a learner reviews available information about alternatives and then makes a decision based on feedback from anticipated rewards.

1. Informative Feedback

This cognitive interpretation of reinforcement has led to an increased interest in informational feedback theory as it applies to classroom learning. As has been pointed out elsewhere (Phye, 1977, 1979), whether the improvement in performance is the result of informational or motivational consequences depends in part on the type of task the learner is asked to practice. When the task is of a verbal nature and meets the criterion of classroom learning, informational consequences appear to predominate. "Informative feedback can serve two functions. In the case of a correct answer, feedback serves to confirm the correctness of the response. In the case of an error, feedback would provide information which could be used to correct the error" (Phye, 1979, p. 385). In the same vein, Kulhavy (1977) has suggested that "applied to written instruction, we can say that feedback will have one of two effects on each response that a student makes: (a) to let him know when he is right and, (b) to correct him (or let him correct himself) when he is wrong" (Kulhavy, 1977, p. 219).

When students study a reading assignment in an educational psychology text, they frequently have access to a study guide. Typically, the study guide contains a practice test over the assignment. The practice test is intended to be used by the learner so that she or he can evaluate how effective study has been. In this regard, the practice test is viewed as a study aid and is assumed to promote learning and retention. In most cases, practice tests in study guides follow a multiple-choice format. Following completion of the practice test, the learner turns to the back of the study guide in order to obtain feedback concerning the correctness or incorrectness of individual items. This information is then used to determine if more study is required, or if learning is satisfactory and review should be employed in order to retain what was learned.

2. Error Analysis

Because a practice session is a period of acquisition and refinement of knowledge or skill, learning is not perfect. In other words, errors occur that must be corrected in order for there to be further improvement in performance. As would be suggested by the iterative model, a practice model should contain a diagnostic component that would serve the purpose of error identification and correction. In some respects, this could be considered a metacognitive monitoring strategy or function. From a purely practical classroom perspective, error diagnosis and correction should be a skill demonstrated by teachers.

As a student, I was always struck by the fact that after an assignment was made, I did not need a teacher unless I made an error I could not correct. As a teacher, I have come to believe that the most important role I play is one of providing feedback that either confirms a correct solution or provides the basis for correcting an erroneous solution. This perspective would suggest that a classroom teacher must be a diagnostician. However, diagnostic skills should not be limited to providing correct answers. One of the greatest talents a teacher can possess is the ability to develop an accurate picture of a student's misguided thinking or reasoning that produces an error. This involves being aware of a student's knowledge, including the faulty reasoning. This understanding on the part of a teacher is a necessary prerequisite for successful remediation.

3. Error Types

There are several types of errors that can typically be made in a learning situation. While some errors reflect faulty information or reasoning, other errors are categorized as action slips. According to Norman (1981), "A slip is the error that occurs when a person does an action that is not intended" (p. 1). This is a type of error that produces performance that was not intended. These slips often appear to be the result of a conflict between or among several possible actions or thoughts. This is the interesting case of an error that occurs even though a person's knowledge or reasoning is correct. The problem resides in the performance or commission of the action. Norman further suggests that "a complete error theory seems likely to require autonomous, subconscious processing with intentions, past habits, thoughts, and memories all playing some role in corrupting the intended behavior" (Norman, 1981, p. 2). In the classroom, one can see instances of slips in all academic tasks. When the learner is confronted with a slip, it is usually attributed to carelessness. A frequent comment might be "I knew that— what a stupid mistake."

Error types that reflect faulty information or procedural knowledge (strategy, algorithm, etc.) are much more frequent and of most concern to teachers. A subject matter area that has paid attention to procedural errors is mathematics. The arithmetic skills of addition and subtraction are procedural in nature and provide a learning task where systematic procedural errors can be observed. A learner's errors are systematic if there exists a procedure that produces the error. "In nearly all cases, we have found that systematic errors are minor perturbations from the correct procedure for that skill" (Brown & Van Lehn, 1980, p. 380). In observing children's errors in subtraction and addition, several investigators (Ashlock, 1976; Brown & Burton, 1978; Cox, 1975) have classified errors as slips, systematic, or random. Of these errors, the random error is the most difficult to remediate because no pattern can be determined. The error may be due to a lack of knowledge about basic facts or about procedures. A student who repeatedly gives 14 as the answer to $8 + 5 = ?$, is making a systematic basic fact error. On the other hand, a child who responds in the following manner: (1) $37 - 4 = 23$; (2) $43 - 1 = 32$; and (3) $85 - 3 = 72$; is making a systematic procedural error. This child has "borrowed" from the tens column when it was unnecessary. In both cases, remediation is possible because a teacher can diagnose the reason for the error.

Errors in writing have also been classified. Whereas we spoke of basic fact and procedural errors in arithmetic, a similar distinction in writing is made between sentence-level errors and errors of discourse or matters beyond the level of a sentence. Sentence-level errors involve errors in punctuation, mechanics, spelling, syntax, and grammar. Errors beyond the level of a sentence would be errors in organization, logic, or style. Again we see an apparent distinction between factual-information errors and procedural errors. It could also be assumed that a writing sample can be assessed for action slips and for random or systematic errors whether at the sentence or the discourse level.

In the preceding examples, the writing and arithmetic errors are domain specific. This is not the case with slips or other types of error analysis. Phye (1979) has identified three types of executive errors that are made when students practice a word list and informative feedback about individual items is provided. Students were asked to practice a 40-item word list presented using a multiple-choice format of the following type:

1 Something given a customer   2 Provincial speech:
   for good measure:
   flume   leman
   lagniappe   uncial
   coeval   patois

Following a complete trial of the forty items, answer sheets were collected and feedback in the form of definition and correct answer was provided for all items. When feedback was completed, a second trial was begun. This practice schedule was one of Trial 1 – feedback–Trial 2–et cetera. Using this particular practice schedule, three types of errors are observed: *same errors*, *different errors*, and *new errors*. A *same error* is a perseverative error where an item is missed on at least two consecutive occasions, and the same alternative is selected each time. This gives the appearance of a systematic error resulting from a failure to use feedback for corrective purposes. A *different error* is observed when the same item is missed on two or more occasions, but different alternatives are selected each time. This would give the appearance of a random error. Whereas, the same error could result from misinformation, the different error appears to result from a lack of information. The *new error* is observed when an item is first answered correctly and then incorrectly on the second trial. While this type of error may be the result of a slip, it might also simply reflect a lucky guess on the first trial.

Why be concerned with errors? What can a child's error tell a teacher? At the very least, it makes clear that instruction in the form of feedback is necessary. A student who answers a problem correctly may know the solution or may have made a lucky guess. This child may or may not need further instruction. The child who errs clearly needs help. It is not enough to simply provide the information that a learner's response is in error. In this situation, the learner can only continue in a trial-and-error manner if no additional feedback is given. This not only is counterproductive with most academic tasks, but also will probably lead to a lack of perseverance. An awareness of error type can help a teacher better understand the learner's problem. A systematic error can provide the teacher insight into how a procedure is being misapplied. A random error can well denote a lack of relevant background for problem solution or task completion. A slip or new error may denote a lack of concentration (cognitive monitoring?) and might not be considered critically when evaluating overall performance.

At a theoretical level, Norman (1981) has called for the development of an error theory that involves more than a theory of action slips. Such a theory could provide the framework for a cognitive theory of feedback and practice in the acquisition of complex academic tasks. Inherent in the notion of an error theory is the need for feedback mechanisms. These mechanisms could be a part of the learner's cognitive structure that functions when a person corrects himself or herself. In this instance, feedback mechanisms seem a necessary part of a self-corrective system. "In cognitive psychology, feedback mechanisms have played almost no role, probably because the emphasis has been on the reception of information rather than the performance of acts" (Norman, 1981, p. 11).

At an early stage of academic skill development, it would seem logical to assume that a teacher would provide the feedback necessary to help a learner correct errors. At a later point in one's educational career, it is assumed that the learner has acquired the skills necessary to obtain feedback (dictionary use, new information, metacognitive monitoring) when practicing (e.g., doing homework or seatwork).

IV. SUMMARY

From the research literature reviewed, it is apparent that practice involves the effective use of appropriate cognitive skills. The question remains, however, as to how such skills are acquired. In a general sense, one can say that any skill requires practice in order for it to become automatically applied at the appropriate time. Also, because cognitive skills like inductive or deductive thinking are a complex procedure, errors will occur and need to be corrected before mastery can be reached. In the course of practice when errors occur, feedback must be provided (or obtained) in order for an error to be efficiently corrected (as contrasted with trial-and-error learning). This practice of academic skills is assumed to occur either in the classroom or at home when homework is being completed.

According to one review (Rohwer, 1984), parents presume that academic learning results not only from instruction supplied by the teacher but also from study (practice) that is supplied by the learner. "Broadly conceived, studying is the principal means of self education through life. It consists of all those activities, both covert and overt, that individuals independently engage in in order to acquire knowledge or skill" (Rohwer, 1984, p. 1).

How does the current consideration of practice and skill acquisition relate to an educational psychology of studying? Rohwer (1984) has provided a preliminary framework for research on studying that organizes the ways course and student factors relate to study activities. The present chapter did not pursue the issue of student factors or their interaction with study variables. Rather, the present efforts have been focused on aspects of study activities referred to by Rohwer as covert cognitive procedures (e.g., selection, rehearsal, elaboration, organization, and mental review) and response management and use (e.g., time and effort allocation, consulting ancillary texts, consulting teachers, study conditions). Specifically, the present discussion of practice and skill acquisition fit nicely into the category of study activities called covert cognitive procedures and arranging study conditions.

REFERENCES

Anderson, J. R. (1976). *Language, memory, and thought.* Hillsdale, NJ: Erlbaum.

Anderson, J. R. (1982). Acquisition of cognitive skill. *Psychological Review,* 89(4), 369–406.

Anderson, J. R. (1985). *Cognitive psychology and its implications* (3rd ed.). New York: Freeman.

Anderson, J. R., & Bower, G. H. (1973). *Human associative memory.* Washington, D.C.: Hemisphere.

Ashlock, R. B. (1976). *Error patterns in computation.* Columbus, OH: Bell & Howell.

Ausubel, D. P. (1968). *Educational psychology: A cognitive view.* New York: Holt.

Ausubel, D. P., & Robinson, F. G. (1969). *School learning.* New York: Holt.

Bloom, B. S. (1982). The role of gifts and markers in the development of talent. *Exceptional Children,* 48(6), 510–522.

Bloom, B. S. (1986). The hands and feet of genius. *Educational Leadership,* 43(4), 70–77.

Brackbill, Y., Bravos, A., & Starr, R. H. (1962). Delay-improved retention of a difficult task. *Journal of Comparative and Physiological Psychology,* 55, 947–952.

Brown, A. L. (1981). Metacognition: The development of selective attention strategies for learning from texts. In M. L. Kamil (Ed.), *Directions in reading: Research and instruction* (pp. 21–43). Washington, DC: National Reading Conference.

Brown, J. S., & Burton, R. R. (1978). Diagnostic models for procedural bugs in basic mathematical skills. *Cognitive Science,* 2, 155–192.

Brown, J. S., & VanLehn, K. (1980). Repair theory: A generative theory of bugs in procedural skills. *Cognitive Science,* 4, 379–426.

Chase, W. G., & Simon, H. A. (1973). The mind's eye in chess. In W. G. Chase (Ed.), *Visual information processing.* New York: Academic Press.

Cox, L. S. (1975, February). Diagnosing and remediating systematic errors in addition and subtraction computations. *The Arithmetic Teacher,* 22(2), 151–157.

Estes, W. K. (1972). Reinforcement in human behavior. *American Scientist, 60*, 723–729.

Fitts, P. M. (1964). Perceptual-motor skill learning. In A. W. Melton (Ed.), *Categories of human learning* (pp. 244–285). New York: Academic Press.

Gagne, E. D. (1985). *The cognitive psychology of school learning.* Boston: Little, Brown.

Hayes-Roth, F., Klahr, P., & Mostow, D. J. (1981). In J. R. Anderson (Ed.), *Cognitive skills and their acquisition* (pp. 231–254). Hillsdale, NJ: Erlbaum.

Hudgins, B., Phye, G. D., Schau, C. G., Theisen, G. L., Ames, C., & Ames, R. (1983). *Educational psychology.* Itasca, IL: Peacock.

Kulhavy, R. (1977). Feedback in written instruction. *Review of Educational Research, 47*, 211–232.

Kulhavy, R., & Anderson, R. C. (1972). Delayed retention effect with multiple-choice tests. *Journal of Educational Psychology, 63*, 505–512.

Langley, P., & Simon, H. A. (1981). The central role of learning in cognition. In J. R. Anderson (Ed.), *Cognitive skills and their acquisition* (pp. 361–380). Hillsdale, NJ: Erlbaum.

Larkin, J. H., McDermott, J., Simon, D. P., & Simon, H. A. (1980, June). Expert and novice performance in solving physics problems. *Science, 208*, 1335–1342.

Lewis, C. (1981). Skill in algebra. In J. R. Anderson (Ed.), *Cognitive skills and their acquisition* (pp. 85–110). Hillsdale, NJ: Erlbaum.

Luchins, A. S. (1942). Mechanization in problem solving. *Psychological Monographs, 54* (No. 248).

McGeoch, J. A., & Irion, A. L. (1952). *The psychology of human learning* (2nd ed.). New York: McKay.

Merrill, P. F., Salisbury, D. (1984). Research on drill and practice strategies. *Journal of computer-based instruction, 11*(1), 19–21.

Newell, A., & Rosenbloom, P. S. (1981). Mechanisms of skill acquisition and the law of practice. In J. R. Anderson (Ed.), *Cognitive skills and their acquisition* (pp. 1–55). Hillsdale, NJ: Erlbaum.

Newman, M. I., Williams, R. G., & Hiller, J. H. (1974). Delay of information feedback in an applied setting: Effects on initially learned and unlearned items. *Journal of Experimental Education, 42*(4), 55–59.

Norman, D. A. (1981). Categorization of slips. *Psychological Review, 88*(1), 1–15.

Peeck, J., & Tillema, H. H. (1978). Delay of feedback and retention of correct and incorrect responses. *Journal of Experimental Education, 47*, 171–178.

Phye, G. D. (1977). *The role of informative feedback in productive learning.* Paper presented at the annual meeting of the American Educational Research Association, New York.

Phye, G. (1979). The processing of informative feedback about multiple-choice test performance. *Contemporary Educational Psychology, 4*, 381–394.

Phye, G., & Baller, W. (1970). Verbal retention as a function of the informativeness and delay of informative feedback: A replication. *Journal of Educational Psychology, 61*, 380–381.

Phye, G., Gugliemella, J., & Sola, J. (1976). Effects of delayed retention on multiple-choice test performance. *Contemporary Educational Psychology, 1*, 26–36.

Rohwer, W. D., Jr. (1984). An invitation to an educational psychology of studying. *Educational Psychologist, 191*(1), 1–14.

Salisbury, D. F. (1984). *Cognitive psychology and its implications for designing drill and practice programs for computers.* Paper presented at the annual meeting of the American Educational Research Association, New Orleans.

Sassenrath, J. M., & Yonge, G. D. (1969). Effects of delayed information feedback and feedback cues in learning on delayed retention. *Journal of Educational Psychology, 60*, 174–177.

Schneider, W., & Shiffrin, R. M. (1977). Controlled and automatic human information processing: I. Detection, search attention. *Psychological Review, 84*(1), 1–66.

Shiffrin, R. M., & Dumais, S. T. (1981). The development of automatism. In J. R. Anderson (Ed.), *Cognitive skills and their acquisition* (pp. 111–140). Hillsdale, NJ: Erlbaum.

Shiffrin, R. M., & Schneider, W. (1977). Controlled and automatic human information processing: II. Perceptual learning, automatic attending and a general theory. *Psychological Review, 84*(2), 127–190.

Skinner, B. F. (1968). *The technology of teaching.* New York: Appleton.

Stroud, J. B. (1942). The role of practice in learning. In *The psychology of learning: 41st yearbook of the National Society for the Study of Education* (Part II, pp. 353–376). Chicago: University of Chicago Press.

Sturges, P. T. (1969). Verbal retention as a function of the informativeness and delay of informative feedback. *Journal of Educational Psychology, 60*, 11–14.

Sturges, P. T. (1978). Delay of informative feedback in computer assisted testing. *Journal of Educational Psychology, 70*(3), 378–387.

Thorndike, E. L. (1935). *The psychology of wants, interests, and attitudes.* New York: Appleton.

Voss, J. F., Tyler, S. W., & Yengo, L. A. (1983). Individual differences in the solving of social science problems. *Individual Differences in Cognition, 1*, 205–232.

White, K. (1968). Delay of test information feedback and learning in a conventional classroom. *Psychology in the Schools, 5*, 78–81.

Zechmeister, E. B., & Nyberg, S. E. (1982). *Human memory.* Monterey, CA: Brooks/Cole.

PROBLEM SOLVING AND EDUCATION

Thomas Andre

Department of Psychology
Iowa State University
Ames, Iowa 50011

I. CONTEXT AND INTRODUCTION

It is 3:00 p.m. on a Wednesday afternoon, and with a flourish our hero types in the last correction on the chapter manuscript. The chapter is due Thursday at the publishers, and our hero has procrastinated so long that normal mail won't get there in time. What to do? Our hero thinks of several alternatives, "Call Superman, drive to New York, take a plane, U.S. Express Mail, use a modem, Come Quick Express Service." Cogitating further, our hero reasons, "Superman would be nice, but isn't very practical. Driving will take too long. Taking a plane will cost too much. U.S. Express Mail means that the chapter must be delivered to the post office by 5:00 p.m.— not enough time for that. Come Quick seems like the best bet; they claim to come to the house." Having made that trial decision, our hero thinks, "Never used Come Quick before, I wonder how you get them. Check the phone book." Finding the number, our hero calls and finds that she can get the package picked up and delivered in time for a reasonable fee. "Problem solved!" she thinks.

Mundane as it is, this problem situation illustrates several important features of human problem solving. The situation shows that problem solving starts with a desired goal (e.g., getting the manuscript to New York). It also shows that we look for and consider alternative possible solutions (e.g., Superman or Come Quick?), and that we call heavily on our memory and knowledge store in problem solving (e.g., remembering that phone books let us contact places).

Much of education is intended to make people better problem solvers. The justification for teaching children to read, write, or reckon is usually couched in some variant of: *These skills will be useful in solving problems later.* The arguments for a liberal college education usually have a future problem-solving component implicit within them. While problem solving is central to education, the study of problem solving has historically received only sporadic attention from educators and educational psychologists. An explicit theory of problem solving has not been available and educators interested in promoting problem solving have primarily been engaged in guesswork when designing programs. Since the late 1960s or early 1970s, the study of thinking and problem solving has become respectable for psychologists, and the issues of promoting problem-solving skills has become an important one for educators. While a complete theory of problem solving does not yet exist, we have learned much about the kinds of thinking that goes on when individuals solve problems and about the kinds of factors that facilitate problem solving.

This chapter has two basic purposes: (1) to provide an overview of psychological research and theory in the area of problem solving, and (2) to discuss ways in which students can better be taught to become effective problem solvers. The general approach taken is to first provide a description of historically interesting theories of problem solving to provide background and then to focus the present chapter on a cognitive information-processing, schema-theoretic view of problem solving. A model for teaching of problem-solving skills is proposed in which problem solving is assumed to be similar to the development of other intellectual skills. This model is used to analyze the instructionally important elements of intellectual skill acquisition and to provide a description of things teachers can do to promote the development of problem solving.

II. THE NATURE OF PROBLEM SOLVING
AND APPROACHES TO STUDYING PROBLEM SOLVING

A. What Is a Problem?

While all of us know what a problem is at an intuitive level, a definition of what a problem is provides a useful place to start a discussion of problem solving. Most discussions of problem solving are usually consistent with this definition: *A problem is a situation in which the individual wants to do something but does not know the course of action needed to get what he or she wants* (Newell and Simon, 1972).

Problems have four components (Hayes, 1981; Mayer, 1983; Newell and Simon, 1972).

1. The Goal or Goals

This is what you want to do in a situation. A situation can have many goals or a single goal. The goal(s) can be very well defined or ill defined. Most arithmetic story problems have very well-defined goals, as in: *Mother has 10 dollars, John asks her for 60 cents to buy a treat from the ice cream vendor. How much money does Mother have left?* Many life problems have more fuzzily defined goals: *What would be fun to do on a date?*

2. The Givens

Givens are what is available to you to start in a problem situation. Givens can be many or few and also can be well or ill defined. In the preceding arithmetic problem, Mom having 10 dollars and the treat costing 60 cents are well-defined givens. Givens can also be implicit; the arithmetic problem has an implicit given in that arithmetic is supposed to be used to provide the answer. Answering *"Mom has $10 left because she says no to John because ice cream is bad for teeth"* would probably not be regarded as an acceptable answer by most teachers. The givens in the fun-date problem are undefined.

3. The Obstacles

These are elements or factors that get in the way of a solution. The fact that Mom has dollars and the price is in cents is an obstacle in the arithmetic problem. Again, obstacles can be well or ill defined and explicit or implicit.

4. The Methods or Operations

These refer to the procedures that may be used to solve the problem. Often in solving problems, the kinds of procedures you may use are constrained in some way. If our author hero, in the first paragraph of this chapter, had had enough money, then many other solutions might have been possible. The range of methods may also be explicitly described as part of the problem or may be implicit in the context.

B. WHAT IS PROBLEM SOLVING?

Problem solving consists of the mental and behavioral activities that are involved in dealing with problems. Problem solving may involve thinking (cognitive) components, emotional or motivational components, and behavioral components. Mentally transforming cents to dollars would be an example of a thinking component, a feeling of confidence in one's ability to solve the problem would represent an emotional component, and looking up something in a dictionary or library would be a behavioral component. This chapter focuses on the cognitive components of problem solving, but it is important to realize that motivational and behavioral components are involved in real-life problem solving. For example, a professional advertising photographer may take a series of trial Polaroid photographs to test the lighting and get an actual visual impression of a setup before the actual usable images are made. If someone gives you a puzzle, and you do not feel that solving it is worth your effort, you are unlikely to engage in problem solving. Psychological research has mostly been involved with cognitive approaches to problem solving, and a theory that integrates motivational and behavioral components into a comprehensive view of problem solving is still in the future.

C. HISTORICAL APPROACHES TO PROBLEM SOLVING

1. The Behavioral Approach

The behavioral approach to psychology was the dominant force in American psychology during the first 60 years of the twentieth century, and problem solving was involved in some of the earliest studies of behavioral psychology. Thorndike (1898) studied the behavior of cats placed in a box whose door could be opened if a lever was pressed. When first placed in the box, the cats would engage in a variety of behaviors such as trying to squeeze through an opening, biting at the wire, etc. Eventually, the cat would press the lever, open the door, and escape. When placed back in the box, the cat would engage in less random behavior before escaping. Finally, the cat would come to be able to escape immediately upon entering the box. Thorndike explained the cat's problem solving by invoking the concepts that have come to be called reinforcement and extinction. Solution-irrelevant behavior was gradually extinguished or eliminated because it did not lead to reinforcement, while the response of lever pressing was gradually strengthened by being reinforced by escape. In solving the problem, the cat did not show thought or planning of activities, so Thorndike called the process *trial-and-error learning* and used that basic model as a description of problem solving in general. With some quibbling among behaviorists as to the exact nature of such trial-and-error learning, Thorndike's view has provided the basic behavioral model of problem solving (Campbell, 1960; Davis, 1973; Mayer, 1983; Skinner, 1966; Staats, 1966).

According to behavioral views, trial-and-error learning occurs when a stimulus situation demands a response, but the correct response is not dominant in the response hierarchy for that situation. By *response hierarchy* is meant the set of responses a learner might make in that situation. A *dominant response* is the response that is most likely in a situation. The learner tries out responses in their order of dominance. Incorrect responses are extinguished, and the correct response reinforced until it becomes dominant in that situation. This behavioral view allows little room for thought and planning in problem solving. But it is clear that in many situations, humans do think about problems before engaging in behavior. Human activity does not seem to be totally random. Behaviorists argue that such thinking consists of internal trial-and-error learning (Davis, 1973). Such trial-and-error learning can be mediated by discriminative stimuli produced by verbal responses (language) (Skinner, 1966; Staats, 1966).

2. The Gestalt Approach to Problem Solving

Partly in reaction to American behaviorism and partly in reaction to other German schools of psychology, a group of German psychologists, called *Gestalt psychologists*, developed an approach to psychology that emphasized the role of mental structure and organization in perception and thinking. With respect to problem solving, they emphasized the role of a sudden reorganization of mental elements into a structure that provides a solution to a problem. This sudden reorganization was called an *insight experience*.

The first Gestalt study of problem solving was provided by Kohler (1925), who studied problem solving in chimpanzees and other animals. Kohler presented chimpanzees with problems such as the two-stick problem. In this problem, the chimp needed to fit one stick into a second to make a stick long enough to reach a banana placed outside its cage. Kohler noted that the behavior of the chimp did not seem to involve random trial and error, but rather it studied the problem, with a sudden solution emerging. Kohler called the sudden restructuring of the problem an *insight*. He argued that human problem solving also was based on thinking about a situation and rearranging the mental elements into a structure that provides a solution to the problem. Other Gestalt psychologists investigated the effects of mental habits in preventing problem restructuring and insight (Duncker, 1945; Katona, 1940; Luchins, 1942; Maier, 1930, 1970). These studies demonstrated that prior habits could interfere with the discovery of problem solutions and raised the issue of discovery versus expository learning.

3. The Stages of Problem Solving

Several authors have analyzed problem solving into a series of stages. Wallas (1926) described the stages of (1) preparation, (2) incubation, (3) inspiration, and (4) verification. In the *preparation stage*, the problem solver analyzes the problem, tries to define it clearly, and gathers relevant facts and information. In the *incubation* stage, the problem is considered subconsciously while the problem solver is relaxing or considering something else. During the *inspiration* stage, the solution to the problem comes to the learner unexpectedly in the sort of "light bulb lights" experience illustrated in cartoons. The inspiration stage corresponds to the insight experience of the Gestalt psychologists. The *verification* stage involves checking the solution and working out the details.

Wallas's stages of problem solving are well illustrated by the descriptive reports of chemists involved in solving problems, which were collected by Platt and Baker (1931, reported in Symonds, 1936). Here is a sample case history:

> After intense concentration and many vain attempts to overcome this difficulty, I reluctantly decided to abandon the method. . . . I decided to go down town and have a thick beefsteak at Charley Wirth's and completely forget my work for the time being. Freeing my mind of all thought of the problem I walked briskly down Fremont Street, when suddenly . . . an idea popped into my head as suddenly and emphatically as if a voice had shouted it in these words: "In pharmacy and in industry, we clarify emulsions by means of a high-speed centrifuge; such a method would be impractical in a thermostat. But if rapid whirling for a brief time will do it, why will not slow rotation for a longer time accomplish the same result? (Symonds, 1936, p. 140)

Not all stage descriptions place a strong emphasis on the subconscious processes of incubation and inspiration. Many describe a rational series of steps that the problem solver presumably goes through in solving a problem (Adams, 1974; Hayes, 1981; Kingsley & Garry, 1957; Osborn, 1963). An intuitive average of these stages is shown in Fig. 1. Descriptions such as shown in Fig. 1 are both very rational and gross. They are *rational* in the sense that they emphasize conscious thought and a logical analytic approach to problem solving. They are *gross* in the sense that they provide a molar and imprecise description of the mental activities in problem solving. They do not say what the mind or brain does when problems are noticed or solutions are generated. An adequate theory of problem solving will have to explain how problems are noticed or solutions generated, etc. However, these stage descriptions may be a useful starting place for an adequate theory.

Stage descriptions may also have a heuristic value in teaching learners to be more effective problem solvers. The steps can be considered as directions to learners to engage in activities that might facilitate problem solving. When considered as directions, such steps form a basis for most problem-solving training courses. Training with such directives has also been used to help individuals to solve interpersonal and emotional problems in counseling (Craighead, Kazdin, & Mahoney, 1981; Goldfried & Goldfried, 1980).

4.   The Piagetian Approach to Problem Solving

Piaget and his followers have developed an approach to problem solving that focuses on the mental logic that supports problem solving and how that logic develops. Because of the extensive research and theoretical development in the area of cognitive development and problem solving, it is discussed separately in Chapter 10 by Lunzer. The interested reader is referred to that discussion.

1. Problem noticing: Some discrepancy between what you have and want is noted.
2. Problem specification: A more precise description of the problem is worked out.
3. Problem analysis: The parts of the problem are figured out, and relevant information is gathered.
4. Solution generation: Possible solutions are considered.
5. Testing of solutions: The various possible solutions are considered and evaluated for likelihood of success.
6. Solution selection and implementation: The most likely solution is implemented in detail and evaluated for success.
7. Solution revision as necessary.

FIG 1.   Analytic stages of problem solving.

III. A COGNITIVE INFORMATION-PROCESSING MODEL OF PROBLEM SOLVING

Since the early 1960s, the dominant position in American psychology has moved from a behavioral position to a cognitive information-processing position. This position is based on a metaphor that the brain is like a programmed computer. From this position, problem solving is viewed as the processing of information by an information-processing system (brain, computer), such that the information in an initial state is transformed into the information of a desired end state. An adequate theory of problem solving would consist of (1) a complete description of the architecture and capabilities of the information-processing system and (2) a description of the step-by-step processes by which a problem-solving activity is carried out. The level of description in such a theory would be sufficiently precise to simulate the entity being described in an actual or conceptual computer (see Chapter 1 for a more complete description of these concepts). Often information-processing descriptions are actually programmed into a computer (e.g., Newell & Simon, 1972), and the adequacy of the description is tested by comparing the computer simulation to the behavior of humans. Unlike the behavioral position, the cognitive focus has mostly been on the description of how problem solving occurs rather than how individuals learn to become problem solvers. Only recently has learning received attention within the information-processing tradition.

A.   A GENERAL PROBLEM-SOLVING MODEL

Most cognitive psychologists would agree to a description of problem solving that is similar to that described in Fig. 2 (Anderson, 1980; Hayes, 1981; Mayer, 1983; Newell & Simon, 1972). The description in Fig. 2 is similar in some ways to the steps of problem-solving notions described above, but has the advantage of telling us issues that need to be investigated

1. A problem consists of a situation where you want something and do not know the precise steps to get it.
2. The problem solver analyzes the problem into goals and givens as defined in Fig. 1 and forms an initial representation of the goals and givens in memory.
3. The problem solver operates on the representations of the givens and the goals in order to reduce the discrepancy between the givens and the goals. A solution to the problem consists of the path of operations that can transform the givens into the goals.
4. In operating on the givens and goals, the problem solver may use the following, not necessarily exclusive, approaches:
   a. Information or schemata (productions) in long-term memory
   b. Heuristic approaches to solving problems
   c. Algorithms for problem solution if they are available
   d. Metaphorical relationships with other representations.
5. The process of operating on an initial representation to find a problem solution is called *search*. As part of the solution-search process, the representation may be transformed into other representations.
6. Search continues until either a solution is found or the problem solver gives up.

FIG. 2.   An information processing description of problem solving

in order to understand problem solving. If this description of problem solving is accurate, then areas to be researched include

1. The processes by which a problem description is converted to an internal representation
2. The role of representation in problem solving
3. The role of prior knowledge in problem solving—this issue subsumes questions about
   a. The nature of knowledge in our memory
   b. Factors that cause stored knowledge to be activated
   c. Differences between verbal knowledge and skill knowledge
   d. The arrangement of knowledge in memory.

B.   COMPONENT PROCESSES IN PROBLEM SOLVING

Let us examine more fully what is meant by each of these components in problem solving.

1.   Representation

Representation consists of a transformation of the presented information into a model in memory. It consists of identifying the goal, identifying the important givens, and forming a representation of these elements. Perhaps the issues of representation can be illustrated more clearly with the following story that I use in my undergraduate classes. I ask you a question after the story.

A bus leaves the bus barn in the morning. It stops at the first stop and picks up 5 people. It proceeds to the next stop and 6 people get on. It goes to the next stop and 4 people get on. At the next stop, 3 people get on and 2 get off. At the next stop, 5 people get on and 4 get off. At the next stop, 6 people get on and 1 gets off. Next time, 3 people get on and 2 get off. At the next stop, 2 get off and no one gets on. At the next stop, no one is waiting so the bus doesn't stop. At the next stop, 10 people get on and 3 people get off. At the next stop, 3 people get on and 6 people get off. Finally, the bus reaches the end of the route.
NOW FOR THE QUESTION.
How many stops are there on the bus route?

If you are like most of my undergraduate students, you are probably able to tell me how many people are left on the bus, or how many people got on the bus, etc. To do this, you selected the numerical information as important and represented it internally in the form of arithmetic operations. Almost never is someone able to tell me the number of stops. In terms of the information-processing model, why does this happen? I have given you an ill-defined goal and some pretty definite numerical givens. The emphasis on the numbers of people getting on and off makes a probable goal something having to do with those numbers. So you represent the goal as a total of some kind. The decision lets you select as relevant information the numbers of people getting on or off the bus and to ignore the stops.

2. Research on Representation

The importance of representation on problem solution is shown in a variety of studies. Studies on logical reasoning problems (such as syllogisms of the form, *All/Some As are Bs, All/Some Bs are Cs, X is a A, must it be a C?*) have found that children and adults often have difficulty with such problems. If the problem is presented in abstract form or contradicts the person's beliefs, the difficulty is greater. The hypothesis that people reason illogically when beliefs are threatened has been advanced by many researchers and is seemingly supported by much research (Feather, 1965; Gordon, 1953; Janis & Frick, 1943; Janis & Terwilliger, 1962; Kaufman & Goldstein, 1967; Lefford, 1946; Morgan & Morton, 1944; Parrott, 1967, 1969; Revlin & Leirer, 1978; Wilkins, 1928; Wilson, 1965).

Revlin and Leirer (1978) proposed an alternative hypothesis that they called the conversion hypothesis. Revlin and Leirer believed that rather than reasoning illogically, subjects formed an incorrect representation of the statements that made up the syllogism and then reasoned logically from that incorrect representation. They were able to show that incorrect representations could account for many of the errors subjects make in such problems.

Supporting research was provided by Simpson and Johnson (1966). To make clear what is meant by an incorrect representation, consider the state-

Panel A	The Himoots are farmers.
	The farmers are valley people.
	The valley people are warlike.
	GUGU is warlike. Is he a farmer?
Panel B	The himoots are people included within the group of farmers.
	The farmers are included in the group of valley people.
	The valley people are included in the set of warlike people.
Panel C	The Himoots is the name given to the farmers, so every one who is a farmer is a Himoot and vice versa.
	All of the farmers live in the valley and all of the valley people are farmers.
	All of the people living in the valley are warlike and all the warlike people live in the valley.

FIG. 3.   Class inclusion statements

ments in Panel A of Fig. 3. If you interpret these statements as a logician would, you would translate them to the statements in Panel B of Fig. 3 which represent the set relationships illustrated in Fig. 4a. If this is your representation then you would answer the problem, "Is GUGU a farmer?" by saying that the answer is indeterminate because people other than farmers are included in the set of warlike people. This is the answer a logician would give.

On the other hand, you might interpret the statements in Panel A as shown in Panel C of Fig. 3 and illustrated in Fig. 4b. If you form this latter interpretation, it is logically true that if someone is warlike, then he or she is a farmer.

Braine (1978) has argued that errors such as the preceding may not be errors at all but may represent ways in which the logic of natural English is different from logicians' use of English. Some work in linguistics offers support for this notion (Gordon & Lakoff, 1971; Horn, 1972). Revlis (1975) presents evidence that when features are added to make the correct interpretation more likely, logical errors are reduced. However, Fisher (1981) has demonstrated that, while such errors of representation occur in syllogistic reasoning problems, they cannot account for all the errors subjects make on such problems. Fisher found evidence for errors occurring also because of limited working-memory capacity and faulty deductive reasoning.

Additional evidence for the role of representation in solving logical problems is provided by Egan and Grimes-Farrow (1982). They showed that students adopted either an abstract dimensional representation or a concrete representation of features for 3-term linear ordering problems. Three-term linear ordering problems are exemplified by the following:

1. Bob is taller than Bill. Jim is shorter than Bill. Who is tallest?
2. Sandpaper is rougher than cotton. Silk is smoother than cotton. Which is least rough?

Students who represented the position of the objects as abstract positions on a dimension were able to solve the problems more efficiently than the students who visualized the actual objects.

That the representation a person uses in problem solving can greatly facilitate or inhibit solution is so well known that most training programs on problem solving devote considerable attention to alternative representations (e.g., Adams, 1974; Hayes, 1981; Wickelgren, 1974). In a discussion of computer coaching systems to teach problem solving, Goldstein (1980) emphasizes the necessity for the computer coach to understand students' representations and to provide hints for alternative representations. It is easy to provide simple examples of the importance of representation. Consider the following problem: *1951 divided by 61*. While most of us would prefer paper and pencil to solve this problem, we know the algorithm (long division) for solving it. Now consider the following MCMLI/LXI. This is the same problem, but try solving it without reverting to arabic numerals.

3. Representation and Expert–Novice Differences

One of the lines of research on problem solving involves differences between experts and novices in problem solving. Experts and novices recognize and represent problems in different ways. Experts seem to have higher-order mental structures which can be used to classify problems into types. By identifying problems as falling within a particular type, experts can bring to bear more effective representations.

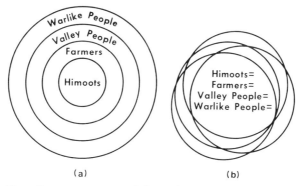

FIG. 4.   Alternative representations of class inclusion statements in Fig. 3, Panel A.

Egan and Schwartz (1979) compared experienced electrical engineers, recently graduated engineers, and student engineers on the ability to remember electrical circuit diagrams. Experienced engineers could remember more because they classified particular diagrams into higher-order schemata (e.g., this is a class A amplifier circuit). The engineers could then use the general structure of that type of circuit to recall the details of the diagram. Novice engineers remembered by looking at individual details, but did not form a representation that captured the type of circuit. While not a direct test of problem solving, this study illustrated differences in the nature of expert and novice knowledge. Similar effects were reported by Chase and Simon (1973) in a study that compared expert and novice chess players. Expert chess players organized board positions into general schemata and were able to reproduce the diagrams better than novice players. When given random board positions that could not be organized into schemata to remember, experts were no better than novices.

Larkin and her co-workers have investigated differences between expert and novice physics problem solvers (Larkin, 1980; Larkin, McDermott, Simon, & Simon, 1980). When given word problems to solve, expert physicists organized the information into larger-scale functional units. Novices treated items of information more individually. The solution time curves for novices seemed to indicate a random search process, whereas the experts' solution times diverged greatly from a random search model (Larkin, 1980, p 119). This indicated that experts organized the information into larger representations. Similarly, Hinsley, Hayes, and Simon (1977) found that subjects were able to classify algebra word problems into particular types. Classification into type seemed to activate a representation that indicated which information would be relevant and which type of solution to try. Similar results are provided by Greeno (1980) and Mayer (1980).

4. Representation and Problems in Problem Solving

Considerable effort has been devoted to the issue of identifying factors that interfere with problem solving. Initial work was done by the Gestalt psychologists, who focused on the role of previously learned habits as interfering factors in problems solving. This interference has been called problem-solving set (Luchins, 1942). Luchins gave problem solvers a series of problems in which they had to get a specified amount of water into a jar, given a supply of water and three jars of different capacities. If the jars are labeled A, B, and C; the problems could be solved by the formula $B - C - 2A$. That is, fill the second jar, fill the third from it, then fill the first twice from the second. The specified amount of water would then be left in the second jar. Across a series of problems, the first n could be solved only by the formula. The remaining problems could be solved either by that formula or by a simpler formula $(A - C)$. Luchins found that with practice on the first n problems, many subjects blindly followed the first formula when the second set of problems was encountered. Subjects without experience on the first set of problems used the more efficient method.

Similar results were presented by Duncker (1945). He demonstrated that the common use of an object could interfere with its use to solve a problem in a different way. For example, when presented with a task of attaching a candle upright on a wall given boxes containing matches, candles, and tacks, subjects given the objects in the boxes were unlikely to discover the solution of tacking an inverted box to the wall to serve as a candleholder. The containment function of the box interfered with finding the solution.

The interfering effects in these cases stems from the influence of previously learned schemata–productions, upon performance in a task that requires a new production. Adams (1974) has called these interfering schemata conceptual blocks and has devoted a speculative book to describing ways of overcoming such blocks. Techniques discussed by Adams basically are general heuristics and are similar to techniques taught in many problem-solving courses.

5.   Search Processes in Problem Solving

Search processes refer to the mental operations that problem solvers employ to think about the representation of goals and givens to try to transform the givens into the goals and find a solution. In the way the term is being used in this chapter, *search* includes both the kind of thinking the problem solver may do to decide on an approach to the problem and also the working out of a solution once a particular algorithm is decided on.

Search processes include heuristics, algorithms, and divergent-thinking processes. *Heuristics* are rules of thumb that problem solvers have found useful. Heuristics indicate likely directions to pursue or approaches to follow. They may lead to a problem solution, but are not guaranteed to do so. *Algorithms* are specific procedures that are guaranteed to produce a solution to a problem so long as the algorithm is relevant to the problem. For example, the long-division algorithm is guaranteed to solve long-division problems, but would be incorrect for multiplication problems. Algorithms usually represent the last phase of problem solving; when we begin to use an algorithm we are usually pretty sure that the approach will work. Under *divergent-thinking* processes, I am classifying procedures that have not been studied much by cognitive psychologists, but that are probably involved in generating alternative approaches and in the "insight/inspiration" phase of creativity.

As with representation processes, search processes are dependent on a store of information and knowledge. As is noted here subsequently, expert problem solvers in particular domains possess a great deal of knowledge relevant to a particular domain that allows them to deal with problems more efficiently and effectively than do novices.

6. Heuristic Processes

Heuristic processes can vary in their generality. Some heuristics are very general and can be applied to a variety of domains; others are very specific and limited to a particular domain of knowledge. Most training programs in problem solving devote considerable emphasis to general heuristics (Adams, 1974; Hayes, 1981; Polya, 1945; Rubinstein, 1975; Wickelgren, 1974). Early research in artificial intelligence and problem solving focused on the use of very general heuristics (e.g., Newell & Simon, 1972). Such general heuristics can be very powerful.

The General Problem Solver program (Ernst & Newell, 1969; Newell & Simon, 1972), for example, was successful in solving a wide variety of logic problems by using a general heuristic called means–ends analysis. The drawback of very general heuristics is that they can be quite inefficient. If more is known about the subject matter, more efficient procedures are usually available (Simon, 1980). More recent work in cognitive psychology and artificial intelligence has emphasized the need for considerable domain-specific knowledge in problem solving. General heuristics are useful when the subject matter of the problem is unfamiliar.

7. Example General Heuristics

Examples of some general heuristic procedures follow. This list is not meant to be exhaustive, for more detail and for other heuristics, consult Hayes, (1976, 1981), Mayer (1983), Polya (1945), Rubinstein (1975), and Wickelgren (1974).

a. *Heuristic: Looking for Alternative Representations.* Because the way one represents a problem can be critical to solving the problem, a useful heuristic is to try to develop alternative representations that might provide a more effective idea about how to solve the problem. Goldstein (1980) provides a good example. In playing the computer game Wumpus, some children kept lists of the features of various rooms in the dungeon. This representation was useful in identifying particular properties of the rooms, but did not provide an overall map of the dungeon and was difficult to scan. Some students used an alternative visual representation that was more useful for some aspects of the game. Actually both the list and the visual representations were useful in given situations; the point is that changing representations was useful in solving particular problems of play.

b. Heuristic: Working Backward. This heuristic involves starting with the goal and trying to change it into the givens. Most people who have taken high school geometry remember using this procedure in proving at least some theorems. One assumed the theorem and tried to work back to the postulates. Hayes (1981) provides another example taken from Katona (1940), and it is shown in Fig. 5. If you try to solve this problem directly by arranging the deck, you will have difficulty. However, if you try working backwards by laying out the cards in an alternating sequence and picking them up backwards, you will find the task easier.

c. Heuristic: Hill Climbing. *Hill climbing* (Mayer, 1983) involves taking the next move that seems to bring you closest to your goal. In the jargon of artificial intelligence, hill climbing is taking the move that makes the current given state most like the desired goal state. As a simple example, in a chess game, the final goal state would involve putting the opponent's king in check. A hill climbing routine would choose a check-making move over other moves. The problem with hill climbing is that problems sometimes require that the given state be changed so that there is greater rather than lesser discrepancy between givens and goal. In chess, there are many times when taking a check is a disastrous move. Atwood and Polson (1976) demonstrated that subjects seem to use this kind of hill climbing procedure in solving water-jug problems.

d. Heuristic: Means–Ends Analysis. This heuristic consists of breaking down problems into subgoals, picking a subgoal to work on, deciding how a subgoal is different from the current given state, and removing obstacles between the subgoal and the given state. According to Mayer (1983), the problem solver continually asks three questions: "What is my goal? What obstacles are in my way . . . what operators are available for overcoming these obstacles?" (p 175). Mayer (1983) reports data from Greeno (1974), Thomas (1974), and Larkin, McDermott, Simon, and Simon (1980) that a means–ends approach can simulate at least some aspects of problem solving, but that other procedures such as hill climbing are often combined with

---

Your task is to arrange a deck of four red and four black cards so that you may deal them out as follows:

1. You place the top card on the table, face up. It is black.
2. You place the next card (now on the top of the deck) on the bottom of the deck.
3. You place the next card on the table, face up. It is red.
4. You place the next card on the bottom of the deck.
5. You continue in this way until all card are dealt out in an alternating black/red pattern. (Hayes, 1981, p 19)

FIG. 5. A card trick problem from Katona (1940)

means–ends analyses. In addition, individuals who know a lot about a particular subject matter will often use more efficient procedures (Larkin et al., 1980; Larkin, 1980).

  e. *Additional General Heuristics.* Additional heuristics include hypothetical reasoning (Hayes, 1981), solving parts of a problem one can solve, solving a similar problem (Polya, 1945), looking for an analogous problem, and random trial-and-error search. Readers interested in more details on particular general heuristics should consult Groner, Groner, and Bischof (1983), Hayes (1981), Polya (1945), and Wickelgren (1974).

  f. *Specific Heuristics and Domain-Specific Knowledge.* While early studies of problem solving emphasized general heuristics, more recent work has recognized that expert problem solvers amass a large amount of domain-specific knowledge. Such knowledge can include larger structures for recognizing problems, more complicated algorithms, and a large number of specific heuristics. Lenat (1983) developed a computer simulation that was able to learn and discover fundamental laws of basic arithmetic from an initial base of fundamental mathematical facts. The program consisted of only a few basic facts but a large number of quite specific heuristics that controlled the exploration process. In addition, the program had to develop new specific heuristics as it learned about the subject matter. Champagne, Klopfer, and Chaiklin, (1984) studied what physics students needed to know to solve transfer problems. They found that the learners needed much more domain-specific knowledge than is commonly given in physics instruction. Without such knowledge, students were not able to do much more than rotely memorize solutions to problems and were unable to transfer what they had been taught to new situations. For example, Simon (1980) estimates that a chess master has approximately 50,000 general patterns of chess pieces stored in memory. Each pattern includes a pattern of pieces and a procedure to follow when that pattern is encountered. Simon estimates a minimum of 8 seconds of learning are required to master each chunk. More complicated chunks would take longer; Simon believes that expertise in a subject matter area probably requires 10 years of study of that area. Other authors (Goldstein & Papert, 1977; Norman, 1980] also support the notion that efficient problem solving requires considerable domain–specific knowledge.

  To illustrate the kinds of knowledge necessary for a particular domain, consider the kinds of knowledge Mayer (1983) identifies as necessary knowledge for solving mathematical story problems. Mayer's list includes

  1. Linguistic knowledge—recognizing words, parsing sentences, etc.
  2. Semantic knowledge—knowledge of the world relevant to the problem
  3. Schematic knowledge—knowledge of problem types

4. Procedural knowledge—knowledge of the algorithms necessary for problem solution

5. Strategic knowledge—techniques for using types of knowledge and heuristics.

As an example of how these kinds of knowledge are necessary, consider this use of semantic knowledge that Mayer borrows from Paige and Simon (1966). Subjects are presented with the following problem. *The number of quarters that a man has is seven times the number of dimes he has. The value of the dimes exceeds the value of the quarters by two dollars. How many has he of each coin?* While some subjects attempted to solve this problem by constructing equations based on the problem (e.g., $7 \times Q = D; D - Q = 250$), others used some general semantic knowledge and realized that the value of the dimes cannot exceed the value of the quarters. The point of this discussion of domain-specific knowledge is that search processes (and indeed, representational processes) are as dependent on domain-specific knowledge as they are on general problem-solving techniques. Superficial analyses of problem solving have often given the impression that much creativity and problem solving depends on the unlocking of hidden potential and general tricks of thinking (Andre, 1979). Rather effective problem solving in a domain relies both on considerable domain-specific knowledge and on general heuristics. This fact emphasizes the importance of the preparation stage of problem solving discussed by Wallas (1926). It also argues that education must provide learners with an extensive knowledge base if they are to develop problem-solving skills.

IV. THE NATURE OF DOMAIN-SPECIFIC KNOWLEDGE— INTELLECTUAL SKILLS

If domain-specific knowledge is critical to understanding problem solving, an important question is how knowledge is stored and organized in memory to facilitate problem solving. The basic approach that cognitive psychologists and artificial intelligence researchers have adopted is the production system. A production system consists of a network of condition–action sequences. The *condition* refers to the set of circumstances that will activate the production; the *action* refers to the set of activities that will occur if the production is activated. Both the conditional and the action part of a production can vary from simple to complex. Consider the example of a production given in Fig. 6.

This if–then conditional might represent a production for the application of a behavioral treatment for eliminating an undesired behavior. Current theory in problem solving would argue that the mind of a behavioral psychol-

Conditional part
    If: 1. The issue has to do with a change in behavior, and
           2. The behavior is to be decreased, and
           3. Adversive consequences cannot be applied,

Action part
    Then: 1. Determine the frequency and occurrence of reinforcements of the behaviors
           2. Determine the frequency of occurrence of antecedent eliciting conditions
           3. Eliminate or reduce the frequency of reinforcement
           4. Eliminate or reduce the frequency of antecendent conditions
           5. Determine the frequency of occurrence of an antagonistic desirable behavior
           6. Determine the frequency of reinforcements to the antagonistic desirable behavior
           7. Determine the frequency and occurrence of the eliciting antecedents of the desired behavior
           8. Increase the frequency of reinforcement and eliciting antecedents for the desired behavior

FIG. 6.   Example of production—decreasing behavior.

ogist, despite his or her protestation not to have a mind, would consist of a network of such productions.

Hull–Spence behavioral psychologists will recognize production systems as mediated stimulus–response hierarchies. The condition for a production can be conceptualized as a set of discriminative stimuli that give rise to a response chain. Note that in a mediated stimulus–response system, there is no requirement that discriminative stimuli be entirely external or that responses all be observable. Models based on such systems have been used to explain complex human behavior (Osgood, 1957; Staats, 1966).

Perhaps in the zeitgeist change to cognitive psychology, many distinctions between cognitive and behavioral psychology were overdrawn. However that may be, the idea of a production is a powerful computational tool for representing precisely ideas that were discussed more fuzzily in the English-based language of S–R psychology. The notion of the production has been found to be essential to developing artificial systems that can successfully solve real-life problems such as medical or dental diagnosis (Simon, 1980). Such systems were not buildable using S–R concepts.

A. Productions, Schemata, and Intellectual Skills

I believe that the idea of a production system provides a unifying theme for representing *what* one knows when one knows concepts, principles, mental skills, and problem-solving abilities. Gagne (1977) has called knowledge of such entities *intellectual skills*. The word *schemata* is also commonly used. The formalism of a production can be used to represent each of these notions. This section describes what individuals know when they know concepts, principles, and mental and problem-solving skills, and it shows how the general idea of a production can be used to represent that information in memory.

Concepts

In the traditional psychological view, concepts are generally viewed as rules for classifying (Anderson & Faust, 1973; Gagne, 1977). In knowing a concept, a person is assumed to have knowledge of the rule that defines the critical features of the concept and to be able to use these critical features to recognize unfamiliar instances of the concept. Both philosophical analysis (Wittgenstein, 1953) and recent research in cognitive psychology suggests that this traditional view is insufficient. One prediction of a strict critical-feature model would be that all instances of the category should be recognized equally quickly because each instance should be tested against the same critical features.

However, this is not the case. For example, Rosch (1973) demonstrated that individuals' knowledge of the concept *bird* seemed to be dependent on a having a prototype of the concept *bird*. A *prototype* is a sort of generalized image, not necessarily visual, of the concept. Birds closer to the prototype (e.g., robins, sparrows) were recognized more quickly, while nontypical birds (e.g., owl, ostrich) took a longer time to identify. Clear nonbird silhouettes were quickly dismissed as noninstances quickly. Supporting findings are reported by McCloskey and Glucksberg (1978), Rosch (1975), Rosch (1977), and Walker (1975). (See Anderson, 1980, for a comprehensive discussion.) While there is considerable discussion about the precise nature of prototypes (Anderson, 1980); exposure to instances does play a critical role in acquiring a prototype.

In cognitive psychology, prototypes/concepts are often called *schemata* (frames, scripts, patterns, gestalts). A *schema* is an organizational form for the knowledge we have about a particular concept. A schema usually has default values for the parts of the concept. The totality of the default values would represent the prototype for the schema.

One metaphor that may help to conceptualize what a schema/prototype might be like is to imagine making black-and-white silhouette slides of a variety of birds so that the birds are about the same height. Then imagine projecting a very bright light through the entire set of slides. What would emerge would be a centralized dark image (the prototype) that would be the most typical bird. Nontypical birds would be represented by lighter gray fuzzy boundaries around the central prototype.

I am generally comfortable with the idea of a schema/prototype for most naturally acquired concepts. However, I think that many school-learned concepts may be acquired both as a set of learned critical features and as a prototype. The prototype is used to identify instances that are fairly typical, as well as clear noninstances. Typical instances possess many commonalities with the prototype, while noninstances possess few commonalities. However, for examples that are ambigious, learned critical features are used to determine if the example is valid (or we attempt to generate a set of critical features to use if we have not learned them previously). For concepts not learned in school, subjects would have difficulty making decisions about ambiguous instances. This is precisely what McCloskey and Glucksberg (1978) found with respect to individual category judgment for ambiguous instances of common categories. For example, about half of the subjects agree that stroke was a disease, while half did not.

The idea that conceptual knowledge may include both prototypical information and critical-feature information is consistent with the research on conceptual development carried out by Klausmeier and his associates (Klausmeier & Allen, 1978; Klausmeier, Ghatala, & Frayer, 1974; Tennyson & Park, 1980). Klausmeier and his co-workers see conceptual development occurring in four stages, running from discrimination of individual instances, through classifying instances as category members, to being able to verbally and formally describe the concept and relate it to other concepts. In a longitudinal study of conceptual development in children, they show that this is how children acquire concepts (Klausmeier & Allen, 1978).

Concepts also relate to other concepts by means of superordinate, coordinate, and subordinate relationships (Klausmeier & Allen, 1978; Klausmeier, Ghatala, & Frayer, 1974; Tennyson & Park, 1980). Acquiring a knowledge of such relationships is necessary to gaining an understanding of the concept (Tennyson & Park, 1980). In addition, concepts may be related metaphorically to other concepts. The implications and importance of such metaphorical relationships are just beginning to be understood. Such metaphorical relationships may represent a fundamental process in understanding new situations and acquiring new concepts (Ortony, 1980).

B. RULES, PRINCIPLES, AND SKILLS

Rules or principles are statements that relate concepts and tell how changes or alterations in one concept influence other concepts. A person who knows a rule has an "inferred capability that enables the individual to respond to a class of stimulus situations with a class of performances" (Gagne, 1977). Just as do concepts, principles and skills have a set of critical features that give rise to their operation or identify situations to which they apply. For example, critical features of the problem, $45 + 134 + 76 = ?$, such as the $+$ and the $=$ signs, prompt the operation of addition skills. For behavioral psychologists, the situation, "Explain why a rat that gets a food pellet for standing on its head stops doing so when food is no longer applied," will activate an explanation based on the principle of extinction, which relates the concepts *removal of reinforcement* and *strength (probability) of response*. Thus principles, rules, and skills can be analyzed into condition–action sequences just as can concepts.

The nature of rules can be illustrated by work on story schemata (Bower, Black, & Turner, 1979; Schank & Abelson, 1977). Schemata have been used to explain how we understand language and events in the world. Consider the following story: "A man enters a building. He picks up a loaf. He walks to a counter. He picks up his change. He leaves the building and drives away." When I use this example in my classes, I ask students to tell me what this story is about. Invariably they tell me it is about a man picking up a loaf of bread in a store. Then I ask if, as I read the story, they envisioned shelves with racks of bread on them, aisles with food on them, a counter containing a conveyer belt, a woman clerk near a cash register, etc. Most students answer yes. Then I ask where all those details came from. They certainly were not in the original story, rather they were in the schema for buying in a supermarket. I also point out that like ambiguous perceptual figures (e.g., the famous vase–faces figure from Gestalt psychology) this story is subject to multiple interpretations. For example, the person might have been buying gasoline and picking up a meatloaf baked for him by the gas-station owner's wife. While this latter scenario is less likely, it is still perfectly plausible. This use of schemata has been called *instantiation* by Anderson, Pichert, Goetz, Schallert, Stevens, and Trollip (1976). Anderson et al. (1976) argue that language is understood by constructing plausible instantiations from learned schemata. The instantiation applied determines what is remembered and learned from a text.

Schemata are also used to tell us what to do in particular situations. Schank and Abelson (1977) discussed the role of schemata in determining appropriate behavior in a restaurant. When we enter a restaurant, we have certain expectations: a waiter will come with a menu, we will order food, etc. These schema-based expectations determine our behavior. It may make this more clear to note that we have schemata for different classes of restaurants. You probably have no trouble identifying schemata for plastic fast food place, fine restaurant, greasy spoon, bar and grill. We have a different schema for each of these different categories of restaurants which allows us to recognize the type and tells us how to behave in that type of restaurant. We would not expect to order wine at McDonald's and we would not expect to stand at a counter for food at the Ritz. Perhaps a more interesting example is the work on sexual scripts. We have schemata for sexual activities: marriage, love affair, one-night stand, etc. These schemata define appropriate behavior in these situations (Delameter, 1983; Gagnon & Simon, 1973; Mosher, 1980).

Productions and Education

As noted, I believe that it is valuable to think about the learning of concepts, principles/rules, skills, and problem-solving abilities as the development of production systems. Each of these intellectual skills is activated by some set of conditions (the *conditional* part of a production), carries out some task (the *action* part of a production), and is associated in particular ways to other productions in memory. By thinking about knowledge as a production system, we have a unified means of describing what students must acquire to learn intellectual skills and what teachers and instruction should do to help the acquisition of intellectual skills. The conception of concepts, rules, and problem-solving skills as elements in a production system is consistent with Gagne's (1977) common description of these as intellectual skills and with current cognitive models of learning (Anderson, 1980; Anderson, Kline, Beasley, 1979; Goldstein, 1980, Lenat, 1983; Simon, 1980).

C. DECLARATIVE AND PROCEDURAL KNOWLEDGE

Production-system learning models make a distinction between declarative versus procedural knowledge. The distinction is usually described as the distinction between *knowing that* and *knowing how*. *Knowing that* refers to being able to talk about something; *knowing how* refers to being able to do that something (e.g., being able to describe a tennis service versus being able to hit one). The importance of this distinction is not that declarative and procedural knowledge are fundamentally different in the way that they are stored in memory, but rather that they involve two different aspects of teaching intellectual skills or productions. Teaching someone to hit a serve is different from teaching them to describe a tennis serve. For most school-learned intellectual skills, the objectives of instruction involve both declarative and procedural knowledge about a skill. For example, physicists certainly want students to be able to discuss weight (declarative knowledge) and to measure it (procedural knowledge); psychologists wants students to discuss reinforcement, recognize examples of it, and to use it to change behavior.

Acquiring procedural knowledge does *not* ensure that declarative knowledge will be acquired and vice versa. Keeping the distinction in mind helps teachers and instructional designers to focus on the need to develop instruction that leads to *both* procedural *and* declarative knowledge and not to the slighting of one for the other. I might raise the point that subject matter fields tend to differ in their emphasis on one or the other. On the basis of my own experiences and discussions with students in teaching about this topic, courses in mathematics and the mathematically oriented sciences seem to focus primarily on procedural knowledge, while at the introductory level at least; courses in the humanities and social sciences seem to focus on declarative knowledge. This difference may lead to the common stereotypes of such domains. Are math and the "hard" sciences perceived of as difficult in part because insufficient declarative knowledge in the form of literal and metaphorical description are taught in such courses? Are the humanities and social sciences regarded as fuzzy because lots of words but few specific procedures for doing anything are taught? Perhaps instructional designers in both areas need a more careful analysis of their subject matter in terms of its declarative and procedural knowledge and to consider these more carefully in the design of instruction.

D.   RESEARCH ON LEARNING OF PRODUCTIONS

If the acquisition of concepts, rules, skills, and problem-solving abilities can be viewed as the learning of productions, it is useful to ask what sorts of factors may facilitate or inhibit the learning of productions. The purpose of this section is to discuss research on such factors. This review of research is not exhaustive; it is meant to illustrate important procedures that may facilitate or inhibit the acquisition of intellectual skills. Each procedure is illustrated by one or two major studies.

1.   Providing Students with a Metaphorical Representation

This variable has been investigated in several studies. Royer and his associates have demonstrated that providing students with a concrete analogical passage prior to an instructional passage facilitates learning from the target passage (Perkins, 1978; Royer & Cable, 1975, 1976; Royer & Perkins, 1977).

Mayer (1975, 1976, 1980) has demonstrated that providing students with an analogy or model by which to understand a computer programming language facilitates learning to solve problems using the language. In the 1980 study, students in one condition related terms in a file-management programming language to familiar office functions such as filing, sorting, writing on a note pad, etc. This analogy led to an increased ability to solve far transfer problems compared to students given practice in using the concepts without understanding them.

The difference between *near* and *far transfer* refers to the similarity of the test problems to the problems given in instruction. Near problems are pretty much like the problems in instruction with minor variables changed. Far transfer problems would involve problems in which the dimensions of the problem were changed. For example, if one had practiced using the language to print out labels for individuals in the data base who were in the insurance industry, an example of a near transfer problem would be to print out labels for people in the airline industry. A problem involving far transfer might be to print out an address list of all individuals making more than $40,000 per year. The first problem merely involves a change in the same dimension (type of industry); the second problem involves two changes, in the nature of the output (labels to address book) and the dimension by which individuals are selected (industry to income).

While such analogies can be useful as instructional tools, Royer and Feldman (1984) caution that developing analogies is a truly creative and difficult act. In addition, analogies are never perfect—the topic to be learned is never exactly like the old previously known comparative materials. The difference may lead to confusion on the part of the student because the student cannot know how far to continue the analogy. Instruction that uses analogical representations to promote understanding in teaching intellectual skills must be careful to also lead students to draw distinctions between the analogy and the to-be-learned material. An analogy with the behavioral concept of prompting may be apropos; an analogical representation may be considered a prompt to allow the students to make correct responses (e.g., begin to understand) the subject matter; but it must be faded over practice if the student is to fully understand the new subject matter.

2. Verbalization during Problem Solving

A number of studies have found that verbalization of thought processes during problem solving can facilitate problem solution and learning. Gagne and Smith (1962) demonstrated that subjects who stated what they did while working Tower of Hanoi problems did better on the final problem than students who did not. Stinessen (1975) replicated this finding and demonstrated that the effect was greater when the task was abstract than when it was concrete. Stinessen (1974) demonstrated that verbalization has a greater effect when subjects are given explicit information about the problem-solving situation than when they were given nonexplicit information. Neither Gagne and Smith nor Stinessen provide an adequate theoretical explanation for this result. Webb (1983) discusses this issue in regard to group effects on learning intellectual skills (discussed below). One explanation may be that verbalization induces greater elaboration and cognitive structuring of the presented material. The effect is greater if the learner expects to teach the material to others (Webb, 1983). Further research is needed on this issue.

3. Using Questions

Asking students to try to use productions in the process of learning them has been shown to be facilitative of intellectual skill acquisition. Watts and Anderson (1971) found that asking students to apply concepts in the process of learning them facilitates learning of the concepts. While similar research has sometimes produced conflicting findings (Andre, 1979; Andre, Mueller, Womack, Smid, & Tuttle, 1980); such findings probably were due to the time interval between study and test and to insufficient practice given on the problems. Andre and Reiher (1983) found that the effect of asking questions that required students to practice concepts was enhanced on a delayed test. Tennyson and his co-workers (1975, 1980) have found that students generally require several practice examples to learn a concept.

In an interesting study, McKenzie and Herrington (1981) had students answer questions that asked them to apply an intellectual skill over several school days. Compared to a group that answered factual questions, the application-questions group transferred the skill to new material. In a study mentioned previously, Mayer (1980) had students answer questions that asked them to relate the terms in the file-control computer language to typical office functions. Students who answered these types of questions while learning did better on problem solving on the posttest. As part of a program on training the skill of learning from scientific text, Larkin and Reif (1976) trained students to ask application questions about scientific principles being taught. These student acquired a better ability to apply the material.

4. Providing Examples

In learning productions, students need worked-out examples from which to develop their understanding of the material to be learned. While this may seem like a truism to many, it has often been ignored by instructional designers and teachers. Pepper (1981) studied texts in computer programming. A text preferred by programming instructors was particularly terse and void of examples. By comparing the performance of learners who used the standard text and a modified text with many well-worked-out examples, Pepper demonstrated that examples facilitated the learners' ability to use the language in solving problems. Simon (1980) similarly emphasized the role of examples. Simon (1984) described instructional materials for teaching algebra concepts that involved mostly presented examples. Students who worked independently with these materials learned the algebra concepts in less than half the time as teacher-taught students.

In a review of research on teaching concepts, Tennyson and Park (1980) point out that the examples presented should constitute a rational set (Markle & Tiemann, 1969). A *rational set* provides examples that illustrate the variability of the irrelevant attributes of a production while sharpening focus on the relevant attributes of the production. Acquisition is facilitated when presentation of examples follows these rules: (1) examples should be ordered from easy to difficult; (2) subsequent examples should diverge in variable attributes from previous examples; and (3) examples should be matched to nonexamples on the basis of similarity of variable attributes (Tennyson & Park, 1980, p. 59). The function of these rules is to ensure that the learner acquires an accurate conditional part of the production.

5. Coordinate Ideas

Within a given subject matter domain, productions are often coordinate. For example, under the superordinate concept of behavioral learning theory, one might find the coordinate productions (or rules), *operant conditioning* and *classical conditioning*. Over a number of studies, simultaneous presentation of coordinate productions (or rules), in which nonexamples of one production (rule) are examples of coordinate productions, has been found to be facilitative of production acquisition (Tennyson & Park, 1980; Tennyson & Tennyson, 1975).

6. Discovery versus Expository Learning

In rule-induction experiments, discovery learning has often been found to facilitate transfer and problem-solving skills when compared to expository learning. For example, Katona (1940) found that learners who discovered solutions to problems were more likely to be able to successfully perform on far transfer tasks. In a study of solving cryptograms, Guthrie (1967) reported a similar finding. Such findings have led to the generalization that discovery learning produces better far transfer, while expository learning produces better near transfer or learning of the original task (Bruner, 1961; Suchman, 1961).

Andre (1979) criticized this conclusion because comparison of the methods had not ensured that the procedures were attempting to teach the same outcomes. In particular, while discovery methods force students to search for generality, expository methods may or may not require the student to process the information for generality. If the expository method is used to focus students on the acquisition of a particular response category, it is not surprising that students do poorly on transfer tasks. But it is certainly not an inherent feature of the expository method that students be focused on mindless learning. For example, as noted earlier, the presentation of analogical models for understanding, certainly an expository act, has facilitated far transfer (Mayer, 1975). The real issue is not expository or discovery learning, but the nature of the processing students engage in while learning (Andre, 1979). Discovery methods may offer students a way to ensure processing that leads to far transfer, and for this reason they are instructionally important, but they are not the only methods to ensure processing for far transfer. As in the aforementioned Mayer work, the nature of the expository instruction is critical. When expository instruction focuses the learner on understanding the underlying productions by fitting them to a cognitive structure, expository description may facilitate far transfer. When the expository description focuses the learner on repetition of a verbal chain or the repetitive application of a production, then exposition may interfere with transfer.

7. Giving a Verbal Description

An issue related to the discovery–expository issue is whether or not having students learn a verbal description of a principle or rule is facilitative. Typically, learning a verbal description has been facilitative of at least near transfer (Craig, 1956; Kersh, 1962). These results suggest that when the instructional objective involves near transfer, a procedure of giving a rule should be followed.

8. Training the Learner to Learn Better

Learners differ in the extent to which they try to understand and use material they are exposed to. Higher-ability learners seem to use techniques to help them develop understanding, see applications, and make use of learned ideas. Less able learners do not do so. One line of research related to the development of problem solving and intellectual skills involves attempts to produce better learners by giving training in appropriate processing strategies. An example of this line of research is presented by Larkin and Reif (1976). Other research has been done by Dansereau and his associates (1979, 1984), Weinstein and her associates (1983), and by Annis (1984). This research demonstrates that it is possible to train learners to use more effective learning strategies. This research is discussed more fully in Chapter 8 by Duell and Chapter 9 by Snowman in this text.

9. Group Learning Effects

A number of studies have found that small-group learning procedures may be useful for training in intellectual skills (Webb, 1982b). For example, Webb (1982a) found that learning in groups of four promoted near transfer in learning exponentiation and scientific notation among seventh- and eight-grade students. Skon, Johnson, and Johnson (1981) reported that group learning facilitated the acquisition of cognitive reasoning skills. There are some difficulties in the latter study, in that the learning tasks also served as the measure of performance, and transfer was not demonstrated. However, other studies have reported that group-learning experience can facilitate concept learning, conservation, and reasoning strategies (Johnson & Johnson, 1979; Johnson, Skon, & Johnson, 1980; Laughlin, 1978).

Webb (1982a, 1982b) argues that the facilitation of performance comes from the opportunity to receive explanations and feedback from other group members. In the Webb (1983) study, not receiving an explanation when it was requested was the strongest predictor of the transfer test performance. Receiving an explanation correlated positively with performance. Giving explanations also led to better performance. This latter effect is particularly interesting.

Consistent with academic folklore, having to teach something facilitates learning of it. Webb (1983) discusses two possible explanations of the teaching effect. One explanation is based on the aforementioned verbalization studies; often verbalization during learning facilitates learning. A second explanation is that preparing to teach forces the learner to elaborate on the material to a greater degree and to develop a more organized cognitive structure for the topic. This interpretation is consistent with studies by Durling and Schick (1978), who found that learners who prepared to teach to actual students learned more than than learners who taught to the teacher. Webb (1983) and Slavin (1980) provide comprehensive reviews of this literature; the interested reader is referred to those sources for more information.

10. Emotional Factors in Problem Solving

It is well known that anxiety can inhibit performance on complex tasks (Anderson & Faust, 1973). Some studies have suggested that anxiety-reduction procedures may be useful in problem solving. Collins, Dansereau, Garland, Holley, and MacDonald (1978) examined the influence of relaxation procedures in learning from prose. A combination of relaxation techniques to maintain concentration and positive self-talk techniques facilitated learning from a prose passage. While not directly related to the learning of productions, this study is suggestive that reduction of anxiety may facilitate such learning.

Gross and Mastenbrook (1980) examined the effects of state anxiety on problem-solving efficiency under high- and low-memory conditions. The task consisted of a concept-identification task using cards containing geometric figures varying in several dimensions. When no external memory aid was provided, high-anxious subjects did worse than low-anxious subjects. When a memory aid was provided, there was no difference between highly anxious and low-anxious subjects. Other research similarly demonstrates a reduction of the anxiety effect when memory aids are provided (Leherissey, O'Neil, & Hanson, 1971; Sieber, Kameya, & Paulson, 1970). The specific mechanism by which memory aids operate is not clear from this research. Webb (1983) discussed the role of groups in problem solving and argued that when learners receive explanations and teaching from other group members instead of a teacher, there may be a reduction in anxiety, leading to improvements in performance.

Mild levels of stress may or may not improve problem-solving performance (Davis, 1968). For example, Fine, Cohen, and Crist (1960) found that working under humid and hot conditions improved anagram-solution times. Similarly, time pressure improved anagram performance (Nance & Sinnot; 1964). Phillips, Griswold, and Pace (1963) found that reduced oxygen levels (14,250 ft altitude conditions) did not reduce performance in arithmetic computation problems but did in solving word-rhyme problems. Whether or not stress will influence performance may be related to the complexity of the task. Because stress may increase anxiety, it should help performance on simple tasks and reduce performance on more complex task. Of course, complexity must be assessed relative to the abilities and knowledge base of the individual learner.

V. FACILITATING THE LEARNING OF INTELLECTUAL SKILLS

One reasonable question to ask after this review of the cognitive structures we use to problem solve and the instructional factors that influence problem solving is; *Can we use this information to teach intellectual skills better?* Andre (1984) suggested that such a review would be useful by leading to a set of general guidelines developing instruction on intellectual skills. In Andre's view, every time a production (concept, rule, skill, or problem-solving ability) is to be taught, the production needs to be analyzed into its three components and the instruction should ensure that the learner acquires each of the components. In Andre's model, once the components are identified, then instructional moves can be planned. The model is presented in Fig. 7.

The recommendations in Fig. 7 are still very general. To be used, they have to be operationalized in a particular educational situation. The list in Fig. 7 should be considered a checklist of possible activities in which a learner may engage in order to promote the development of productions that represent intellectual skills. Instructional developers should use this list to consider possible instructional moves. In addition, the model provides a program for future investigation on instructional processes.

Step 1. Analyze the subject-matter domain for intellectual skills required in that domain, and develop a map of skills and their relationship. Develop a behavioral–cognitive task analysis for each skill.

Step 2. Provide for an appropriate emotional–motivation setting.

Step 3. Acquire the conditional component of the production.

  a. Identify the subcomponents of the conditional (identify the critical features of exemplar situations that will activate the concept insofar as possible. Collect exemplar situations that represent the range of situations that will activate the conditional).

  b. Test students to determine if they have the subcomponents available to them. Provide training as necessary.

  c. Activate relevant prior learning by
   i. Subsumatory or comparative advanced organizers
   ii. Meaningful metaphors that provide a model for understanding.

  d. Provide a range of examples that illustrate the discriminative features of exemplar situations that activate the conditional to allow development of a prototype.

  e. Lead the student to attend to discriminative features of examples by appropriate adjunct aids, such as
   i. Inserted questions that ask why examples are examples
   ii. Text cues
   iii. Diagrams/illustrations.

  f. Lead the student to attend to discriminative features by activating relevant learning strategies or tactics.

Step 4. Acquire the network relationships of a production by
  a. Presenting an organizer that demonstrates relationships between superordinate, coordinate, and subordinate concepts
  b. Leading the student to analyze relationships between productions by requiring him/her to respond to compare–contrast type questions
  c. Providing metaphors that illustrate relationships among concepts
  d. Teaching related productions simultaneously to illustrate relationships
  e. Using pictorial–graphic material that illustrates relationships.

Step 5. Acquire the action part of a production
  a. Identify the steps in the action, and communicate the steps to the learner—this may involve both behavioral and cognitive task analysis.
  b. Provide the learner with sufficient opportunity to practice the skills so that its use becomes relatively automatic.
  c. Provide feedback to the learner about the quality of his/her action.

FIG. 7. Model for developing instruction for training in intellectual skills.

REFERENCES

Adams, J. L. (1974). *Conceptual blockbusting*, New York: Norton.
Anderson, J. R. (1980). *Cognitive psychology and its implications*, San Francisco: Freeman.
Anderson, J. R., Kline, P. J., & Beasley, C. M. (1979). A general learning theory and its application to schema abstraction. In G. H. Bower (Ed.), *The psychology of learning and motivation*, Vol. 13, (pp. 249–296). New York: Academic Press.
Anderson, R. C., & Faust, G. W. (1973). *Educational psychology*, New York: Dodd, Mead.
Anderson, R. C., Pichert, J. W., Goetz, E. T. Schallert, D. L., Stevens, K. V., & Trollip, S. R.

(1976). Instantiation of general terms, *Journal of Verbal Learning and Verbal Behavior*, 15, 667–680.

Andre, T. (1979). On productive knowledge and levels of questions. *Review of Educational Research*, 49, 280–318.

Andre, T. (1984). *Adjunct aids and the acquisition of concepts, principles, and problem-solving skills from text*. Paper presented at the annual meeting of the American Educational Research Association, New Orleans.

Andre, T., Mueller, C., Womack, S., Smid, K., & Tuttle, M. (1980). Adjunct application questions facilitate later application, or do they? *Journal of Educational Psychology*, 72, 533–543.

Andre, T., & Reiher, T. (1983). *Type of question, delay interval, and learning from prose*. Paper presented at the annual meeting of the American Educational Research Association, Montreal.

Annis, L. F. (1984). *Improving college study skills and reducing anxiety: The effects of a model course*. Paper presented at the annual meeting of the American Educational Research Association, New Orleans.

Atwood, M. E., & Poison, P. G. (1976). A process model for water jug problems. *Cognitive Psychology*, 8, 191–216.

Bower, G. H., Black, J. B., & Turner, T. J. (1979). Scripts in memory for text. *Cognitive Psychology*, 11, 177–220.

Braine, M. D. S. (1978). On the relations between natural logic and reasoning and standard logic. *Psychological Review*, 85, 1–21.

Bruner, J. S. (1961). The act of discovery. *Harvard Educational Review*, 31, 21–32.

Campbell, D. T. (1960). Blind variation and selective retention in creative thought as in other knowledge processes. *Psychological Review*, 67, 380–400.

Champagne, A. B., Klopfer, L. E., Chaiklin, S. (1984). *The ubiquitous quantities*. Paper presented at the annual meeting of the American Educational Research Association, New Orleans.

Chase, W. G., & Simon, H. A. (1973). Perception in chess. *Cognitive Psychology*, 4, 55–81.

Collins, K. W., Dansereau, D. F., Garland, J. C., Holley, D. D. & MacDonald, B. A., (1978). Control of concentration during academic tasks. *Journal of Educational Psychology*, 73, 122–128.

Craig, R. C. (1956). Directed versus independent discovery of established relations. *Journal of Educational Psychology*, 47, 223–234.

Craighead, W. E. Kazdin, A. E., & Mahoney, M. J. (1981). *Behavior Modification*. Boston: Hougton Mifflin.

Dansereau, D. F. (1984). *Computer-based learning strategy training modules: A progress report*. Paper presented at the annual meeting of the American Educational Research Association, New Orleans.

Dansereau, D. F., McDonald, B. A., Collins, K. W., Garlind, J. C., Holley, C. T., Kiekhoff, G. M., Evans, S. H. (1979). Evaluation of a learning strategy system. In H. F. O'neil, Jr., and C. D. Spielberger (Eds.), *Cognitive and affective learning strategies* (pp. 3–79). New York: Academic Press.

Davis, G. A. (1968). Current status of research and theory in human problem solving. *Psychological Bulletin*, 66, 36–54.

Davis, G. A. (1973). *Psychology of problem solving*. New York: Basic.

Delamater, J. (1983). *Cultural scenarios and sexual desire: A sociological perspective on human sexuality*. Paper presented at the annual meeting of the Society for the Scientific Study of Sex, Chicago.

Duncker, K. (1945). On problem solving. *Psychological Monographs*, 58(5, Whole No. 270).

Durling, R. & Schick, C. (1978). Concept attainment by pairs and individuals as a function of vocalization. *Journal of Educational Psychology, 68,* 83–91.

Egan, D., and Schwartz, B. J. (1979). Chunking and recall of symbolic drawings. *Memory and cognition, 7,* 149–158.

Egan, D. E., & Grimes-Farrow, D. D. (1982). Differences in mental representation spontaneously adopted for reasoning. *Memory and Cognition, 10,* 297–307.

Ernst, G. W., & Newell, A. (1969). GPS: A case study in generality and problem solving. New York: Academic Press.

Ewert, P. H., & Lambert, J. F. (1932). Part II: The effect of verbal instructions upon the formation of a concept. *Journal of General Psychology, 6,* 400–411.

Feather, N. (1965). Acceptance and rejection of arguments in relation to attitude strength, critical ability, and intolerance of inconsistency. *Journal of Abnormal and Social Psychology, 69,* 127–136.

Fine, B. J., Cohen, A., & Crist, B. (1960). Effect of exposure to high humidity at high and moderate ambient temperature on anagram solution and auditory discrimination. *Psychological Reports, 7,* 171–181.

Fisher, D. L. (1981). A three factor model of syllogistic reasoning: The study of isolable stages, *Memory and Cognition, 9,* 496–514.

Gagne, R. M. (1977). *The conditions of learning,* New York: Holt.

Gagne, R. M., & Smith, E. C. (1962). A study of the effects of verbalization on problem solving. *Journal of Experimental Psychology, 63,* 12–18.

Gagnon, J. H., & Simon, W. (1973). *Sexual conduct: The sources of human sexuality.* Chicago: Aldine.

Goldfried, M. R., & Goldfried, A. P. (1980). Cognitive change methods. In F. H. Kanfer & A. P. Goldstein (Eds.), *Helping people change* (pp. 97–130). New York: Pergamon.

Goldstein, I., (1980). Developing a computational representation for problem-solving skills. In D. T. Tuma, and F. Reif (Eds.), *Problem solving and education* (pp. 53–80). Hillsdale, NJ: Erlbaum.

Goldstein, I., & Papert, S., (1977). Artificial intelligence, language, and the study of knowledge. *Cognitive Science, 1,* 84–124.

Gordon, D., & Lakoff, G. (1971). Conversational postulates. In *Papers from the seventh regional meeting of the Chicago Linguistic Society.* Chicago: University of Chicago Press.

Gordon, R. (1953). Attitudes toward Russia on logical reasoning. *Journal of Social Psychology, 37,* 103–111.

Greeno, J. G. (1974). Hobbits and orcs: Acquisition of a sequential concept. *Cognitive Psychology, 6,* 270–292.

Greeno, J. G. (1980). Trends in the theory of knowledge for problem solving. In D. T. Tuma & F. Reif (Eds.), *Problem solving and education: Issues in teaching and learning* (pp. 9–24). Hillsdale, NJ: Erlbaum.

Gross, T. F., & Mastenbrook, M. (1980). Examination of the effects of state anxiety on problem-solving efficiency under high and low memory conditions. *Journal of Educational Psychology, 72,* 605–609.

Guthrie, J. T. (1967). Expository instruction versus a discovery method. *Journal of Educational Psychology, 58,* 45–49.

Hayes, J. R. (1976). It's the thought that counts. In D. Klahr (Ed.), *Cognition and instruction* (pp. 235–244). Hillsdale, NJ: Erlbaum.

Hayes, J. R. (1981). *The compleat problem solver.* Philadelphia: Franklin Institute Press.

Hinsley, D., Hayes, J. R., & Simon, H. A. (1977). From words to equations. In P. Carpenter & M. Just (Eds.), *Cognitive processes in comprehension* (pp. 139–164). Hillsdale, NJ: Erlbaum.

Horn, L. (1972). *On the semantic properties of logical operators in English.* Unpublished doctoral dissertation, University of California, Los Angeles.

Janis, I., & Frick, P. (1943). The relationship between attitudes toward conclusions and errors in judging logical validity of syllogisms. *Journal of Experimental Psychology, 33*, 73–77.

Janis, I., & Terwilliger, R. (1962). An experimental study of psychological resistances to fear arousing communications. *Journal of Abnormal and Social Psychology, 65*, 403–410.

Johnson, D. W., & Johnson, R. (1979). Cooperative, competitive, and individualistic learning. *Journal of Research and Development in Education, 12*, 3–15.

Johnson, D. W., Skon, L., & Johnson, R., (1980). Effects of cooperative, competitive, and individualistic learning on problem-solving performance. *American Educational Research Journal, 77*, 83–94.

Katona, G. (1940). *Organizing and memorizing.* New York: Columbia University Press.

Kaufman, H., & Goldstein, S. (1967). The effects of emotional value of conclusions upon distortions in syllogistic reasoning. *Psychonomic Science, 7*, 367–368.

Kersh, B. Y. (1962). The motivating effect of learning by directed discovery. *Journal of Educational Psychology, 49*, 282–292.

Kingsley, H. L., & Garry, R. (1957). *The nature and conditions of learning* (2nd ed.). Englewood Cliffs, NJ: Prentice-Hall.

Klausmeier, H. J., & Allen, P. S. (1978). *Cognitive development of children and youth: A longitudinal study.* New York: Academic Press.

Klausmeier, H. J., Ghatala, E. S., & Frayer, D. A. (1974). *Conceptual learning and development: A cognitive view.* New York: Academic Press.

Kohler, W. (1925). *The mentality of apes.* New York: Harcourt Brace Jovanovich.

Larkin, J. H. (1980). Teaching problem solving in physics: The psychological laboratory and the practical classroom. In D. T. Tuma & F. Reif (Eds.), *Problem solving and education: Issues in teaching and research* (pp. 111–126). Hillsdale, NJ: Erlbaum.

Larkin, J. H., McDermott, J., Simon, D. P., & Simon, H. A. (1980). Expert and novice performance in solving physics problems. *Science, 208*, 1335–1342.

Larkin, J. H., & Reif, F. (1976). Analysis and teaching of a general skill for studying scientific text. *Journal of Educational Psychology, 68*, 43–440.

Laughlin, P. (1978). Ability and group problem solving. *Journal of Research and Development in Education, 12*, 114–120.

Lefford, A. (1946). The influence of emotional subject matter on logical reasoning. *Journal of General Psychology, 34*, 127–151.

Leherissey, B. L., O'Neil, H. F. & Hansen, D. N. (1971). Effects of memory support on state anxiety and performance in computer-assisted learning. *Journal of Educational Psychology, 62*, 413–420.

Lenat, D. B. (1983). Toward a theory of heuristics. In R. Groner, M. Groner, & W. F. Bischof (Eds.), *Methods of linguistics* (pp. 351–404). Hillsdale, NJ: Erlbaum.

Luchins, A. S. (1942). Mechanization in problem solving. *Psychological Monographs, 54*(6), Whole No. 248.

Maier, N. R. F. (1930). Reasoning in humans I: On direction. *Journal of Comparative Psychology, 10*, 115–143.

Maier, N. (1970). *Problem solving and creativity: In individuals and groups.* Belmont, CA: Brooks/Cole.

Markle, S. M. & Tiemann, P. W. (1969). *Really understanding Concepts.* Champaign, IL: Stipes.

Mayer, R. E. (1975). Different problem-solving competencies established in learning computer programming with and without meaningful models. *Journal of Educational Psychology, 67*, 725–734.

Mayer, R. E. (1976). Some conditions of meaningful learning for computer programming: Advanced organizers and subject control of frame order. *Journal of Educational Psychology*, 68, 143–150.

Mayer, R. E. (1980). Elaboration techniques that increase the meaningfullness of technical text: An experimental test of the learning strategy hypothesis. *Journal of Educational Psychology*, 72, 770–784.

Mayer, R. E. (1983). *Thinking, problem solving, cognition*. New York: Freeman.

McCloskey, M. E., & Glucksberg, S. (1978). Natural categories: Well-defined or fuzzy sets? *Memory and Cognition*, 6, 462–472.

McKenzie, G. R., & Herrington, L. M. (1981). *Effects of adjunct application questions on forward transfer of a cognitive strategy.* Paper presented at the annual meeting of the American Educational Research Association, Los Angeles.

Morgan, J. J. B., & Morton, J. T. (1944). The distortion of syllogistic reasoning produced by personal convictions. *Journal of Social Psychology*, 20, 39–59.

Mosher, D. L. (1980). Three dimensions of depth of involvement in human sexual response. *The Journal of Sex Research*, 16, 1–42.

Nance, R. D., & Sinnot, W. (1964). Level of difficulty and consistency of performance in anagram solving. *Psychological Reports*, 14, 895–898.

Newell, A., & Simon, H. (1972). *Human problem solving.* Englewood Cliffs, NJ: Prentice-Hall.

Norman, D. A. (1980). Cognitive engineering and education. In D. T. Tuma & F. Reif (Eds.). *Problem solving and Education* (pp. 97–110). Hillsdale, NJ: Erlbaum.

Ortony, A. (1980). Metaphor. In Spiro, R. J., Bruce, B. B., & Brewer, W. F. (Eds.). *Theoretical issues in reading comprehension* (pp. 349–361). Hillsdale, NJ: Erlbaum.

Osborn, A. F. (1963). *Applied imagination.* New York: Scribner's.

Osgood, C. E. (1957). A behavioral analysis of perception and language as cognitive phenomena. In J. S. Bruner (Ed.), *Contemporary approaches to cognition* (pp. 257–293). Cambridge, MA: Harvard University Press.

Page, J. J., & Simon, H. A. (1966). Cognitive processes in solving algebra word problems. In B. Kleinmuntz (Ed.), *Problem solving: Research, method and theory* (pp. 77–109). New York: Wiley.

Parrott, G. (1967). *The effects of premise content on accuracy and solution time in syllogistic reasoning.* Unpublished master's thesis, Michigan State University.

Parrott, G. (1969). *The effects of instructions, transfer, and content on reasoning.* Unpublished doctoral dissertation, Michigan State University.

Pepper, J. (1981). Following student's suggestions for rewriting a computer programming textbook, *American Educational Research Journal*, 18, 259–270.

Perkins, M. R. (1978). *Measures of cognitive structure: Do they really assess learning at the level of comprehension?* Unpublished doctoral dissertation, University of Massachusetts, Amherst.

Phillips, L. W., Griswold, R. L., & Pace, N. (1963). Cognitive changes at high altitude. *Psychological Reports*, 13, 423–430.

Platt, W. & Baker, R. A. (1931). The relations of the scientific "hunch" to research. *Journal of Chemical Education*, 8, 1969–2002.

Polya, G. (1945). *How to solve it.* Garden City, N.Y.: Doubleday.

Revlin, R., & Leirer, V. O. (1978). The effects of personal biases on syllogistic reasoning: Rational decisions from personalized representations. In R. Revlin and R. E. Mayer (Eds.), *Human reasoning* (pp. 51–82). Washington, DC: Winston.

Revlis, R. (1975). Two models of syllogistic reasoning: Feature selection and conversion. *Journal of Verbal Learning and Verbal Behavior*, 14, 180–195.

Rosch, E. (1973). On the internal structure and perceptual and semantic categories. In T. E.

Mooze (Ed.), *Cognitive development and the acquisition of language* (pp. 213–253). New York: Academic Press.

Rosch, E. (1975). Cognitive representations of semantic categories. *Journal of Experimental Psychology: General, 104*, 192–223.

Rosch, E. (1977). Human categorization. In N. Warren (Ed.), *Advances in Cross-Cultural Psychology* (Vol. 1, pp. 171–197). London: Academic Press.

Royer, J. M., & Cable, G. W. (1975). Facilitated learning in connected discourse. *Journal of Educational Psychology, 67*, 116–123.

Royer, J., & Cable, G. W. (1976). Illustrations, analogies, and facilitative transfer in prose learning. *Journal of Educational Psychology, 68*, 205–209.

Royer, J. M., & Feldman, R. S. (1984). *Educational Psychology.* New York: Knopf.

Royer, J. M., & Perkins, M. R. (1977). Facilitative transfer in prose learning over an extended time period. *Journal of Reading Behavior, 9*, 185–188.

Rubinstein, M. F. (1975). *Patterns of problem-solving.* Englewood Cliffs, NJ: Prentice-Hall.

Schank, R. C., & Abelson, R. P. (1977). *Scripts, plans, goals, and understanding.* Hillsdale, NJ: Erlbaum.

Sieber, J. E., Kameya, L. I., & Paulson, F. L. (1970). Effect of memory support on the problem-solving ability of test-anxious children. *Journal of Educational Psychology, 61*, 159–168.

Simon, H. A. (1980). Problem solving in education. In D. T. Tuma & F. Reif (Eds.), *Problem solving and education: Issues in teaching and research* (pp. 81–96). Hillsdale, NJ: Erlbaum.

Simon, H. (1984). Talk presented at the Nobel Conference, Gustafus Adolphus College, St. Peter, MN.

Simpson, M. E., & Johnson, D. M. (1966). Atmosphere and conversion errors in syllogistic reasoning. *Journal of Experimental Psychology, 72*, 197–200.

Skinner, B. F. (1966). An operant analysis of problem solving. In B. Kleinmuntz (Ed.), *Problem solving: Research, method and theory* (pp. 127–159). New York: Wiley.

Skon, L., Johnson, D. W., & Johnson, R. T. (1981). Cooperative peer interaction versus individual competition and individualistic efforts: Effects of the acquisition of cognitive reasoning strategies. *Journal of Educational Psychology, 73* 83–92.

Slavin, R. E. (1980). Cooperative learning in teams: State of the art. *Educational Psychologist, 15* 93–111.

Staats, A. W. (1966). An integrated–functional learning approach to complex human behavior. In B. Kleinmuntz (Ed.), *Problem solving: Research, method and theory* (pp. 261–298). New York: Wiley.

Stinessen, L. (1973). Effect of different training on solution of Katona's match stick problem. *Scandinavian Journal of Psychology, 14*, 106–110.

Stinessen, L. (1974). Explicit and inexplicit guidance in problem solving and ability to state principles. *Psychological Reports, 34*, 515–518.

Stinessen, L. (1975). Conditions which influence acquisition and application of verbal representations in problem solving. *Psychological Reports, 36*, 355–42.

Suchman, J. R. (1961). Inquiry training: Building skills for autonomous discovery. *Merrill-Palmer Quarterly, 7*, 147–169.

Symonds, P. M. (1936). *Education and the psychology of thinking.* New York: McGraw-Hill.

Tennyson, R. D., & Park, O. (1980). The teaching of concepts: A review of instructional design literature. *Review of Educational Research, 50*, 55–70.

Tennyson, R. D., & Tennyson, C. L. (1975). Rule acquisition design strategy variables: Degree of instance divergence, sequence, and instance analysis. *Journal of Educational Psychology, 67*, 852–859.

Thomas, J. C., Jr. (1974). An analysis of behavior in the hobbits–orcs problem. *Cognitive Psychology, 6,* 257–269.

Thorndike, E. L. (1898). Animal intelligence: An experimental study of the associative processes in animals. *Psychological Monographs, 2*(No. 8).

Walker, J. H. (1975). Real-world variability, reasonableness judgements, and memory representation for concepts. *Journal of Verbal Learning and Verbal Behavior, 14,* 241–252.

Wallas, G. (1926). *The art of thought.* New York: Harcourt Brace Jovanovich.

Watts, G. H., & Anderson, R. C. (1971). Effects of three types of inserted questions on learning from prose. *Journal of Educational Psychology, 62,* 387–394.

Webb, N. M. (1982a). Group composition, group interaction, and achievement in cooperative small groups. *Journal of Educational Psychology, 74,* 475–484.

Webb, N. M. (1982b). Peer Interaction and learning in small groups. *Journal of Educational Psychology, 74,* 642–656.

Webb, N. M. (1983). Predicting learning from student interaction: Defining the interaction variables. *Educational Psychologist, 18,* 33–41.

Weinstein, C. E., Schulte, A. C., & Cascallar, E. C. (1983). *The learning and study strategies inventory (Lassi): Initial design and development.* Unpublished manuscript, University of Texas, Department of Educational Psychology, Austin.

Wickelgren, W. A. (1974). *How to solve problems: Elements of a theory of problems and problem solving.* San Francisco: Freeman.

Wilkins, M. C. (1928). The effect of changed material on ability to do formal syllogistic reasoning. (Archives of Psychology, No. 102).

Wilson, W. (1965). The effect of competition on the speed and accuracy of syllogistic reasoning. *Journal of Social Psychology, 65,* 27–32.

Wittgenstein, I. (1953). *Philosophical investigations.* New York: Macmillan.

8

METACOGNITIVE SKILLS

Orpha K. Duell

College of Education
Wichita State University
Wichita, Kansas 67208

I. INTRODUCTION

Sally's teacher announces that tomorrow the class will have an essay exam on Chapter 2. Sally believes she will fail unless she studies, so she decides to study. She opens her book to Chapter 2, glances at the title of the chapter and then stares into space while attempting to recall all of the major pieces of information she knows about that topic. Next, she examines the names of the chapter divisions and discovers she had omitted three of them. She closes the book and repeatedly recalls the major topics, being careful to include the three previously omitted. Convinced she knows all the major topics, she summarizes everything she knows about the first major topic. She then turns to that part of the chapter and rereads passages from the book she had underlined as she initially read the chapter, paying special attention to those she had not recalled from memory and checking to see that what she is reading makes sense to her. She repeatedly checks the underlined passages, attempts to put them in her own words and only looks at the text when she must. After closing the book and recalling all she can from this division of the chapter, she returns to the book to check her recall. Once she is convinced she knows the material in this division of the chapter, she moves on to the next.

The information Sally enters into her memory while studying will be content in her memory which she hopes she will be able to recall when she takes the exam. Her belief that she needed to study and her decisions about when and how to study, as well as her estimates of her readiness to recall the information when she takes the exam, are called *metacognition*. The purpose of this chapter is to consider metacognition, some of the research which has been done in this area, and what it may suggest to classroom teachers. To this end, the chapter first describes what metacognition is within the context of information-processing theories of learning, reviews relevant research literature, and draws conclusions concerning classroom practices.

COGNITIVE CLASSROOM LEARNING:
UNDERSTANDING, THINKING,
AND PROBLEM SOLVING

II. DEFINITIONS AND THEORIES

Learning theorists who attempt to explain how people learn by viewing them as continually processing information and making decisions about it are called information-processing learning theorists. Such theorists have often developed their theories by either writing computer programs (step-by-step directions that tell the computer what it is to do), which attempt to simulate or copy the way humans perform, or by using computer terminology plus some of the basic concepts coming from computer simulation research. Most assume three basic parts in the memory system, although some assume additional parts and not all use exactly the same names. One part is *sensory memory*, which registers incoming information as the learner experiences it. Sensory memory is assumed to be very brief (a fraction of a second), and so if information is to be used by the learner, it must move from the sensory memory to the second part of the memory system, *short-term memory*. From a classroom teacher's point of view, short-term memory is also very brief, usually thought to last about 20 seconds. Unless the learner does something with the information in short-term memory, such as rehearse it, it will be lost. Finally, there is *long-term memory*, which is relatively perma-nent. What classroom teachers hope will happen is that students will interact with the material being presented in class in such a way that it will move from short-term memory into long-term memory. Once information is in long-term memory, the learner must retrieve the information when it is needed. The knowledge the learner has about his or her learning system and the decisions the learner makes about how to act on information coming into the learning system is called *metacognition.*

John Flavell (1979) defines metacognitive knowledge as "that segment of your [a child's, an adult's] stored world knowledge that has to do with people as cognitive creatures and with their diverse cognitive tasks, goals, actions, and experiences" (p. 906). An example would be Sally believing she learns information better if she puts it in her own words than if she repeats the information word for word as it appears in the study materials. Another example would be Sally believing she can learn a list of words faster if she groups similar words (for example, she puts all clothing terms together, food terms together, etc.).

Baker and Brown (cited in Brown, 1981) distinguish two types of metacog-nition: (1) knowledge about cognition and (2) regulation of cognition. *Knowl-edge about cognition* includes such things as knowledge about one's own cognitive resources, and knowledge about how compatible the demands of learning situations are with one's own resources. They believe knowledge about cognition (1) is stable over time (if Bob believes today that he can learn better by putting information into his own words, it is likely he will continue to believe that tomorrow), (2) can be stated by the learner, (3) may not be accurate, and (4) is late-developing and so is more complete in the older learner. The later development of the ability to think about and be aware of one's own actions during problem solving, reading, and writing means that the teacher may be working with learners who are unaware of their capabilities and limitations as learners. Such learners are therefore not always able to take the most appropriate actions in any given learning situation. The second type of metacognition, regulation of cognition, "consists of the self-regulatory mechanisms used by an active learner during an ongoing attempt to solve problems" (Brown, 1981, p. 21). These activities are thought to be (1) relatively unstable (the learner may use them on some occasions but not on others), (2) rarely statable (learners know how to do many things they cannot describe in words), and (3) relatively independent of the learner's age. Brown (1981) provides the following examples of these regulatory metacognitive activities: "*planning* one's next move, *checking* the outcome of any strategies one might use, *monitoring* the effectiveness of any attempted actions, *testing, revising,* and *evaluating* one's strategies for learning" (pp. 21–22). Although these two types of metacognition may be distinguished conceptually, Brown (1981) argues that they are closely related and should not be separated if one is to understand metacognition.

Metacognition includes knowledge about and regulation of various cognitive processes. For example, knowledge about and regulation of understanding communications is labeled *metacomprehension* and knowledge about and regulation of memory is labeled *metamemory*. If Sally believes that a good way to find a "misplaced" item, such as a pen she has lost, is to mentally retrace her steps until she recalls the last place she had the item, this would be an example of metamemory because it deals with what Sally knows about how to use her memory system.

Although John Flavell (1971) only recently introduced the term *metamemory*, the focus of its attention on self-awareness and self-control in learning is not new. Since the beginning of this century, educational psychologists have recognized that processes such as self-awareness and self-control are important components in reading (Brown, 1981). The increased attention given to self-awareness and self-control in learning since Flavell introduced the term *metamemory* has led to differences over what metamemory and metacognition include (Wellman, 1983). These concepts are relatively new and not precisely defined at this time. The review of the literature which follows gives a sampling of the areas researchers have investigated relative to metacognition. More studies on metamemory than other metacognitive areas are covered because that area has produced a large number of studies.

If the reader has detected a similarity between what we have been describing as metacognition and what you might want to call "study skills," you are not the first one to recognize it. Brown (1978) pointed out this similarity in her review of selected parts of this literature. This means the chapter concentrates on cognitive processing basic to the development of study skills.

III.   LITERATURE REVIEW

This section reviews studies that have examined various aspects of meta-cognition. It looks at studies on metamemory, studies of metacognition in communication and comprehension, observations about metacognition in problem solving, studies describing attempts to teach metacognitive skills, studies looking at the relationship between metacognition and behavior, and hypotheses about how metacognition is acquired.

Because all subareas of metacognition are interrelated, it was not always easy to decide where to include a study. Studies using text-like prose materials are reviewed in the section on metacognition in communication and comprehension, although some of those studies are clearly extensions of studies reported in the earlier metamemory section.

A.   METAMEMORY RESEARCH

Much research has been done in the area of memory since the mid-1970s. One reason is that memory is viewed as consisting of many cognitive processes, making it impossible to separate memory from the others. For example, memory includes the cognitive processes of encoding or storing information, retrieving stored information, rehearsing information that has entered short-term memory, searching for information that may be stored in memory, and using learning strategies such as clustering similar items to be learned and elaborating information to be learned by creating sentences, phrases, and/or mental images which aid in the storage of that information. Hence, the reader should not attempt to draw distinct lines between learning and memory while reading this chapter.

This section reviews studies on metamemory. It is organized according to the classification scheme developed by John Flavell and Henry Wellman (1977). The taxonomy has two main categories (sensitivity and variables), each of which is further subdivided. The first category recognizes that learners need to have an understanding or awareness of how to behave most appropriately in different learning situations. For instance, is this a situation where I should attempt to recall (retrieve) something I should be able to find in my memory? Is this a situation where I should be studying information so that I will be able to recall it at a future time? Is this a situation when I should arrange my environment (e.g., leave my school books beside the door) so it will be easy for me to later locate an object or recall something? We call this the *sensitivity category* because it addresses the need for learners to be sensitive to the most appropriate way of approaching situations.

The second category recognizes that how the learner performs "in a memory situation or task is influenced by a number of factors the nature of which a person might know" (Flavell & Wellman, 1977, p. 5). We call this the *variables category* because it draws attention to several factors or variables the learner might benefit from knowing about. For example, knowing that it is easier to recall the main ideas from a passage than to recall it word-for-word is a task variable learners could benefit from knowing.

1. Sensitivity Category

Flavell and Wellman (1977) divide the sensitivity category into two sub-categories. The first, *elicited activities*, consists of activities learners engage in when asked to retrieve information from memory or to prepare for retrieval at some future time. The second, *spontaneous activities*, consists of activities learners spontaneously engage in when they believe it may be to their advantage to attempt to retrieve some information or to be able to retrieve information at some future time.

a. Elicited Activities. According to the "differentiation hypothesis" (Appel, Cooper, McCarrell, Sims-Knight, Yussen, & Flavell, 1972), young children do not differentiate between a request to memorize information for future recall and a request to look at the information carefully. That is, they do not understand that when they are told to memorize information for future recall, this request implies that they should do something special with that information so that they will be able to retrieve it at a future time. Young children must acquire the ability to recognize that instructions to memorize are requests for them to engage in present activity that will prove useful at some future time. Appel et al. (1972) presented 4-, 7-, and 11-year-olds two sets of pictures and instructions. When shown one set, the children were instructed to memorize the items for future recall. When presented the other picture set they were instructed to look carefully at the pictures. The 11-year-olds did differentiate between the two sets of instructions. They knew the memorization instructions requested special activities like rehearsal and the grouping of similar items, were more apt to use these strategies, and recalled more when told to memorize than when told to look carefully. On the other hand, the 7-year-olds seemed to understand that memorization instructions were a request for special activities since they were more likely to name and point to the items when instructed to learn them, but they were unable to increase their recall. Four-year-olds appeared to behave the same regardless of the instructions. Subsequent research (Salatas & Flavell, 1976a; Yussen, Gagne, Gargiulo, & Kunen, 1974) revealed many 7-year-olds will process items differently when told to memorize than when told to look at them, provided they can think of a strategy they can use to facilitate their learning of the items. There is some evidence that children as young as 3 years understand what it means to intentionally remember the location of an object (Acredelo, Pick, & Olsen, 1975; Wellman, Ritter, & Flavell, 1975). Wellman, Ritter, and Flavell (1975) hid a toy under one of a series of identical cups, and the 3-year-old was told either to wait with the toy until the experimenter returned or to remember where the toy was while the experimenter left the room for 45 seconds. Children told to remember where the toy was not only recalled its location better than the other children, but also engaged in planful activity to retain that information by doing such things as touching the relevant cup, making it distinctive in some way, or apparently rehearsing which one hid the toy. One child was observed going down the series of cups nodding her head "no" for empty cups and "yes" for the cup the toy was under.

Whether a distinction between instructions to learn or to look is made by learners appears to be related to whether the task presented is one with which they are familiar (Brown, 1981). In a review of the literature on the differentiation hypothesis, Flavell (1978) concluded that although it is possible to observe when a child makes a behavioral differentiation between inspecting and learning instructions, we have not yet found a way to empirically demonstrate that for any memory task there is a time when a child can conceptually differentiate activities but is unaware that this has behavioral implications.

b. Spontaneous Activities. Little is known about spontaneous activities and their development (Flavell & Wellman, 1977). One study (Siegler & Liebert, 1975) found that more 13-year-olds than 10-year-olds kept written records of the possible solutions they had attempted for the problem of discovering which setting of four switches (each of which could be in an up or down position) would make an electric train run. Subjects who chose to keep written records tended to generate more different combinations than those who did not. However, because all subjects were supplied with paper and pencil and told, "There are many possibilities and you don't want to repeat the same choices you already made, so you might want to keep a record of which choices you have tried and found not to work," their behavior cannot be considered totally spontaneous. Additional examples of spontaneous activities have been found in studies using school-like prose material. These are reviewed in the subsection on metacognition in communication and comprehension.

2.   Variables Category

Flavell and Wellman (1977) divided the variables category into four sub-divisions, each of which identifies factors that can affect the quality of performance on retrieval problems. These include (1) *person variables* ("all temporary and enduring personal attributes and states that are relevant to data retrieval" [p. 10]); (2) *task variables* (qualities of the task itself which influence retrieval); (3) *strategy variables* (ways of going about storing and retrieving information from memory); and (4) the *interaction among variables* (the fact that the actions a learner engages in in any one setting can be a function of the combination of what she or he knows about all three classes of variables).

a.   *Person Variables.*   Person variables include both enduring properties that change little over time, such as being able to predict about how many items a learner will be able to recall after studying them for a brief period of time, and temporary properties, such as the learner being able to say whether at this time she or he can correctly recall all items on a study list. This section first describes research on enduring person variables and then studies about temporary person variables.

There is evidence that older children have a better understanding of their memory abilities and limitations than younger children. Several studies have looked at learners' abilities to predict their memory spans (the number of items a learner can correctly recall immediately after being shown a group of items). In these experiments, the usual procedure has been to show the subject a horizontal presentation of two pictured objects. The subject is then asked if she or he could remember these objects in the order they appeared if they were covered up. The process is repeated with one more picture being added each trial until the learner says she or he does not believe she or he would be able to recall the sequence of objects or until the number of pictures has become so large that it is unrealistic for anyone to predict recall (e.g., 10 pictures). The actual memory span of the learner is then tested. Flavell, Friedricks, and Hoyt (1970) found over one-half of their 4- to 6-year-olds unrealistically predicted they would be able to recall as many as 10 pictured objects while fewer than one-fourth of the 7- to 10-year-olds made similar unrealistic predictions. Yussen and Levy (1975) tested 4-, 8-, and 20-year-olds. The older subjects made more accurate predictions than the younger subjects, who overestimated their memory spans. In fact, the 20-year-olds were remarkably accurate—the mean predicted span was 5.89 and the actual mean span was 5.52.

Brown, Campione, and Murphy (1977) made one change in the procedure when testing educable mentally retarded children. After a child first said she or he would not be able to remember a list of the length shown, the experi-

menter continued to show the child longer lists. As many as 32% of the
subjects were inconsistent in that after they had first declared a list too long,
they later declared a longer list to be one they could recall. These results
raise questions about what would have been found in the prior studies if they
too had continued questioning after the first "too difficult" response. Regardless, consistent with the results of the prior studies, more older educable mentally retarded children (mental age 8) made accurate span estimates
than younger mentally retarded children (mental age 6).

The studies all suggest that a learner's ability to accurately predict memory span for verbal units increases with age. However, Kelly, Scholnick,
Travers, and Johnson (1976) failed to find a similar trend when people predicted their ability to recall the location of an object. These researchers
suggest that differences in spatial and nonverbal memory abilities may account for their different findings. Markman (cited in Flavell & Wellman,
1977) found 5-year-olds can predict the motor skill of how far they can jump
much more accurately than they can predict how many objects they will be
able to recall. In addition, 5-year-olds predict others' recall with about the
same average accuracy as they predict their own recall, believe teen-agers
can recall more than 5-year-olds, and believe 5-year-olds can recall more
than 2-year-olds.

It is conceivable that practice activities can provide hints about what
predictions learners should make. Some of the 5-year-olds in Markman's
study (cited by Flavell & Wellman, 1977) improved their ability to predict
their memory spans with practice at the task even when provided with no
feedback; however, other 5-year-olds did not improve even when they were
provided feedback about the accuracy of their predictions. Also, Yussen and
Levy (1975) had 4- and 8-year-olds attempt to recall sequences of 9 and 10
items before they were asked to predict their memory spans for sequences of
10 or fewer items. The actual mean memory spans were 3.34 for the 4-year-
olds and 4.71 for the 8-year-olds. These practice experiences did not affect
their predictions.

Investigators have also looked at learners' awareness of enduring person
variables. Kreutzer, Leonard, and Flavell (1975) individually interviewed 20
children in each of four grade levels (kindergarten, first, third, and fifth).
The older children seemed more aware that a learner's memory ability may
differ from one setting to another, and that learners of the same age differ in
memory abilities; they believed older learners will study differently when
preparing for future recall. The younger children appropriately used such
terms as *remember* and *forget*; knew that if they were given a rote piece of
information, such as a telephone number, they would remember it for only a
very short time; and knew that relearning information forgotten over the

summer would take less time than learning information for the very first time.

Hale (1983) attempted to determine whether high school students could predict how much they would forget over time. He had 11th- and 12th-graders study a 24-paragraph passage on the history of China, take a 12-item multiple-choice test over half of the main ideas in the passage, and score their own exams. Then subjects predicted how they would have scored on the exam if they had read the passage today but had not been tested until 1, 8, or 15 days later. Later, students were administered a surprise 12-item multiple-choice test over the remaining half of the main passage ideas. Tests were administered 1, 8, or 15 days later. Students predicted that 1 day later they would score over two points lower than on the immediate test, even lower 8 days later, and about three points lower 15 days later. The actual retention scores indicated they scored only about a half a point lower 1 day later, just over one point lower 8 days later, and not quite two points lower 15 days later. An analysis of the data from students who predicted for the same delay they had actually experienced indicated they predicted significantly more forgetting than actually occurred. Hale (1983) suggests the inaccurate expectations may result from the students' lack of experience with similar settings. Students are seldom tested over only main points rather than memorized details, are seldom tested without having studied during the interval between learning and testing, are seldom tested both immediately after learning and again at a later time, and are seldom asked to think about their memory performance.

In addition to the more general, enduring person variables, there are also temporary variables of which a learner may be aware. One such variable is the ability to monitor when one is ready to recall information. Flavell, Friedrichs, and Hoyt (1970) found 7- to 10-year-olds were much better at judging their readiness to recall a set of items than were 4- to 6-year-olds. The children were told to study a set of items until they were sure they could recall all of the items without making an error. The children studied until they indicated they were ready to recall, and were immediately tested. They were given three such episodes. The older children were usually able to recall the lists without error while the younger children could not and did not improve their estimates over the three episodes. Subsequent research (Neimark, Slotnick, & Ulrich, 1971) found that 6-year-olds are rather poor at estimating their readiness to recall. Denhiere (cited by Flavell & Wellman, 1977) found that even adults are not perfect at this task.

Another temporary variable is the ability to monitor how well one has done on a memory task. Geis and Lange (cited in Flavell & Wellman, 1977) observed that although both younger and older children may be aware that they have or have not recalled all items they were asked to recall, older children are better at this than younger ones. Immediately after recall, both first- and third-graders are able to accurately report how many items they have correctly recalled, although third-graders are more accurate than first-graders (Moynahan, 1976). Berch and Evans (1973) showed kindergartners and third-graders an initial set of items consisting of pictures of common objects, followed by a longer second set which contained the initial set plus additional items. The children not only had to indicate whether each item in the second set had been seen before, but also had to rate how much confidence they had in their response. Both groups could to some extent assess the accuracy of their responses; again, the third-graders were more accurate than the kindergartners.

Another area of research on temporary person variables is that of tip-of-the-tongue or feeling-of-knowing experiences. Wellman (1977) asked kindergartners, first-graders, and third-graders to name the objects shown in a series of pictures. If children could not name an item, they were asked both whether they thought they knew it (despite the fact they could not name it) and would therefore be able to recognize its name, and whether they had seen the item before. Later, the subjects were tested to see if they could recognize the names of the objects when they heard them. Older children more accurately predicted those items for which they were or were not able to recognize the names. For the kindergartners, their response as to whether they had seen the item before was a better predictor of whether they would recognize the item name than was their prediction of that behavior. The opposite was true for the 9-year-olds. College students can accurately predict which question answers they will be able to correctly recognize even though they cannot at that time recall the answer (Hart, 1965, 1967).

b. Task Variables.   Research on task variables has shown that some types of information are more difficult to learn and later retrieve than others. Knowledge of the relative difficulty of different types of information could be a part of a learner's metamemory. Such information could include how the make-up of individual items affects retrievability and could also include the nature of the relationships among items. There is evidence that some kindergartners and first-graders correctly believe familiar items are easier to remember (Kreutzer et al., 1975), and that 7-year-olds correctly believe that easily named or identified items are easier to remember (Moynhan, 1973). Interview data (Kreutzer et al., 1975) suggest that even most kindergartners are aware that increasing the length of a list of items makes it more difficult to recall.

In addition to knowledge about the individual units of information to be learned, metamemory might contain knowledge about how the relationships between items affect the retrievability of the information. Moynahan (1973) found third- and fifth-graders were significantly more likely than first-graders to correctly predict that sets of strongly categorized items would be easier to recall than sets of items that were the same length but conceptually unrelated. Salatas and Flavell (1976a) told first-graders the names of the categories and the items within each category, thus identifying the categorical organization. Later, the first-graders were shown an array which grouped the items into categories and one which mixed them, and then they were asked which, if either, would be easier to remember. Nine of the 12 first-graders who had been instructed to look at the items while the experimenter presumably prepared for another task, failed to select the categorically organized items as the array which would be easier to remember. So even when first-graders have been made aware of the categories, they are not sensitive to the fact a categorized list is easier to remember. Tenney (1975) had kindergartners, third-graders, and sixth-graders generate and recall lists of words. Although the kindergartners could generate lists of words in the same category as a target word provided by the experimenter, they were less apt than the older students to generate words in the same category as the provided target word when they were told to make a list of words that would be easy to remember. This again suggests the younger children were not aware of the advantage categorical organization provides when retrieving information.

When interviewing children, Kreutzer et al. (1975) explored the possibility that they understood the relative ease of learning and retrieving a word that is the opposite of the word presented by the experimenter as opposed to learning and retrieving a word that is unrelated to the word presented by the experimenter. They found most kindergartners and first-graders were unaware of this advantage for opposites while the third- and fifth-graders were not only aware of it but could also often explain why.

Instead of examining organization of single items, Danner (1976) examined children's sensitivity to the organization of sentences. Children heard and attempted to recall two passages, each consisting of 12 sentences. Within the 12 sentences, there were 4 sentences on each of three topics. Sometimes the four sentences on each topic were grouped together and sometimes they were not. As would be expected, based on prior research with categorized materials, children showed better recall and were more apt to group information by topic in their recall when the presented sentences were grouped by topic. Later, the children were shown all 12 sentences, each written on a separate card. They were told to select three cards to serve as notes for future retrieval of the stories. Of 24 children at each age level, 21 twelve-year-olds, 15 ten-year-olds, and only 5 eight-year-olds selected one sentence from each topic (the optimal strategy because it shows an understanding that one item from a group can help one remember other items from that same group).

Research on organization has also been conducted with other types of materials. Moynahan (1973) found 7-year-olds believed they could more easily recall the order of a sequence of colored blocks if all blocks of the same color were grouped together than if they appeared randomly in the sequence. These data indicate that although children this young are not sensitive to the facilitation that categorization provides when recalling verbal materials, they are when working with a physical dimension like color. Kreutzer et al. (1975) asked kindergartners, first-graders, third-graders, and fifth-graders whether it would be easier to recall a sequence of pictured objects if the pictures were simply presented in order or if the presenter made up a story which connected the pictures. Significantly more of the older children selected the story condition and gave an appropriate reason for this choice. Once more, the older children were more sensitive to the advantage of using words to organize the materials to be recalled. All the children understood that the amount of space appearing between pictures does not affect how hard or easy it will be to remember them. Interviews (Myers & Paris, 1978) revealed that both second- and sixth-graders believe stories they prefer to read will be easier to remember than nonpreferred stories.

Thus far, our discussion of task variables has involved research on the nature of the to-be-learned materials. Another factor that could affect the difficulty of retrieval is the demands made by the retrieval task. In Kreutzer et al.'s (1975) interview study, the third- and fifth-graders, but neither the kindergartners nor the first-graders, understood that it might be harder to correctly learn a second list of people's names immediately after learning a similar list of other people's names. This shows the third- and fifth-graders appreciated the potential of confusing the two lists. Although only about half of the kindergartners appeared to think that studying longer would result in recalling more of the objects pictured, almost all of the older children did. Correspondingly, interviews by Myers and Paris (1978) found significantly more sixth-graders than second-graders were aware that knowing whether the goal of reading was to be able to recall the story word for word or in their own words (gist recall) can lead the reader to use different strategies. Significantly more sixth-graders reported they would or might do something differently if given one rather than the other task. The majority of both the second- and the sixth-graders were aware that recalling a story in their own words would be easier and require less preparation than recalling it word-for-word.

Older children adjust how long they study to the length of the recall interval (Rogoff, Newcomb, & Kagan, 1974); 4-, 6-, and 8-year-olds studied a group of pictures and then attempted to recall them a few minutes later, 1 day later, or 7 days later. The children were then shown 40 pictures and told they had to remember them for the length of time they had previously experienced. The 8-year-olds, but not the 6- or 4-year-olds, studied longer if they were in the 1-day or 7-day conditions than if they were in the few-minutes-later condition.

The ability to predict performance also varies, depending on the nature of the task. Levin, Yussen, DeRose, and Pressley (1977) had first-graders, fifth-graders, and college students predict how many nouns they would be able to recall or recognize from a list pronounced to them. The older the subjects, the more accurate their predictions of their recall. Subjects of all ages tended to underestimate the number of items they would correctly recognize. Speer and Flavell (1979) found some kindergartners and many first-graders know they are apt to score better on a recognition test than on a recall test. Data indicate the older elementary school children know that recognition tests are less demanding than recall tests and that they elect to study differently for them (Naus, Ornstein, & Kreshtool, 1977).

c. *Strategy Variables.* Learners may develop knowledge of strategies for storing information in their memories and for retrieving it. Flavell and Wellman (1977) point out that in real life, people are most apt to encounter open-book rather than closed-book problems—that is, they are free to search external sources such as books, magazines, and other persons' memories, in addition to their own memories. School appears to be the main setting where a premium is placed on closed-book retrieval.

The children interviewed by Kreutzer et al. (1975) were asked what they could do to be sure they did not forget to take their skates with them the next day. Older children were able to think of more different things they could do to remind themselves, and all the children thought of more ways external to themselves (putting the skates next to the door, having their mother remind them, writing a note) than internal (thinking about the skates, doing a mental check the next morning of things they should do). A second interview item, which asked them how they would go about remembering a birthday party to which they were invited yielded similar results. Yet another interview item asked them what they did when they wanted to remember a phone number. One third-grader clearly showed the use of cognitive strategies when she described using her age, her brother's current age, and her brother's age last year for remembering it. When presented a set of pictures of clothing, food, and body parts and asked how they would go about learning them, most third- and fifth-graders described something planful and strategic, such as grouping the similar items or rehearsing them.

Children as young as 3 and 4 years have been observed to use appropriate strategies to recall a location. Ritter (cited in Flavell, 1978) had young children watch as a piece of candy was hidden under one of six identical cups, hide their eyes while the turntable holding the cups was turned, and then attempt to find the cup under which the candy had been placed. Children as young as four showed some understanding that it was useful to use one of the markers provided by the experimenter to mark the cup hiding the candy before the turntable was turned and that it would not help to add markers to the other cups. Also, when Wellman et al. (1975) asked 3-year-olds to remember for 45 seconds which of several identical cups hid a toy, they observed 3-year-olds using strategies such as touching the relevant cup and rehearsing which one hid the toy to aid their memories.

Masur, McIntyre, and Flavell (1973) found that third-graders and college students who were given an opportunity to select half of a list of items for additional study after they had attempted to recall them selected items they had missed on the previous recall attempt, while first-graders appeared to randomly select items. The older subjects displayed the strategy of concentrating on items they did not already know; however, among those who chose this strategy, only the college students consistently gained from using that strategy. Brown (1981) suggests that perhaps the younger students who used this strategy were unable to keep alive previously recalled items while studying the previously unlearned items. This would have produced losses which counterbalanced the gains made through the use of the strategy.

Brown, Campione, Barclay, Lawton, and Jones (cited in Brown, 1978) examined the ability of children to predict the outcome of using different study strategies. Children viewed a four-segment video tape of a 12-year-old engaging in the study strategies of categorizing, rehearsing, labeling, and looking as ways to learn a 12-item list of pictures. The majority of the first- and third-graders correctly predicted that categorization and rehearsal would be the more effective study strategies while, although a majority of the 4-year-olds selected either categorization or rehearsal, their choices were fairly evenly spread across the four strategies.

Several studies have investigated the use of rehearsing as a strategy. Flavell, Beach, and Chinsky (1966) gave 5-, 7-, and 10-year-olds seven pictures and then pointed to three that were to be remembered on that trial. The children were observed for signs of verbal rehearsal by an experimenter who could read lips. The observer saw only 10% of the 5-year-olds engage in rehearsal on any of the trials while 60% of the 7-year-olds verbalized at least once and 25% regularly did so. Of the 10-year-olds, 85% verbalized at least once and 65% regularly did so. Not only did more of the older children rehearse, they also correctly recalled more of the pictures than the younger ones. Alternative procedures have been used by investigators to measure rehearsal. For example, Ornstein and Naus (1978) told their subjects that if they thought about the stimuli, they should do so aloud. Although this procedure makes it easier to measure rehearsal, it may also encourage the children to engage in behaviors they might not use without the directions. Locke and Fehr (1970) made electromyographical recordings which detect inaudible verbalizations but do not detect their content. Regardless of the procedure used to measure rehearsal, the studies find that rehearsal becomes a common learning activity at about 9 or 10 years (Kail & Hagen, 1982).

Rather than use direct measures of rehearsal, other studies (Hagen & Kail, 1973; Hagen & Kingsley, 1968; Hagen, Meachman, & Mesibov, 1970) have examined rehearsal inferentially by looking at how children recall a list that must be recalled in the order presented. Adults generally recall the initial stimuli in the list more accurately than subsequent ones. It is assumed that this superiority is the result of their rehearsing these items. The fact that a distinct advantage for the initial items is rarely found among children 8 or younger lends additional support for the conclusion that rehearsal is not common in children younger than 9 or 10.

More complex strategies have also been investigated. For example, Pressley and Levin (1977) had fifth-, seventh-, and ninth-graders learn a list of 25 paired concrete nouns. Afterwards, they were asked how they had tried to study them. Finally they were given three more pairs and were to describe how they would have gone about learning the new pairs had they been a part of the original list; 47% of the fifth-graders, 74% of the seventh-graders, and 93% of the ninth-graders reported some use of elaboration strategies such as forming sentences or verbal phrases to link the pairs together or forming interactive visual images to link them together. When tested over them, students who consistently used elaboration correctly recalled more of the 25 pairs. Hence, the older the children, the larger the number selecting the more effective elaboration strategies.

Although most older students use some elaborative strategies, they are not always able to predict which strategies are apt to aid retention. Hale (1983) had 11th- and 12th-graders read a 24-paragraph passage on the history of China and then complete and self-score a 12-item multiple-choice test over half of its main ideas. Students incorrectly predicted that they would have probably scored at about the same level if they had also taken notes while they were studying. Students who wrote a summary of the main ideas after reading each paragraph incorrectly predicted they would have probably scored at about the same level if they had only read the passage. The students' incorrect predictions show they were not sensitive to the positive effect this strategy had on the immediate retention scores of those who had written summaries. Similarly, the reading-only group failed to predict that if they had used the strategy of underlining during study they would have scored higher; however, the reading-only group did predict that they would have scored higher if they had tested themselves while studying. It should be noted that these students' failure to predict higher scores for the strategies of underlining and note-taking differs from the predictions reported by Brown and Smiley (1978) for similar aged students.

Until now, we have been discussing planning for future retrieval of information. Now we turn to knowledge people have of strategies they can use to retrieve previously stored information. Flavell and Wellman (1977) suggest a good first move is to sit and wait for the information to come to mind. Once it becomes apparent that will not work, a deliberate search of memory for related information which might bring to mind the sought-for information is a good second move. Finally, they say the most elaborate strategy consists of using what one can recall to reconstruct "what must have been." Kreutzer et al. (1975) asked children what they could do to find a jacket they had lost. The older children thought of more things they could do and described more complicated strategies (a step-by-step retracing of their whole day's activities or returning to the spot they last remembered having the jacket and retracing their movements after that). Drozdal and Flavell (1975) found that although 9- to 10-year-olds understand if an article is missing, the segment of activities that must be searched to locate it is that which begins with the last place the article is remembered and ends with the first place where it is missed, 5- to 6-year-olds do not. When Kreutzer et al. (1975) asked children what they could do to determine which Christmas they had received a dog as a present, an often-suggested strategy for the first-, third-, and fifth-graders was to ask the help of others. Not surprisingly, the fifth-graders gave some of the more complex strategies such as checking the dog's papers or dog tag, searching their memory Christmas by Christmas backwards until they reached the Christmas when they had received the dog, and remembering other things that had happened at the same time the dog arrived such as other Christmas presents received.

One useful retrieval skill is to realize the need for and know how to conduct a thorough search for the needed information. Salatas and Flavell (1976b) asked kindergartners, third-graders, and college students to name all items from a set of items that had a certain property (for example, were breakable or could be used outside). Only the college students spontaneously used the strategy of recalling each of the items and deciding whether each exhibited the specified property, thus being careful to not omit any of the items. Interviews (Kreutzer et al., 1975; Yussen & Levy, 1977) with elementary school children and older students show they will often report it is important to conduct a thorough search in which they look everywhere. However, as indicated in the prior paragraph, these interviews also show older students can think of more strategies to use in attempting to recall information. Older students are also more apt to develop plans that include an ordering of subplans they could try (first I would do this, and if that does not work, then I would do this).

Flavell (1978) suggests another thing learners must come to understand is using a piece of information they do not want to recall as a cue which may lead to recalling the desired piece of information. He concludes that several studies show learners gradually develop an understanding of how to use retrieval cues. One example comes from the Kreutzer et al. (1975) interviews where 20 of the 24 fifth-graders reported this type of approach to remember which Christmas they received a dog as a present (recalling other Christmas gifts from that year). Yet another example comes from the Salatas and Flavell (1976b) study where kindergartners, third-graders, and college students first learned lists of tools, clothing, and toys so that they always recalled all items from a single category together and they always recalled the categories in the same order. Next, the students were asked to name all the items that had a certain property (for example, were breakable or could be used outside). The majority of the college students silently recalled each item in order and said aloud those that exhibited the identified property. By using this strategy, the college students were using each item to help cue the next item in the list they had learned to ensure none were missed even though this meant considering items that did not have the identified property. Their strategy also had the effect of turning the recall task into a recognition task. Although third-graders could use this strategy when they were instructed to use it, they did not spontaneously think of using it.

Brown (1978) identifies checking and monitoring as strategies learners may use to ensure their recall is logical and consistent. Brown (1976) found many preschoolers were not bothered by inconsistencies in their answers. Specifically, they correctly said they had seen four pictures while hearing a story but selected six of the eight pictures provided when asked to select the ones they had seen. Sensitivity to inconsistencies appears to develop at different ages for different subject matters, for even though Thieman and Brown (cited in Brown, 1978) found children as young as second-graders refused to accept meaningfully inconsistent sentences as being in the same story, Holt (1964) found children as old as fifth-graders accepted such inconsistencies as saying both $245 + 179 = 424$ and $245 + 179 = 524$ are correct. Yet another example of students failing to monitor their recall for reasonableness comes from an experiment where Morris and Resnick (cited in Resnick & Glaser, 1976) first taught 5- and 6-year-olds how to use blocks to find the area of rectangles. When the 24 children were next given a parallelogram, 19 began to put the blocks on it as if it were a rectangle, evidently not checking to determine whether the figure was a rectangle. When the experimenter said "That's wrong, you can't do that," 12 persisted in leaving the blocks on the parallelogram and simply rearranged them in an attempt to achieve a closer fit. They blindly applied the rule they had learned without checking to determine if their strategy was consistent with the problem they had been given. Yet another study on learners' checking and monitoring is one Brown (1978) described, which investigated retarded learners' flexibility at selecting the appropriate strategy when the situation called for a change. The children were presented several lists they were to recall. Changes in the situation included suddenly presenting the same list over and over, ending the need for active work on the items; and then suddenly presenting a new list, reinstating the need for the memorizing strategy being used. The data indicate that when compared with older children and adults, the younger children took more time (1) to initially select the memorizing strategy they would use for learning the lists, (2) to stop using the selected strategy when it was no longer needed, and (3) to reinstate the strategy when it was again needed.

Based on a review of the literature on the use of strategies, Kail and Hagen (1982) conclude a general developmental trend emerges in the use of strategies consisting of "(1) infrequent use of strategies among five- and six-year-olds; (2) a transitional stage from seven to ten years of age, when strategies may appear depending upon factors related to the strategy itself and to the context in which the strategy is to be used; and (3) the first inkling of mature strategy use at approximately ten years of age" (p. 351). Later, they modified this conclusion to include the stipulation that "Even very young children seem to have the intent to behave strategically; whether they will be able to effect that intention will depend on the particular memory problem and the strategies appropriate to its solution" (p. 352). They identify such nonverbal motor activities as pointing and looking as being areas that are more apt to be in the strategic repertoire of young children. Regardless of when strategic behavior initially appears, its use continues to develop. Older learners are more flexible at selecting memory strategies that fit specific memory problems. It is likely that the developmental changes are linked to the growing child's increased *metamemory*, that is, knowledge about memory and knowledge about the regulation of memory.

    d.   Interaction among Variables.   Flavell and Wellman (1977) point out that it is unlikely that people consider the person, task, and strategy variables in isolation. It is much more likely that they consider them jointly and adjust their activities to take into account the combined impact of the variables in any given situation. As an example, they cite the response from one of the children in Kreutzer et al.'s study (1975), who, when asked whether she would choose to study a list of words she was shown for 1 or 5 minutes, responded "There's quite a lot of words here, you know, and it would be kind of hard to learn in just one minute." The response indicates that the child knew the variable of length-of-study could be adjusted to take into account another variable, the length-of-the-list. Wellman (1978) looked at children's ability to combine variables. He found that while both 5- and 10-year-olds could correctly handle single variables (longer lists would be harder to remember than shorter lists, and it would be harder to remember for longer periods of time than for shorter periods of time), only the 10-year-olds could combine these variables to make correct predictions about the relative difficulty of remembering lists of varying length to be recalled after varying time intervals. Hence, the available data suggest the ability to consider variables jointly also improves with age.

e. *Summary.* The metamemory research indicates learners become more knowledgeable about memory and more skillful in using appropriate strategies to enhance memory and retrieve information from memory as they mature. This growth was found in learners' knowledge of both enduring and temporary person variables, knowledge of and response to task variables, knowledge and use of strategies, and in their ability to consider the joint effects of these variables. However, this growth is uneven (for example, the ability to predict motor skill performance emerges earlier than the ability to predict performance on verbal tasks).

B.   METACOGNITION IN COMMUNICATION AND COMPREHENSION

Although much work in metacognition has been done in the area of memory, work has occurred in other areas, most notably the areas of communication and comprehension. Flavell (1978) reports that the classification system for metamemory has been applied to the area of communication and may be applied to the area of metacomprehension. This implies that people must learn, for example, that messages may be incomplete, vague, or inaccurate; or may be interpreted in different ways. If such metacognitions must be acquired, then young children should not be as skilled as older learners at monitoring communications. Based on a review of the literature, Flavell (1978) points to evidence that young children will say they have understood a message even when it is ambiguous or lacks critical information, are less apt to question a speaker and ask for additional information than are older ones, and tend to blame all communication failures on the listener.

An example study from the area of communication is one by Markman (1977), who told 6-, 7-, and 8-year-olds she was trying to develop directions to teach children how to play games and do magic tricks. The children were to judge the adequacy of her instructions for a magic trick and were to suggest revisions. The younger children did not discover anything wrong with her very incomplete directions until they attempted to do the trick. Evidently, when they listened to the instructions, they did not atempt to think through the steps the instructions told them to do in order to test their completeness and clarity.

A review (Wong, 1985) of studies on self-questioning instructional research reported that instruction which led high school seniors to locate important ideas in text and to formulate questions which required new examples of that main idea or a paraphrased version of the main idea led to improved comprehension in low-verbal-ability students. Ann Brown (1981) and her associates have completed a series of studies which have looked at learners' study strategies when they are studying school-like information. They found that the ability to identify the main ideas in a passage is a gradually developed skill. Brown and Smiley (1977) had the 55 idea units in fifth-grade reading level folk stories rated 1–4 in terms of their importance to the theme of the story. This was accomplished by first having the subjects listen to the story which had been recorded on tape while they read the story. The written story had each idea unit printed on a separate line. After a second reading, the subjects were instructed to mark out with a blue pencil about one-fourth of the idea units which they judged to be least important. The process was repeated two more times with different colors of pencils, producing four levels of rated importance. Younger subjects were run individually and given more specific practice before data were collected. Eight-year-olds were unable to make reliable distinctions between levels of importance as determined by an independent group of college raters; 10-year-olds only distinguished between the highest level of importance and the rest of the idea units; 12-year-olds accurately identified the most important and the least important units, but were unable to distinguish between the two intermediate levels of importance; while 18-year-olds could distinguish among all four levels of importance. When these students read and recalled another story, all age groups most often recalled the important idea units and least often recalled the unimportant idea units as identified by an independent group of college raters. Pilot data (Brown, 1978) show an identical trend for nursey-school children and kindergartners. Based on these data, Brown (1981) concludes that "Apparently we spontaneously abstract the main ideas of an oral or written communication even when no deliberate attempt to do so is instigated" (p. 24). If this conclusion is correct, if learners are to remember more than the main ideas, they must planfully use strategies to attend to and interact with other less important idea units which would otherwise not be retained. Younger learners are at a disadvantage because if they cannot distinguish important from unimportant ideas, they do not know which ideas need this extra attention.

It is also true that learners can improve their recall of important ideas through additional study time only if they can identify which ideas are the more important ones. Brown and Smiley (1978) found seventh-graders and older students given a passage to study in a study period equivalent to three times their reading rate, improved their recall of the important ideas within the passage but exhibited no improvement for the less important ideas. Their recall included little trivia and most of the important ideas. On the other hand, younger children did not profit as much from the extra study time. If their recall of ideas improved, improvement occurred at the same rate for ideas at all levels of importance so that their recall omitted important ideas and included trivia. Fifth-graders and older students sometimes spontaneously took notes or underlined sections of the passage as they studied. When they did so, they isolated ideas crucial to the theme of the passage. Interestingly, students encouraged to underline and/or take notes failed to show the same level of preference for important idea units shown by those who spontaneously used these study strategies, and these students' recall was inferior to that of the spontaneous students.

Brown (1981) says that once efficient learners are sure they have understood the main ideas, they will start filling in the details. This can be done by testing what one knows and giving attention to those ideas one does not know (the process Sally used in the opening example in this chapter). Researchers (Brown & Campione, 1979; Brown, Smiley, & Lawton, 1978) had students study prose materials, select a subset of idea units that were printed on cards and could be kept to aid them during recall (retrieval cues), asked them to recall the material, gave them a rest period, and then repeated the whole process. On the first trial, the majority of the learners at all grade levels selected the most important idea units to keep as retrieval cues during recall. Learners below high school and as young as fifth-graders continued to select the most important idea units to keep as retrieval cues for all trials while older students did not. On the second trial, college students selected to keep the second most important idea units and on the third trial selected to keep the third most important idea units and never elected to keep the fourth level or least important idea units. Eleventh- and twelfth-graders kept the most important idea units on both the first and second trials, even when their recall showed they knew as much of the passage material as the college students, and moved to the second most important idea units on the third trial. Brown (1981) believes that the ability to select the most efficient retrieval cue (the most important idea units the student is not currently able to recall) when studying text develops late in learners' school careers since, to use it, learners must (1) ascertain what parts of the text they do and do not know, (2) be able to distinguish among all levels of importance of idea units, and (3) know that the best strategy is to select retrieval cues consisting of the most important idea units they were unable to recall on their last recall attempt. It appears that although learners who are as young as third-graders (Masur et al., 1973) can accurately select for additional study pictures of objects they failed to recall (a version of the strategy used by the older students), only much more experienced learners can apply the strategy to text learning.

Yet another important study skill that has been studied by Brown and her associates is the skill of writing summaries of information. Just as the selection of the most efficient retrieval cues is dependent on decisions about the relative importance of idea units, so are the decisions about what to include and what to omit in a summary. In order to differentiate between what the researchers (Brown, Day, & Jones, 1983) believed to be the automatic result of comprehension (a bare outline of the main points of a passage) and the results of deliberate planful activities of the learner, they used relatively complex study materials consisting of 500-word 60-idea-unit folk stories written at the fifth-grade level. Fifth-graders, seventh-graders, eleventh-graders and first-year-college students who volunteered for the study were instructed to learn two of the folk tales perfectly by studying them at home for 1 week. Students were asked to write both stories from memory and only those who recalled 70% or more of the story idea units were used for the data analyses. After a break, they were given a sheet of paper plus some scratch paper and a copy of the story. They were asked to write a summary of one of the two stories they had learned. The story was randomly selected by the experimenter. After a break, the students were asked to write a second summary limited to 40 words. They were provided a sheet of paper containing 40 blanks at the bottom with blank space on top where they could write drafts if they wished. Finally, they were provided with a similar sheet and asked to write one more summary of the story; only this time, they were limited to 20 words. The idea units in the folk stories had been rated 1–4 for importance to the story by independent groups of college students. In all the summaries, the seventh-graders, eleventh-graders, and college students primarily included idea units from the top two levels of importance. Less important idea units showed up in the first, unlimited summary but disappeared from the limited summaries. College students were able to include more idea units in the same number of words than the younger students. The youngest students, the fifth-graders, performed differently. In their unlimited summaries, they included more of the most important idea units (level 4 units) but showed no preference for the next most important level of idea units (level 3) over the lesser ideas (levels 2 and 1); however, when limited to 40 words in their summaries, they included more level 4 units than any other level, and more level 2 and 3 units than level 1 units. When limited to 20 words, they dropped the level 2 units and ended up with summaries similar to those of the older students. Of the idea units in the summaries of the fifth- and seventh-graders, 27% were verbatim and 57% were near verbatim from the original story, while only 28% of the idea units in summaries of the eleventh-graders and college students were verbatim or near verbatim. Brown et al. (1983) point out that the copy–delete strategy used in the younger students' summaries is also the most common strategy used by students in grades five through seven when taking notes or outlining.

In a series of three experiments, Brown and Day (1983) examined more closely how students go about writing summaries and found students at different grades use different strategies for summarizing texts. Fifth-graders, seventh-graders, tenth-graders, and college students were equally efficient at using the strategies of deleting trivia and deleting redundancy from the original text and used these strategies almost every time they could appropriately be used. The older students more frequently used effective superordinates to replace strings of similar specifics (for example, "flowers" for "daisies, poppies, marigolds, and lilies") than the younger students, and students of all ages more frequently did so when the summaries were limited to 60 words than when no limit was given. The older the students, the more likely they were to select topic sentences from the text to be included in their summaries. When college students' summaries were limited, they contained fewer of the topic sentences, perhaps because they, like experts, resort more to combining across paragraphs when limited. The fifth- and seventh-graders seldom invented or created topic sentences appropriate for the text but not found in it, and tenth-graders used this strategy on only about 33% of the appropriate occasions while college students used it on only about 50% of the appropriate occasions. These strategies of deleting trivia, deleting redundant information, selecting topic sentences, and inventing new topic sentences could be a part of students' metacognition. Are learners aware of these strategies for summarizing information? Brown and Day (1983) found fourth-year graduate students in a university's English department who had taught freshman rhetoric courses at least twice were unable to specifically identify these rules which they used when writing summaries until after they had engaged in summarizing a text while simultaneously talking aloud about the steps they were taking.

Yet another difference (Brown et al., 1983) found between younger and older students' summarizing behaviors was that significantly more eleventh-graders and college students showed evidence of planning (preparation of rough drafts) before writing their summaries than fifth- and seventh-graders. Fifth- and seventh-graders who planned wrote summaries that contained as many idea units from the second half of the passage as from the first half, while those who failed to plan included significantly fewer idea units from the second half of the passage suggesting they quit when they ran out of spaces for words on their answer sheets. The older students, on the other hand, were able to include idea units from both halves even when they did not plan.

Ryan (1984) asked 90 undergraduate students, predominantly freshmen, enrolled in a Fundamentals of Psychology course to describe how they determined they had understood reading material assigned for the course. Of the 15 different monitoring criteria found in their responses, 7 involved recalling information from the text, and 8 involved more complex processing (e.g., "Integrate different parts of the text into a common framework," "Devise examples of principles and concepts," and "Determine relationship between each text section and its heading" [p. 252]). The most frequently reported criteria were "Recall information from text in response to study guide questions" ($n = 30$), "Recall information from text as part of mental review" ($n = 23$), "Determine the meaning of individual sentences" ($n = 23$), and "Paraphrase the text" ($n = 21$) (p. 252). Nine or fewer students reported the remaining criteria; 54% of the students reported more than one criterion. Those reporting criteria involving both recall of text information and more complex processing earned higher course grades than did students reporting only criteria involving recall. Since 40% of the students reported only recall-monitoring criteria, we may conclude that many college students could develop better text-comprehension-monitoring criteria.

Consistent with the metamemory research, metacognitive research indicates that as learners mature, they gradually become more effective at communicating and comprehending. For example, they are better able to identify main ideas, to use their knowledge of main ideas to direct study, and to summarize text. Improvement was evident among college students, indicating growth continues to occur after students complete high school.

C. METACOGNITION IN PROBLEM SOLVING

People doing research on metacognition hope to identify strategic processes that will apply generally to all types of problem solving, rather than to specific areas such as memory and comprehension. Brown (1978) identified several strategic processes learners might acquire to assist them in being effective problem solvers. These are (1) predicting one's limits as a learner, (2) being aware of the strategies one knows how to use and when each is appropriate, (3) identifying the problem to be solved, (4) planning and scheduling the appropriate strategies, (5) monitoring and supervising the effectiveness of the plans that are used, and (6) evaluating the effectiveness of the preceding five strategies so that the problem solver knows when to end work on this problem. In fact, she speculates that the metacognitive processes of problem solving are not necessarily different from those used in intelligent control of one's actions for remembering and hence those described in this chapter.

D.   Teaching Metacognition

Researchers have attempted to teach metacognition. Many early attempts focused on teaching very specific metamemory knowledge and strategies. For example, Brown (1978) described a series of studies in which mildly retarded children with mental ages of 6 and 8 were taught to know when they were ready to recall, to select previously missed items as those for additional study when learning a list, and to accurately estimate their memory spans. She summarizes them by saying that the teaching must be very explicit about what the child is to do, and the teacher may need to continually remind the child to use what was taught. She also observed that in all the studies, the teaching effects were short-lived for the younger children but more durable for the older children. Brown (1978) summarizes the research on older children's ability to generalize what they had been taught to similar yet different situations as follows: "the only tangible effect of two years of training was to alert the children to their own memory deficiencies, but not to possible methods of overcoming them, a less positive outcome than we would have wished" (p. 126).

More recently, there have been more successful attempts to teach more general metacognitive strategies. Two examples are described. In the first example, students were taught how to ask questions while reading text, which would increase their comprehension of that text, whereas in the second, students were taught strategies which would make them better able to summarize information they read to possibly aid their comprehension of it.

Palincsar (cited in Brown, 1981) worked every day for about 40 days with 4 seventh-grade minority children who could decode fifth- to seventh-grade reading materials but comprehended at the second-grade level. The sessions alternated between baseline sessions and teaching sessions. During baseline sessions, the children read stories and answered comprehension questions over them. During the first baseline session the children correctly answered about 15% of the comprehension questions. For the first teaching session, the children were given corrective feedback in which they were asked questions about a story they had read, and then were provided with the correct answer, the location of the answer in the text, and were told whether the information was in the text or had to be inferred from the text. Each day following the teaching, the children independently read another passage and answered comprehension questions over it. During the corrective feedback phase of the study, they gave correct answers to approximately 50% of the comprehension questions over the independently read passages; however, their performance varied considerably from day to day. During a second baseline phase, the children maintained their performance at the 50% correct level. The second teaching phase consisted of strategy instruction in which the teacher and student took turns asking one another questions about the story the child had read. The teacher asked two types of comprehension questions: hypothesis testing and prediction making. She was serving as a model the students could copy when they asked their questions of her. At least one of the children was provided a second strategy teaching phase after a third baseline period. By the end of the strategy teaching phase(s), the children's comprehension on the passages they read independently following the daily teaching sessions rose to 80–90% correct. The teacher's modeling of comprehension questions changed the children's comprehension of stories they read independently of the teacher.

Day (cited in Brown, 1981) taught junior college students to use the summarization strategies of deleting redundant information, deleting trivial information, writing superordinates for any lists, underlining topic sentences found in the text, and inventing topic sentences when none were provided in the text. Prior research (Brown & Day, 1983) had shown that although junior college students effectively used the two deletion strategies when summarizing text, their use of the remaining three strategies was comparable to that of seventh-graders and below that of college freshmen. In one study, Day (cited in Brown, 1981) gave normal students (defined as those who had no diagnosed reading or writing problems) and remedial writers (defined as students with diagnosed writing problems but no diagnosed reading problems) 3 days of instruction in small groups. Each student received one of four types of instruction. Students provided "self-management" instruction were encouraged to write good summaries by including main ideas and omitting trivia and unnecessary words. "Rules" instruction consisted of explicit instructions and modeling in the use of the five strategies being taught. Students in the "rules plus self-management" group were provided a combination of the first two approaches, while students in the "control plus monitoring" group were not only taught to use the strategies but were also shown how to check whether they had used each of the rules every place they could. In a second study, a third group of junior college students who were diagnosed as having both reading and writing problems was provided individualized instruction for an unspecified length of time. All the students given instruction on the rules showed significant improvement in their use of the strategies following instruction; however, the more explicit the instruction, the greater the gains. For all types of students, rules plus monitoring was best, rules plus self-management next best, and rules was next best, while self-management produced nonsignificant gains. Poor writers only achieved at the level of 4-year-college freshmen if they had received the most explicit instruction—that is the rules plus monitoring. At least some of the gains were still evident 2 weeks after instruction. A significant interaction revealed that average writers profited the most from the instruction, poor writers the next most, and students who were both poor writers and poor readers profited the least.

Brown (1981) believes the five strategies taught to these junior college summary writers are specific examples of the macrorules of deletion, superordination, selection, and invention. Furthermore, she believes that these macrorules "are general rules underlying comprehension of texts" (Brown, 1981, p. 31). If students have mastery of these rules or forms of these rules, they can understand text and hence should be able to be successful in school.

In the examples of teaching metacognitive strategies described thus far, learners have been taught specific metacognitive strategies but have not been explicitly taught information about how the strategies work. Pressley, Borkowski, and O'Sullivan (1984) describe and review relevant literature on three different methods for adding to strategy instruction information about how strategies work. This information about strategies can include "knowledge about a strategy's goals and objectives, tasks for which it is appropriate, its range of applicability, the learning gains that can be expected from consistent use, effort associated with its deployment, and whether the strategy is fun to use" (Pressley, Borkowski, and O'Sullivan, 1984, p. 96). Their three methods are (1) the *laissez-faire* method, which provides learners experience with strategies from which they can draw conclusions about the strategies, (2) the *explicit provision of metamemory* method, which provides learners with explicit information about how strategies work, and (3) the *metamemory acquisition procedures* method, which has learners use procedures designed to produce understandings about how the strategy works.

The studies reviewed in this section thus far have been examples of the laissez-faire method because students were given experience with strategies and could draw conclusions about the strategies from those experiences. A series of five experiments (Pressley, Levin, & Ghatala, 1984) using the laissez-faire method to teach strategies indicate when learners are taught to use two different strategies for different examples of the same learning task, both adults and fifth- and sixth-graders tend to select for a new, similar task the strategy they have been told is more effective if their selection is made before they have been tested over the material they learned using the two strategies. However, if they select the strategy for the new, similar task after they have been tested over the original materials, adults select the strategy by which they learned the most even when it disagrees with what they have been told, while the fifth- and sixth-graders tend to persist in selecting the strategy they were told was better despite the evidence to the contrary.

Only when children in grades 5–7 were provided feedback which told them how many correct answers they had given with each strategy did they select the more effective elaborative strategy. Thus, the available data suggest the laissez-faire approach is more effective for adults than for children.

A taught strategy is useful only if the learner continues to use the strategy. Elliott-Faust and Pressley (1986) examined various ways of teaching third-graders to detect inconsistencies in stories they heard. Three of the groups were initially asked to give an example of something that did not make sense, given feedback as to the correctness of the example, and provided a meaning for what making sense is. Two of these groups were then provided strategy instruction. One strategy group was taught to compare each pair of sentences they heard to see if they made sense and to check the whole story they heard to see if what they had just heard made sense when compared with earlier parts of the story. Children in the other strategy group were given identical instruction, plus they were taught to ask themselves a series of four questions designed to help them self-monitor strategy use ("What am I supposed to do?" "What is my plan?" "Am I using my plan?" and "How do I do?" [p. 29]). Both strategy instruction groups correctly detected more inconsistencies in stories they heard immediately after instruction than did the group given only a definition. However, only the third-graders provided self-monitoring training maintained that superiority on a delayed post-test one week later. Continued use of the strategy was dependent upon the inclusion of instruction on how and when to apply the strategy.

In another study (Ghatala, Levin, Pressley, & Lodico, 1985) which examined continued use of strategies, second-graders were first taught that some ways of playing games are better than others because they result in better performance, or that some ways of playing games are better because they are more fun, or no criteria for selecting between ways of playing games. After learning a list of paired concrete nouns using any strategy they chose, students were taught the strategy of making up sentences to connect words in each pair. When they used this strategy to learn a second list of paired nouns, they learned more words clearly indicating the sentence strategy was effective. When given the freedom to use any strategy they wanted to help them remember as many words as possible on a third list given immediately after the second list, a fourth list given one week after the initial session, and a fifth list given nine weeks after the initial session, students who were first taught that some strategies are better because they result in better performance were more likely to continue using the sentence strategy than children in either of the other two groups. Strategy maintenance was enhanced by teaching the children to monitor how effective strategies are.

In addition to durability, a strategy's usefulness depends upon whether the learner applies it to many different situations for which it is appropriate. Using a strategy in a new and different situation is called transfer. An example of the explicit provision of metamemory method, a study by O'Sullivan and Pressley (cited in Pressley, Borkowski, & O'Sullivan, 1984), examined its effects on transfer. Fifth- and sixth-graders were provided instruction on an elaborative strategy for learning pairs of items (a list of city–product pairs). Children whose instruction either included telling them both when the strategy could appropriately be used and how it could be applied to other types of materials or the preceding information plus experience with applying the strategy to three diverse situations learned more of the items on a new, transfer list consisting of Latin vocabulary words than children whose instruction either included only experience with applying the strategy to three diverse situations or experience with the steps in using the elaborative strategy taught to all experimental groups. Based on these data and those from related studies, Pressley, Borkowski, and O'Sullivan (1984) conclude that "transfer is more likely when strategy instructions include information about how, when, and where to use a strategy" (p. 101).

In the metamemory acquisition procedures method for teaching strategies, the instruction includes exercises designed to help the learner derive information about the strategy being taught. For example, Lodico, Ghatala, Levin, Pressley, and Bell (1983) taught 7- and 8-year-olds to monitor or evaluate their performances when using different ways of accomplishing the same task. Subjects drew circles freehand and with the aid of a cookie cutter; then they memorized lists of letters which were in a random order and which were organized so they spelled the children's names. Following each pair of activities, subjects given monitoring instruction were asked questions which made them evaluate their relative performances and helped them identify which of the two ways was more effective for that task. This gave these subjects practice at monitoring or evaluating the effectiveness of the alternative strategies they had used. All subjects were then given two additional types of tasks. One was learning pairs of items and the other was learning a list of items which could be recalled in any order. For each of these tasks, the subjects were taught two different strategies, which were applied by the children to different examples of each task. After using both strategies for one of the tasks, the children were asked which list they had learned better and why they had learned it better. For both tasks, the majority of the children who had and had not been given monitoring instruction correctly identified the list on which they had given the better performance; however, a greater percentage of the children who had been given monitoring instruction referred to the strategy as the reason for their better performance than did those who had not been provided monitoring instruction. Finally, a third example list was learned for each task, with the children free to use either strategy they wished. On these third lists, a larger percentage of the monitoring-trained children used the more effective strategy and said they chose it because they thought it would help them learn more of the list. Hence, there is evidence that providing learners with experiences which can provide information about the strategies (in this example, questions which forced the learners to compare the effectiveness of the two strategies taught) can help learners select the more effective strategy for future, similar tasks. However, Pressley, Borkowski, O'Sullivan (1984) point out that not all research using the metamemory acquisition procedures method has resulted in similar facilitation.

In summary, various metacognitive strategies have been successfully taught to learners. There is evidence that incorporating into the instruction information about when a strategy may be used, how to modify the strategy for different situations, and its effectiveness for promoting learning may facilitate the continued use of the strategy and its transfer to new, appropriate settings.

E.   Relationship between Metacognition and Behavior

Much of the interest in metamemory came from the assumption that learners' knowledge about how memory works would influence their memory-related behavior. Studies have shown discrepancies between learners' responses to metacognitive questions and their behaviors. Brown, Campione, Barclay, Lawton, and Jones (cited in Brown, 1978) found that although the majority of 4-year-olds, first-graders, and third-graders correctly predicted that the study strategies of categorization or rehearsal would be superior to the strategies of labeling or looking for learning a list of 12 pictures, only 22% of the 4-year-olds, 36% of the first-graders, and 77% of the third-graders who had made correct predictions proceeded to use the strategy they had predicted to be best when they were asked to study the 12 pictures using any strategy they wished to learn as many of them as possible. Flavell, Beach, and Chinsky (1966) found 25% of 31 five-, seven-, and ten-year-olds who were observed verbalizing the names of pictures, an effective memory behavior, did not report that they had. Salatas and Flavell (1976a) had first-graders either look at or study with the intent to remember a group of pictures which could be categorized. They were then shown an array which was organized by categories and one which mixed the categories and were asked which, if either, would be easier to remember. Six weeks later, the children were given a new set of pictures which could be categorized. Those first-graders who had said the categorized list would be easier to remember did not tend to categorize the new list any more frequently than those who had not. These studies demonstrate that researchers have not always found a clear correspondence between awareness and behavior.

Flavell and Wellman (1977) argue that the relationship between metacognition and behavior is likely to be quite complex and variable because memory behavior in any one situation will reflect the interrelationship of the situation, the possible behaviors, and the subject's awareness or knowledge about memory. They detail several reasons why there might not be a one-to-one correspondence between behavior and metamemory, including the notion that we do not always do what we know we ought to do. Flavell (1978) suggests that on some occasions no metamemory occurs; that is, something is accidentally stored in memory or accidentally retrieved without the student intending to. A learner may engage in strategies such as rehearsal that are so habitual that they may be used without being initiated by metacognitive processes. He also suggests that if new knowledge about how memory works (metamemory) is not yet well established, it may not be used when appropriate occasions present themselves. It is also possible that metamemory may occur too late to influence behavior; that is, after a learning episode is over, the learner may think of some strategy she or he could have used that would have been more effective. Sometimes the learner may be unwilling to invest the time and effort necessary to enact the strategy metamemory says would be best. Metamemory should influence behavior when that knowledge will help the learner accomplish a goal and when the learner wants to accomplish that goal badly enough to exert the time and energy dictated by the metamemory.

One of the problems in determining the relationship between metacognition and behavior is selecting a way to accurately measure metacognition. Brown, Day, and Jones (1983) found that when fifth-graders were forced to limit summaries they wrote of folk stories they had learned to 20 words, they included only idea units that had been rated by independent groups as being the most important (level 4) and next most important (level 3) idea units and omitted idea units rated least important (levels 2 and 1), indicating that fifth-graders are sensitive to small differences in levels of importance. This countered prior findings from studies on note-taking, underlining, and selection of cues for help in recalling information, which had suggested fifth-graders can differentiate the most important (level 4) ideas from the rest but are unable to differentiate between ideas of lesser importance (levels 1–3). Also, as reported earlier in Section III.B, Brown and Day (1983) found fourth-year university English graduate students who had taught freshman rhetoric courses at least twice were unable to clearly identify strategies they had used to write summaries of text 2 weeks earlier, but they were able to identify them when asked to talk aloud while summarizing a second passage. Findings such as these clearly indicate that how researchers go about measuring awareness influences whether researchers find learners are aware of information they could have as a part of their metacognition.

F. Acquisition of Metacognition

It is generally assumed that metacognition is gradually acquired throughout development as learners experience new and varied demands on their cognitive skills. Hagen (1971) suggests that through learning experiences, learners come to realize that they can control how much they learn by the activities or strategies they use. Flavell and Wellman (1977) hypothesized that metamemory might develop through a process like Piaget's "reflective abstraction," which they interpret as "the child abstracts and permanently incorporates into his cognitive structure generalizations or regularities concerning the properties of his own actions vis-a-vis the environment, as contrasted with knowledge about the environment itself that derives from 'physical abstraction'" (pp. 29–30).

Salatas and Flavell (1976a) had one group of first-graders simply inspect a set of pictures and had another group do whatever they wanted to help them remember the pictures. Both groups were asked to recall the pictures. Children told to do whatever they wanted to do to remember the pictures were more apt to spatially group pictures in the same category than were children told to inspect the pictures. Subsequently, when asked to judge whether a categorized or an uncategorized set of items would be easier to remember, children who had been instructed to remember the list were more apt to select the categorized set of items. It is possible that their prior experience with categorizing the pictures influenced their subsequent judgment.

In a series of five experiments, Pressley, Levin, and Ghatala (1984) taught subjects two different strategies for learning the meanings of foreign vocabulary words. One strategy was an ineffective strategy and the other was an effective, elaborative strategy. While being taught the strategies, some of the subjects were incorrectly told that the ineffective strategy was more effective than the other, truly effective strategy. The subjects then learned the meanings of a list of 24 foreign vocabulary words using each of the two strategies for half of the words. After they had learned these words, the subjects were informed that they would be given a second list of vocabulary items and told they could elect to use only one of the two strategies to learn this new list. If adults were asked to select the strategy for the new list before they were tested on the original list, those who had been misinformed about the effectiveness of the two strategies tended to choose the ineffective strategy. On the other hand, if the adults were asked to select their strategy for the new list after they were tested on the original list, the majority of the adults selected the effective strategy. Interviews indicated that their performances on the test over the original list told the adults that the effective strategy had produced greater recall. When fifth- and sixth-graders experienced these same conditions, they persisted in choosing the ineffective strategy even if they chose after they had been tested on the initial lists. These data suggest fifth- and sixth-graders are not as proficient as adults in using the results of their experiences to aid them in selecting the more effective strategy for future learning situations.

Kail and Hagen (1982) and Brown (1978) indicate some theorists argue that schools' unique demands for the use of memory strategies results in children developing the metamemory necessary for school success. Kail and Hagen (1982) report that cross-cultural research consistently shows that "uneducated persons generally behave in ways akin to young Western children— that is, these individuals rarely use mnemonics on memory tasks when it would be advantageous to do so" (p. 353). There are possibilities other than the lack of schooling which could account for these differences; however, they point to studies that rule out the two alternative explanations that school children might do better because they are more familiar and more at ease with laboratory-like tasks and settings, and that uneducated persons' failure to use strategies is but one instance of deficient cognitive skill in illiterate people. They conclude their discussion with two cautions: (1) we know little about how schooling fosters children's acquisition of strategies and the associated mnemonic knowledge, and (2) data indicate young children are capable of at least some forms of strategic behavior long before they enter elementary school.

IV. IMPLICATIONS FOR PRACTICE

What emerges from the review of the literature on metacognition is a description of learners becoming increasingly knowledgeable about their memory capabilities, how various factors influence their memories, how various variables work jointly to influence their memories, and the strategies which may be used to facilitate various types of learning and memory. They become increasingly skillful at monitoring what they do and do not know, monitoring what they have and have not recalled, monitoring their productions for logic and consistency, identifying a variety of approaches to take in a given situation, planning a systematic approach for a given situation, selecting strategies which fit the situation, identifying when a strategy is no longer useful, selecting appropriate retrieval cues, and conducting thorough memory searches. The skillful use of strategies emerges at different ages for different types of materials. Although children as young as 3 years have been observed using appropriate strategies to aid the recall of the physical location of an object, and although the use of appropriate strategies for verbal items becomes common by age 10 years, the ability to use appropriate strategies for more complex text material continues to improve during college.

When compared with older persons, school children not only have less background information to which they can relate the new information they are being taught, they also know less about how to go about learning new information. During their school years they are not only learning new information about their world and the understandings and insights of those who have lived before them, they are also learning about themselves as learners and how to efficiently go about learning and remembering information. Admonitions to study the important information from the material they read will not be helpful to students who are unable to distinguish between the levels of importance of the ideas being studied. Telling students to underline as they read to aid them in their study or to take notes while studying may not be very helpful if they are not able to select the more important ideas for underlining or outlining. Advising students to concentrate their study on the parts they do not yet know will be of little help to students who cannot accurately judge what they are and are not capable of recalling. Teachers must be sensitive to and alert for the possibility that their students may not know how to go about studying, and may not have the prerequisite knowledge and skills needed to profit from general advice on how to study.

In an area as new as metacognition, one must be especially cautious when attempting to generalize to typical classrooms. The following are tentative suggestions based on the literature. As the literature in the area continues to grow, more specific and less tentative recommendations will become possible.

If a teacher decides to allocate instructional time to metacognitive or study skills, the literature would suggest that the teacher specifically identify the skills to be taught and develop a plan whereby they are explicitly taught, not implied or generally described. When selecting study skills to teach, the teacher would be wise to consider how generally applicable they are. More general skills like those for summarizing or comprehending text would be more useful to students than more discrete skills such as being able to predict how many objects one will be able to recall after briefly looking at them. When teaching the skills, the teacher might begin by demonstrating the behaviors for the students. Additionally, the teacher should provide the students with opportunities to practice the behaviors, give the students feedback on how successful their attempts are, show the students how to monitor their own work to see if they have successfully implemented the new skills, and include information on when and where to use the new skills.

There is evidence that if learners are made aware of the fact that a strategy does enhance their learning, they are more apt to start using the strategy (Paris, Newman, & McVey, 1982) and are more apt to continue using it (Cavanaugh & Borkowski, 1979). Additionally, research suggests that including information about both when to use a strategy and how to modify it for various situations may increase the probability students will transfer the strategy to new, appropriate settings; hence, the teacher would be wise to provide the students with that kind of information.

As you read the remainder of this text, you will learn some of the things skilled learners are known to do to help them encode and retrieve information. These are strategies and understandings you might select to teach your students if they lack them.

REFERENCES

Acredolo, L. P., Pick, H. L., Jr., & Olsen, M. G. (1975). Environmental differentiation and familiarity as determinants of children's memory for spatial location. *Developmental Psychology, 11*, 495–501.

Appel, L. F., Cooper, R. G., McCarrell, N., Sims-Knight, J., Yussen, S. R., & Flavell, J. H. (1972). The development of the distinction between perceiving and memorizing. *Child Development, 43*, 1365–1381.

Berch, D. B., & Evans, R. C. (1973). Decision processes in children's recognition memory. *Journal of Experimental Child Psychology, 16*, 148–164.

Brown, A. L. (1976). Semantic integration of children's reconstruction of narrative sequences. *Cognitive Psychology, 8*, 247–262.

Brown, A. L. (1978). Knowing when, where, and how to remember: A problem of metacognition. In R. Glaser (Ed.), *Advances in instructional psychology* (Vol. 1, pp. 77–165). Hillsdale, NJ: Erlbaum.

Brown, A. L. (1981). Metacognition: The development of selective attention strategies for learning from texts. In M. L. Kamil (Ed.), *Directions in reading: Research and instruction* (pp. 21–43). Washington, DC: National Reading Conference.

Brown, A. L., & Campione, J. C. (1979). The effects of knowledge and experience on the formation of retrieval plans for studying from texts. In M. M. Gruneberg, P. E. Morris, & R. N. Sykes (Eds.), *Practical aspects of memory* (pp. 378–384). London: Academic Press.

Brown, A. L., Campione, J. C., & Murphy, M. D. (1977). Maintenance and generalization of trained metamnemonic awareness in educable retarded children. *Journal of Experimental Child Psychology, 24*, 191–211.

Brown, A. L., & Day, J. D. (1983). *Macrorules for summarizing texts: The development of expertise* (Technical Report No. 270). Champaign, IL: Center for the Study of Reading.

Brown, A. L., Day, J. D., & Jones, R. S. (1983). *The development of plans for summarizing texts* (Technical Report No. 268). Champaign, IL: Center for the Study of Reading.

Brown, A. L., & Smiley, S. S. (1977). Rating the importance of structural units of prose passages: A problem of metacognitive development. *Child Development, 48*, 1–8.

Brown, A. L., & Smiley, S. S. (1978). The development of strategies for studying texts. *Child Development, 49*, 1076–1088.

Brown, A. L., Smiley, S. S., & Lawton, S. C. (1978). The effects of experience on the selection of suitable retrieval cues for studying texts. *Child Development, 49,* 829–835.

Cavanaugh, J. C., & Borkowski, J. G. (1979). The metamemory–memory "connection": Effects of strategy training and maintenance. *Journal of General Psychology, 101,* 161–174.

Danner, F. W. (1976). Children's understanding of intersentence organization in the recall of short descriptive passages. *Journal of Educational Psychology, 68,* 174–183.

Drozdal, J. G., Jr., & Flavell, J. H. (1975). A developmental study of logical search behavior. *Child Development, 46,* 389–393.

Elliott-Faust, D. J., & Pressley, M. (1986). How to teach comparison processing to increase children's short- and long-term listening comprehension monitoring. *Journal of Educational Psychology, 78,* 27–33.

Flavell, J. H. (1971). First discussant's comments: What is memory development the development of? *Human Development, 14,* 272–278.

Flavell, J. H. (1978). Metacognitive development. In J. M. Scandura & C. J. Brainerd (Eds.), *Structural/process theories of complex human behavior* (pp. 213–245). Rockville, MD: Sijhoff & Noordoff.

Flavell, J. H. (1979). Metacognition and cognitive monitoring: A new area of cognitive-developmental inquiry. *American Psychologist, 34,* 906–911.

Flavell, J. H., Beach, D. R., & Chinsky, J. M. (1966). Spontaneous verbal rehearsal in a memory task as a function of age. *Child Development, 37,* 283–299.

Flavell, J. H., Friedrichs, A. G., & Hoyt, J. D. (1970). Developmental changes in memorization processes. *Cognitive Psychology, 1,* 324–340.

Flavell, J. H., & Wellman, H. M. (1977). Metamemory. In R. B. Kail, Jr., & J. W. Hagen (Eds.), *Perspectives on the development of memory and cognition* (pp. 3–33). Hillsdale, NJ: Erlbaum.

Ghatala, E. S., Levin, J. R., Pressley, M., & Lodico, M. G. (1985). Training cognitive strategy-monitoring in children. *American Educational Research Journal, 22,* 199–215.

Hagen, J. W. (1971). Some thoughts on how children learn to remember. *Human Development, 14,* 262–271.

Hagen, J. W., & Kail, R. V. (1973). Facilitation and distraction in short-term memory. *Child Development, 44,* 831–836.

Hagen, J. W., & Kingsley, P. R. (1968). Labeling effects in short-term memory. *Child Development, 39,* 113–121.

Hagen, J. W., Meachman, J. A., & Mesibov, G. (1970). Verbal labeling, rehearsal, and short-term memory. *Cognitive Psychology, 1,* 47–58.

Hale, G. A. (1983). Students' predictions of prose forgetting and the effects of study strategies. *Journal of Educational Psychology, 75,* 708–715.

Hart, J. T. (1965). Memory and the feeling of knowing experience. *Journal of Educational Psychology, 56,* 208–216.

Hart, J. T. (1967). Memory and memory monitoring process. *Journal of Verbal Learning and Verbal Behavior, 6,* 685–691.

Holt, J. H. (1964). *How children fail.* New York: Dell.

Kail, R., & Hagen, J. W. (1982). Memory in childhood. In B. B. Wolman (Ed.), *Handbook of developmental psychology* (pp. 350–366). Englewood Cliffs, NJ: Prentice-Hall.

Kelly, M., Scholnick, E. F., Travers, S. H., & Johnson, J. W. (1976). Relations among memory, memory appraisal, and memory strategies. *Child Development, 47,* 648–659.

Kreutzer, M. A., Leonard, C., & Flavell, J. H. (1975). An interview study of children's knowledge about memory. *Monographs of the Society for Research in Child Development, 40* (1, Serial No. 159).

Levin, J. R., Yussen, S. R., DeRose, T. M., & Pressley, G. M. (1977). Developmental changes in assessing recall and recognition memory capacity. *Developmental Psychology, 13,* 608–615.

Locke, J. L., & Fehr, F. S. (1970). Young children's use of the speech code in a recall task. *Journal of Experimental Child Psychology, 10,* 367–373.

Lodico, M. G., Ghatala, E. S., Levin, J. R., Pressley, M., & Bell, J. A. (1983). The effects of strategy-monitoring training on children's selection of effective memory strategies. *Journal of Experimental Child Psychology, 35,* 263–277.

Markman, E. M. (1977). Realizing that you don't understand: A preliminary investigation. *Child Development, 48,* 986–992.

Masur, E. F., McIntyre, C. W., & Flavell, J. H. (1973). Developmental changes in apportionment of a study time among items in a multitrial free recall task. *Journal of Experimental Child Psychology, 15,* 237–246.

Moynahan, E. D. (1973). The development of knowledge concerning the effect of categorization upon free recall. *Child Development, 44,* 238–246.

Moynahan, E. D. (1976). The development of the ability to assess recall performance. *Journal of Experimental Child Psychology, 21,* 94–97.

Myers, M., II, & Paris, S. G. (1978). Children's metacognitive knowledge about reading. *Journal of Educational Psychology, 70,* 680–690.

Naus, M. J., Ornstein, P. A., & Kreshtool, K. (1977). Developmental differences in recall and recognition: The relationship between rehearsal and memory as test expectation changes. *Journal of Experimental Child Psychology, 23,* 252–265.

Neimark, E., Slotnick, N. S., & Ulrich, T. (1971). The development of memorization strategies. *Developmental Psychology, 5,* 427–432.

Ornstein, P. A., & Naus, M. J. (1978). Rehearsal processes in children's memory. In P. A. Ornstein (Ed.), *Memory development in children* (pp. 69–99). Hillsdale, NJ: Erlbaum.

Paris, S. G., Newman, R. S., & McVey, K. A. (1982). Learning the functional significance of mnemonic actions: A microgenetic study of strategy acquisition. *Journal of Experimental Child Psychology, 34,* 490–509.

Pressley, M., Borkowski, J. G., & O'Sullivan, J. T. (1984). Memory strategy instruction is made of this: Metamemory and durable strategy use. *Educational Psychologist, 19,* 94–107.

Pressley, M., & Levin, J. R. (1977). Developmental differences in subjects' associate-learning strategies and performance: Assessing a hypothesis. *Journal of Experimental Child Psychology, 24,* 431–439.

Pressley, M., Levin, J. R., & Ghatala, E. S. (1984). Memory strategy monitoring in adults and children. *Journal of Verbal Learning and Verbal Behavior, 23,* 270–288.

Resnick, L. B., & Glaser, R. (1976). Problem solving and intelligence. In L. B. Resnick (Ed.), *The nature of intelligence* (pp. 205–230). Hillsdale, NJ: Erlbaum.

Rogoff, B., Newcombe, N., & Kagan, J. (1974). Planfulness and recognition memory. *Child Development, 45,* 972–977.

Ryan, M. P. (1984). Monitoring text comprehension: Individual differences in epistemological standards. *Journal of Educational Psychology, 76,* 248–258.

Salatas, H., & Flavell, J. H. (1976a). Behavioral and metamnemonic indicators of strategic behaviors under remember instructions in first grade. *Child Development, 47,* 81–89.

Salatas, H., & Flavell, J. H. (1976b). Retrieval of recently learned information: Development of strategies and control skills. *Child Development, 47,* 941–948.

Siegler, R. S., & Liebert, R. M. (1975). Acquisition of formal scientific reasoning by 10- and 13-year-olds: Designing a factorial experiment. *Developmental Psychology, 11,* 401–402.

Speer, J. R., & Flavell, J. H. (1979). Young children's knowledge of the relative difficulty of recognition and recall memory tasks. *Developmental Psychology, 15,* 214–217.

Tenney, Y. J. (1975). The child's conception of organization and recall. *Journal of Experimental Child Psychology, 19*, 100–114.

Wellman, H. M. (1977). Tip of the tongue and feeling of knowing experiences: A developmental study of memory monitoring. *Child Development, 48*, 13–21.

Wellman, H. M. (1978). Knowledge of the interaction of memory variables. *Developmental Psychology, 14*, 24–29.

Wellman, H. M. (1983). Metamemory revisited. In M. T. H. Chi (Ed.), *Contributions to human development: Trends in memory development research* (Vol. 9). New York: Karger.

Wellman, H. M., Ritter, K., & Flavell, J. H. (1975). Deliberate memory behavior in the delayed reactions of very young children. *Developmental Psychology, 11*, 780–787.

Wong, B. Y. L. (1985). Self-questioning instructional research: A review. *Review of Educational Research, 55*, 277–268.

Yussen, S. R., Gagne, E., Gargiulo, R., & Kumen, S. (1974). The distinction between perceiving and memorizing in elementary school children. *Child Development, 45*, 547–551.

Yussen, S. R., & Levy, V. M., Jr. (1975). Developmental changes in predicting one's own span of short-term memory. *Journal of Experimental Child Psychology, 19*, 502–508.

Yussen, S. R., & Levy, V. M. (1977). Developmental changes in knowledge about different retrieval problems. *Developmental Psychology, 13*, 114–120.

LEARNING TACTICS AND STRATEGIES

Jack Snowman

*Department of Educational
 Psychology
Southern Illinois University at
 Carbondale
Carbondale, Illinois 62901*

I. INTRODUCTION

Previous chapters in this volume have described in detail the information-processing view of learning. The importance to learning of such cognitive processes as metacognition, attention, encoding, schema formation, and retrieval were well documented. The purpose of this chapter is to discuss how these processes can be used by students as learning tactics and strategies. In general, learning tactics and strategies are specific techniques (in the case of tactics) and general plans (in the case of strategies) that facilitate the achievement of one or more instructional objectives.

Although most research on learning tactics and strategies is of fairly recent origin, having been published since 1970, it represents a long-standing, basic goal of inquiry in educational psychology—understanding and improving classroom learning. That goal was well expressed by John Carroll (1963), who wrote,

> The primary job of the educational psychologist is to develop and apply knowledge concerning why pupils succeed or fail in their learning at school, and to assist in the prevention and remediation of learning difficulties. (p. 723)

Despite some conceptual and methodological problems that are discussed throughout the chapter, research on learning tactics and strategies gives every indication of making a major contribution to that goal.

A. WHAT ARE LEARNING TACTICS AND STRATEGIES?

Although learning may or may not be thought of as the educational equivalent of war, it should be recognized that tactics and strategies are military concepts with very specific and different meanings.

Webster's New World Dictionary of the American Language (1972) defines *strategy* as "the science of planning and directing large scale military operations, specifically . . . of maneuvering forces into the most advantageous position *prior to* [italics added] actual engagement with the enemy" (p. 1407).

Tactics, on the other hand, is defined as "the science of arranging and maneuvering military and naval forces *in action* [italics added] or before the enemy, especially . . . with reference to short-range objectives" (p. 1448). A secondary meaning given by Webster's is any methods used to gain an end.

Learning is defined as "the change in a subject's behavior or behavior potential to a given situation brought about by the subject's repeated experiences in that situation" (Bower & Hilgard, 1981, p. 11). Such changes, according to James Jenkins (1979) and John Bransford (1979) are governed by the following four classes of interacting variables:

1. *Learner activities:* The cognitive processes learners use to encode, store, and retrieve information.

2. *Learner characteristics:* The enduring attributes individuals possess that affect the encoding, storage, and retrieval of information.

3. *Learning material:* The type and structure of material that must be encoded, stored, and retrieved.

4. *Criterial task:* The type of assessment that is used to evaluate learning.

Jenkins (1979) and Bransford (1979) refer to these four classes of variables as constituting a tetrahedral model of learning. An important aspect of the tetrahedral model is that these classes of variables are interactive. For example, a particular learner activity may enhance performance considerably more for low-ability than high-ability students, may be more effective with expository text than with narrative materials, and may augment performance on essay tests to a greater extent than it affects performance on multiple-choice tests.

From the preceding definitions, a *learning strategy* might be described as a general plan one formulates for determining how to best achieve a set of academic objectives *prior to* dealing with the learning task itself and a *learning tactic* as a specific technique one uses in the service of the strategy *while confronted* with the task. A specific approach to strategy formulation and use that I would propose for now is composed of the following five steps:

1. *Analyze:* Any workable plan must be based on relevant information. By using the preceding tetrahedral model, the strategic learner can generate this information by playing the role of an investigative journalist and asking questions that pertain to what, when, where, why, who, and how. In this way, the learner can identify salient aspects of the learning task (what, when, where), understand the nature of the criterion task (why), identify relevant

personal characteristics (who), and identify potentially useful learning tactics (what).

2. *Plan:* Assuming that satisfactory answers can be gained from the preceding analysis, the strategic learner would formulate a learning plan by thinking, "Given this type of task (e.g., understanding a biology text, memorizing mathematical formulas), to be accomplished at this time and location (e.g., 6 weeks from now, in class), according to this criterion (e.g., comprehension, verbatim recall), and given these personal attributes (e.g., low motivation, distractible), I should use these learning tactics (e.g., mnemonic devices, note-taking, text analysis, distributed practice)."

3. *Implement:* At this step, the learner skillfully employs one or more tactics aimed at enhancing memory and/or comprehension of the learning materials.

4. *Monitor:* Once the learning process is underway, the strategic learner assesses the degree to which the chosen tactics are having their intended effect.

5. *Modify:* If the monitoring assessment is positive, the learner may decide no changes are needed. If, however, attempts at memorizing and/or understanding the learning material seem to be producing unsatisfactory results, the learner will need to reevaluate and modify the analysis, the plan, the implementation, or some combination of those steps.

These five steps can be grouped to form two general components of a three-component learning strategy model. The first component is labeled strategic skills. *Strategic skills* involve effectively analyzing a learning situation using the tetrahedral model as a guide and formulating a learning plan. The second component, called *tactical skills* because they occur only after the learner has effectively engaged the task, involve skillfully using various learning techniques, monitoring one's progress, and making modifications in one or more of the preceding components. The third component, which has not yet been mentioned, is metacognitive knowledge. According to Ann Brown (1978, 1980), *metacognition* involves being aware of how one thinks and knowing how to appropriately use one's thought processes in order to achieve a learning goal. The metacognitive knowledge necessary to become a strategic learner would include knowing one has to carry out all five of the previous steps, knowing why each step is necessary, knowing when to carry out each step, and knowing how well one is prepared to perform each step. These components and their interrelationships are displayed in Fig. 1.

B. CURRENT STATUS OF RESEARCH ON LEARNING TACTICS
    AND STRATEGIES

The research described in this chapter can be found in the educational–psychological literature under such diverse phrases as knowing how to

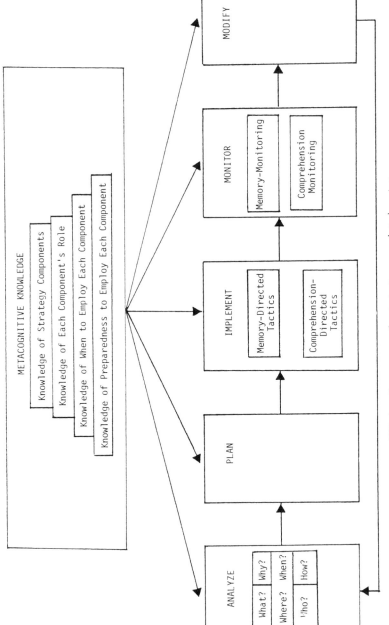

FIG. 1.   Components of a strategic approach to learning.

know, knowing when, where, and how to remember, learning to learn, intellectual skills training, study skills, study strategies, learning strategies, mnemonic strategies, and cognitive elaboration strategies. While all of these studies seek to enhance one or more cognitive processes in order to increase the probability of mastering particular instructional objectives, it is important to note their differences and that some of them are misnamed in light of the definitions given at the beginning of this chapter. Researchers who claim to be investigating the efficacy of a learning strategy or a memory strategy are, more often than not, investigating the efficacy of one or more learning or memory tactics. If one wants to investigate the utility of a learning strategy and/or the conditions under which its training can be optimized, one must plan to investigate the interactions among metacognitive knowledge, strategic skills, and tactical skills. To do otherwise is to conceptualize this process so narrowly that its ultimate utility may never be known.

Given this distinction, the literature reviewed for this chapter was divided into two major groups: learning tactics and learning strategies. Using the criterion of popularity among students and/or researchers, the six tactics chosen to represent the first group were underlining, summarizing, mnemonic devices, questioning, note-taking, and text analysis. For each tactic, attempts were made to locate and include studies whose primary purpose was to investigate its basic utility (i.e., does it work?) and studies whose primary purpose was to investigate the conditions under which its training and transfer would be enhanced. In addition, the preceding six tactics were subdivided in terms of whether their primary purpose was seen as retrieval or comprehension. These subgroups were labeled memory-directed tactics and comprehension-directed tactics, respectively (Levin, 1982). According to Levin (1982), the primary emphasis of memory-directed tactics (e.g., underlining, summarizing, mnemonics) is on the storage and retrieval of ideas, whereas the primary emphasis of comprehension-directed tactics (e.g., questioning, note-taking, text analysis) is on understanding the meaning of ideas and their interrelationships. Two points made by Levin (1982) about these subgroups should be kept in mind. First, they are not mutually exclusive. It is well documented that the meaningfulness and comprehensibility of information help determine its retention and retrieval (see Bransford, 1979). Second, they are the result of subjective judgement. The decision of which category was most appropriate for each tactic was made largely in terms of the criterion measures used by each experimenter. Other individuals using different classification criteria will likely produce different groupings.

The second group of studies included those whose main focus was the effectiveness of a learning strategy. As mentioned earlier, a learning strategy should combine metacognitive knowledge with strategic and tactical skills.

Attempts were made to locate studies that matched or approximated this description.

One reason why research on learning tactics and strategies has become so popular is because large numbers of students at all levels of education have demonstrated severe deficiencies in their knowledge of these processes and how to use what they do know to their advantage. Ann Brown (1978) and her colleagues (Brown & Campione, 1977; Brown, Campione, & Day, 1981) have found, for example, that children with marginal academic skills are deficient in such elementary cognitive skills as planning, implementing, and monitoring the success of rote recall strategies. They argued that most children need to be systematically taught the general strategy of (1) analyzing a learning situation, (2) deciding on a course of action, (3) carrying their plan out in a skillful manner, (4) monitoring its success, and (5) making any necessary modifications before large increases in classroom learning can be expected by educators. The same could be said of older students. According to surveys conducted by Annis and Annis (1979) and Davis and Annis (1978–1979), most high school and college students employ a narrow range of learning tactics over a wide range of learning materials and objectives.

II. RESEARCH ON MEMORY-DIRECTED LEARNING TACTICS

A. Underlining

Although underlining (and its equivalent, highlighting) is a very popular learning tactic among high school and college students (Annis & Annis, 1979; Davis & Annis, 1978–1979), it apparently has been the object of only a modest number of investigations. A fairly comprehensive search of the literature turned up a total of nine studies conducted between 1942 and 1979 in which underlining was compared with such other tactics as note-taking, outlining, and reading or rereading under a variety of conditions.

Of these nine studies, four (Arnold, 1942; Hoon, 1974; Idstein & Jenkins, 1972; Stordahl & Christensen, 1956) reported no significant differences among the treatment groups regardless of the nature of the reading passage or the nature and timing of the criterion test. One study (Davis & Annis, 1978–1979) found reading produced better results than underlining or note-taking when reading was preferred by the subjects and used in conjunction with familiar material.

The remaining four studies found positive but modest effects for underlining under certain conditions. Fowler and Barker (1974) reported no overall difference on a multiple-choice test given 1 week later for subjects instructed to highlight whatever they felt was important from two reading passages versus subjects who read prehighlighted versions versus subjects who read nonhighlighted versions. However, when the analysis was conducted on highlighted versus nonhighlighted item material, Fowler and Barker found that a highlighted item was passed more often by active highlighting subjects than when that same item was not highlighted whereas passive highlighting subjects showed no such difference.

Kulhavy, Dyer, and Silver (1975) had high school students complete both multiple-choice and constructed response exams over an 845-word passage on which they either took notes or underlined critical information. Each subject could underline or take up to only three lines of notes per page of text. A third group simply read the text once. In addition, one-half of the subjects in each condition were told to expect either a multiple-choice test or a constructed response test. Although notetakers generally performed better on the criterion test and performed best of all in the absence of any test instructions, subjects who underlined with instructions to expect a multiple-choice test retained more than subjects who underlined with instructions to expect a constructed response test or the read-only subjects who received no test instructions.

Rickards and August (1975) examined the effect on free recall of subject-generated versus experimenter-provided underlining of sentences (one per paragraph) that were least or most important to the overall structure of the passage presented. Additionally, some readers were instructed to underline any one sentence per paragraph while others were asked to simply read the passage. Those who could underline any one sentence recalled more total information, more underlined information, and more nonunderlined information than subjects who were directed to underline either the most important sentence, the least important sentence, who were given passages with the most or least important sentence already underlined, or who read the passage once.

Finally, Todd and Kessler (1971) compared underlining, note-taking, and reading across three levels of reading-passage difficulty for males and females of high and low reading ability. Underlining and note-taking subjects were told to underline or write down important words and phrases but not whole sentences unless they felt them to be especially important. Of the four dependent measures analyzed (number of words recalled, number of ideas recalled, number of identical words recalled, number of eight-word sequences recalled), underlining was superior to reading and note-taking only for the number of eight-word sequences recalled.

The main reasons for the differential success of underlining appear to be the extent of underlining and the appropriateness of criterion. All five studies that failed to support the utility of underlining (Arnold, 1942; Davis &

Annis, 1978–1979; Hoon, 1974; Idstein & Jenkins, 1972; Stordahl & Christensen, 1956) allowed subjects to underline as much as they pleased and assessed their performance in terms of global retention. The remaining studies, by contrast, limited the amount of underlining in which subjects could engage (Kulhavy, Dyer, & Silver, 1975; Rickards & August, 1975; Todd & Kessler, 1971) and/or assessed performance with criteria that may have better matched the nature of the tactic (Fowler & Barker, 1974; Kulhavy, Dyer, & Silver, 1975; Todd & Kessler, 1971).

From the present limited findings, it appears as if underlining should be used sparingly and judiciously—that is, in conjunction with material that relates directly to the teacher's objectives. Such a conclusion is consistent with Thomas Anderson's (1980) earlier review and analysis of this literature. Anderson pointed out that researchers have typically ignored the role of the learner's knowledge of the criterion task in producing a good match between the encoding processes required during study and the retrieval processes required for performance. Telling learners little or nothing about the nature of the criterion forces them to guess at what is important and how it should be processed. Perhaps underlining will produce stronger and more consistent findings where learners are made aware of its strengths and limitations and then trained in its use. Apparently, such a study has yet to be done.

B. SUMMARIZING

Summarizing is another popular learning tactic that has garnered little empirical support among the relatively few studies that have made it an object of investigation. Of seven studies that have compared summarizing with other tactics, two (Arnold, 1942; Stordahl & Christensen, 1956) found no differences among subjects who engaged in either summarizing, underlining, outlining, or reading–rereading on objective tests of simple recall, recognition, and comprehension. The nonsignificant finding reported by Arnold (1942) is interesting because his subjects were given 3 weeks of instruction, practice, and feedback prior to testing.

Three studies found reading or rereading to be superior to summarizing. Germane (1921) found that sixth-, seventh-, and eighth-grade children who were given 10 minutes of instruction in summarizing performed slightly worse on a test of recall than a comparison group directed to read–reread. An interesting comment made by Germane was that the eighth-grade summarizers seemed handicapped by the tactic because their summaries included large numbers of isolated facts, whereas the test called on the ability to see and remember relationships among ideas. In this case, it seems clear that the poor performance of the summarizers may have been largely due to the discrepancy between how the information was processed and the demands of the test. Repetitive readers, without the burden of deciding what to record, may have had more time to think about and integrate more of the information. Similar results were reported by Howe and Singer (1975). They found that college students who were allowed to read a relatively short passage (286 words) as often as possible within a 10-minute period, performed better on an immediate and a 1-week-delayed, free-recall test than students who were directed to write a summary of each paragraph. A third group that was directed to copy the article word for word performed significantly worse than either of the other two groups. Finally, Dyer, Riley, and Yekovich (1979) had college students read a 2000-word passage with or without taking notes. Then, one-half of the students wrote summaries from memory while the rest completed an unrelated task. Students then either reread the passage or engaged in a placebo task. All students took a 30-item completion test immediately and 1 week later. Those who took notes or reread recalled more than those who summarized. The combination of note-taking and rereading was no more effective than either tactic alone. There was only one effect of summarizing that might be viewed positively. If an item of information was mentioned in the summary, the corresponding test question was more likely to be answered correctly.

One study that did find facilitative effects for summarizing was conducted by Ross and DiVesta (1976). One-half of their college student sample read a 2200-word passage with the expectancy that they would present an oral summary shortly afterward. The rest of the students read the same material without this expectancy. The students (all females) were told to expect short-answer and multiple-choice test questions 1 week later on general concepts and specific details. After reading the passage, one-third of the students in each group presented oral summaries, one-third listened to the summaries of other students, and one-third did not engage in any review activity. The results indicated that giving a verbal summary enhanced retention relative to hearing a summary or simply reading the passage regardless of whether one expected to give a summary. The effect was greater for cued recall (short-answer) than for recognition (multiple-choice) items and for longer summaries than for shorter ones.

A second study reporting positive effects for summarizing was conducted by Bretzing and Kulhavy (1979). They found that high school students who were directed to either summarize the main points from each page of a 2000-word passage after it was read or to write down main points from each page as it was read (with a limit of three lines in both cases), recalled more than students who simply read the passage. The criterion test was composed of 25 short-answer items that were described as requiring the integration of facts rather than simple verbatim responses.

There is no question that the preceding findings are generally disappointing. However, the remarks that were made in the section on underlining apply here as well. In no study were students given detailed information about the nature of the criterion, the nature of the reading passage, or the best way to construct summaries for particular types of test items. The two studies that did report favorable results (Bretzing & Kulhavy, 1981; Ross & DiVesta, 1976) seemed to provide their subjects with somewhat more than the typical amount of information about the nature of the criterion. In addition, Bretzing and Kulhavy (1981) may have produced a better match between encoding and retrieval by limiting summaries to three lines. If this constraint induced subjects to integrate information into more general, higher-order propositions, it would be reasonable to expect them to perform better on short-answer items requiring integration of facts. The performance of Germane's (1921) eighth-graders is consistent with this interpretation. If future studies also show that summarizing has its greatest effect on higher-level outcomes, it may be necessary to reclassify it as a comprehension-directed tactic. The Bretzing and Kulhavy (1981) study also suggests that better results might be obtained by training learners how to construct good summaries. Studies by Christopherson (1981) and Kintsch and Kozminsky (1977) on the characteristics of summaries provide some support for this notion.

C. MNEMONIC DEVICES

A *mnemonic* is a memory-directed tactic that helps a learner transform and/or organize material in order to enhance its retrievability. These devices are typically used to learn and remember individual items of information (e.g., names, facts) or collections of information in list form.

Although the origins of certain mnemonic devices are over 2000 years old (see Yates, 1966 for a detailed discussion of the history of mnemonics), they were rarely made the object of scientific study until the 1960s. Since that time, however, they have been frequently and intensively studied by researchers. In recent years, reviews of the mnemonic literature have been conducted by Bellezza (1981), Higbee (1979), Pressley, Levin, and Delaney (1982), and White (1983). Because the literature on mnemonic devices is quite large and space here is limited, this section is based largely on White's (1983) review and analysis. The specific mnemonic devices that are discussed include the acronym, sentence, narrative story, pegword, method of loci, and keyword.

1. Acronym

This mnemonic (also known as the first-letter mnemonic) combines the first letters of the to-be-learned material into a word that can be easily stored in memory and used later as a set of retrieval cues. For example, the first letters of the five great lakes can be arranged to form the word "HOMES" or the colors of the light spectrum, taken in their natural sequence (longest to shortest wavelengths), can be encoded as ROY-G-BIV. Surveys of mnemonic devices among college students have found this technique to be one of the most well known and widely used (e.g., Blick, Buonassissi, & Boltwood, 1972; Blick & Waite, 1971).

According to White (1983), it appears as if the acronym is likely to be most effective when one must recall items, particularly abstract or familiar items, in a certain order. White (1983), however, cautions against drawing premature conclusions about acronym effectiveness because many critical variables have yet to be investigated. Using the tetrahedral model as a theoretical framework, he points out that acronym researchers have not fully investigated the role of such important learner characteristics as age or intellectual ability. In addition, none of the researchers provided much of an opportunity for subjects to become proficient with the mnemonic nor did they assess how often the method was actually used.

2. Sentence

This mnemonic enhances learning and memory by incorporating separate items of information into a sentence, with the sentence then serving as a retrieval cue. One version of this technique is used, like the acronym, to learn lists of items and is often referred to as an acrostic. One simply constructs a sentence by using the first letters of the to-be-remembered items as the first letters of the words making up the mnemonic sentence. For example, music teachers have long taught students to remember the notes on the staff (E, G, B, D, F) by remembering the sentence, "Every good boy does fine." A second version is typically used to learn pairs of items. In this situation, the subject embeds a pair of items (e.g., fowl–gun) in a meaningful sentence (e.g., "The hunter shot the fowl with his gun"). It is the latter version that is reviewed here because it has more often been studied by researchers.

Based on two studies conducted by Rohwer (1973; Rohwer, Raines, Eoff, & Wagner, 1977), White (1983) concluded that for paired-associate learning (PAL) tasks, the sentence mnemonic is more effective than rote repetition for younger (through 6th grade) middle-class subjects of all ability levels and older (through 11th grade) middle-class subjects of low and moderate ability than it is for younger upper-class subjects or older high-ability subjects.

When variations in learning materials were examined (e.g., Paivio & Foth, 1970), better results were obtained with abstract words than with concrete words.

The results of studies that examined subject-generated versus experimenter-supplied sentences (e.g., Bower & Winzenz, 1970; Garten & Blick,

1974; Pines & Blick, 1974; Rohwer, 1973) are inconclusive, although the evidence leans in favor of the former. Whether subjects who are well trained in generating good sentences would consistently outperform naive subjects who are supplied with good sentences is still an open question.

Regardless of age, the mnemonic seems to facilitate delayed cued and delayed free recall relative to control subjects told to use their own learning method or told to repetitively rehearse (e.g., Bower & Winzenz, 1970; Lowry, 1974; Negin, 1978; Pines & Blick, 1974).

White (1983) maintains that future studies should focus on the applicability of this method to other tasks besides PAL and the extent to which training enhances performance over the levels achieved by naive subjects.

3. Narrative Story

The story mnemonic is like the sentence mnemonic in that it organizes separate items of information into a meaningful unit. In this case, the unit is a set of sentences constructed as a story and based on the to-be-remembered items.

White (1983) found the technique to be effective with elementary school children (e.g., Gripe, 1979; Kulhavy, Canaday, Haynes, & Schaller, 1977) and college students (e.g., Borges, Arnold, & McClure, 1976; Bower & Clark, 1969; Cunningham & Snowman, 1975; Hermann, Geisler, & Atkinson, 1973) for immediate and delayed free recall, serial recall, and recognition. Better results have been obtained with concrete items of information than with abstract items (e.g., Cunningham & Snowman, 1975; Manning & Bruning, 1975; Santa, Ruskin, & Yio, 1973). Presenting the items to-be-remembered one at a time rather than as a set does not seem to limit the mnemonic's effectiveness (e.g., Kulhavy & Heinen, 1974).

On the basis of this and other evidence, White (1983) concluded that the narrative story mnemonic is very effective for a wide range of subjects and recall criteria. Future studies, he felt, should investigate its utility for tasks other than list learning.

4. Pegword

The *pegword* mnemonic requires the learner to memorize a simple set of objects that rhyme with integer names: one–bun, two–shoe, three–tree, four–door, five–hive, six–sticks, seven–heaven, eight–gate, nine–wine, ten–hen. To use the mnemonic, the learner first generates images of the to-be-remembered material. Then, each image is linked with an image of one of the peg words. The image of the pegword and its associated number serves as the retrieval cue. If, for example, a grocery list contains eggs, milk, and butter as its first three items, images integrating eggs and a bun, milk and a shoe, and butter and a tree would be formed.

Based on the preceding description, one would expect the pegword mnemonic to be most effective with material that lends itself to visual imagery. White (1983) found this to be the case in studies that compared concrete and abstract nouns (e.g., Foth, 1973; Griffith & Atkinson, 1978; Santa, Ruskin, & Yio, 1973; Wortman & Sparling, 1974).

The role of ability in pegword use is not clear, as one study (Smith & Noble, 1965) found low-ability subjects remembered more nonsense syllables than high-ability subjects, whereas another study (Griffith & Atkinson, 1978) reported the opposite pattern for recall of nouns.

The technique has been proven effective with children (e.g., Higbee, 1976), military personnel (e.g., Griffith & Atkinson, 1978), and graduate students (e.g., DiVesta & Sunshine, 1974), and for a variety of retention measures (e.g., Foth, 1973; Roediger, 1980; Smith & Noble, 1965). Typically, it is used to learn word lists, although one study (Higbee, 1976) showed it to be useful for learning and 10 commandments.

White's (1983) main criticisms of pegword research are the insufficient training that is often provided and the lack of assessment of actual mnemonic use by subjects. This last criticism is especially telling because Persensky and Senter (1970) long ago reported the pegword to be effective only with subjects who reported using it.

5. Method of Loci

This mnemonic is sometimes called the place method because the word *loci* means places. To use this method, the learner first forms a set of highly familiar loci for which visual images can be formed, such as the rooms of one's house. Then, images of the to-be-remembered items are generated and embedded within the locations. During retrieval, the learner mentally walks through the locations, retrieves each image, and decodes it into a response. As you can see, this technique is basically the same as the pegword mnemonic.

White (1983) reports that the method of loci is an effective memory-directed tactic for children (e.g., Brown, 1973), college students (e.g., Bellezza & Reddy, 1978; Weinstein, Cubberly, Wicker, Underwood, Roney, & Duty, 1981), and senior citizens (e.g., Tchabo, Hausmann, & Arenberg, 1976). Most of the learning tasks involve word lists, although some evidence exists (e.g., Snowman, Krebs, & Kelly, 1980) that when combined with an outlining tactic, the loci mnemonic facilitates recall from prose. Performance with subject-generated loci is superior to experimenter-provided loci among college students (e.g., Bellezza & Reddy, 1978; Montague & Carter, 1974). Loci users score better than nonusers on immediate and delayed free recall tests (e.g., Snowman et al., 1980), immediate and delayed serial recall (e.g., Weinstein et al., 1981) and recency judgements (e.g., Brown, 1973).

6. Keyword

The *keyword* mnemonic was devised in the 1970s as a means of learning foreign language vocabulary (e.g., Atkinson, 1975; Atkinson & Raugh, 1975). The technique involves two steps. First, the learner extracts a meaningful, concrete English word (called the keyword) from the pronunciation of the to-be-learned foreign word and constructs a visual image for it. Second, this image is integrated with an image representing the English translation of the foreign word. For example, to learn that the Spanish word *pato* (pronounced pot-o) means *duck*, the learner might imagine a duck wearing a pot on its head. At recall, the word *pato* will bring the preceding image to mind. The image, in turn, will serve as a cue for the correct response.

White (1983) has found the keyword to be effective with preschoolers (e.g., Pressley, Samuel, Hershey, Bishop, & Dickinson, 1981), elementary school children (e.g., Miller, Levin, & Pressley, 1980; Pressley & Levin, 1978), adolescents (e.g., Pressley & Dennis-Rounds, 1980), and college students (e.g., Atkinson & Raugh, 1975), although younger subjects must be given the keyword and a picture incorporating the keyword and the English translation in order to profit from the technique.

The keyword has proven to be very flexible, as it also facilitates the recall of cities and their products (e.g., Pressley & Dennis-Rounds, 1980), states and their capitals (e.g., Levin, Shriberg, Miller, McCormick, & Levin, 1980), medical definitions (Jones & Hall, 1982), and famous people's accomplishments (e.g., Shriberg, Levin, McCormick, & Pressley, 1982). Some researchers (e.g., Pressley, Levin, & Miller, 1981) have found that a sentence variation of the keyword was as effective as the standard version for helping fifth-graders remember concrete and abstract word lists.

III. RESEARCH ON COMPREHENSION-DIRECTED
LEARNING TACTICS

A. QUESTIONING

As stated earlier, comprehension-directed tactics are geared more toward understanding the meaning of ideas and their interrelationships than toward ensuring reliable recall of those ideas. Levin (1982) feels that the tactic of learner-generated questions could fall into either category, depending on the nature of the questions. For example, generating questions that require verbatim recall or recognition of simple details might reasonably be considered a memory-directed tactic. On the other hand, if the questions assess comprehension, application, or synthesis of main ideas or other high-level information, they probably belong in the comprehension-directed category. Given the criterion measures used by most researchers of learner-generated questions, this tactic is usually meant to foster comprehension. The benefits of learner-generated questions are presumed to be due to students being forced to notice and think meaningfully about specific segments of text. Several factors may need to be considered in order to realize these benefits.

Crouse and Idstein (1972) found that college students who were told to generate short-answer questions from the underlined segments of three 200-word passages because the criterion test would be made up of 22 similar questions from those segments performed no better than subjects who simply read the passages, read the passages with the relevant sections underlined, or read the passages with the actual test items provided after the underlined material. Because those results may have been due to passage brevity, a second experiment compared a read-only group with an experimenter-supplied underlining group on recall of a 6000-word passage. Under these circumstances, underlining resulted in an 87% improvement over the read-only. It is tempting to think that a learner-generated questions group would have performed as well as the underlining group.

Prior to reading four 550-word passages, Duell (1978) provided college students with directions on how to write test questions that matched the specifications of knowledge level and application level objectives. The students then read the objectives, read the passages, wrote relevant multiple-choice questions, and took a 32-item multiple-choice test based on the objectives. A second group simply read the objectives, read the passages, and took the test. Overall, question writers scored significantly higher than non-question writers. However, all students answered significantly more knowledge-level questions correctly than application questions. Duell (1978) noted that extended training in question writing and the use of longer passages might increase ability to correctly answer application questions.

In the first of two experiments, Frase and Schwartz (1975) presented pairs of high school students with a 1200-word biographical passage. At different times, each member of the pair would either generate questions for the other member to answer, respond to the partner's questions, or simply read. The students were instructed to ask the kinds of questions that would help one do well on a test. The posttest, which was not described to the students, contained short-answer questions. More than 99% of the questions generated by the students required specific, verbatim responses. Test scores under the answering and the questioning conditions did not differ although both exceeded scores obtained under the study condition. For both the questioning and the answering conditions, recall was higher on posttest items for which questions were generated than on posttest items unrelated to student questions.

A tentative conclusion that could be drawn from the three preceding studies is that students need to be trained in how to frame good questions if the tactic is to be effective. The few studies that have attempted to investigate the benefits of training have produced mixed results.

André and Anderson (1978–1979) found that low-ability high school seniors who were given extensive practice and feedback on how to generate comprehension questions from a 450-word passage scored significantly higher on a short-answer test than low-ability students who read the passage more than once. High-ability students scored equally well regardless of treatment condition. The probability of answering an item correctly after having generated a good question during training was .78. When a less-than-adequate question was generated, the probability of correctly responding fell to .39. In a follow-up experiment that included an untrained question-generation group, similar results were obtained despite the fact that the trained subjects wrote a significantly greater percentage of good comprehension questions.

Dreher and Gambrell (1982) conducted a training study with sixth-grade boys that was a replication and extension of the André and Anderson (1978–1979) study. For 2 days, students either wrote questions following André and Anderson's training procedures, wrote questions with no training, or engaged in a read–recite–review tactic. For both questioning groups, only one-third of the questions that were written elicited main ideas as a response. Four days later, all students were given two passages to read and a short-answer test requiring main idea and detail responses. No differences among the three groups were found. One week later, the classroom teacher repeated the procedure. Again there were no differences. One week after the second test, the students were asked to describe how they would tell another student to study for a test. Only about 20% in each group described the technique they had been taught.

Singer and Donlan (1982) taught a group of high school students to analyze short stories according to a five-element problem-solving schema and to generate story-specific questions based on the schema. A comparison group responded to teacher-posed questions. Both groups received 2 days of instruction per week for 3 weeks. Short multiple-choice tests were administered after each training session. There was no difference between the groups for the first two sessions. Although the schema group outscored the comparison group for sessions 3–6, the difference was significant only for the fifth session.

Overall, these findings provide only weak support for learner-generated questions as an effective comprehension-directed tactic. For high school and college students, question asking was as effective as question answering for test items based on the questions, although either activity led to better test scores than just reading (e.g., André & Anderson, 1978–1979; Frase &

Schwartz, 1975; Singer & Donlan, 1982). Although Duell (1978) found that question writers outscored non-question-writers, the effect was limited largely to low-level knowledge questions. For elementary grade students, question asking proved no more effective than a simple read–recite–review tactic, even when the students were trained to write appropriate questions (e.g., Dreher & Gambrell, 1982). It should be pointed out, however, that most of the preceding studies used passages of less than 1500 words. It may have been possible for most students to meaningfully process most of the information in such relatively brief passages in spite of the treatment condition to which they were assigned. Given the strong improvement in recall reported by Crouse and Idstein (1972) when subjects in an underlining treatment went from a 200-word passage to a 6000-word passage, future research on learner-generated questions might include passages in the neighborhood of 5000 or more words. Finally, the failure of the training studies to produce strong effects may have been due to the brevity of the training and the omission of a metacognitive component. André and Anderson (1978–1979) have noted that effective self-questioning should force learners to pause frequently in their reading, deal with an understanding question, determine whether or not comprehension has occurred, and decide what action should be taken next. Apparently, none of the preceding studies assessed the degree to which students were aware of and engaged in these activities.

B. NOTE TAKING

Of the 10 studies comprising this section, 4 found note taking to be no more effective than or less effective than rereading for such criterial tasks as short-answer questions for main ideas and details, multiple-choice questions, essays, and free recall (Davis & Annis, 1978–1979; Dyer, Riley, & Yekovich, 1979; Hoon, 1974; Todd & Kessler, 1971). Perhaps the best way to explain these failures, as well as the successes, is in terms of the tetrahedral model. In at least two of the preceding cases, the learning materials appeared to have been inappropriate for a note-taking tactic. For example, Dyer et al. (1979) had college students read a 2000-word anthropological description of a fictional African tribe called the Himoots. Although the passage is of reasonable length, it is highly concrete, fact-filled, and somewhat simply structured. In all likelihood, such a passage could be adequately comprehended by the more passive tactic of rereading. The opposite problem appeared in the Todd and Kessler (1971) study. Their passage was the brief "War of the Ghosts" used by Bartlett (1932) in his studies of memory. This story would be very difficult to understand unless one was familiar with the myths and legends of the North American Indians on which it was based.

In addition, all four studies may have been subject to another shortcoming mentioned by Anderson (1980) in an earlier review of note-taking research. Anderson offered two reasons to explain the failure of note taking in several of the studies he reviewed. First, subjects may not have processed the right information with respect to the criterion task because of limited study time (note taking takes longer than rereading) and/or insufficient knowledge of the criterion task (leading subjects to guess what to record). Second, subjects may have copied information verbatim from the passage instead of constructing a more personally meaningful paraphrase. Both reasons imply a failure to induce transfer-appropriate processing. This idea holds that the best type of processing at the time of encoding is that which produces knowledge that matches the demand of the criterion test. In terms of the tetrahedral model, transfer-appropriate processing involves at the very least an interaction between learner activities and the nature of the criterial task.

Studies that have found facilitative effects for note taking have usually been designed such that the relationship between the demands of the criterion task and the encoding processes invoked by note taking was more consistent. Peper and Mayer (1978), for example, found that note takers outscored non–note takers on test items measuring far transfer, whereas the opposite pattern prevailed on test items of near transfer, especially for low verbal ability subjects. Barnett, DiVesta, and Rogozinski (1981) found that college students who were instructed to take notes on an 1800-word taped passage by identifying main headings and related key ideas outscored non–note takers on a set of short-answer items designed to parallel the text and students' notes. Hale (1983) told high school students who either read–reread or took notes over a 1300-word passage that they would be given a multiple-choice test on the passage's main points and that each paragraph contained a main point. Note taking subjects were additionally told to think about the main point of each paragraph and write it down. The criterion test consisted of 12 items, 6 of which covered one-half of the passage's main points. The other 6 questions covered lower-level details. Unannounced delayed tests were given 1, 8, and 15 days later. Note takers outscored non–note takers on the immediate test but not on the delayed tests. Only the results of a study reported by Kulhavy, Dyer, and Silver (1975) are at odds with the explanation that note-taking is useful only when something is known about the criterion test. They found that high school students who took notes over an 845-word passage (no more than 3 lines of notes per page) and were given no information about the criterion test, outscored subjects who underlined, subjects who simply read, and other note taking subjects who were told to expect either a multiple-choice or a short-answer test.

An example of how the categories of learner characteristic, learning material, and criterial task can determine the effectiveness of note taking can be seen in a study reported by Annis (1979). After reading or taking notes over an organized or scrambled 16-paragraph article, field-independent and field-dependent college students took 1-week-delayed recall and completion tests. The latter test required students to fill in an essential word or phrase omitted from sentences rated high or low in importance to the structure of a paragraph. Field-independent learners outscored field-dependent learners on high-importance completion items, whereas no differences occurred on low-importance items. Notes taken on an organized learning passage were of higher average structural importance than notes taken on an unorganized learning passage.

In a similar vein, Bretzing and Kulhavy (1981) found that the free recall protocols of note-taking college students who read a low-formality passage (written at a more familiar and concrete level) contained significantly more paraphrased statements than the free recall protocols of note takers who read the high-formality version. A conditional probability analysis showed that an idea was more likely to be recalled if it had been written in notes than if it had only been read.

Of the 10 note-taking studies reviewed here, not one made a serious attempt to train students to take notes more effectively. The need for such training, at least among high school students, was pointed out by Hale (1983). Many of his subjects did not realize how helpful a tactic like note taking could be to foster comprehension and reduce forgetting. Thus, study skills programs would do well to provide concrete experiences that can help students develop a realistic sense of the forgetting process and the utility of learning tactics.

C. TEXT ANALYSIS

Prose materials often produce different learning outcomes than simpler verbal materials under more or less identical conditions. This discontinuity is largely due to the fact that prose materials present a more complex structure and often involve a greater degree of abstractness. Because many school learning tasks involve working with such material, researchers have tried to determine if learner awareness of text structure and use of text-structure analysis methods is a useful comprehension-directed tactic. While a variety of text analysis techniques have been investigated, most involve the identification of various idea units and a method for specifying their interrelationships. The research reviewed in this section has been organized into two categories: training in the use of text structure analysis and training in the use of headings and topic sentences.

1. Training-in the Use of Text-Structure Analysis

For 1 hour a day for 12 consecutive days, Armbruster and Anderson (1980) taught 11 eighth-graders a text analysis technique called mapping. This technique identifies up to seven basic relationships among idea units (e.g., example, compare/contrast, temporal) and represents them in an interconnected diagram. For immediate recall of two brief passages, the experimental group recalled a significantly greater percentage of idea units than a control group (34% versus 15%) from the first passage. No differences occurred for the second passage or for a second posttest administered 3 days later. A conditional probability analysis of the immediate recall scores revealed that the probability of recalling idea units that were mapped was significantly greater than the probability of recalling idea units that were not mapped. Moreover, the effect was most pronounced for ideas rated high in structural importance (i.e., the more superordinate ideas). The conditional probability analysis of the delayed recall scores revealed no differences between the groups. Armbruster and Anderson offered three reasons for these mixed results. First, not all of the relationships were learned equally well. Understanding cause–effect relationships was particularly difficult for many students. Second, students generally did not try to integrate all the relationships into one map; instead, they mapped subsections independently. Third, there was a general lack of interest in the task.

Holley, Dansereau, McDonald, Garland, and Collins (1979) provided 17 college students with $5\frac{1}{2}$ hours of training on a hierarchical mapping technique similar to that of Armbruster and Anderson (1980). Following training, the students used the technique to study a 3000-word passage taken from a geology text. A control group simply read the passage. Five days later, all subjects took four tests: essay, concept cloze, multiple-choice, and short-answer. The experimental group significantly outperformed the control group on the combined concept cloze and essay scores, both of which were designed to tap main ideas. There was no difference between the groups on the combined multiple-choice and short-answer scores, both of which were designed to tap details. An additional analysis indicated that the technique may be more beneficial for low-ability students.

Snowman, Krebs, and Kelly (1980) provided 15 weeks of training for 3 hours per week to college students on the use of a simple, four-element text-analysis scheme. Students were trained to identify the main idea of a passage, note the ways in which the main idea was discussed, and then list characteristics and examples. These ideas were then arranged from top to bottom and left to right on a sheet of paper, yielding a simplified hierarchical structure. Similar groups received the same amount of training in the method of loci mnemonic or a combination of the two techniques. Students who received training in either the text-analysis technique alone or the text-analysis-plus-loci techniques recalled significantly more idea units than students who were trained in just the method of loci mnemonic.

Taylor (1982) provided fifth-graders with 7 weeks of training for 1 hour each week in the formulation of a three-level hierarchical outline. Control subjects were exposed to the more conventional procedure of answering questions after reading. After training, students studied a pair of 800-word passages using their respective techniques. The text-analysis group scored significantly higher than the conventional-instruction group for free recall and organization of recall. Both groups scored equally well on a short-answer test. A replication of this experiment, however, produced mostly nonsignificant findings.

2. Training in the Use of Headings and Topic Sentences

The utility of *intact headings* (an outline presented prior to reading) and *embedded headings* (headings interspersed throughout the passage) as encoding and retrieval aids was examined by Holley, Dansereau, Evans, Collins, Brooks, and Larson (1981). They found that college students who were instructed in how to use either intact or embedded headings recalled significantly more information on a delayed test from an unfamiliar passage than students whose passage contained neither aid. The text-with-headings students recalled approximately 11% more information on an immediate test and 44% more information on a delayed test than the text-without-headings students.

An evaluation of the effects of intact and embedded headings over a wider range of outcome measures was made by Brooks, Dansereau, Spurlin, and Holley (1983). In the first of two experiments, college students who read a 2400-word passage with embedded headings scored better on essay and create-an-outline tests administered 5 days after reading than students who received either intact headings, intact and embedded headings, or a passage with neither type of heading. No differences among the groups were observed for the multiple-choice test or for any of the immediate tests. Presumably, the headings provided the same kind of information about superordinate–subordinate relationships that was assessed by the first two criterion measures. The second experiment compared the effects of instructing or not instructing field-dependent and field-independent college students in how to use embedded text headings on the same outcome measures. The instructions were to (1) develop expectations about the passage based on the headings, (2) understand why each heading was appropriate for its section of text, (3) memorize the headings, and (4) use the headings as recall aids. The instructed group significantly outscored only the control group (no headings) on the delayed essay test. The scores of the uninstructed headings group and the control group were equivalent. All comparisons on the delayed multiple-choice and outline tests were nonsignificant. The effect of cognitive style was nonsignificant.

In order to determine if better results might be obtained by having students generate their own headings, Brooks, Dansereau, Holley, and Spurlin (1983) either instructed college students in how to construct good headings, provided a passage with embedded headings but without instructions, or provided a passage without embedded headings. The instructed group was told that good headings emphasize the hierarchical structure of the text and was given an opportunity to practice the technique. Five days later, students were given a free-recall test, an outline test, a multiple-choice test, and a short-answer test. The students who generated their own headings generally outscored the other groups on the various measures of recall (e.g., free-recall content, outline content, short-answer) but scored about as well on the comprehension measures (e.g., free-recall organization, outline organization, multiple-choice).

In a similar study, Dee-Lucas and DiVesta (1980) compared the effects of topic sentences, headings, related sentences, and unrelated sentences on learning from text when they were either generated by the students or provided in the text. A topic sentence related the topic of a paragraph to that of a previous paragraph and was intended to highlight the hierarchical structure of the text. The headings were one or two words that captured the general topic of a paragraph. A related sentence paraphrased information from another sentence of that paragraph. An unrelated sentence was related to the passage topic but not to any other sentence in the paragraph. Performance was measured by a knowledge-of-passage-structure test, a free-recall test, and a matching test. For the passage-structure test (recalling paragraph topics and placing them in appropriate slots in a hierarchical tree structure), there were no differences among the four experimenter-provided conditions. For the subject-generated conditions, the topic-sentence group significantly outscored the other three. For the free-recall test, the headings group outscored the topic sentence and unrelated sentence groups but not the related-sentence group under subject-generate and experimenter-provide conditions. For the matching test, experimenter-provided headings and related sentences led to equal performance, although both groups significantly outscored the experimenter-provided unrelated sentences group. All experimenter-provided groups significantly outscored their subject-generated counterparts on this measure.

In general, it seems fair to conclude that training students in the use of various types of text structure analysis schemes seems to enhance comprehension as measured by the recall of superordinate ideas. However, it is likely to be a difficult undertaking. In order to assess just how useful text structure analysis training can be, future studies should (1) provide training for as long as it takes each subject to demonstrate mastery of the techniques; (2) keep interest and motivation high by employing various incentives; (3) measure the effects of training over several types of measures, materials, and time periods; (4) identify subjects for whom such training is likely to be most beneficial; and (5) make sure the training is comprehensive. For example, the mixed results of Armbruster and Anderson (1980) and Taylor (1982) points up what happens when children are trained in the use of a tactic as opposed to an overall strategy. As outlined in the beginning of this chapter, a strategy should include tactics training plus metacognitive training so that students know, in terms of appropriate learning behaviors, what, when, where, how, and why. Brown, Campione, and Day (1981) refer to this as self-control training. Apparently, many students do not understand why a tactic is useful and why it should be mastered.

As measured by a variety of criteria, the use of headings, particularly embedded headings, and topic sentences seem to be useful comprehension-directed tactics, although the evidence is not consistent. Some of this inconsistency was likely due to differences in procedures and materials. For example, the failure of the uninstructed embedded headings group to outperform the control group in Experiment 2 of Brooks et al. (1983) as it did in Experiment 1 was attributed to students being more aware of the headings in Experiment 1 because they received both immediate and delayed passages and tests. The positive findings reported by Dee-Lucas and DiVesta (1980) for topic sentences may have been due in part to their use of a brief (about 500 words), highly structured passage (15 hierarchically related topics, each of which was discussed in a three-sentence paragraph).

IV. LEARNING-STRATEGY RESEARCH

The learning strategy model on which this chapter is based is, as was mentioned earlier, composed of five steps. This model is consistent with the analysis of strategic behavior made by Paris, Lipson, and Wixson (1983). They describe the strategic learner as being in possession of declarative knowledge, procedural knowledge, and conditional knowledge. Declarative knowledge includes information about various task characteristics and one's abilities. Procedural knowledge includes information about how to use learning tactics and other intellectual skills. Conditional knowledge includes knowing when and why to apply one or another of the preceding tactics and skills. Regardless of the specific approach and terms used, the critical element of a learning strategy is, as Paris, Lipson, and Wixson (1983) point out, the intentional, effortful, self-selection of a means to an end. After careful deliberation, the learner must choose one action (or a sequence of actions) from among several in order to reach a goal. The factors that contribute to this capability, and whether or not they can be taught, are examined in the next group of studies.

The learning-strategy model described earlier implies that as individuals increase their metacognitive awareness, they are more apt to use effective strategic and tactical skills and thus enhance their performance on learning tasks. The validity of these causal links for a paired-associate learning task among eighth- and tenth-graders was investigated by Waters (1982). For both groups, knowledge of appropriate tactics (e.g., visual elaboration, verbal elaboration) was positively related to tactics use, which, in turn, was positively related to recall performance. Tenth-graders recalled significantly more pairs than eighth-graders because of increased tactics use.

The role of various types of metacognitive feedback on maintenance of an instructed-recall tactic among first-, third-, and fifth-graders was investigated by Ringel and Springer (1980). The learning task was to sort 20 familiar pictures into different semantically related groups (e.g., foods, toys) and then free recall as many of the picture names as possible. Subjects in Group 1 were uninstructed and sorted in any manner they chose. Subjects in Groups 2, 3, and 4 were shown how to do the sorting task and were told that figuring out which pictures go together might help them learn the pictures. Group 2 subjects received no feedback about their performance. Group 3 subjects were told they did better than the other children in the class. Group 4 subjects were told that their improved performance was due to the sorting technique they were taught. Only those third-graders provided with sorting instruction plus metacognitive feedback (Group 4) exhibited maintenance of the technique, improved sorting style, and improved recall on a near transfer task. Few instructed first-graders showed improved sorting styles and recall following explicit feedback, whereas instructed fifth-graders improved despite receiving no feedback. These results indicate that children as young as 8 years old can profit from explicit feedback regarding the utility of a tactic for accomplishing a particular goal. Such feedback illustrates the value of understanding the effects of tactical behavior on the task at hand. Ringel and Springer may have obtained more positive findings for their other subjects had they also included instruction and feedback on the value of understanding the potential usefulness of learning tactics on a variety of tasks and assessed the effects on a variety of near and far transfer measures (see Barclay, 1979).

The fact that few learning strategy studies have examined the effect of pointing out to subjects the diverse applications of a strategy and the benefits of strategy transfer was noted by Kramer and Engle (1981). Hence, they manipulated the metacognitive awareness of normal and mentally retarded children with a mental age of 8 years by providing information about the nature of a rehearsal tactic, its general utility, and examples of its use in the presence and absence of rehearsal training. Although rehearsal training was effective in improving recall scores on the training task, neither rehearsal training, memory awareness, nor their combination significantly improved performance on the generalization tasks. Kramer and Engle concluded that future learning strategy studies may be more successful if they directly train those metacognitive processes involved in generalization. The process of self-monitoring was mentioned as a particularly promising candidate for training.

To a large degree, the findings reported by Ringel and Springer (1980) and Kramer and Engle (1981) are consistent with a phenomenon known as a production deficiency for mnemonic strategies. That is, children who do not spontaneously generate mnemonic strategies will, after being given appropriate instruction, use the demonstrated strategy to improve recall on a subsequent task. However, in the absence of explicit prompts, young children typically abandon the strategy on later, similar tasks. Paris, Newman, and McVey (1982) ascribe these findings to a lack of awareness that a direct relationship exists between cognitive means (strategy use) and ends (recall consequences). Like Kramer and Engle (1981), they felt that the lack of effectiveness of strategy training over time, particularly among first-graders, pointed up the need for more elaborate interventions with young children. Further, they hypothesized that children would not behave strategically until they understood the significance of various optional actions. Paris et al. (1982) tested their hypothesis by asking 7- and 8-year-old children to study and recall 24 pictures twice each day for 5 days. Days 1 and 2 were baseline, practice trials. Day 3 included strategy training. Days 4 and 5 involved how to label, rehearse, and group the pictures as well as how to self-test one's memory and use blocked recall. Half of the children were shown the actions and told to do them. The other half received elaborated feedback on the usefulness and appropriateness of the techniques for remembering. The elaborated-instructions group exhibited significantly greater recall, clustering, strategic study behavior, and metamemory regarding the mnemonic techniques than the other group.

Finally, the effects of training college students in the use of a complex learning strategy in the context of a learning skills course was assessed by Dansereau, Collins, McDonald, Holley, Garland, Diekhoff, and Evans (1979). The learning strategy program developed by Dansereau and his associates was composed of two mutually supportive components. The first component, called *primary strategies*, was designed to facilitate the comprehension and retention of information as well as its subsequent retrieval and use. The second component, called *support strategies*, was designed to help students set goals, schedule study activities, create a positive emotional state, monitor progress, and diagnose learning difficulties. In short, the support strategies involved a moderate degree of metacognitive training. Thirty-eight undergraduates were given 2 hours of strategy training each week for 12 weeks. During the last 6 weeks, the students were divided into three subgroups according to their stated preferences for a particular comprehension–retention tactic. Each subgroup received about 4 hours of training on one of the following prose learning tactics: paraphrase–imagery, identification of key ideas, and networking (a text-analysis tactic). After training, all subjects read and were tested over a 3000-word passage. The results indicated that students who received the training exhibited significantly greater positive precourse–postcourse changes on short-answer and multiple-choice tests than did students in the control group. The benefits were particularly pronounced for networking students as measured by the short-answer test.

V. CONCLUSIONS

A. LEARNING TACTICS

The preceding review was begun with the intent of answering two questions: Do learning tactics and strategies enhance retention and comprehension of information? Can students be trained to use learning tactics and strategies more effectively? The answers, as usual, are not straightforward. Depending on the tactic or type of strategy being considered, the answer may range from strongly affirmative to uncertain to doubtful.

Underlining appears to be a modestly effective memory-directed tactic when the learner knows what parts of the reading material are important and should be underlined. Unfortunately, nothing is known about the extent to which training can enhance the effectiveness of underlining because such studies have apparently never been conducted. Training studies that might be conducted in the future should teach students to recognize the conditions under which underlining is likely to be most effective and provide training for as long as it takes each subject to demonstrate mastery of the technique.

Summarizing does not appear to be an effective memory-directed tactic. However, it should be remembered that the subjects in most of the summarizing studies were given relatively little information about the nature of the criterion task, the nature of the reading passage, or the best way to construct summaries for particular types of test items. Until studies on summarizing incorporate such procedures, there is little that we can say for sure about its usefulness as a memory-directed tactic. Furthermore, the possibility exists that summarizing enhances comprehension more than it does verbatim recall. As with underlining, nothing is known about the effects of training, although related evidence (e.g., Christopherson, 1981; Kintsch &

Kozminsky, 1977) suggests it might help learners summarize more effectively.

Of the three memory-directed tactics discussed in this chapter, mnemonic devices are, with some necessary qualifications, clearly the most effective. The acronym or first-letter mnemonic is quite useful for remembering a relatively short list of items, particularly abstract items, in serial order. The sentence mnemonic is quite effective for recalling pairs of items. As with the acronym, the effect is more pronounced with abstract pairs than concrete pairs. The narrative-story mnemonic is a very effective tactic for recalling lists of moderate length regardless of whether the criterial task demands serial or free recall. If serial recall is important and if the material to-be-learned is relatively concrete, the pegword mnemonic is an effective tactic for children, adolescents, and adults. The method of loci can be used by most learners to serially recall rather extended lists of items. Finally, the keyword mnemonic has proven to be a highly effective memory tactic for children, adolescents, and adults for a variety of association tasks (e.g., foreign language vocabulary, cities and their products, states and their capitals, medical terms and their definitions, famous people and their accomplishments). Despite these positive findings, there is still much research on mnemonic devices that can and should be done. Few researchers, for example, have explored the effects of combining two or more of the preceding mnemonics for various types of tasks. Also to be determined is the effect of extended training on maintenance and generalization.

Learner-generated questions has not yet proven its worth as an effective comprehension-directed tactic, although it may not have been given a fair test in every case. Future studies should examine the role of such variables as passage length, knowledge of the criterial task, and ability to write appropriate questions. An appropriate question is one that relates to the demands of the criterial task.

Note taking has been shown to be an effective comprehension-directed tactic when the encoding process invoked by note taking is consistent with the demands of the criterial task. Thus, students should be given clear, detailed knowledge of course objectives and the nature of test questions if note taking is to be of any value. Whether students should take notes while they read (or while the teacher lectures) or after they read a segment of text is open to question at this point. Likewise, whether students should take notes or be given the instructor's notes is unclear. Whether or not the efficiency and/or effectiveness of note taking can be improved through training has apparently not been investigated.

The use of various text-structure analysis schemes is an effective, if time-consuming, comprehension tactic among college students. Because of the complexity and abstractness of text-structure analysis, students who have not attained the formal operational stage of cognitive development, and this would include many high school and junior high school students, are not as apt to understand and use the tactic as effectively as possible. However, it may be possible to teach such students the related but simpler tactics of generating embedded headings and topic sentences.

B. LEARNING STRATEGIES

Learning strategy research, which means combining strategic and tactical skills with metacognitive knowledge, is a relatively new area of exploration, and so there are few studies from which to draw definitive conclusions. Nevertheless, the early results are encouraging. Students as young as 7 and 8 years old who have been taught to implement and monitor a simple strategy have demonstrated the ability to maintain the strategy over time and apply it to similar tasks. Similarly, college students have been taught to implement and monitor a complex-prose-learning strategy with moderate success.

Future research on learning strategy training and use should continue to examine the utility of the tactics discussed in this chapter for certain learners, materials, and outcomes. So far, only the tactic of text-structure analysis has been looked at in conjunction with metacognitive training. Based on the results of the present review, mnemonic devices, summarizing, and note-taking might be useful tactics to incorporate into a learning strategy. In addition, researchers might further explore the utility of combining a memory-directed tactic (e.g., mnemonic devices) with a comprehension-directed tactic (e.g., text-structure analysis), as well as the combination of memory-directed tactics, comprehension-directed tactics, and metacognitive awareness.

Finally, despite the limited and sometimes tentative knowledge that has been generated about the use and training of tactics and strategies, researchers should continue to assess their utility under typical classroom conditions. In a recent discussion of what is and is not known about training students to use cognitive strategies for classroom use, Peterson and Swing (1983) reached the same conclusion and offered the following four reasons for their decision. First, some questions about the feasibility of classroom implementation of learning strategies can be answered only by research in an actual classroom setting. Second, results obtained under laboratory conditions may differ from results obtained in the classroom. Third, classroom learning may be qualitatively different from laboratory learning. Fourth, learning strategy use in the classroom has the potential to enhance such basic skills as vocabulary learning, reading comprehension, and problem solving.

REFERENCES

Anderson, T. H. (1980). Study strategies and adjunct aids. In R. J. Spiro, B. C. Bruce, & W. F. Brewer (Eds.), *Theoretical issues in reading comprehension*. Hillsdale, NJ: Erlbaum.

André, M. E. D. A., & Anderson, T. H. (1978–1979). The development and evaluation of a self-questioning study technique. *Reading Research Quarterly, 14*, 605–623.

Annis, L. F. (1979). Effect of cognitive style and learning passage organization on study technique effectiveness. *Journal of Educational Psychology, 71*, 620–626.

Annis, L. F., & Annis, D. (1979, April). *A normative study of students' preferred study techniques*. Paper presented at the annual meeting of the American Educational Research Association, San Francisco.

Armbruster, B. B., & Anderson, T. H. (1980). *The effect of mapping on the free recall of expository text* (Tech. Rep. No. 160). Urbana-Champaign: University of Illinois, Center for the Study of Reading. (ERIC Document Reproduction Service No. ED 182 735)

Arnold, H. F. (1942). The comparative effectiveness of certain study techniques in the field of history. *Journal of Educational Psychology, 33*, 449–457.

Atkinson, R. C. (1975). Mnemotechnics in second-language learning. *American Psychologist, 30*, 821–828.

Atkinson, R. C., & Raugh, M. R. (1975). An application of the mnemonic keyword method to the acquisition of a Russian vocabulary. *Journal of Experimental Psychology: Human Learning and Memory, 7*, 126–133.

Barclay, C. R. (1979). The executive control of mnemonic activity. *Journal of Experimental Child Psychology, 27*, 262–276.

Barnett, J. E., DiVesta, F. J., & Rogozinski, J. T. (1981). What is learned in note taking? *Journal of Educational Psychology, 73*, 181–192.

Bartlett, F. (1932). *Remembering*. Cambridge, England: Cambridge University Press.

Bellezza, F. S. (1981). Mnemonic devices: Classification, characteristics, and criteria. *Review of Educational Research, 51*, 247–275.

Bellezza, F. S., & Reddy, B. G. (1978). Mnemonic devices and natural memory. *Bulletin of the Psychonomic Society, 11*, 277–280.

Blick, K. A., Buonassissi, J. V., & Boltwood, C. E. (1972). Mnemonic techniques used by college students in serial learning. *Psychological Reports, 31*, 983–986.

Blick, K. A., & Waite, C. J. (1971). A study of mnemonic techniques used by college students in free recall learning. *Psychological Reports, 29*, 76–78.

Borges, M. A., Arnold, R. C., & McClure, V. L. (1976). Effect of mnemonic encoding techniques on immediate and delayed serial recall. *Psychological Reports, 38*, 915–921.

Bower, G. H., & Clark, M. C. (1969). Narrative stories as mediators for serial learning. *Psychonomic Science, 14*, 181–182.

Bower, G. H., & Hilgard, E. R. (1981). *Theories of learning* (5th ed.). Englewood Cliffs, NJ: Prentice-Hall.

Bower, G. H., & Winzenz, D. (1970). Comparison of associative learning strategies. *Psychonomic Science, 20*, 119–120.

Bransford, J. D. (1979). *Human cognition: Learning, understanding, and remembering*. Belmont, CA: Wadsworth.

Bretzing, B. B., & Kulhavy, R. W. (1979). Note taking and depth of processing. *Contemporary Educational Psychology, 4*, 145–153.

Bretzing, B. B., & Kulhavy, R. W. (1981). Note taking and passage style. *Journal of Educational Psychology, 73*, 242–250.

Brooks, L. W., Dansereau, D. F., Holley, C. D., & Spurlin, J. E. (1983). Generation of descriptive text headings. *Contemporary Educational Psychology, 8*, 103–108.

Brooks, L. W., Dansereau, D. F., Spurlin, J. E., & Holley, C. D. (1983). Effects of headings on text processing. *Journal of Educational Psychology, 75,* 292–302.

Brown, A. L. (1973). Mnemonic elaboration and recency judgements in children. *Cognitive Psychology, 5,* 233–248.

Brown, A. L. (1978). Knowing when, where, and how to remember: A problem of metacognition. In R. Glaser (Ed.), *Advances in instructional psychology* (Vol. 1). Hillsdale, NJ: Erlbaum.

Brown, A. L. (1980). Metacognitive development and reading. In R. J. Spiro, B. C. Bruce, & W. F. Brewer (Eds.), *Theoretical issues in reading comprehension.* Hillsdale, NJ: Erlbaum.

Brown, A. L., & Campione, J. C. (1977). Training strategic study time apportionment in educable retarded children. *Intelligence, 1,* 94–107.

Brown, A. L., Campione, J. C., & Day, J. D. (1981). Learning to learn: On training students to learn from text. *Educational Researcher, 10*(2), 14–24.

Carroll, J. B. (1963). A model of school learning. *Teachers College Record, 64,* 723–733.

Christopherson, S. L. (1981). Effects of knowledge of semantic roles on summarizing written prose. *Contemporary Educational Psychology, 6,* 59–65.

Crouse, J. H., & Idstein, P. (1972). Effects of encoding cues on prose learning. *Journal of Educational Psychology, 63,* 309–313.

Cunningham, D. J., & Snowman, J. (1975, March). *Imagery and narrative stories as mediators for one trial serial and free recall list learning.* Paper presented at the annual meeting of the American Educational Research Association, Washington, DC.

Dansereau, D. F., Collins, K. W., McDonald, B. A., Holley, C. D., Garland, J. C., Diekhoff, G., & Evans, S. H. (1979). Development and evaluation of a learning strategy training program. *Journal of Educational Psychology, 71,* 64–73.

Davis, H. K., & Annis, L. F. (1978–1979). The effects of study techniques, study preferences, and familiarity on later recall. *Journal of Experimental Education, 47,* 92–96.

Dee-Lucas, D., & DiVesta, F. J. (1980). Learner-generated organizational aids: Effects on learning from text. *Journal of Educational Psychology, 72,* 304–311.

DiVesta, F. J., & Sunshine, P. M. (1974). The retrieval of abstract and concrete materials as functions of imagery, mediation, and mnemonic acids. *Memory and Cognition, 2,* 340–344.

Dreher, M. J., & Gambrell, L. B. (1982, March). *Training children to use a self-questioning strategy for studying expository prose.* Paper presented at the annual meeting of the American Educational Research Association, New York.

Duell, O. K. (1978). Overt and covert use of objectives of different cognitive levels. *Contemporary Educational Psychology, 3,* 239–245.

Dyer, J. W., Riley, J., & Yekovich, F. R. (1979). An analysis of three study skills: Notetaking, summarizing, and rereading. *Journal of Educational Research, 73,* 3–7.

Foth, D. L. (1973). Mnemonic technique effectiveness as a function of word abstractness and mediation instructions. *Journal of Verbal Learning and Verbal Behavior, 12,* 239–245.

Fowler, R. L., & Barker, A. S. (1974). Effectiveness of highlighting for retention of text material. *Journal of Applied Psychology, 39,* 358–364.

Frase, L. T., & Schwartz, B. J. (1975). Effect of question production and answering on prose recall. *Journal of Educational Psychology, 67,* 628–635.

Garten, J. A., & Blick, K. A. (1974). Retention of word pairs for experimenter-supplied and subject-originated mnemonics. *Psychological Reports, 35,* 1099–1104.

Germane, L. E. (1921). The value of the written paragraph summary. *Journal of Educational Research, 3,* 116–123.

Griffith, C., & Atkinson, T. R. (1978). Mental aptitude and mnemonic enhancement. *Bulletin of the Psychonomic Society, 12,* 347–348.

Gripe, J. (1979). Investigating techniques for teaching word meanings. *Reading Research Quarterly, 14*, 624–644.

Hale, G. A. (1983). Students' predictions of prose forgetting and the effects of study strategies. *Journal of Educational Psychology, 75*, 708–715.

Hermann, D. J., Geisler, F. V., & Atkinson, R. C. (1973). The serial position function for lists learned by a narrative story mnemonic. *Bulletin of the Psychonomic Society, 2*, 377–378.

Higbee, K. L. (1976). Can young children use mnemonics? *Psychological Reports, 38*, 18.

Higbee, K. L. (1979). Recent research on visual mnemonics: Historical roots and educational fruits. *Review of Educational Research, 49*, 611–630.

Holley, C. D., Dansereau, D. F., Evans, S. H., Collins, K. W., Brooks, L., & Larson, D. (1981). Utilizing intact and embedded headings as processing aids with nonnarrative text. *Contemporary Educational Psychology, 6*, 227–236.

Holley, C. D., Dansereau, D. F., McDonald, B. A., Garland, J. C., & Collins, K. W. (1979). Evaluation of a hierarchical mapping technique as an aid to prose processing. *Contemporary Educational Psychology, 4*, 227–237.

Hoon, P. W. (1974). Efficacy of three common study methods. *Psychological Reports, 35*, 1057–1058.

Howe, M. J. A., & Singer, L. (1975). Presentation variables and students' activities in meaningful learning. *British Journal of Educational Psychology, 45*, 52–61.

Idstein, P., & Jenkins, J. R. (1972). Underlining versus repetitive reading. *Journal of Educational Research, 65*, 321–323.

Jenkins, J. J. (1979). Four points to remember: A tetrahedral model of memory experiments. In L. S. Cermak, & F. I. M. Craik (Eds.), *Levels of processing in human memory.* Hillsdale, NJ: Erlbaum.

Jones, B. F., & Hall, J. W. (1982). School applications of the mnemonic keyword method as a study strategy by eighth graders. *Journal of Educational Psychology, 74*, 230–237.

Kintsch, W., & Kozminsky, E. (1977). Summarizing stories after reading and listening. *Journal of Educational Psychology, 69*, 491–499.

Kramer, J. J., & Engle, R. W. (1981). Teaching awareness of strategic behavior in combination with strategy training: Effects on children's memory performance. *Journal of Experimental Child Psychology, 32*, 513–530.

Kulhavy, R. W., Canaday, J. O., Haynes, C. R., & Schaller, D. L. (1977). Mnemonic transformations and verbal coding processes in children. *Journal of General Psychology, 96*, 209–215.

Kulhavy, R. W., Dyer, H. W., & Silver, L. (1975). The effects of notetaking and test expectancy on the learning of text material. *Journal of Educational Research, 68*, 363–365.

Kulhavy, R. W., & Heinen, J. R. L. (1974). Mnemonic transformations and verbal coding processes. *Journal of Experimental Psychology, 102*, 173–178.

Levin, J. R. (1982). Pictures as prose-learning devices. In A. Flammer, & W. Kintsch (Eds.), *Advances in psychology: Vol. 8. Discourse processing.* Amsterdam: North-Holland.

Levin, J. R., Shriberg, L. K., Miller, G. E., McCormick, C. B., & Levin, B. B. (1980). The keyword method in the classroom: How to remember states and their capitals. *Elementary School Journal, 80*, 185–191.

Lowry, D. H. (1974). The effects of mnemonic learning strategies on transfer, interference, and 48-hour retention. *Journal of Experimental Psychology, 103*, 16–20.

Manning, B. A., & Bruning, R. H. (1975). Interactive effects of mnemonic techniques and word-list characteristics. *Psychological Reports, 36*, 727–736.

Miller, G. E., Levin, J. R., & Pressley, M. (1980). An adaptation of the keyword method to children's learning of foreign verbs. *Journal of Mental Imagery, 4*, 57–61.

Montague, W. E., & Carter, J. (1974, April). *The loci mnemonic technique in learning and memory.* Paper presented at the annual meeting of the American Educational Research Association, Chicago.

Negin, G. A. (1978). Mnemonic and demonic words. *Reading Improvement, 15,* 180–182.

Paivio, A., & Foth, D. L. (1970). Imaginal and verbal mediators and noun concreteness in paired-associate learning: The elusive interaction. *Journal of Verbal Learning and Verbal Behavior, 9,* 384–386.

Paris, S. G., Lipson, M. Y., & Wixson, K. K. (1983). Becoming a strategic reader. *Contemporary Educational Psychology, 8,* 293–316.

Paris, S. G., Newman, R. S., & McVey, K. A. (1982). Learning the functional significance of mnemonic actions: A microgenetic study of strategy acquisition. *Journal of Experimental Child Psychology, 34,* 490–509.

Peper, R. J., & Mayer, R. E. (1978). Notetaking as a generative activity. *Journal of Educational Psychology, 70,* 514–522.

Persensky, J. J., & Senter, R. J. (1970). The effects of subjects conforming to mnemonic instructions. *Journal of Psychology, 74,* 15–20.

Peterson, S. L., & Swing, S. R. (1983). Problems in classroom implementation of cognitive strategy instruction. In M. Pressley & J. R. Levin (Eds.), *Cognitive strategy research: Educational applications.* New York: Springer-Verlag.

Pines, M. S., & Blick, K. A. (1974). Experimenter-supplied and subject-originated mnemonics in retention of word pairs. *Psychological Reports, 34,* 99–106.

Pressley, M., & Dennis-Rounds, J. (1980). Transfer of a mnemonic keyword strategy at two age levels. *Journal of Educational Psychology, 72,* 575–582.

Pressley, M., & Levin, J. R. (1978). Developmental constraints associated with children's use of the keyword method of foreign language vocabulary learning. *Journal of Experimental Child Psychology, 26,* 359–372.

Pressley, M., Levin, J. R., & Delaney, H. D. (1982). The mnemonic keyword method. *Review of Educational Research, 52,* 61–91.

Pressley, M., Levin, J. R., & Miller, G. E. (1981). How does the keyword method affect vocabulary comprehension and usage? *Reading Research Quarterly, 16,* 213–226.

Pressley, M., Samuel, J., Hershey, M. M., Bishop, S. L., & Dickinson, P. (1981). Use of a mnemonic technique to teach young children foreign language vocabulary. *Contemporary Educational Psychology, 6,* 110–116.

Rickards, J. P., & August, G. J. (1975). Generative underlining strategies in prose recall. *Journal of Educational Psychology, 67,* 860–865.

Ringel, B. A., & Springer, C. J. (1980). On knowing how well one is remembering: The persistence of strategy use during transfer. *Journal of Experimental Child Psychology, 29,* 322–333.

Roediger, H. L. (1980). The effectiveness of four mnemonics in ordering recall. *Journal of Experimental Psychology: Human Learning and Memory, 6,* 558–567.

Rohwer, W. D., Jr. (1973). Elaboration and learning in childhood and adolescence. In H. W. Reese (Ed.), *Advances in child development and behavior* (Vol. 8). New York: Academic Press.

Rohwer, W. D., Jr., Raines, J. M., Eoff, J., & Wagner, M. (1977). The development of elaborative propensity in adolescence. *Journal of Experimental Child Psychology, 23,* 472–492.

Ross, S. M., & DiVesta, F. J. (1976). Oral summary as a review strategy for enhancing recall of textual material. *Journal of Educational Psychology, 68,* 689–695.

Santa, J., Ruskin, A., & Yio, A. (1973). Mnemonic systems in free recall. *Psychological Reports, 32,* 1163–1170.

Shriberg, L. K., Levin, J. R., McCormick, C. B., & Pressley, M. (1982). Learning about "famous" people via the keyword method. *Journal of Educational Psychology, 74*, 238–247.

Singer, H., & Donlan, D. (1982). Active comprehension: Problem solving schema with question generation for comprehension of complex short stories. *Reading Research Quarterly, 17*, 166–186.

Smith, R. K., & Noble, C. E. (1965). Effects of a mnemonic technique applied to verbal learning and memory. Perceptual and Motor Skills, *21*, 123–134.

Snowman, J., Krebs, E. W., & Kelly, F. J. (1980, April). *Enhancing memory for prose through learning strategy training.* Paper presented at the annual meeting of the American Educational Research Association, Boston.

Stordahl, K. E., & Christensen, C. M. (1956). The effect of study techniques on comprehension and retention. *Journal of Educational Research, 49*, 561–570.

Taylor, B. M. (1982). Text structure and children's comprehension and memory. *Journal of Educational Psychology, 74*, 323–340.

Tchabo, E. A., Hausman, C. P., & Arenberg, D. (1976). A classical mnemonic for older learners: A trip that works. *Educational Gerontology, 1*, 215–226.

Todd, W. B., & Kessler, C. C. (1971). Influence of response mode, sex, reading ability, and level of difficulty on four measures of recall of meaningful written material. *Journal of Educational Psychology, 62*, 229–234.

Waters, H. S. (1982). Memory development in adolescence: Relationships between meta-memory, strategy use, and performance. *Journal of Experimental Child Psychology, 33*, 183–195.

Webster's new world dictionary of the American language (2nd college ed.). (1972). New York: World.

Weinstein, C. E., Cubberly, W. E., Wicker, F. W., Underwood, V. L., Roney, L. K., & Duty, D. C. (1981). Training versus instruction in the acquisition of cognitive learning strategies. *Contemporary Educational Psychology, 6*, 159–166.

White, M. W. (1983). *An analysis of six mnemonics via the tetrahedral model of learning.* Unpublished manuscript.

Wortman, P. M., & Sparling, P. B. (1974). Acquisition and retention of mnemonic information in long-term memory. *Journal of Experimental Psychology, 102*, 22–26.

Yates, F. A. (1966). *The art of memory.* London: Routledge.

COGNITIVE DEVELOPMENT: LEARNING AND THE MECHANISMS OF CHANGE

Eric Lunzer

School of Education
The University of Nottingham
University Park, Nottingham,
  England NGF ZRD

I. INTRODUCTION

It could be said that during the first part of this century, developmental psychology was largely a matter of describing what children could reasonably be expected to do at successive ages or stages. Its orientation was normative, and its primary function was to provide adequate descriptions for the behaviors and aptitudes of ordinary children to act as standards against which one might evaluate the strengths and deficits of exceptional children. A secondary aim was to establish correlations and groupings of correlations among the various characteristics of children, and between such groupings of abilities and character traits on the one hand and possible antecedents on the other, especially parental abilities, parental circumstances, and parental treatment. Developmental psychology was therefore clinical or psychometric or both.

As to the mechanism governing progressive gains in cognition, it was assumed that this was simply a matter of learning in accordance with the principles established by behaviorist learning theories, the rate of such learning being modulated by more or less innate individual differences in a more or less general basic intelligence. Of course, adverse circumstances were seen as possible suppressors of learning, and it was the job of psychologists and educators to uncover these where they existed and to take appropriate remedial action.

Not all of these aims are unworthy, nor could it be gainsaid that at least part of the business of developmental psychology remains as it was. There is no substitute for a rich and representative data base, to distinguish the exception from what is the rule. Also such a data base, although not sufficient, is one essential for the invention of explanatory theories. However,

COGNITIVE CLASSROOM LEARNING:
UNDERSTANDING, THINKING,
AND PROBLEM SOLVING

explanatory theory was lacking in this phase of developmental psychology—
except in Europe, and especially in Geneva under the influence of Jean
Piaget. At that time, this work was hailed by a few, criticized by a few more,
but for the most part ignored.

It was a situation which changed radically following publication in English
of a whole series of Piaget's works, mainly during the years 1950 to 1960.
Particularly influential were the books on the general theory of intelligence
(1950), on the child's conception of number (1952a), on the early development of intelligence (1952b), on moral development (1962), and on adolescent thinking (Inhelder & Piaget, 1958). Such was the persuasiveness of
these and other works that from 1960 on, if not before, developmental
psychology has been largely a matter of agreeing with Piaget or of disagree-
ing with him. One could be more precise by specifying two phases: agreement up to about 1968, and disagreement from then on.

II.   A RESUME OF PIAGET'S THEORY

Piaget's account of cognitive development consists of two sets of constructs: functional invariants and structural elements which evolve in a fixed
progression.

A.   FUNCTIONAL INVARIANTS

The central construct among the functional invariants is the notion of
scheme. The scheme, for Piaget, is the psychological source of behavioral
differentiation. When a scheme is evoked by environmental stimulation,
that scheme determines the interpretation of the object: how it is perceived
and how the individual will respond to it.

Schemes are the residue of previous experience, and the totality of
schemes represents the subject's world knowledge at any given time. But
Piaget did not think of schemes as merely passive. Instead, they were rooted
in action, inasmuch as even the categorizations derived from perceptual
behavior were arrived at because of their relevance to other forms of behavior. Thus, the earliest schemes take the form of innate reflexes like sucking
or grasping or visual focusing, while the earliest differentiations made among
objects correspond to the different things a baby can do with them: movable
or fixed, graspable, noisy, biteable, etc.

When the pattern of stimulation—itself the outcome of an activity which
results from some scheme—results in the evocation of a new scheme, the
process is termed *assimilation*. Piaget believes that every existing scheme
seeks to assimilate to itself any object: For instance, a child of 9 months may

be observed to try out all sorts of schemes on a new object, picking it up, rattling it, biting it, etc. Assimilation can, however, be distorting. Thus, there is distortion in treating a brick as if it were a car (or vice versa) as is quite typical in the play of nursery age children.

If Piagetian assimilation were to proceed unchecked, we might well end up in an extreme form of schizophrenia. But there is a corrective, and Piaget calls this *accommodation*. Accommodation of a scheme begins as the trial-and-error adaptation of a scheme to counter any element of novelty inherent in the current situation. Accommodation can also result in the differentiation of a scheme to form two new schemes. One of Piaget's favorite examples is the discovery that coveted objects can be obtained by acting on their support. There are different ways of doing this: you can pull a cloth, while something like a turntable has to be rotated. Accommodation is thought of as the mechanism of all learning, be it through trial-and-error or systematic inquiry or logical inference.

The last construct to note is the notion of *equilibration*. Suppose two schemes are to be activated by the same stimulus—there is conflict if they lead to contrary interpretations or to contrary behaviors or both, and such conflict must be resolved. The two schemes therefore tend to accommodate to one another, by differentiation or by fusion, and the outcome can be the birth of a third scheme more comprehensive than either—without actually destroying the original pair. Piaget maintained that the processes of mutual accommodation continued until all conflict was resolved by the formation of these more differentiated and all embracing schemes, and it is that tendency which he called *equilibration*.

The concept of equilibration has much in common with the theory of cognitive dissonance and its resolution (Festinger, 1957), and this may have contributed to the acceptability of Piagetian theory in the 1960s.

According to Piaget, the universal tendency to equilibration of schemes results in their structurization. A set of schemes is relatively unstructured if each represents an alternative action sequence that results in a new state, i.e., one that cannot be predicted from the results of other schemes. Conversely, the set of schemes is structured in the measure that the outcome of any one scheme is precisely related to the effects of others because there are well-defined links between them. Imagine a toddler who knows his way to the park starting from home, and also the way to the local shops. Furthermore, although he also knows his way back home from the corner, he fails to notice that he has to pass this corner on the way to the shops or the park. What this child has is a set of unstructured schemes. They become more and more structured as he learns his way back and forth, the limit being an internalized map of the neighborhood. To take another example, a child who knows how to add and how to subtract but does not know the relation between these two operations may be said to have two unstructured schemes. There is gain in structure with the realization of commutativity (e.g., $3 + 5 = 5 + 3$), and further gain with an understanding of the inverse (e.g., $5 + 3 = 8$ implies both $8 - 3 = 5$ and $8 - 5 = 3$).

It should be clear that wherever there are equivalent routes between two points, or equivalent action sequences between two states, there is structure. Also, there is structure whenever an action has an inverse. Piaget laid particular stress on the second of these, which he termed *reversibility*. Of course, not all schemes can be reversible, simply because not all of reality is reversible—for instance, many biological processes are irreversible. However, Piaget chose to concentrate on the development of mathematical and logical thinking, and these he thought do have structures which are potentially reversible. What is more, he considered that the kinds of reversibility that were observable at successive periods in development were distinct from each other and could therefore be used to identify each of three stages. They are the sensorimotor stage, the stage of concrete operations and the stage of formal operations, and they are held to be reached on average at 18 months, 7 or 8 years, and at some time between the ages of 11 and 15 years.

B.   STRUCTURES IN PIAGETIAN THEORY

Piaget was strongly committed to the view that each of these stages is characterized by the emergence of new structures. The idea of structure is essential to an understanding of Piaget's view on equilibration and learning.

The idea of distinct structures is one that he adapted from mathematical set theory, and can best be illustrated by reference to an example: the structure of a commutative group. The set of positive and negative integers $(1, 2, 3, \ldots ; -1, -2, -3, \ldots ; 0)$ has this structure under the operation of addition.

> Addition is a binary operation which combines two numbers and produces another number, e.g., "add $(5, 2) \rightarrow 7$"; "add $(5, -2) \rightarrow 3$"; "add $(-5, 2) \rightarrow -3$"; etc. This structure has five key properties.

1. The first is *closure:* the result of any operation or sequence of operations, however long, is always a member of the set, i.e., a single positive or negative number.
2. The second is the *identity element:* there is one and only one such element, 0, and when this element is combined with any other element under "add," the result is the original element.
3. The third is the *inverse:* every element has just one inverse and combining this with itself produces the identity element. For addition, the

inverse of any number is obtained by change of sign, and we have "add (3 −3) → 0", etc.

4. The fourth is *associativity:* A sequence of operations can be permuted in any way without altering the result. For instance, "add (5, (add (3, −2)))" means execute the bracketed operation first, which yields 1, then execute the outer operation, yielding 6; exactly the same result will be obtained from "add ((add (5, 3)), −2)."

5. The last property is *commutativity:* the elements combined under the operation can be taken in either order with the same result; e.g., "add (5, 2) → 7," and likewise "add (2, 5) → 7" (which would not hold of the operation "subtract").

All this would be somewhat trivial if it were the only instance of group structure. But there are many others. Most notably, the set of rational numbers under the operation "multiply," when the identity element is 1 and not 0, and the inverse of any number is obtained by "inverting" it ($\frac{5}{3}$ for $\frac{3}{5}$, etc.). Both the additive and the multiplicative groups involve operations on infinite sets, but the same structure can be found in a set with just two elements, namely, 1 and −1 under multiplication. Structures like the group have considerable power in mathematics, in that they assist in the discovery of new relations. They also make for elegance and help to contribute to freedom from contradiction.

Piaget maintains that at each stage of development the child's understanding in any domain is associated with the structure of the equivalences that he can recognize. At the formal stage, the principal form of structure is the group. However, at the previous stage, the key structures are not groups, but a special form devised by Piaget himself, called *grouping.* A grouping is similar to the group in regard to most of its properties, but not all. Piaget describes four classificatory groupings and four seriatory groupings, but for our present purpose it is sufficient to give a brief account of one, the structure of hierarchical classifications, as instanced by the class-inclusion problem. A much fuller account, but one that is still very readable, is given by Flavell (1963).

The structure of inclusion can be followed quite easily with reference to a concrete example, like the class of all flowers. Suppose we label this class D. This can be split up in many ways, all of which would yield the same structure. For instance one can focus on spring flowers as a major subclass and label this C, leaving other flowers as the complementary C'. Within C, we might select primulas for special attention, B, leaving daffodils and other spring flowers as B'. As our immediate focus, we take primroses, and label this A, leaving A' as other varieties of primula. Any action involving these classes and subclasses can be represented by an equation. For instance, putting the primroses together with the other primulas to produce the complete set of primulas is represented as A + A′ = B. The grouping structure accounts for equivalences between sequences of these actions implied by a proper understanding of class inclusion. Its properties are

Composition. (A + A′ = B) + (B + B′ = C) = (A + A′ + B′ = C). In other words, any sequence of classificatory unions can be combined.

Associativity. The actions can be performed in any order with the same result.

Identity. In practice, the action that consists in leaving things as they are: 0 + 0 = 0.

Reversibility. Every action has a unique inverse, e.g., (A + A′ = B) + (−A − A′ = −B) = (0 + 0 = 0), (putting a sequence of subclasses together then removing them one at a time will leave you where you started).

Special identities. (A + B + B′ = C) = (B + B′ = C); i.e., the addition of A has no effect on the result because A is already included in B.

Children of 7 or 8 years and older do show an ability to anticipate the effects of classificatory actions and their interrelations, and Piaget takes this to mean that they have constructed such groupings and can apply them to problems when they are needed.

Both classification and ordering are interpreted by Piaget as arguing a more limited degree of structurization than the group. Nevertheless, he maintains that even at the stage of concrete operations, children's understandings of equivalence relations exhibit a true group structure in two domains: number and spatial displacements. Thus the successful attainment of number conservation in a variety of situations is taken to imply the additive and multiplicative groups as described previously, while the mastery of measurement operations together with the conservation of length and area argue the presence of an analogous structure for geometrical reasoning, the group of spatial displacements (Piaget, 1952a; Piaget, Inhelder, and Szeminska, 1960).

It is supposed that at the stage of formal operations, group structures are more ubiquitous. However, in order to show why this is believed to be so, we need to consider what are the elements which enter into the structure of groupings and to compare these with the elements of adolescent thinking. The former, it will be recalled, can be thought of as equations anticipating the effects of combining classes and comparing their properties. Related classes are contrasted by the presence or absence of relevant properties. For instance, the two properties of gender and graduate status combine to yield four categories of student: using the symbols p and q for the properties and overbar for negation, we have pq = male graduates, $p\bar{q}$ = *male undergraduates*, $\bar{p}q$ = female graduates and $\bar{p}\bar{q}$ = female undergraduates.

Now beginning with these four categories, one can go on to make up combinations like male graduates and female undergraduates, $pq \cdot \bar{p}\bar{q}$ (*where · means and*). The total number of possible combinations is 16, including "all" ($pq \cdot p\bar{q} \cdot \bar{p}q \cdot \bar{p}\bar{q}$) and none ($\phi$). Piaget maintains that each of these combinations can be taken to correspond to a hypothesis about what instances one can expect to meet up with. For instance $pq \cdot \bar{p}q \cdot \bar{p}\bar{q}$ corresponds to "p implies q," because it excludes $p\bar{q}$. One might imagine a women's university which accepts male students, but only if they are graduates. Less trivially, the symbolism is used to represent the construction of hypotheses when exploring a scientific principle.

One example used by Piaget is an experiment on what causes variation in the rate of oscillation of a pendulum. If p stands for change in length and q represents change in weight, we need a third symbol r for change in rate. Intuition may suggest that change in length is a necessary and sufficient cause ($pqr \cdot p\bar{q}r$, excluding $\bar{p}qr$) or that weight is critical ($pqr \cdot \bar{p}qr$), or perhaps both are required (pqr). None of these can be read off by inspection. Instead, the young scientist must design the experiments needed to decide among the alternatives, and to do this systematically, Piaget believes he or she will have to anticipate all possible hypotheses and their interrelations. Younger children may well be able to read off simple classifications (there are eight of these for three variables), but they cannot anticipate combinations, which means they are unable to design experiments or understand scientific methodology. In the pendulum experiment, Inhelder found that younger subjects habitually tried to verify their hypotheses by maximizing any possible effect (ignoring alternative interpretations). For instance they would vary both weight and length. Older subjects realized the need to vary each of these separately through a series of mini-experiments.

Knowing how to make the move from one combination to another is thought by Piaget to argue the underlying intervention of a mental structure termed the *INRC* group. To understand why, we introduce the symbol $\lor$ (or), together with · (and) and overbars (negation), allowing us to have a set of related statements for each of the 16 combinations, e.g., $p \lor q, p.q, p \lor \bar{q}$, etc. ($q \lor \bar{p}$ is equivalent to $pq \cdot \bar{p}q \cdot \bar{p}\bar{q}$, or p implies q). We can now define four operations for transforming one hypothesis into another. They are

N = change all signs and substitute $\lor$ for · and vice versa
R = change all signs
C = substitute $\lor$ for · and vice versa
I = do nothing

e.g., for p implies q, which is the same as $q \lor \bar{p}$, we have

$$I = q \lor \bar{p}$$
$$N = \bar{q} \cdot p$$
$$R = \bar{q} \lor p$$
$$C = q \cdot \bar{p}$$

Here the letters I, N, R, C stand for *identity, negation, reciprocal,* and *correlative,* and the operation that combines them is simply *and.* Under this operation, any two elements of the set may be combined to form another, as shown in Table 1.

Operations in the lefthand margin, when followed by an operation at the head of a column produce the operation shown at the appropriate intersection. If we denote N and N as N^2, we find that $N^2 = R^2 = C^2 = I^2 = I$; $NR = C$, $NC = R$, $RC = N$, NCR (in any sequence $= I$ and I is the identity element, so that $IN = N$, etc.

In this way, Piaget sought to demonstrate that the gains of adolescent thinking derive from the characteristic structure of reasoning. Although there is no space to develop it here, he believed that a similar argument will show how the same *INRC* group also underlies an understanding of proportionality relations in science and mathematics.

C. LEARNING AND EQUILIBRATION

We find little in Piaget's writings about learning in the sense of the acquisition of skills or learning as an accumulation of facts. His learning theory is concerned almost exclusively with the growth of understanding, which he takes to be synonymous with the changing structures of knowledge. These are seen as stable coordinations among mental actions. They are stable because they allow one to take cognizance of a network of related mental actions while avoiding contradictions.

Throughout his writings on the subject (e.g. especially, Piaget, 1959a, 1959b), Piaget insists that these structures are not learned in the conventional sense, through direct instruction and reinforcement; they are elabo-

TABLE 1 Structure of the *INRC* Group

	I	N	R	C
I	I	N	R	C
N	N	I	C	R
R	R	C	I	N
C	C	R	N	I

rated by a process of equilibration. In essence, this means that conflicting alternative schemes will coexist so long as they are not simultaneously active, but increasing familiarity makes their coexistence inevitable, and when this happens there is mutual accommodation resulting in the formation of a new overall scheme which is free from contradiction.

One example is *conservation*. The liquid from one of two identical glasses has been poured into a tall thin glass, and the subject is asked whether this still contains the same amount as the glass which has been left intact. Piaget maintains that there are four theoretical stages in his response. In stage 1, the only active scheme is to use the more salient cue, which is height of liquid, and so the tall glass is said to have more. In stage 2, which is less probable, but which may be favored by some chance circumstance, the less salient cue will be attended to, and the child will therefore say the thin glass (which is also the tall one) has less. To begin with, because it is not primed by the perceptual stimulus, this response is rare, but with practice it becomes more common, and when this happens the child oscillates between the two conflicting responses, more and less. This is the third stage. The fourth stage comes when the oscillation is so rapid as to be quasi-simultaneous. The child now becomes aware of the conflict and resolves it by recognizing the equality: looked at one way, the new glass has more, looked at another it has less, but in reality it has the same amount. (Piaget, 1977).

Broadly speaking, the same principles can be invoked to explain the gradual mastery of class inclusions. Here the younger child may be thought to fail because he or she is unable to focus simultaneously on the whole class (e.g., all primulas) and the part (primroses); primroses are opposed to other primulas, or alternatively, they are merged with primulas and opposed to other flowers. Only when the two schemes are entertained at once is the child in a position to reconcile them by constructing the more embracing scheme of a hierarchical structure. Now if Piaget's description of this and other groupings is taken as a true representation of equivalences that are recognized by the child, all of which are essential for avoiding contradiction when dealing with the properties of things and events, then it makes sense to imagine that the grouping itself and later the *INRC* group are the inevitable forms toward which thinking must approximate.

The essential condition for this development seems to be the familiarity of the constituent schemes, which must be sufficient to allow them to be compared and integrated within a single act of attention.

This last point is one that is strongly urged by Pascual-Leone (Pascual-Leone & Smith, 1969) and by Case (1974, 1978a). In Piaget's own work, it is at best implicit. However, the notion of spontaneous equilibration and the role of conflict are explicit and central. They underlie the Genevan view of learning: that it must be spontaneous because it must arise out of schemes that are familiar; that it is produced by conflict; that intervention is effective only when introduced when the subject is on the brink of unaided discovery. Above all, the notion of powerful and stable structures underlies the most controversial tenets of Piagetian theory: that instruction in isolated competences (e.g., teaching conservation) is relatively useless and cannot create true understanding; and that the spontaneous development of structures results in distinct stages marked by different kinds of equilibrium, each ushered by a more limited phase of disequilibrium.

III.   THE POSITIVE LEGACY OF PIAGET: LEVELS OF CONSTRUCT

I have already said that since about 1968 if not before, most of the literature on cognitive development has been critical of Piaget. Nevertheless, a large section of recent and current research continues to draw on his work, if only in that the same research paradigms are used, whether to urge some modification of his theories, or to expose them as invalid and substitute an alternative approach (Modgil & Modgil, 1982; Siegel & Brainerd, 1978). It is for this reason that I elected to begin this chapter with an overview of his ideas. We do not, as at present, possess any alternative theory of comparable sweep. Few would deny that the questions Piaget asked were important and remain so. Equally, there are certain aspects of his approach that were far in advance of his predecessors and more consonant with current psychological theory. There is no going back to the old-style learning theories so well described and analyzed by Hilgard (1958). Finally, while many contemporary psychologists are critical of Piaget's interpretations, the data that he established remain valid within limits, and they continue to pose a challenge.

We begin with the "functional invariants." It is interesting to note what was revolutionary about Piaget's notion of schemes and why this made his approach so acceptable some 30 years after the ideas first evolved (during the 1920s and 1930s). In putting forward the concept of the scheme, Piaget was denying the stimulus–response approach of behaviorism and substituting a central cognitive initiator for the control of behavior and learning. Perceptual stimulation, information pick-up, is dependent on ongoing behavior and hence on the activity of some ongoing scheme. Thereafter, the interpretation of the stimulus is a function both of the original scheme and of the new schemes that it evokes. Such ideas might have seemed strange in the 1930s, but by the 1960s, they had become commonplace. The model for the brain had been, implicitly, the telephone exchange; now it was, explicitly, the computer. Much more needs to be established about the scheme than was said by Piaget, but in outline such a notion is basic to contemporary cognitive psychology. It should be added that the term *schema* has greater currency than Piaget's *scheme*. Again, while the terms *assimilation* and *accommodation* have not gained wide acceptance, this approach to perception and learning is in line with most current thinking in psychology.

However, despite the centrality of *functional invariants*, most of Piaget's writing and all of his research have been concerned with structural development. (Notions such as the scheme are not directly researchable; functional invariants belong to the realm of metatheory: they are not testable but they help to point the researcher in particular directions, thereby developing theories that are). In the next section, I argue that the central notion of structure is unacceptable. Nevertheless, the work on structural growth has produced a very considerable body of evidence on children's achievements at successive ages. Within limits, and the qualification is important, the experimental findings have been corroborated over the years. At the same time, while there are undoubted gaps in the areas chosen for investigation—as in the relative neglect of cognitive development in the preschool years, most of the research paradigms devised by the Genevan school remain significant and fruitful: the development of conservation, classification, and seriation, followed by the acquisition of inferential strategies, including especially the control of variables in experimentation and the use of simple functions such as proportionality. Piaget's choice of these problems derives from his appreciation of what it is that needs to be explained: the origin of logical thinking, especially as this appears in scientific and mathematical reasoning.

There remains the vexed issue of Piaget's developmental stages. The idea of relatively discontinuous stages has little support from research, nor is there much evidence for two phases of accelerated intellectual growth, one occurring at 6–8 years and the other at about 11–13 years, these being bounded by longer periods of equilibrium marked by a slower rate of development. What evidence there is would suggest the not-very-exciting view that the acquisition of cognitive schemes is a gradual business, whether or not it is assisted by instruction and example, and new competences always build on old. Nevertheless, if we look at the kind of content with which the individual must come to terms in the course of acculturation to the demands of our society, we are bound to recognize the need for the intervention of constructs. What is more, these constructs can readily be classified as belonging to one of three successive levels of abstraction.

1. First-Order Constructs

The lowest degree of abstraction belongs in the first instance to unanalyzed objects (mother, dog, pencil, etc.) and to unanalyzed properties of objects (red, large, long, hot, etc.). Psychologically, it would be incorrect to admit a distinction of level between these two categories because both correspond to discriminations that are acquired well before the meaningful use of words. To these we need to add perceptual judgments of relation, and in particular the notion "greater than," and with it "more." Thus, Bryant has shown conclusively that very young children learn to discriminate in terms of relative rather than absolute size in making choices between two otherwise similar objects. Both *more* and *a lot* seem to belong to the same category as *greater*, and Donaldson and Balfour's finding that young children are apt to confuse the two words *more* and *less* (1968) should not be taken to imply that they have no conception of either but rather that they cannot decide, out of context, which is which. The phrase *out of context* is worth dwelling on, for the most general characteristic of unanalyzed constructs is that they function only in context. It is in this same sense that one can interpret many aspects of children's responses to relational concepts in language such as the meaning of the prepositions *in, on, under* (Clark, 1973), and the interpretation of passives. Children of 3 years do not analyze the precise form of an utterance to decide on its meaning. Rather they assign to it whatever meaning seems most suited to the context. For instance, because cats catch mice and not vice versa, little children take this to be the meaning of every one of these sentences: "The cat catches the mouse," "The mouse catches the cat," "The cat is caught by the mouse," and "The mouse is caught by the cat" (Strohner & Nelson, 1974).

The use of unanalyzed constructs will get us a long way, for they are essential and quite adequate to interpret the familiar world of objects and events in terms of a commonsense one-directional set of expectations corresponding to rather simple laws of causality. Such a representation is developed in terms of behavioral expectations before the intervention of representation and language, which is partly why in his later writings, Piaget does not acknowledge an intuitive stage.

2. Second-Order Constructs

The second level of abstraction belongs to constructs that do not denote everyday objects, but properties and relations that are defined on these. The sense of *defined* can best be illustrated by reference to two sets of examples. One is the familiar conservations. The number of a set of discrete objects is defined by the action of counting each element once and once only; the relative length of two lines is defined by putting them in parallel with one pair of ends in alignment; relative weights are defined by placement on a balance; etc. Given a recognition of transitivity, such constructs may be taken to underlie the relevant conservations. In each case, the construct is typically the outcome of a precise sequence of actions performed on objects, which of course does not exclude the continued use of perceptual and contextual estimates where these are appropriate and sufficient.

The second example is classificatory behavior. In most simple classificatory tasks, the constructs do not need to be related to specific action sequences, but they do require the subject to establish clear relations between the various properties of objects. It is thus no cause for surprise that the most effective tasks of classificatory adequacy involve the handling of two criterial dimensions, either simultaneously, as in matrix classification, or successively, as in classification and reclassification. In a very well-thought-out study, Halford (1980) demonstrated that 3-year-olds could learn to carry out one-way classifications but made no significant progress in two-way classifications. The set-up consisted of a series of cards like the one shown in Table 2, using different colors and shapes for successive problems. One-dimensional problems required the child to fill in one column (or one row) at a time, and all distractors were different in the relevant dimension. Two-dimensional problems involved choices from distractors which agreed with one of the two dimensions needed but not both. From the age of $4\frac{1}{2}$ years onward, most children were able to learn this form of the task. It may be noted that 4 is very much younger than the age given by Piaget as the lower bound for concrete operations. However, Halford (1980) took pains to provide maximal guidance, where the situations devised by Piaget and his co-workers are essentially test of the subject's ability without much guidance, and even to resist a degree of miscueing.

3. Third-Order Constructs

The third level of abstraction belongs to constructs that cannot be defined directly on objects and their properties because they entail a relationship between different constructs of that order. Weight can be defined by an action on objects, and so too can area, but pressure cannot, because it involves a relation between them. The number of a set of objects can be obtained directly by counting its members, but a proportion is a relation between the ratios of two numbers, not two objects. The price of a commodity is defined with reference to specific actions with an object, what you

TABLE 2   Structure of a Multiplication Task

Green triangle	Green circle	Green cross
Red triangle	Which one comes here?	
Pink triangle		

Note. After Halford (1980).

must pay for it, where inflation can only be defined by reference to changes in such things as prices, wages, etc.

Such constructs may denote new ideas. Thus, inflation is a concept for which there is no more primitive parallel. But this is not always the case. For instance we can experience a sense of pressure different from weight if another person's stiletto heel is brought to bear on our sandalled toe. It follows that third-order constructs (like second-order constructs before them) do not always denote new ideas. However, they do entail new ways of defining them and more precise relations between them. One example is the case of length and area and the relation between these. Both length and area are properties of things, and either will be used as a response cue from a very early age. Yet they also figure as second-order constructs when they denote the results of mensuration, using differing, but precise actions, and different unit measures. But area becomes a third-order construct when it is seen as the product of linear dimensions. Thus, Piaget, Inhelder and Szeminska (1960) noted a considerable increase in difficulty in area measurement when the constraints of the task were changed. It was easy enough to find out how many tiles would be needed to line the floor of a pool, as long as there were enough tiles available to put out one row and one column, and both of these were unit multiples of the square tiles. The task was much harder when the tiles had to be placed outside the perimeter of the pool when measuring it. In a recent survey of mathematical performance among British secondary school children, a similar step-up was found when the calculation of area required a multiplication of lengths involving one decimal place (Hart, 1981).

Such considerations should help to introduce a further characterization of levels of abstraction. How one arrives at one's constructs and how one combines them is the decisive factor influencing the way one conceives of the possible and its relation to the real. Inhelder and Piaget (1958) maintain that the critical distinction between the adolescent's way of thinking and that of the younger child is that while the latter thinks of the possible as a modification of the real, the former sees the real as an instantiation of the possible. This makes sense when taken to mean that, for certain purposes, whatever aspect of things is under investigation needs to be treated as if it were a construct rather than a primary datum. A first example is the separation of variables. In the pendulum experiment the subject is forced to set up events by selecting appropriate lengths and weights and comparing their performance. Children who maximize differences begin by imagining a real event (i.e., a pendulum in motion) and then decide on what sorts of adjustment can be made to produce a desired effect. Those who select equal weights to test the effect of varying length and vice versa are treating the total pendulum as a construct, i.e., a product of its constituents. The central problem then becomes What are the possible variations of the set-up, what are the limits on their realization in combination, and how does the construction affect the outcome?

Another instance, first described by Collis (1975, 1978), and replicated in Hart (1981), concerns the notion of variable in algebra. Children who are introduced to algebra begin by thinking of letters as things that stand for a unique unknown number, the business being to discover what it is. They have no difficulty in solving problems like "$g + 3 = 7$. What is the value of g?" But they cannot always solve problems like "$c + d = 10$. $c > d$. What is the value of c?" Such problems do not allow for just one solution. But there is a solution set which can be found quite easily by trying out successive numbers in a calculation which could involve real objects. As a result, the increase in difficulty is not very large. However, there are problems which present far more difficulty, although they are superficially quite simple. Such a problem is "When is $2n$ less than $n + 2$? (always, never, when . . .)." Trying out a value like $n = 3$, $n = 12$, etc. can only lead to the chance solution $n = 1$, ignoring all other values between 0 and 2 as well as all the negatives. The correct solution path demands that the subject forgets that the numbers he is looking for stand for real things and thinks of them as values that can satisfy a relation. Instead of beginning with the numbers and establishing the relation, one has to start with the relation. Once that decision is made, the further step of looking at $2n - (n = 2)$ is probably obvious, and the further step of considering $2n - (n + 2) + 0$ will follow by virtue of previous experience in algebra.

All the foregoing can be taken as constituting a strong case for the recognition of distinct levels of abstraction among the constructs needed to solve particular problems or to arrive at certain kinds of explanations of things. It does not mean that individual subjects will invariably select the same level of construct for all problems.

IV.   ERRORS OF PIAGETIAN THEORY: LOGICISM AND DISCONTINUITY

In the last section, I have been at some pains to show that there is a good deal that is valuable underlying Piaget's theory of stages. Yet that theory has been the subject of severe criticism along two lines. The first is directed at the inherent logicism in Piagetian theory, whie the second concerns the question of continuity.

Logicism is usually taken to denote a too-ready assumption by a psychologist that because a given line of inference is valid and important in logic, it is also a correct description of actual thought processes. Even the very brief account of Piagetian structures given in Section II.A will have raised the suspicion that such a charge is not without foundation. Could it be that not all of the equivalences entailed by the eight concrete operational groupings have their counterparts in children's inferences? As Flavell (1963) has shown, only a minority of the groupings are instantiated by the observations of Inhelder and Piaget (1958). What is the evidence that all of the equivalences involved in any one grouping are interdependent and that they develop simultaneously? The Genevan work contains no relevant evidence because each inquiry involved different subjects. Kofsky (1966) offers some evidence for a sequential development of classificatory behavior culminating in class-inclusion. Although the behaviors that were studied were taken from Piaget, the dependences cut across the groupings and, if Kofsky is right, they are hierarchical. In other words, if class-inclusion requires all of the inferences involved in cross-tabulation and some that are additional, then success in class-inclusion presupposes success in cross-tabulation, but not vice versa. This is not interdependence in the sense required by Piaget's theory of equilibration. Other work, such as the studies of Tuddenham (1970) show only very moderate correlations between success in different Piagetian tasks. Our own studies (Lunzer, Wilkinson, & Dolan, 1976) yielded slightly higher correlations, sufficient to allow one to speak of "operativity" as a reliable construct that can be measured. However, even though this was also shown to have good predictive validity (Lunzer, Dolan, & Wilkinson, 1976), there was no evidence for distinct structures; indeed the only differentiation that could be made by factor analysis was a factor loading on all conservation tasks, doubtless reflecting the very obvious similarities in procedure.

At the formal level, likewise, Piaget's structural interpretations are open to serious objections. For instance, the separation of variables entails neither a complete combinatorial nor the INRC group of transformations because it argues no more (and no less) than the ability to compare two ways of looking at the same range of phenomena (cf. Lunzer, 1965). No less damaging is the criticism of logicians like Parsons (1960) and Ennis (1978), who have demonstrated that Piaget's treatment of implication, based on the combinatorial, carries implications that are contrary to both logic and science.

Logical structures play a central part in Piaget's theory because they justify the notion of spontaneous equilibration. But that notion is plausible only when taken as a loose description. Thus, two of its subordinate principles are often helpful to understanding. These are the role of conflict in overcoming the resistance of well-established schemes, and what appears to be a built-in negative response to contradiction. The first theme has been recognized by many educators. The second may be a useful pointer for the study of the origins of logic. However, Piaget's detailed account of the mechanism of equilibration is far from convincing. In particular, Piaget supposes that conflict between existing schemes is resolved by the emergence of a new scheme that integrates them. The new scheme is endogenous in origin in the sense that the child's experience of conservation situations is all that he needs to make the jump, or rather, experience together with a kind of self-constructing logic—equilibration itself. What evidence we have suggests that new constructs are more often exogenous in origin. They tend to be exogenous both in the sense that the germ of the new scheme is to be found in a different context, and also in the sense that adult modelling, adult prompting, and adult instruction play a far greater role than Piaget would allow.

In the case of number conservation, Piaget would have us believe that counting is irrelevant, citing the evidence that children who can count do not always conserve. But what this ignores is the ubiquitous observation that a judgment once reached is very often resistant to infirming evidence, especially when the line of reasoning used in reaching the judgement is different from that followed in its refutation (cf. Evans, 1982; Wason and Johnson-Laird, 1972). Within the field of number itself, the fact that counting ability does not guarantee conservation does not prove that counting is irrelevant to eventual success, but only that in certain cases the child either fails to count (indeed he may be discouraged from counting on the grounds that, in the end, and in some conditions including the artificial setting of conservation experiments, conservation will free him from the need to count), or fails to reconcile the numerical evidence with the perceptual. More recently, Gelman and Gallistel (1978) have carefully traced the development of children's understanding of number, noting that counting involves matching the word with the action (little children are apt to get the numbers out of phase with the tagging or pointing), an appreciable load on memory (keeping count of the last number reached), and a recognition that each element must be taken once and once only. Such coordinations are impressive and demanding, although clearly they are actively encouraged by parents and others. Now, it is at least as credible that, in the end, it is the number concept that becomes decisive for number conservation as is Piaget's belief that counting is mere mumbo-jumbo until conservation has been reached, at which point counting will be learned as something rather trivial.

Another aspect of Piaget's excessive formalism is the failure to pay sufficient regard to the role of analogy in thinking at every level, and especially in children's conceptions concerning phenomena that cannot be directly observed. Recent research by science educators has shown the prevalence of a wide array of misconceptions about such things as the movement of light and heat, the distribution of molecules in a gas, what happens when we see, and the nature of an electrical circuit (Driver & Easley, 1978). These misconceptions cannot be explained in terms of the structure of children's reasoning. Some notions, such as the idea that light is concentrated in the vicinity of a candle, are fairly easy to shift (there being plenty of evidence of light rays traveling a very long way), but others, such as the idea that electric current is used up as it travels round a circuit, prove far more intractable. I believe this to be because electric current is an abstract third-order construct and a particularly difficult one at that, because it is related to several other constructs of the same order and has few relations with more elementary constructs. Be that as it may, it is clear that all such misconceptions arise because we interpret experience by analogy. And in trying to coordinate experience in a new area, we build up a model based on another that is more familiar. But these are dynamic content-models of what happens to what and how, rather than formal relations between arguments.

Piagetian theory lays particular stress on supposed discontinuities in development associated with the emergence of the concrete and formal stages. Yet there is now a considerable body of evidence pointing to a relatively unbroken continuity. Much of this has accumulated in the course of the 1970s.

To take one example, where the structuralist view argues for a more or less sharp break between the intuitive and the concrete levels at about the age of 7 years it is now clear that the relevant problems can be tackled with success at much younger ages, following on apparently modest alterations in procedure. Thus Rose and Blank (1974) showed that failure in conservation can be reduced by not repeating the question "Are they the same?" thereby implying (apparently) that they are not. Likewise, Donaldson and her associates showed that if the transformation can be made to appear accidental rather than deliberately initiated by the adult, conservation appears much earlier (Light, Buckingham, & Robbins, 1979; McGarrigle & Donaldson, 1974).

If we turn to studies of classification, we may note the evidence of Odom (1978), who found that matrix completion could be advanced by as much as 2 years by ensuring that the relevant dimensions are the most salient in each configuration. One recalls the aforementioned work of Halford.

Finally, there are the many studies of the effect of teaching on the acquisition of operational behavior. Here again, there is a wealth of evidence against the traditional Piagetian view that operational thinking cannot readily be taught. Much of the work has been revised by Brainerd (1978), who comments: "The four tutorial methods on which adequate evidence is available have produced improvements in the trained concepts that satisfy all the usual Genevan learning criteria" (p. 88). The criteria referred to are superior performance on pretest items, superior performance on at least one new type of item, an acceptable verbal justification of a correct response, evidence of transfer, and stability as shown by a late posttest (usually following an interval of 2–4 weeks.)

From such evidence, one is led to conclude that there is no one turning point for the acquisition of concrete operational behavior—or, as I would prefer to term it, the differentiation and stabilization of second-order constructs. Well-adapted and successful solutions to relevant problems may be obtained as early as 4, or even 3 years, given optimal cueing and/or appropriate training. Consistent and flexible use of such constructs, including the search for relevant criteria in the face of some degree of miscueing by the situation or the adult is not something that comes suddenly, but only as a result of progressive transfer over a period of years.

Similar evidence for the gradual acquisition of third-order constructs comes from studies such as those of Markman (1978) and Lunzer (1973). Taken together, the arguments and findings reported in this section seem to me to require a substantial revision of Piagetian theory, along the lines indicated in Fig. 1. The first representation, Figure 1a, may be said to represent orthodox Piagetian theory. Three domains (three orders of constructs) are figured, each in the form of three bands designed to portray the availability of adequate solution procedures for all the tasks that might be set within the domain at each of the three Piagetian levels: intuitive or preoperational, concrete, and formal. The domains in question might be hier-

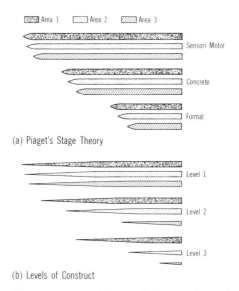

FIG. 1. Changing images of the world. See text for explanation.

archical classification, number concepts, and experimentation. The thickness of these bands increases to a maximum, which denotes complete competence, with the horizontal axis corresponding to chronological or mental age. I have deliberately shown the increase in thickness as quite rapid. Also, while there is a certain decalage for the onset of the two higher levels as between the two domains, the extent of this is limited. Figure 1b is the corresponding representation of the position I have been urging in this section. The increase in thickness of each band is more gradual, and the new band corresponding to the next level of construct emerges about the time when gains at the lower level are becoming minimal. There is no necessary and prolonged period of static equilibrium. Decalage, too, may be greater than might be thought compatible with orthodox Piagetian theory.

V.   MECHANISMS OF COGNITIVE CHANGE

Let me begin this final section by summing up the argument thus far. The child's growing interpretation of the world is a function of the constructs at his disposal. These may be categorized by distinguishing three levels of abstraction, which are necessarily successive within any given domain. There is no necessary synchronicity for their attainment in different domains, and even within domains, the availability of the relevant constructs for the solution of particular problems is a gradual acquisition and not a sudden development.

There is no need to rehearse the debt to Piaget, and differences have been adequately set out in earlier sections. However, I have also argued that Piaget's theory of equilibration should be rejected, and because equilibration was the mechanism by which he sought to explain the process of cognitive changes, its rejection means that the modified statement I have just formulated is now purely descriptive. What are the processes which contribute to the emergence of new constructs, and especially of higher-order constructs? More generally, are there any fundamental developments, beyond the accumulation of innumerable bits of learning, which help to explain the fact that there are changes in cognitive attitude as well as accretions to knowledge and skill. Construct levels constitute one such change: The older and more sophisticated learner looks for different kinds of answers. There are others: For instance, we know from recent developments in metacognition that the individual becomes a more effective learner to the extent that he can plan his own activity once he has discovered just what he is doing in the course of learning and what it is that could make these things easy or difficult.

Such are the questions I address in the present section. However, were I to attempt a complete answer, I would certainly need to treble the length of this chapter, and even then I would end up with a very inadequate statement. Instead, I do three things. First, I give a highly condensed resume of four bodies of theory, which I take to be relevant to the questions just raised. They are frame theory, metacognition theory, working memory, and production-system theory. Next, I say something about how each of these perspectives may be needed for a better understanding of cognitive development. To that end, I define cognitive development as a change in process, i.e., a second-order change, so allowing me to explore a model of knowledge acquisition, which is the first-order process. This is because, having rejected equilibration theory, one is thrown back on the assumption that what is learned is learned during learning episodes and not by a process of consolidation and restructuring which takes place in the periods between such episodes. (The last statement is too extreme, and some reservations are necessary). Finally, I say a few words about some questions which I think are still unanswered but not unimportant.

A. ALTERNATIVE APPROACHES

1. Frame theory

The concept of cognitive frames and their role in the interpretation of experience is one which was first evolved within the context of artificial intelligence theory as a way of accounting for the fact that a finite system like the brain can recognize an infinite variety of situations by assigning each new complex to some familiar category, which already incorporates a necessary structure and an equally necessary flexibility. The construct has been fruitfully applied to the interpretation of visual scenes, which change in lawful ways as a function of movements of the viewer and of the object (Minsky, 1968, 1975), and to the interpretation of spoken and written discourse (Rumelhart & Ortony, 1977; Schank & Abelson, 1977). A *frame* is a network of related elements (which can be thought of as ideas), which has the added characteristic that not only the elements but also the links among them are distinctive and defined. If you have a frame, you know what goes with what, and also how. By way of example, the frame for *give* is one in which an object passes from the possession of one person to that of another as a result of an action performed by the former. Each of the elements (donor–agent, gift, and recipient) enter as necessary constituents in the transaction, and they are marked by distinctive features: donor and recipient are human, gift is an article which has value, and so on. The relations too are distinctive: the donor does not stand in the same relation to the gift as the recipient, etc. Not all of the elements in a frame are equally central. For instance, the bestowal of a gift may or may not be linked to some appropriate occasion or circumstance, such as a birthday. Even if it exists, such a link may not be situationally relevant. In a narrative, elements that are irrelevant are omitted; in day-to-day transactions, they are ignored. Whether central or peripheral, the elements in a frame may be thought of as slots (following Minsky) which may be filled by entities that have the appropriate characteristics, or left unfilled when irrelevant. If a relevant element is not supplied or if a previously irrelevant element becomes relevant, the empty slot is filled by default: One assumes that it is there and that it has the typical characteristics. For instance, we may not be told what the donor gave the recipient in some instance; if it then transpires that the gift was "the most precious of all: love," we accept this as a legitimate metaphor—but only after a double take: it is not what we expected to hear.

The notion of frame was introduced to help in accounting for the many inferences that are made in the interpretation of everyday experience, including the things that we hear and read. In order to do this satisfactorily, there have to be many of them, and they need to exist at many different levels. For instance, there have to be frames for the parts of the body, frames for faces and frames for eyes; or again, we need frames for retail establishments, frames for restaurants, and frames for menus. More than this, because the objects of experience enter into many different relations, we may need frames for facial expressions, frames for facial types and frames for facial afflictions, to name but a few. Nor is this enough, because in addition to such content frames, it is abundantly clear that there are formal frames, which are used in the interpretation of all kinds of communication (Lunzer & Gardner, 1984; van Dijk and Kintsch, 1983). Familiarity with typical sequences of information, whether in narrative or in expository passages, helps us to make sense of the argument. The Rose and Blank experiment (1974) provides a good example of such frame-induced expectation. Teachers do not usually repeat a question if the pupil had it right the first time and the situation has not basically altered.

Because experience is complex and many-sided, frames have a parallel complexity. Because their function is explanatory, that complexity presents a challenge. How do interlocking frames work together? Unlike dictionary definitions, frames are networks of relations and not lists of properties (Rumelhart & Ortony, 1977), but that means not only that they have more interconnections, but also that these connections are active. If frames activate one another, where does the activation end? How much of our knowledge can we maintain at the alert at any one time? Or are there degrees of alertness. Obviously, not all of the face frames are active each time I see a face or hear the word. In watching a play, I can switch my attention from content to form or quality of the acting or whatever. How are these things achieved?

The notion of frame has much in common with Piaget's notion of a scheme, especially in its more general formulations and as used to describe the behavior of babies. (In many of his later writings, Piaget uses the idea of a scheme when referring to logical structures, and these have received little attention in frame theory). But frames are better spelled out than Piagetian schemes, which is why they make one face questions like how and when frames are switched off, and what triggers the switching mechanism. One useful pointer is the suggestion that, at least in narrative contexts, subordinate frames activate their superordinates, but not vice versa (Abbot & Black, 1980, quoted by van Dijk and Kintsch, 1983). In other words, frames are used to locate the current contents of experience within some more general schema, but wherever possible, we operate with unanalyzed chunks of information. We do not unpack parcels unless we have to.

It is clear that frame theory is still in its infancy, and there are many questions yet unanswered. In our present context, one of these is how content frames interact with form frames and another concerns the origin of frames. How frames originate and how they change is one way of describing all that this chapter is about. More specifically, one would like to have a better understanding of the process whereby individual experiences give rise to generalized knowledge, or, to put the matter another way, how episodic memories become transformed into semantic knowledge (Tulving, 1972). Broadly speaking, one must assume that the process is akin to the assimilation and accommodation described by Piaget. At a slightly more detailed level, it is interesting to speculate that at some time in the course of an experience or thereafter, we can and do arrive at some conclusions about what is specific to the occurrence and what is apt to be found again in at least some future happenings, and such metacognitive episodes may be more or less far-reaching and more or less conscious and directed.

2. Metacognition

Because this volume includes a separate chapter on metacognition, I can confine myself here to raising a single question, which is the role of metacognition in cognitive development as a whole. This of course is the issue adumbrated a few sentences back.

Even the most cursory study of the most frequently quoted references in the metacognition literature make it apparent that the term is used in a number of rather different senses (Brown, 1978; Flavell, 1979; Lefebvre-Pinard, 1983). First, there is procedural knowledge, which I call metacognition 1. Metacognition 1 begins as an understanding that a procedure P will facilitate attainment of a goal G in the context of some task T. It is here that the original insights were made by Flavell and his associates, in the context of memory and rehearsal. Within megacognition 1, however, one finds a further bifurcation, which arises inevitably out of the difficulty of deciding on the precise relation between procedural knowledge and metaprocedural strategy. That P facilitates G in context T is a part of megacognition proper, and is now designated as MC1a. How can we establish that this obtains of a particular subject in a given context? One way is to invite the subject to talk about the task and how it can be resolved. But there is another, which is to observe how he or she sets about actually doing it. The ability to access P in the presence of T, and especially to vary it as appropriate may be evidence of MC1a. But it is also part of the solution itself. I call this MC1b. Strictly speaking, MC1b is a part of cognitive behavior proper. Often MC1a and MC1b go hand in hand. However, it is perfectly possible for MC1a to be present without MC1b, as when one knows what to do in principle but cannot always apply it in practice. Likewise, there may be MC1b without MC1a. This is presumably the case when one has been taught a routine for doing a job. Of course the ability to vary that routine may be evidence of metacognition or of understanding, but variations too can be learned, which means that these are fuzzy categories. The purist might wish to assert that MC1b is not a part of metacognition at all but an aspect of cognition itself.

The second group of inquiries under the general heading of metacognition comprises a growing number of studies dealing with the child as psychologist. They include some aspects of Flavell and Wellman's work on metamemory (1977). Yussen's work on children's concepts of intelligence (Yussen and Kane, 1984) and a recent study by Pramling on the child's conception of learning (1983). I call these MC2 studies. Although interesting in their own right, they are not always of direct concern to our present interest, which is the potential role of metacognition in cognitive evolution as a whole, and especially in modifying children's constructs and their cognitive attitudes.

There is, however, a third aspect of metacognition, which is closer to MC1a and is perhaps critical in the formation of new constructs. This is the ability to reflect on the steps in one's own thinking, and I call this MC3. Of particular interest is the late work of Piaget on growth of awareness (1977). His principal thesis is that prformance generally precedes awareness. One learns to do something before one learns how one does it. The ability to walk on all fours may be taken as a particularly clear example. Although children manage this before they emerge from babyhood, it is a long while before they can rightly tell the order in which they must move their limbs when doing so. There are many other examples in the motor field, and it might be argued that the phenomenon is special to that field. Verbalized insights are notoriously unhelpful for learning how to steer a bicycle or how to turn on skis. As against this, Brown (1978) reports a number of studies where children's awareness of task characteristics seems to outstrip their performance. For instance, children of 6 years and less are well able to tell one that rehearsing the items in an array helps in their recall, as does an organized arrangement, yet these same children rarely do these things spontaneously when told to memorize, even though they know how. Nevertheless, Brown does not leap to the conclusion that awareness is generally in advance of performance, and it is instructive to note why.

There are other studies in which it is apparent that performance precedes awareness. Perhaps the most striking is an inquiry by Brown and Smiley (1977). This involved four groups of subjects, respectively aged 8, 10, 12, and 18 years. The tasks dealt with comprehension and recall of a written passage: All subjects were asked to rate the idea units in a passage according to their importance and were also required to recall the passages. All four groups, including the youngest, were sensitive to differences in importance, in that the more important units, as judged by an independent group of advanced students, were better remembered by all. But the youngest subjects were unable to make deliberate ratings of importance. Their ratings did not agree with those of the independent judges, yet their relative recall reflected these judgments and not their own.

The data relating to spontaneous rehearsal are really cases of MC1a, as defined earlier, and it is here that judgments are in advance of spontaneous performance. MC1a relates to the child's knowledge about the effects of procedures that can be inserted or omitted. Here, the evidence is that children have to realize the advantages of insertion before they will go to the trouble of putting this realization into practice. Imposing a structure on a story or an argument is not something that one can omit at will: It is a part of comprehension from a very early age (Paris, 1975; Paris & Lindauer, 1977). Here, the metacognitive insight is a true act of reflection on an integral process performed by the subject. MC3, so defined, is not a matter of comparing the presence of something with its absence, but of establishing how something might be varied, how these variations are defined (including the variation actually chosen), and what would be the effect of doing things in a different way. Although MC3 relates to intellective tasks and not motor skills, it still seems to be the case that performance precedes awareness. To quote Shatz (1978): "Metacognitive ability depends on an objectivization of process resulting from the release of consciousness from the major chores of selecting and controlling processing operations" (p. 25). MC3 looks like a good candiate for a more general role in producing the second-order changes postulated at the beginning of this section. At the same time, it appears to be closely bound up with the availability of working memory space, to which we now turn.

3. Working Memory

The thinking that takes place in response to a problem or a question entails a series of decision processes, many of which require conscious attention. These decisions depend on information to which we must attend, information which results from the selection and manipulation of items which need to be available in a short-term, rapid access store, but which derive ultimately from one of two origins, direct sensory information, or the residue of earlier processing retained in long-term memory—perhaps in the form of frame knowledge. Most psychologists are agreed that the decisions, the items that are manipulated and their resultants, as well as the overall plan which determines what happens next, all occupy space in some part of the brain which is functionally akin to the central processing unit in a computer. They would agree further that the items in short-term store also need space, and that the boundaries between these two spaces are not well defined, so that there is some interchange between them: A requirement to hold material in short-term memory may compete for space with the solution of a problem, with detriment to speed or accuracy or both (Baddeley & Hitch, 1974). When these ideas are applied to typical lines of reasoning shown by younger and older children, it is immediately apparent that arguments that are more mature are generally more demanding.

By way of example, a perceptual judgment on a conservation problem demands an interpretation of the task requirement followed by the realization that a comparison is called for: Because both comparands are present, and the cue that is used is salient, there is no demand on short-term memory other than the task as such, and the demand on processing itself amounts to little more than COMPARE. A correct judgment is far more demanding. The initial equality must be recalled, so too must the fact of transposition (one of the elements was moved, and both are otherwise unchanged), and because the cueing is often unhelpful as noted earlier, there has to be a deliberate rejection of a perceptual judgment, which would argue at least an implicit recognition of compensation.

The idea of a link between cognitive development and processing demand is one which was first adumbrated by McLaughlin (1963), who compared the norms for recall of digit sequences of varying lengths with the ages given by Piaget for concrete and formal reasoning, speculating that a concrete reasoner would need to handle four chunks of information while a formal reasoner would need seven. A much more sophisticated version of the notion was given by Pascual-Leone in the late 1960s (see Pascual-Leone & Smith, 1969). When a person faces a problem, the visual display and the instructions he or she receives combined to evoke a number of schemes. Each of these schemes corresponds to some relevant understanding.

For instance, in a sorting task: that this counter is blue, that it is round, that there are red counters and blue, that there are round counters and square, that the counters must be sorted in some sensible way. When several schemes are evoked in this way, the response made by the subject is the one which is compatible with all or most of them. However, not all of the schemes available need to be copresent: some may drop out for good reason, because they have been dealt with already, or because they are known to be irrelevant, but others will drop out simply because the subject is unable to entertain more than a certain number of schemes at any one time. The upper limit on a subject's processing capacity is termed her or his M-power, and a number of experiments and tests are adduced as evidence that the average 3-year-old has an M-power of just 1, and that M-power then increases by one unit for every 2 years of (mental) age, which gives modal values of 2, 3, 4, 5, 6, 7 at the ages of 5, 7, 9, 11, 13, 15, respectively.

For an adequate treatment of this theory, I am bound to refer the reader to the references given earlier, or to a very clear account given by Robbie Case (1974). However, the following points merit some mention here. First, not all active schemes are held to demand M-power. A scheme that is evoked by the sensory display makes no demand when attended to. On the other hand, a perceptual property which is recalled because it is not now being attended to does make a demand, and so too does any psychological act, such as COMPARE or COMBINE, etc. Second, it is acknowledged that children do not always use their full M-power, and there is some evidence of a connection with *field independence* (the ability to maintain a psychological set in the teeth of misleading sensory stimuli, as described by Witkin, Dyk, Paterson, Goodenough, & Karp, 1962): The field-independent child is said to be a high M-processor, while the field-dependent individual is a low M-processor. Third, M-power is not synonymous with short-term memory, nor can it be directly measured by a test of forward digit span. However, a test of backward digit span is said to give a fair approximation, while the best measures involve the subject in making some decision about each of the dimensions in a complex stimulus (see Scardamalia, 1977).

Although this theory is quite refined, it seems to me to be open to two criticisms. First, the stepwise and linear increments in measured M-power seem to cry out for some further explanation; and second, the theory remains uncomfortably vague about the way in which compatible and incompatible schemes interact so as to evoke the final response.

The first criticism would not apply to any of the modifications of the Pascual-Leone theory, such as those of Case (1978a), Halford and Wilson (1980) or Fischer (1980). Thus, Case maintains that attentional capacity itself is unlikely to show any marked increase after the age of about 1. A child enters a new stage when he learns to handle a new kind of content. Within each stage, the succession of substages is held to be a function of the number of such content elements which the child can keep in mind. Tasks that are more complex make heavier demands. The lower ceilings associated with earlier substages are attributed not to structural limitation but to the unfamiliarity of operations involving the elements characteristic of a new stage. Although Case does not say so, there is a plausible alternative, which is that the constructs themselves are less well encoded and therefore occupy more of the available attentional space. It may be that they are also more subject to decay in time.

Differences in cognitive capacity are held to be of two sorts: stage differences and substage differences. The stages derive more or less directly from Piaget and correspond to the sensorimotor, the intuitive, the concrete, and the formal stages. However, the definition of these stages is closer to that which I have offered earlier, because they are given in terms of content, and indeed it seems clear that Case's third and fourth stages involve level two and level three constructs respectively, while his first two stages involve first-level constructs, implicit during his stage 1 and explicit and representational at stage 2. The succession of substages can be illustrated by an example taken at the concrete stage. When asked to compare the amount of water in a tall thin beaker with that contained in a wide glass, the 3- to 4-year-old simply notes one thing and goes for the one that appears to have more, ignoring the other (isolated centration). The 5- to 6-year-old will measure both heights carefully and choose the taller column of liquid (a unidimensional comparison involving two items). At 7 to 9 years the average child notices the height and diameter differences and attempts a qualitative compensation (a bidimensional comparison, arguably requiring three items to be retained and attended to). Finally, at 9 to 10 years, the same child will endeavor to quantify the compensation (arguably involving 4 items to be attended to). At any of these substanges—save the first—the items in question are values of some well-defined dimension, or what I have termed second-order constructs. At the formal stage, one would look for parallel gradations of performance involving third-order constructs, and Joyes (1982) provides a credible instance in an inquiry involving the control of variables. Case himself suggests that sentence repetition, when measured by the number of ideas that are retained and not by word length, is an appropriate example of gradations at his second stage. Because the sentences are simple in content (being taken from the Stanford-Binet tests for young children), the items concerned are first-order constructs.

Fischer's (1980) version is similar to Case's in postulating four levels of complexity repeated in successive tiers. Unlike Case, he insists on the specificity of performance, with each domain involving separate "skills". Interestingly, and not very plausibly, Fischer counts both second and third order constructs within his second tier, and reserves his third tier for more advanced intellective behaviour such as scientific invention. Biggs and Collis (1982) are nearer to Case in their definition of constructs, but they, like Fischer, are happy to consider cognitive achievements as more or less domain specific. Indeed the main interest of their work consists in their attempt to develop a usable scale for measuring the quality of pupil output (essays and compositions, problem solutions, etc.), or learning outcomes. Finally, Halford and Wilson (1980) confine their attention to construct levels, and find three (corresponding exactly to those defined in this chapter), which they relate to short-term memory requirement (a view that is explicitly rejected by others).

It is clear that there are several issues which are either unsolved or unresolved. First, I do not believe there is any reliable way as at present of giving an absolute quantification of processing requirement for any given task—although relative quantifications can be instructive. The magic number four (or three) within stages or levels is only thinly supported by the evidence, since decisions about what shall be counted as an item are generally made ad hoc if not post hoc for each new task. Second, when a person sets about the solution of a problem, there are two sorts of things he or she needs to access: propositions or facts and actions or transformations to be executed. Both of these make demands on working memory, yet attempts at quantification almost invariably ignore the latter. It is no accident that the fine analyses given by Case (1978b) and Scardamalia (1977) relate to a child's ability to profit from very specific and detailed instruction in narrowly defined tasks. Third, the problem of transfer cannot be solved either by taking it for granted (Halford) or by insisting on domain specificity (Fischer). How should one define a domain to avoid overlap?

However, despite the persistence of such problems, I have little doubt that both level of construct and processing requirement are necessary elements in any attempt to elucidate the mechanisms underlying changes in cognitive capacity.

4. Production Systems

Models like those we have just considered highlight the fact that a theory of cognitive development must incorporate some way of accounting for changes in the content which the child can handle, as well as changes in the complexity of the processing sequences that are brought to bear on that content. Within the modelling of the processes themselves, the theory should offer a plausible explication both of the origins of new executives, these being specifications of the sequences just referred to, and of the way the implementation of an executive interacts with the execution of each step. In other words, as we have just noted, the child has to learn new sequences which are flexible enough to be serviceable when applied to a range of related tasks, and while implementing such an executive, he or she needs to keep track of where she or he is at within the task as a whole while simul-

taneously observing the constraints involved in the current step. If we had a
really good theory it would explain all these things. Working memory theories are strong on the distinction between content and process (although
they are not very specific about the way new contents come about). However, their descriptions of process fail to account adequately for the interrelations of executives and their implementation, nor do they tell us a great
deal about how these executives come to be formed when they are not
directly taught. Production systems are models which are very specific about
the implementation of sequence.

A production is a rule which specifies that one or more actions is to be
performed if the conditions are as stated. Individual productions are highly
circumscribed, but sets of productions form systems which regulate the
performance of all kinds of task. A production system for leaving a room
might look like this:

GI = GOAL: LEAVE ROOM

(GI)(GAP IN WALL) → WALK THROUGH
(GI)(DOOR OPEN) → WALK THROUGH
(GI)(DOOR CLOSED)(HANDLE ROTATED) → PULL HANDLE
(GI)(DOOR CLOSED)(HANDLE LOCATED) → ROTATE HANDLE
ANTICLOCKWISE
(GI)(DOOR CLOSED) → LOCATE HANDLE
(GI) → FIND DOOR

The bracketed phrases to the left are conditions, while the injunctions to the
right are actions. Each line is a separate production and the whole sequence
is a production system. Such a system ensures a certain flexibility: for instance, you do not try to open an already open door. Here, all conditions
other than GI are states of affairs which are registered by perception. Systems for the solution of representational problems including any kind of
thought will include conditions relating to two sources of input: perception
and short-term memory. Also, the actions specified by a production system
will frequently include an injunction to store an item in short-term memory.
Again, because production-system theory is designed to model information
processing in human beings, it is assumed that short-term memory capacity
is limited: Putting an extra item in the buffer is liable to knock out one that
was previously present, thereby altering the input state. In these respects,
the theory is at least potentially congruent with the theories described in the
last subsection.

There are, however, important differences. Production-system theories
do not in general provide for separate executives or strategies. Instead, it is
assumed that the adaptiveness of behavior is guaranteed by the specificity of
conditions for each production, taken together with a limited set of rules for

the resolution of conflict between rival productions when more than one set of conditions are met (Newell, 1980). Production-system theory originated with the work of Newell and Simon (1972) as a computer system for modeling human problem-solving. Several versions exist, differing partly in the choice of aspects of performance taken for granted and those which are actually incorporated into the program. In general, systems are written to model fairly specific areas of performance: We do not have an overall production-system model of the brain as a working entity—although Newell (1980) does offer a clear account of what such a model would look like and the features it must incorporate, including specifications for the creation of new productions out of the contents of the short term memory store. Within the field of cognitive development, production systems have been developed for modeling class inclusion (Klahr and Wallace, 1972), conservation of number (Klahr and Wallace, 1976), seriation (Baylor and Gascon, 1974), and geometrical problem solution (Greeno, 1978).

Production-system modeling helps to pinpoint differences in process as between more and less advanced solutions to specific tasks, as well as differences between related tasks of unequal difficulty, such as seriation of length and of weight (Baylor and Lemoyne, 1975). However, the construction of production systems capable of improving their performance by constructing and incorporating new productions remains a problem for the future. Also, few if any existing systems incorporate all of the features that would be necessary for a realistic model, i.e., one which not only does what the human processor does, but does it in a credible way, and fails under conditions where the human operator fails. These features include the distinction between perceptual input and short-term memory, procedures for recognizing and substituting specific entities in productions containing variables, a provision for search productions which will seek out intermediate goals while retaining an overall goal, some limitation on the time during which a given production can retain control, and so on.

It seems to me that when all these features are added, the effect is to blur the distinction between frame theory and production-system theory. However, this should not be taken to imply that this theory is redundant. Because production systems are precise expressions, they are a salutary discipline for the theorist. The danger is the temptation to produce systems that are powerful and effective but lack credibility as models for the human processor, whether child or adult.

B. THE LOGIC OF THINKING

The problem as outlined at the beginning of this section is how to explain the more far-reaching changes in cognition that must underlie the new constructions and far transfer which seem to be necessary to account for such phenomena as the spontaneous development of conservation or class inclusion behaviors or the evolution of higher-order constructs. Four important approaches were considered in the last subsection. Because they are relatively recent in origin, all have as yet unrealized potential. However, none is sufficient on its own, the more so as the processes that are envisaged are not limited to cognitive growth but extend to problems of cognition as a whole. In other words, a proper answer to our question would constitute a comprehensive theory of cognition as well as its development. Needless to say, we do not make the attempt. But it may be helpful to look at the question in the light of the previous discussion, so as to gain some sort of preliminary perspective.

One of the central tenets of Gestalt psychology was the belief that the contents of the mind undergo a gradual process of restructuring while in store. It is a view which has few adherents today. There is physiological evidence of consolidation processes, the effects of which may be protracted over several hours or even days (Deutsch & Deutsch, 1973), the implications of which are by no means clear. Nevertheless, I assume that to all intents and purposes, cognitive changes occur during cognitive episodes or very shortly after. If children learn to learn, it is while learning.

Such is the justification for introducing Fig. 2. This is not designed to be a complete flow-diagram for learning episodes, and indeed there are many others which are much better from that point of view. Instead, it is intended solely to bring out certain significant features which I take to be characteristic of environmental encounters in general and of learning episodes in particular. First is the distinction between routine performances and behaviour in tasks that pose a problem in one form or another. Theories of instruction are concerned mainly with the left-hand loop, because it is assumed that the learner will know what to do if the instruction is adequate. Within the left-hand loop, evaluation often appears as part of a prescription for good teacher behavior. In the context of the present discussion, it is the right-hand loop that holds the greater interest. Figure 2 is an outline of any behavior, including both the skilled operator and the pupil or learner. As such, it includes a provision for revising the experience and its outcome. But it also provides a bypass route. Beginners may be unable to take cognizance of the route they have followed, or they may not see the gain in doing so, although such metacognitive activity may be essential for certain kinds of learning. Similarly, when the right-hand loop is taken (i.e., when there is no ready-made plan available for dealing with the situation as cognised), there are at least two ways of initiating a search for a way out. The beginner's way is to modify the situation in the hope that something will suggest itself in the form of a subgoal and a subplan, or even a substitute goal. A more sophisti-

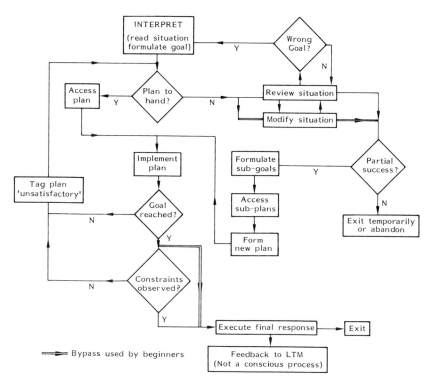

FIG. 2.   Significant features of a learning episode.

cated performer may attempt an analysis, with greater or lesser success, and even if such an analysis leads to an actual modification of the situation, this will feed back to the original review activity before issuing in the sequence which will result in the formation of a new plan.

As to the way in which new plans are formed, we have little to go on save that these must somehow combine fragments of existing plans, that the assembly of an overall plan will often entail an ordering of subplans, and that even when a plan has been formed and control passes to the mechanisms which direct implementation, the subject's hold on the plan itself is likely to be tenuous to begin with, with the result that the goal may never be reached even though the plan was adequate.

However, there is no profit in reiterating the obvious or in parading uncertainties. But it may be instructive to compare Fig. 2 with Table 3. This is really one way of saying that as things stand at present, more than one theoretical approach is needed to advance our understanding of cognitive development but that different contributions illuminate different facets of

TABLE 3   Learning to Learn: A Categorization of Problems
and Relevant Theory

Locus or processing	Relevant theories
INTERPRET	Frame theory
ACCESS PLAN	Frame theory
	Production systems
IMPLEMENT	Working memory theory
	Production systems
REVIEW	
CONSTRAINTS OBSERVED?	Metacognition
FORM NEW PLAN	(Production systems)
	(Frame theory)
	(Levels of construct)
	(Metacognition)
FEEDBACK TO LTM	Traditional learning theory

the problem. Only the principal emphases are indicated in the table, which means that it is not designed to be read in a negative sense. For instance, production system theory may well have relevance for INTERPRET or even for REVIEW, but its principal impact to date has been to further our understanding of the IMPLEMENT phase.

The penultimate insertions of Table 3 are given in brackets as a way of suggesting that there is a long way to go, and we are not sure where to look. Nevertheless, because of the centrality of the problem, it may be worthwhile to consider at least one possible chain of events. We suppose first of all that the role of INTERPRET is partly to match the input to some specific slots in some relevant frames. (It also entails a preliminary code-breaking.) We recall that there are certain kinds of frames, or parts of frames, sometimes called *scripts*, which tell the operator what to do next and what to look out for when it is done. Also, scripts are rules for handling variables, not constants: for instance, "subtract the smaller number from the larger" and not (or not just) "take 3 from 8." The left-hand route of Fig. 2 will then be taken if, despite the novelty of the input situation, there is a mapping of situation features onto script slots, which is sufficient to allow the script to dictate the behavior. (All this could also have been said in production-system language.)

When the mapping is inadequate, control of behavior enters the REVIEW phase, always supposing there are sufficient metacognitive skills available to sustain a review—if not, the MODIFY bypass will be taken and more often than not will result in frustration and task abandonement. Now one of the things the REVIEW phase does is to promote repeated scans through the input features, thereby allowing new frames to be accessed (with luck). Such frames may be of different sorts. For instance, it was argued earlier that there are form frames as well as content frames. By way of example, a child who is asked about the conservation of weight may bring to mind what the things might feel like when lifted, or knowledge about different kinds of scales, or of units for measuring weight, but he may also bring to mind experience of other conservations (and we know that different kinds of conservation correlate as a conservation factor), or general knowledge of measurement. In other words, there are a great many frames which pertain to Level 2 constructs, and these may be thought to facilitate one another. It is not unreasonable to suppose that the greater role of these frames in industrialized societies accounts in part for developmental lag in undeveloped communities.

Frames that are accessed in this manner are unlikely to afford the exact match with input necessary for immediate implementation. Hence, the advantage of a facility for modifying the situation to point up ways of circumventing inadequacies. Modification of the situation is a primitive response, but tentative modifications or mental modifications are not. Such modifications are a form of analytical behavior triggered by the review process, and their results feed back to that process. Even then, we may suppose, the output of the REVIEW will often take the form of a set of partial mappings of features to slots from different frames.

It is possible, but by no means certain that this kind of tentative and inchoate parcel would then be passed on to a FORM NEW PLAN phase, which undertakes the business of selection and ordering, and does this in a more pragmatic way, selecting what can be done given the present state of affairs. This would lead to trial-and-error behavior as opposed to a perfectly thought-out anticipation as the modal form of response to new situations. However, given the further opportunities for correction and refinement implicit in the diamond labeled "CONSTRAINTS OBSERVED?" we may imagine that repeated cycling through the loop will eventually result in the formation of new frames. One presumes that these are constructed by adding slots to existing frames, or by joining frames that were once separate, or both. The end result would be to have available the sort of routine plan which enables the subject to take the left-hand loop through Fig. 2.

Not shown on the figure, but not inconsistent with its intent, is the potential of rehearsal or reminiscence after an interval. Rehearsal of this kind is in any case a reconstructive process which relies on more general frame-like constituents of semantic memory to re-create the remembered episode by supplying missing detail slots with typical or default elements, or even by refashioning the structural outlines in line with knowledge acquired in the interim. This, surely is the most plausible explanation of the phenomenon noted by Piaget and Inhelder (1973) that children who are asked to reconstruct a conservation or a seriation set-up after an interval of several months frequently exhibit better structures and hence apparently superior recall as compared with their own performance immediately after the event.

I have to stress that all of the foregoing is no more than reasonable speculation in the light of the known. However, if it is at all near a correct picture, then much of the fundamental learning and relearning which might be responsible for far transfer takes place in and through metacognitive episodes, either in the REVIEW phase of the original learning incident or through rehearsal after the event. The idea that the reconstructions so achieved may be more reasoned and reasonable than the original solution process would be entirely consistent with dual-process theory of problem solution, according to which there is a sharp distinction between the selection and execution of response which is characteristically unreflecting and the reasoned reconstructions offered by the solver as a rationalization of his efforts (Evans, 1982; Wason & Johnson-Laird, 1972).

All this would imply that, in the end, the emergence of new forms of cognition and problem solution owe a great deal to an innate drive for consistency. I know of no alternative to the metatheory which accords to the infant right from the start certain innate logical functions, including the recognition of sameness (but not of equality), of negation, of variation and comparison, and of the rejection of contradiction (cf. Piaget, Grize, Szeminska, & Bang, 1968). Out of these are born, more or less separately, the kind of logic of thinking which is implicit in the preceding account, and the discipline of logic, which is a slow-developing specialization that relies heavily on teaching as a separate skill (e.g., Bourne & O'Banion, 1971; Lunzer, 1973; O'Brien, Shapiro, & Reali, 1971, and, especially Osherson, 1974). The principal difference between these two is that whereas the former considers only relevant alternatives and their implications, formal logical systems are unable to accept such a limitation. This is mainly because *relevant* is a fuzzy category, and logic exists for the special purpose of eliminating fuzziness or circumventing it.

REFERENCES

Abbott, V., & Black, J. B. (1980). *The representation of scripts in memory* (Tech. Rep.). New Haven, CT: Yale University, Department of Psychology.

Baddeley, A. D., & Hitch, G. (1974). Working memory. In G. H. Bower (Ed.), *The psychology of learning and motivation* (Vol. 8). New York: Academic Press, pp. 47–89.

Baylor, G. W., & Gascon, J. (1974). An informaton processing theory of the development of weight seriation in children. *Cognitive Psychology*, 6, 1–40.

Baylor, G. W., & Lemoyne, G. (1975). Experiments in seriation with children: Towards an information processing explanation of the horizontal dacalage. *Canadian Journal of Behavioral Science, 7,* 4–29.

Biggs, J. B., & Collis, K. F. (1982). *Evaluating the quality of learning: The SOLO taxonomy (Structure of the observed learning outcome)*. New York: Academic Press.

Bourne, L. E., & O'Banion, K. (1971). Conceptual rule learning and chronological age. *Developmental Psychology, 5,* 525–534.

Brainerd, C. J. (1978). Learning research and Piagetian theory. In L. S. Siegel and C. J. Brainerd (Eds.), *Alternatives to Piaget: Critical essays on the theory.* New York: Academic Press, pp. 69–100.

Brown, A. L. (1978). Knowing when, where and how to remember: A problem of metacognition. In R. Glaser (Ed.), *Advances in instructional psychology* (Vol. 1, pp. 77–165). Hillsdale, NJ: Erlbaum.

Brown, A. L., & Smiley, S. S. (1977). Rating the importance of structural units of prose passages: A problem of metacognitive development. *Child Development, 48,* 1–8.

Bryant, P. E. (1972). The understanding of invariance by very young children. *Canadian Journal of Psychology, 26,* 78–96.

Case, R. (1974). Structures and strictures: Some functional limitations on the course of cognitive growth. *Cognitive Psychology, 6,* 544–573.

Case, R. (1978a). Intellectual development from birth to adulthood: A neo-Piagetian interpretation. In R. S. Siegler (Ed.), *Children's thinking: What develops?* (pp. 37–71). Hillsdale, NJ: Erlbaum.

Case, R. (1978b). A developmentally based theory and technology of instruction. *Review of Educational Research, 48,* 439–463.

Clark, E. V. (1973). Non-linguistic strategies and the acquisition of word meanings. *Cognition, 2,* 161–182.

Collis, K. F. (1975). *The development of formal reasoning* (tech. rep.). Newcastle, N.S.W., Australia:

Collis, K. F. (1978). Operational thinking in elementary mathematics. In J. A. Keats, K. F. Collis & G. S. Halford (Eds.), *Cognitive development* (pp. 221–283). New York: Wiley.

Deutsch, J. A. & Deutsch, D. (1973). *Physiological psychology* (rev. ed.). Homewood, IL: Dorsey Press.

Donaldson, M., & Balfour, G. (1968). Less is more: a study of early language comprehension. *British Journal of Psychology, 59,* 461–471.

Driver, R. & Easley, J. (1978). Pupils and paradigms: A review of literature related to concept development in adolescent science students. *Studies in Science Education, 5,* 61–84.

Ennis, R. H. (1978). Conceptualization of children's logical competence: Piaget's propositional logic and an alternative proposal. In L. S. Siegel & C. J. Brainerd (Eds.), *Alternatives to Piaget: Critical essays on the theory* (pp. 201–260). New York: Academic Press.

Ervin, S. (1961). Changes with age in the verbal determinants of word-association. *American Journal of Psychology, 74,* 361–372.

Evans, J. St. B. T. (1982). *The psychology of deductive reasoning.* London: Routledge.

Festinger, L. (1957). *A theory of cognitive dissonance.* Stanford, CA: Stanford University Press.

Fischer, K. W. (1980). A theory of cognitive development: The control and construction of hierarchies of skills. *Psychological Review, 87,* 477–531.

Flavell, J. H. (1963). *The developmental psychology of Jean Piaget.* Princeton, NJ: Van Nostrand.

Flavell, J. H. (1979). Metacognition and cognitive monitoring. *American Psychologist, 34,* 906–911.

Flavell, J. H., & Wellman, H. M. (1977). Metamemory. In R. V. Kail and J. W. Hagen (Eds.),

Perspectives on the development of memory and cognition pp. 3–33. Hillsdale, NJ: Erlbaum.

Gelman, R., & Gallistel, C. F. (1978). *The child's understanding of number.* Cambridge, MA: Harvard University Press.

Greeno, J. G. (1978). A study of problem solving. In R. Glaser (Ed.), *Advances in instructional psychology* (Vol. 1, pp. 13–75). Hillsdale, NJ: Erlbaum.

Halford, G. S. (1980). A learning set approach to multiple classification: Evidence for a theory of cognitive levels. *International Journal of Behavioral Development, 3,* 409–422.

Halford, G. S., & Wilson, W. H. (1980). A category theory approach to cognitive development. *Cognitive Psychology, 12,* 356–411.

Hart, K. M. (Ed.). (1981). *Children's understanding of mathematics* (pp. 11–16). London: John Murray.

Hilgard, E. R. (1958). *Theories of learning* (2nd ed.). New York: Appleton.

Inhelder, B. & Piaget, J. (1958). *The growth of logical thinking from childhood to adolescence.* New York: Basic.

Joyes, G. M. (1982). *Problems in the learning of physics: Development in the control of variables.* Unpublished doctoral dissertation, Nottingham University, Nottingham, England.

Klahr, D., & Wallace, J. G. (1972). Class inclusion processes. In S. Farnham-Diggory (Ed.), *Information processing in children* (pp. 143–172). New York: Academic Press.

Klahr, D., & Wallace, J. G. (1976). *Cognitive development: An information processing view.* Hillsdale, NJ: Erlbaum.

Kofsky, E. (1966). A scalogram study of classificatory development. *Child Development, 37,* 191–204.

Lefebvre-Pinard, M. (1983). Understanding and auto-control of cognitive function: Implications for the relationship between cognition and behavior. *International Journal of Behavioral Development, 6,* pp. 15–35.

Light, P. H., Buckingham, N., & Robbins, A. (1979). The conservation task as an interactional setting. *British Journal of Educational Psychology, 49,* 304–310.

Lunzer, E. A. (1965). Problems of formal reasoning in test situations. In P. H. Mussen (Ed.), European research in cognitive development. *Monographs of the Society for Research in Child Development, 30,* 19–46.

Lunzer, E. A. (1973). The development of formal reasoning: Some recent experiments and their implications. In K. Frey & M. Lang (Eds.), *Cognitive processes and science instruction* pp. (pp. 212–245). Bern: Huber Verlap and Baltimore: Williams & Wilkins.

Lunzer, E. A., & Gardner, W. K. (1984). *Learning from the written word.* Edinburgh: Oliver and Boyd.

Lunzer, E. A., Wilkinson, J. E., & Dolan, T. (1976). The distinctiveness of operativity as a measure of cognitive functioning in five-year-old children. *British Journal of Educational Psychology, 16,* 280–294.

Markman, E. (1978). Empirical versus logical solutions to part–whole comparison problems concerning classes and collections. *Child Development, 49,* 168–177.

McGarrigle, J., & Donaldson, M. (1974). Conservation accidents. *Cognition, 3,* 341–350.

McLaughlin, G. H. (1973). Psycho-logic: A possible alternative to Piaget's formulations. *British Journal of Educational Psychology, 33,* 61–67.

Minsky, M. (Ed.), (1968). *Semantic information processing.* Cambridge, MA: MIT Press.

Minsky, M. (1975). A framework for representing knowledge. In P. Winston (Ed.), *The psychology of computer vision.* New York: McGraw-Hill.

Modgil, S., & Modgil, C. (Eds.), (1982). *Jean Piaget: Consensus and controversy.* New York: Praeger.

Newell, A. (1980). Harpy, production systems and human cognition. In R. A. Cole (Ed.), *Perception and production or fluent speech* (pp. 289–380). Hillsdale, NJ: Erlbaum.

Newell, A., & Simon, H. A. (1972). *Human problem solving*. Englewood Cliffs, NJ: Prentice-Hall.

O'Brien, T. C., Shapiro, B. J., & Reali, N. C. (1971). Logical thinking—language and context. *Educational studies in mathematics, 4,* 201–210.

Odom, R. D. (1978). A perceptual-salience account of decalage relations and developmental change. In L. S. Siegel & C. J. Brainerd (Eds.), *Alternatives to Piaget: Critical essays on the theory* (pp. 111–130). New York: Academic Press.

Osherson, D. N. (1974). *Logical abilities in children: Vol. 1. Organization of length and class concepts: Empirical consequences of a Piagetian formalism*. Hillsdale, NJ: Erlbaum.

Osherson, D. N., & Markman, E. (1975). Language and the ability to evaluate contradictions and tautologiees. *Cognition, 3,* 213–226.

Paris, S. G. (1975). Integration and inference in children's comprehension and memory. In F. Restle, R. Shiffrin, J. Castellan, H. Lindman and D. Pisoni (Eds.), *Cognitive theory* (Vol. 1, pp. 223–246). Hillsdale, NJ: Erlbaum.

Paris, S. G., & Lindauer, B. K. (1977). Constructive aspects of children's cognition and memory. In R. V. Kail & J. W. Hagen (Eds.), *Perspectives on the development of memory and cognition* pp. 35–88. Hillsdale, NJ: Erlbaum.

Parsons, C. (1960). Inhelder & Piaget's 'The growth of logical thinking." *British Journal of Psychology, 51,* 75–84.

Pascual-Leone, J., & Smith, J. (1969). The encoding and decoding of symbols by children: A new experimental paradigm and a neo-Piagetian model. *Journal of Experimental Child Psychology, 8,* 328–355.

Piaget, J. (1950). *The psychology of intelligence*. London: Routledge.

Piaget, J. (1952a). *The child's conception of number*. New York: Humanities.

Piaget, J. (1952b). *The origins of intelligence in children*. New York: International Universities.

Piaget, J. (1959a). Apprentissage et connaissance (premiere partie). P. Greco & J. Piaget, Apprentissage et connaissance. *Etude d'epistemologie genetique* (Vol. 7, pp. 21–67). Paris: Presses Universitaires de France.

Piaget, J. (1959b). Apprentissage et connaissance (seconde partie). In M. Goustard, P. Greco, J. B. Grize, B. Matalon et J. Piaget, La logique des apprentissages. *Etudes d'epistemologie genetique* (Vol. 8, pp. 159–188). Paris: Presses Universitaires de France.

Piaget, J. (1962). *The moral judgement of the child* (M. Gabaith, Trans). New York: Collier.

Piaget, J. (1977). *The equilibration of cognitive structures*. Oxford: Blackwell.

Piaget, J., Grize, J. B., Szeminska, A., & Bang, V. (1968). Epistemologie et psychologic de la fonction. *Etudes d'epistemologie genetique* (Vol. 23). Paris: Presses Universitaires de France.

Piaget, J., & Inhelder, B. (1973). *Memory and intelligence*. New York: Basic.

Piaget, J., Inhelder, B., & Szeminska, A. (1960). *The child's conception of geometry*. New York: Basic.

Pramling, I. The child's conception of learning. (1983). *Goterborg studies in educational science* (Vol. 46). Göteborg, Sweden: Acta Universitatis Gothoburgensis.

Rose, S. A., & Blank, M. (1974). The potency of context in children's cognition: An illustration through conservation. *Child Development, 45,* 499–502.

Rumelhart, D. E. & Ortony, A. (1977). The representation of knowledge in memory. In R. C. Anderson, R. J. Spiro & W. E. Montague (Eds.), *Schooling and the acquisition of knowledge* (pp. 99–135). Hillsdale, NJ: Erlbaum.

Scardamalia, M. (1977). Information processing capacity and the problem of horizontal decalage: A demonstration using combinatorial reasoning tasks. *Child Development, 48,* 128–137.

Schank, R. C., & Abelson, R. P. (1977). *Scripts, plans, goals and understanding.* Hillsdale, NJ: Erlbaum.

Shatz, M. (1978). The relation between cognitive processes and the development of communication skills. In B. Keary (Ed.), *Nebraska symposium on motivation.* Lincoln: University of Nebraska Press.

Siegel, L. S., & Brainerd, C. J. (Eds.), (1978). *Alternatives to Piaget: Critical essays on the theory.* New York: Academic Press.

Strohner, H., & Nelson, K. E. (1974). The young child's development of sentence comprehension: Influence of event probability, non-verbal context, syntactic form and strategies. *Child Development, 454,* 567–576.

Tuddenham, R. D. (1970). A Piagetian test of cognitive development. In W. B. Dockrell (Ed.), *On intelligence. The Toronto symposium, 1969* (pp. 49–70). London: Methuen.

Tulving, E. (1972). Episodic and semantic memory. In E. Tulving & W. Donaldson (Eds.), *Organization of memory* (pp. 382–403). New York: Academic Press.

van Dijk, T. A., & Kintsch, W. (1983). *Strategies of discourse comprehension.* New York: Academic Press.

Wason, P. C., & Johnson-Laird, P. N. (1972). *Psychology of reasoning: Structure and content.* London: Batsford.

Witkin, H. A., Dyk, R. B., Paterson, H. F., Goodenough, D. R., & Karp, S. A. (1962). *Psychological differentiation.* New York: Wiley.

Yussen, S. R., & Kane, P. T. (1984). Children's conception of intelligence. In Yussen, S. R. (Ed.), *The growth of reflection.* New York: Academic Press.

INDEX